THE ORIGINS OF THE RUSSO-JAPANESE WAR

ORIGINS OF MODERN WARS
General editor: *Harry Hearder*

Titles already published:

THE ORIGINS OF THE RUSSO-JAPANESE WAR
  Ian Nish
THE ORIGINS OF THE FIRST WORLD WAR
  James Joll
THE ORIGINS OF THE ARAB-ISRAELI WARS
  Ritchie Ovendale

THE ORIGINS OF THE
RUSSO-JAPANESE WAR

Ian Nish

LONGMAN
London and New York

LONGMAN GROUP LIMITED
Longman House, Burnt Mill, Harlow
Essex CM20 2JE, England
Associated companies throughout the world

*Published in the United States of America
by Longman Inc., New York*

First published 1985

BRITISH LIBRARY CATALOGUING IN PUBLICATION DATA

Nish, Ian
  The origins of the Russo-Japanese war.—
  (Origins of modern wars)
  1. Russo-Japanese War, 1904–1905—Causes
  I. Title II. Series
  952.03′1   DS517
ISBN 0-582-49114-2

LIBRARY OF CONGRESS CATALOGING IN PUBLICATION DATA

Nish, Ian Hill.
  The origins of the Russo-Japanese war.

  (Origins of modern wars)
  Bibliography: p.
  Includes index.
  1. Russo-Japanese War, 1904–1905—Causes. 2. Japan—
Foreign relations—Soviet Union. 3. Soviet Union—Foreign
relations—Japan. I. Title. II. Series.
DS517.N57 1985   952.03′1   84–21296
ISBN 0-582-49114-2 (pbk.)

Set in 10/11pt AM Compset Times
Produced by Longman Group (FE) Ltd
Printed in Hong Kong

CONTENTS

LIST OF MAPS

EDITOR'S FOREWORD

The third volume to be published in this series deals with the origins of a war very different in scope and scale from that of 1914–18 with which Professor James Joll's volume dealt, and very different in character from the Arab-Israeli conflicts with which Dr Ritchie Ovendale's volume deals. The search for common factors in the origins of the three conflicts is perhaps a vain and unrewarding task, yet certain general points of interpretation emerge.

James Joll noted the inadequacies of intelligence and imagination of individual men in positions of supreme authority in 1914, and how those inadequacies helped to lead to the catastrophe. In the present volume Professor Nish shows how Tsar Nicholas II, essentially a man of peace, and sometimes a shrewd observer of what was happening, was for a large part of the time of the crisis on holiday or unobtainable, and was anyhow a weak man who could not halt the impending disaster. There is an irony in the fact that essentially pacific men have often been in authority at the outbreak of wars – Lord Aberdeen in 1854 (a war with which Dr Agatha Ramm will be dealing in the series), Asquith in 1914, Neville Chamberlain in 1939 (a war with which Mr Philip Bell will be dealing in the series). The limitations of Nicholas II contributed in 1904 and 1914 to tragedy on a scale which he certainly did not intend or envisage.

Another question which must be asked about the origins of wars is that of the role of simple miscalculation – the miscalculation regarding the ease with which the war can be won. Ian Nish shows that Russian ministers could not believe that their vast and powerful empire could possibly be defeated by a small upstart Asian nation. The Japanese, ironically in view of their overwhelming victory in the war, were far more cautious. But they were, in Professor Nish's words, 'cool and calculating'. Russian confidence in victory was a proud but somewhat nebulous one; Japanese confidence was less extravagant, but more firmly based on military and naval facts.

That the Arab-Israeli wars with which Ritchie Ovendale dealt in his volume in this series did not lead to a direct Russo-American confrontation was partly due to the very complexity of the situation in the Middle East. Fortunately the Russians and the Americans have never been quite sure whom to back there. Even the basic sympathy which Washington has felt for Israel has sometimes wavered. But the problems dividing Russia and Japan in 1904 were also complex, and the complexity on that occasion did not permit successful bargaining, and so did not prevent war. Yet there was certainly more room for bargaining and negotiating than some of the politicians and diplomats on both sides had the wit to realize. But Professor Nish finds the statement that the war was 'unnecessary' too simplistic. 'If the two sides could not find an agreeable basis for compromise,' he writes, 'it is hard to see how the war can be described as "preventible".' It came to be regarded as necessary in the eyes of both governments, but perhaps not equally necessary in the eyes of all politicians and diplomats concerned. Ian Nish shows very clearly that the holding of a significant post by a certain individual at a particular moment in a crisis may well affect the way the negotiations develop. The foolish belief that the will of individual diplomats or officials can have no influence on developments – that they are all in some mystical way caught up in an inevitable process – is belied by Professor Nish's account. In a classic statement in the early eighteenth century Giambattista Vico pointed out that while it may be true that God made nature, it is certainly true that Man made history: humanity cannot escape that responsibility. Someone – some people – were responsible for wars, and more often than not those people were not all on the same side.

Another general question which can be asked about most wars is whether public opinion was more eager for war than the government, or vice versa. Ian Nish suggests that in 1904 the Japanese people were more eager for war than their government, while the Russian public was less interested in the Far East than were some of their ministers. But Japan was a constitutional state while Russia was still a monolithic autocracy, so that 'public opinion' means something rather different in the two countries. Before a war there is usually a peace party and a war party – doves and hawks. As soon as the war starts the doves appear discredited, but in a defeated nation the hawks in their turn are discredited. Professor Nish tells us, in one of his brilliantly lucid concluding points, that in 1904 'there was in both countries an expansionist group tussling with a more moderate one which was equally determined to pursue national interests but in ways which would avoid confrontation or offense to other powers. The attainment of rational solutions was often lost because of the factional infighting.'

One general point of interest mentioned in this volume relates to the diplomatic paraphernalia of going to war in the nineteenth and early twentieth centuries. A government 'declared' war before waging it, although usually not before mobilizing its armies. Thus Japan was condemned for making war in 1904 without formally declaring it.

Again, half a century later, she was to be condemned for the same reason after her attack at Pearl Harbor, a point which will probably be considered by Professor Akira Iriye in the volume he is writing for this series. In 1914 the Powers went through the formalities of issuing ultimatums and declaring war, as did the British in 1939. Such niceties seem now to have been forgotten. The British and French governments made war on Egypt without declaring it in 1956, and more recently Argentina and Britain have made war on each other in the Falklands without declarations of war.

One final general point is worth noting from Professor Nish's book. When it looked extremely likely that Japan and Russia were going to war the other Powers felt that there was an obligation for them to 'appease' the conflicting parties. Their interests in keeping peace in the Far East were not, however, sufficiently strong for them to take any firm action. Still, 'appeasement' was not yet a dirty word. It became a dirty word only when a gross aberration appeared in world history, the aberration of Nazi Germany. Even then the problem of 'appeasement' was perhaps less simple than the Winston Churchills and the Anthony Edens would have had us believe. The time has surely come for the world to realize that appeasement is better than war, and that crude analogies between the present and 1938 are desperately dangerous. The sense of a duty to 'appease' felt by Western diplomats in 1904 – even though they did not carry out that duty – is not entirely without a message for the present.

HARRY HEARDER

PREFACE AND ACKNOWLEDGEMENTS

I was originally approached by the series editor to write this volume in 1976. I was then engaged in research on Anglo-Japanese relations in the 1920s and 1930s which I set aside for the time being in order to take up this project. It proved to be a more extensive subject of study than I had originally imagined and has taken much longer to reach published form. In pursuing research on this theme, I was fortunate to visit Japan twice – in 1978 (with the help of a Hayter grant) and 1982; Korea in 1982; and Canada and the United States in 1981. This enabled me to consult a number of private papers which added to my understanding of the war.

Many excellent studies of the subject have been published (Malozemoff, White, Warner and Lensen to name but a few). Indeed a number of important new studies appeared as this book was going to press, notably Lieven, Lensen's *Balance of Intrigue* and Quested on Russia in Manchuria. I still thought that the origins of the Russo-Japanese war which was my remit within the series was a worthwhile subject for investigation. On the one hand, the Russo-Japanese war seemed to have characteristics which made it relevant to any series studying the origins of war. On the other, it seemed to me that new materials had been published recently which threw light on these origins.

The new publications on the Japanese side are also particularly rich through the typically thorough coverage of Meiji historical materials by the publisher, Haro Shobō. In addition, several important translations have been published: three volumes of *The Diplomacy of Japan, 1894–1922* by Kajima Morinosuke; Mutsu Munemitsu's *Kenkenroku,* edited by Gordon Berger; and Miyazaki Tōten's *My 33 Years' Dream* by Etō Shinkichi and Marius Jansen. Each of these has vital evidence for our study. We are also grateful for the appearance of selections from the correspondence of four important figures taken from the foreign community engaged on the China coast: the correspondence of Sir Robert Hart in *The I.G. in Peking* (edited by J. K. Fairbank *et al.*); George Lensen's selections from the letters of Baron d'Anethan and Sir

Ernest Satow; and the correspondence of Dr George Ernest Morrison by Dr Loh Hui-min. Each of these sheds important light on the actual operations of Russia and Japan in China; and, while there may be a British or continental bias in them, they were well-informed and perceptive observers.

I was less satisfied by the picture of decision-making in St Petersburg which emerged from my reading. In order to take a fresh look at this problem I consulted the private papers of three British diplomats at the Russian capital: Sir Charles Scott, the ambassador from 1898 to 1904, (Sir) Charles Hardinge, the secretary (1898–1903) and then the ambassador, and (Sir) Cecil Spring-Rice, who was *chargé d'affaires* at the critical juncture of the outbreak of war. In view of the multi-dimensional nature of Russian decision-making, it was necessary to consult these three sources from time to time for contemporary political assessment and for background information. Taken together, they serve as a sort of Greek chorus, making comments on, without being part of, the drama. At the same time, I should stress that this is neither a study of British policy – or indeed of the Anglo-Japanese alliance in another disguise – nor a mere recapitulation of contemporary British attitudes. Perhaps fortunately for my purpose, Scott tended to be receptive to the Russian side of the case, while Hardinge and Spring-Rice were sceptical. The views of these three diplomats on the changing Russian scene will be found in *British Documents on Foreign Affairs: Reports and Papers from the Foreign Office Confidential Print: Russia 1859–1914,* edited by Dominic Lieven (General Editors: K. Bourne and D. C. Watt), 6 vols, University Publications of America, 1984, which, unfortunately, came to hand too late for inclusion in this volume.

I am under a great obligation to a wide variety of people. For help with material, thanks are due to Mrs E. A. Malozemoff of Oakland, California; Professor J. A. White of the University of Hawaii; Mr E. W. Edwards; Mr I. Gow; Mr R. Scoales; Dr Ann Trotter of the University of Otago; Professor-Doctor A. Schwade of the University of Bochum; Dr D. Mills, of Corpus Christi College, Cambridge, and the late Professor G. R. Storry of St Anthony's College, Oxford. I owe debts to my colleagues at the London School of Economics, especially Dr A. Polonsky and Professor M. S. Anderson. I must also thank the series editor, Professor H. Hearder, for many improvements. Among Japanese scholars, Dr Yūichi Inouye of the Foreign Ministry, Mr Setsuya Beppu, Dr Matsumura of the Japan Foundation, Professor Okumura and Emeritus Professor Uchiyama of Keio University, have all assisted me by supplying materials. In the final stages, I have received much help from Mrs Irene Perkin and Mrs Susan Shaw.

To librarians in half a hundred libraries who have helped me beyond the call of duty I express my gratitude and appreciation. In particular, I should thank the British Library of Political and Economic Science; the

Library of the School of Oriental and African Studies, London; the British Library, London, the Public Record Office, Kew; the Houghton Library, Harvard University; the Sterling Library, Yale University; the Diplomatic Records Office, Tokyo; the National Diet Library, Tokyo; and the Libraries of the Nissan Centre, St Antony's College, Oxford, of Churchill College, Cambridge, and of Cambridge University. In cases where citations have been made from papers held by these libraries, permission has been sought from their custodians and given by them. This is gratefully acknowledged. And more particularly, for permission to quote from papers in their custody, I am grateful to the Syndics of Cambridge University Library (Hardinge papers); to Churchill College, Cambridge (Spring-Rice papers); to the Department of Manuscripts, the British Library (Balfour and Scott papers). Public Record Office documents cited in this work are British Crown copyright and are reprinted by permission of Her Britannic Majesty's Stationery Office.

Many thanks are due to my wife who has tolerated my infatuation with this subject over such a long period.

IAN NISH

ABBREVIATIONS

BD	*British Documents on the Origins of the War, 1898–1914* (see under Great Britain in Bibliography)
DDF	*Documents Diplomatiques Français* (see under France)
d'Anethan Dispatches	Albert d'Anethan, *The d'Anethan Dispatches from Japan, 1894–1910*
'Eve of War'	'On the Eve of the Russo-Japanese War' in *Chinese Social and Political Science Review,* a translation of 'Nakanune Russko-Iaponskoi Voiny' in *Krasnyi Arkhiv,* **63** (1934) (see under *Krasnyi Arkhiv*)
FO	Foreign Office: General correspondence, deposited in the Public Record Office, London
Itō Hiroku	*Itō Hirobumi Hiroku* (see under Hiratsuka Atsushi)
NGB	*Nihon Gaikō Bunsho* (see under Japan)
NGNB	*Nihon Gaikō Nempyō narabi ni Shūyō Bunsho* (see under Japan)
Forty Years	Rosen, *Forty Years of Diplomacy*

For Fiona and Alison

INTRODUCTION

Now that peace is assured, the time seems to have arrived for the world to reflect more calmly than ever upon the origin of one of the greatest wars ever recorded in history; and upon the ideals and notions, as well as training and aspirations, of the Japanese, that one of the belligerent parties which had not, perhaps, been sufficiently known to the world before the war. And above all the time has come to observe how faithfully Japan has maintained her ambition of deserving the name of a civilized nation, and to reflect how securely we may take her steady progress of the past, and especially during the last ten years, as a guarantee of her continued advance in the future.[1]

So wrote Baron Suematsu in a semi-official book of essays, published just after the treaty of Portsmouth had brought the Russo-Japanese war to an end. In it he invites his readers in the various European countries to reflect on the origins of the war. It is relatively rare in the history of war for governments to invite enquiries into the origin of wars, more common for them to conceal and distort these origins and to discourage and frustrate the study of their root causes. In this case Japan's readiness to encourage the study of the origins of her war with Russia suggests the existence of great confidence on her part that her war aims were justified and shared by many other countries.

It was of course easier for Japan as the victor to issue such an invitation than it was for the defeated. To be sure, the Russians held that they were the wronged party, against whom warlike steps had been taken without provocation. But for them the war became subsumed in the revolutionary year of 1905. One Russian leader wrote in February 1905: 'If the war had ended in a few months, it would have strengthened Russia's spirit, her international prestige. Even if she had not achieved real benefits from it, she might perhaps have taken heart and her prestige been revived. But the war has grown sour ... and Russia's social fabric has gone to pieces.' The Russians still claimed that they had gone to war in a righteous cause. But they chose not to dwell on the muddled origins of the war unless it was for the purpose of self-justification.

1

Even without an invitation from the parties, there are ample grounds for studying the war's origins. The Russo-Japanese war was an important war of the twentieth century. Although it was confined to two countries, it was significant because of the vast number of those who took part in it: the Russian forces in the area starting at 100,000 troops and growing in 1905 to 1,300,000 and the Japanese starting with 300,000 and growing in 1905 to roughly triple that strength.[3] The war was equally important because of the bitterness of the fighting and the toll it took of the manhood of both countries: the lengthy siege of Port Arthur ended with a loss of 58,000 killed to the victorious Japanese and a loss of 31,000 to the Russians, while the immense battle of Mukden is estimated to have caused casualties of 85,000 to the Russians as against 70,000 to the Japanese. Its sheer scale would justify the description of 'a large and significant war of a bilateral kind'. It attracted the interest of army-navy officers around the world who competed to serve as attachés and its strategic and tactical lessons were soon the staple diet for study in the world's military academies. Most of the European nations deemed it to be sufficiently relevant to them to publish their multi-volume histories of the war.[4]

Even if the Russo-Japanese war was not a world war, it had repercussions throughout the world. Though the outside powers were not belligerents, they were surely 'involved'. France was the reluctant associate of Russia, while Britain and the United States were coming to be increasingly aligned with the cause of Japan. The fact that these countries avoided a declaration of war was sometimes a close-run thing. It will be necessary for us to test the argument often heard that Germany egged on Russia to expand in the Far East, while Britain egged on Japan to resist Russian expansion. The role of European countries in the origins of this war is, therefore, a subtle and complex one. The impact on Asia was equally strong. The war fundamentally changed the balance of power in east Asia and affected the destinies of Russia and Japan in the region. At another level the war was a victory for a coloured race against a white one and thereby shattered many nineteenth-century illusions.[5]

The Russo-Japanese war did not originate purely from a failure of diplomacy, though that was one factor. A diplomatic history would not therefore give an adequate account of its origins. Among its many-sided origins, there was a strong strategic factor. On the military side there were too many Russian troops in Manchuria in 1904 for Japan's conception of her own security and she did not succeed in negotiating for their withdrawal. On the naval side Russia wanted naval supremacy in the Korean straits, and Japan as an aspiring naval power could not accept that.[6] There were also economic origins. It was not so much that Russia and Japan were competitors in trade as that they seemed to be competing for the same raw materials in Korea and Manchuria. The situation looked even more menacing for Japan as the Russian railway empire in north-east Asia came to a state of operational readiness. This improved the position of Russia and necessarily worked to the disadvantage of Japan. There were no basic political incompatibilities between Russia and Japan. Both had elements of stability and instability. Indeed there were resemblances between them and no great ideological differences.

In this introduction we offer certain reflections on the policy-making process in Russia and Japan. This is not the place to undertake a detailed study of the Russian or Japanese state systems, especially as most of the issues which would arise could be highly controversial. We then turn to a brief account of the two areas of political weakness in northeast Asia at the turn of the century: the kingdom (sometimes the empire) of Korea and the empire of China, together with the economically unexploited area of Manchuria. In the age of imperialism these were the natural targets for 'protection' (as it was called) by the stronger powers. These were notably Russia and Japan. We close the introduction with a brief description of the effect of the various railway systems which brought the crisis to a head.

Our story starts in 1894 with the Sino-Japanese war but treats the next six years with brevity. From 1900, the time of Russia's occupation of Manchuria, to the last six weeks of peace in 1904, the subject-matter is treated in increasing detail. Such a deliberate imbalance in treatment seems inevitable when one is considering how attempts to prevent a conflict come eventually to nothing.

RUSSIA AND FAR EASTERN POLICY

In Russia an autocratic emperor had the final say in determining foreign affairs. In the decade covered by this book, there was no prime minister in Russia. For want of this, the emperor had to act as the coordinator to whom all the ministers made direct reference. The state secretaries followed the practice of sending official communications (including of course diplomatic correspondence) to the emperor, attaching their own views and recommendations as to the action that was needed and occasionally (generally too rarely) having audiences with him. There was no automatic opportunity for advance consultation with other ministers in the ordinary course. One consequence of this was that the emperor might receive differing advice from his state secretaries. Without a proper coordinating mechanism, it was not impossible for the emperor to endorse on different occasions courses of action which were mutually contradictory. This led to the accusation that one of the ministries had greater leverage with him and caused jealousies between departments. But at times in our story we shall also find that committees were set up to deliberate on the knotty problems of east Asia and to try to work out a consensus before advising the tsar.

In its formulation, far-eastern policy had to take account of commercial, strategic and diplomatic considerations. The tsar had to weigh the advice of the war ministry, the navy ministry, the finance ministry and the foreign ministry. Those in charge of these offices were not politicians but bureaucrats. Being officials, they did not have to serve constituents; make speeches or answer interpellations in a parliament (before 1905); justify their policies in public; or adjust them in order to make them publicly acceptable. There was not much pressure of public opinion in Russia which affected decisions on east Asia, as distinct from those on the Balkans where pan-slavic doctrines had their influence. Policies could be drawn up more coolly and implemented without fear of stirring up emotional scenes. The reverse of this was, however, that the Russian ministers had little understanding of any system, such as that of the Japanese, where ministers had to make parliamentary speeches and issue white papers on foreign policy. They were also impatient with the critical exposure which Russia received from speeches made in foreign countries.

Much depended upon the personality of the new Autocrat of all the Russias, Nicholas II (r. 1894–1917). He was born in 1868, the son of Alexander III and the Empress Marie from Denmark, and was well educated by private tutors. When his father became tsar, Nicholas was notoriously – and deliberately – kept out of touch with affairs of state. A rare exception to this was his world cruise in 1891 which included visits to India, Japan and Vladivostok. Among his adventures was the episode at Ōtsu in Japan when a disgruntled policeman attacked him with a sword and injured him in the head. The exact cause is still unclear; and the consequence of this incident for Nicholas's later judgements is equally unclear.[7] On his return to Russia, he became engaged in April 1894 to Princess Alexandra of Hesse-Darmstadt. But the euphoria of this event was soon broken by his father's sudden illness which resulted in his death at the age of forty-nine on 1 November. Nicholas acceded to the throne at the age of twenty-six in the midst of the war between China and Japan. His marriage took place later in the month, on the day following his father's funeral. He was formally crowned in May 1896 after a period of court mourning and amid a flurry of diplomatic activity.

What can be said of Nicholas in his first years on the throne? It is important not to read back to earlier times qualities which became manifest later in his reign when personal tragedies affected his mind. The impression left by his performance in the decade before the Russo-Japanese war is that of a dedicated, hard-working sovereign, who was caught up in paperwork, in audiences and ceremonial, and was unable to find a permanent adviser on whose judgement he could rely. Young, shy and diffident, he sought to avoid argument and confrontation and often firm decisions. But he was proud of his role as an autocrat, was strongly nationalistic and had a high sense of duty to his country. Surrounded by intrigue at his own court and swamped by advice from friendly senior monarchs abroad, he was apt to retreat into domestic life as a form of escapism from the harsh decisions which he alone could take.

Nicholas certainly had an unenviable role. In performing it, he seems to have suffered from lack of training and from the protected life he led. Sir Charles Scott, the British ambassador, reported that Nicholas was 'incapable, either from want of sufficient experience or by natural diffidence, of taking a decided initiative on his own judgement and inclined to throw his whole weight of responsibility on Count Mouravieff'.[8] This judgement probably applied equally to his other ministers. It was a dilemma for Russia: the decisions had to be made by the tsar; but he was unsure of himself and untrained for the office. Moreover the environment of his life was not ideal for making judgements. Because of the insecurity felt in court circles since the assassination of Alexander II, Nicholas generally lived in Tsarskoye Selo, some 15 miles from the capital, and never left his palaces without a strong guard. Surrounded by a small intimate coterie, he was cut off from awareness of public opinion and was the victim of those who reported to him. Since he had a self-contained character, he was content with this life of social isolation. Through the narrow window of Tsarskoye Selo he surveyed the affairs of Europe in the diplomatic papers he so conscientiously studied. Because of his world tour in 1891, he kept especially in touch with east Asian affairs and was evidently a strong believer in his country's prospects in Siberia and the far east.

The conduct of foreign affairs was made difficult by the strange pattern of the emperor's calendar. He had the custom of taking very long holidays, considering the crucial place that he occupied in policy-making. Nicholas would go in August to Wiesbaden for the sake of the tsarina; to the imperial hunting lodge at Spala in Poland; and later in the autumn to the Livadia Palace at Yalta in the Crimea. In these places, he was generally attended by some of his ministers, who only chose to stay close to the throne because of jealousy of their colleagues, who might be trying to steal a march with the tsar. Russian diplomats' reports went straight to these holiday places from capitals abroad, though foreign communications were delivered at St Petersburg where the foreign ministry maintained a nominal existence but where policy decisions could rarely be taken. These months (when so many of the crises in the east arose) were therefore a 'close season for diplomacy': the British ambassador generally took furlough from September to just before Christmas, by which time the court had returned to the capital, though this was not feasible for Japanese diplomats.

The fact that diplomacy at the Russian capital was difficult did not mean that the foreign policy pursued by the tsar and his ministers was other than moderate. The emperor frequently professed to be pursuing the object of peace. We know of the personal initiative which he took over the peace conference at The Hague in 1899. If it was regarded by professional diplomats as naïve and innocent, it was none the less representative of his style – and that of Nicholas I before him. It was his own handiwork, not that of his ministers. Contemporary witnesses confirm 'the emperor's innate love of peace'.[9] Indeed the closer people went to the emperor's family circle, the more they were impressed with this peace-loving quality. But Nicholas wanted peace on Russia's terms and failed to understand how objectionable her actions appeared to others or when a conciliatory approach was desirable.

Russia's foreign ministers were officials, not politicians. Whether Nicholas was well served by them is doubtful. He had three foreign ministers during the first ten years of his reign: Prince Lobanov-Rostovskii; M. N. Muraviev; and V. N. Lamsdorf. Lobanov was at the end of a long and distinguished diplomatic career in Europe; but he was 'often in the country and it was almost impossible to see him except on his reception day'.[10] Muraviev was appointed after a less distinguished career in less prominent capitals, while Lamsdorf came to prominence through service in the ministry itself. Their subordinates in the ministry were as always a mixed bag. On the one hand, they could be loyal and competent. On the other, some serious criticisms were made about their lack of professionalism. Thus Dmitrii Abrikosov, himself a junior in the service, wrote that 'the stagnation in the Foreign Ministry is indescribable. Everybody is asleep'.[11] The Germany ambassador also reported: 'Nor have I in my whole life ever seen so much laziness as in the ministries here. All officials arrive at 11 or 12 o'clock and disappear at 4 never to be seen again. During office hours they do nothing but smoke and promenade in the corridors'.[12] There was certainly slackness in the head office; and this reflected itself in some lack of control over legations and consulates overseas.

The weakness of the foreign ministry played into the hands of the already powerful finance ministry. The increasing preoccupation of the Russian state with railway building and industrialization which had been started under his father was a matter beyond Nicholas's competence. He tended to leave the problems associated with it – private capital and foreign loans – to the finance ministry and its new luminary, Sergei Witte (1849–1915). Witte's successful career began in a private railway company from which he had entered government service in 1888. He was chosen to head the railway department in the finance ministry in 1891 and became, first, communications minister and then finance minister in the following year. In this role he succeeded in restoring the state finances, returning the country to the gold standard and arranging state and private loans from abroad. Through his influence with the tsar, he was able to nominate those loyal to him to ministerial positions.[13]

Whether or not the relationship between Nicholas and Witte was one of trust, it was certainly on Nicholas's part one of dependence in the early stages. The power of the ministry of finance bureaucracy and its ability to manage state funds was something that Nicholas could not challenge. It came close to being a superior banking house, channelling the resources of the state into many ventures in Asia, notably the Trans-Siberian railway. Because these undertakings were so wide-ranging in their implications, Witte became the focus of much of the frenzied political activity in the east at the time.[14] Since he was by nature high-handed and self-confident, he often went ahead without due consideration for other political forces and parts of the bureaucracy. Naturally Witte became unpopular. But, so long as he enjoyed the support of the tsar, as he did until 1902, he had not much to fear. Nicholas, inheriting Witte as one of his father's ministers, kept on relatively good terms with him. When, however, the tsar turned against him Witte never forgave him and had many harsh things to write about the young tsar in retrospect in his memoirs, *Vospominaniya*.[15] It is, however, a distortion to believe that this was representative of his sentiments throughout the years he served the tsar.

Like Bismarck before him, Witte had by no means a guarantee of power. Firstly, he was disliked by many of his influential colleagues. Though they were dazzled by his brilliance, they were put off by his overbearing manner and dictatorial intrusions into their preserves. Secondly, his power derived from his ministry of which he had to make a success. The Russian economy being what it was, that could not be guaranteed in the long term. Thirdly, he had to kowtow to the tsar who was fickle in his likes and dislikes. Witte had to lobby to keep his views before his master. Naturally the supreme autocrat resented too much power falling into the hands of any of his subordinates and from 1902 onwards began to keep his distance from Witte, who was having less success with the economy.

There were many competing groups in the Russian court. The ministers, the grand dukes, the armed services – to name but a few. Thus conflicting policies would be put before the tsar with whom the final decision lay. Sometimes the tsar might be won over to one group and be used to do down its rival. On other occasions information might be withheld from the Sovereign: 'In the middle of all the tiraillements between contending Ministers, Grand Dukes and other influences, it is difficult to make out how much the Emperor is told.'[16] It was baffling to the diplomats who had to fathom which voice was speaking for Russia. It came as second nature to them to recognize that there were many voices and many policies operating simultaneously. Was it the voice of the armed services which were not kept under adequate central control? Was it the voice of the grand dukes, the four brothers of Nicholas's father, each an independent, strong-willed man, that carried weight? There was a Babel of voices and little coordination. Russian government was disorganized, inefficient and only kept abreast of the modern industrialized world with difficulty.[17]

In these circumstances it would be unreasonable to expect that Russian 'policy' at the frontier would be crystal clear to the outside observer. There was inefficiency, rivalry and contradiction there too. Yet it has to be said that Russia exhibited remarkable skill in dealing with China, the central problem of east Asia in the 1890s, despite the fact that she had no integrated colonial service and had to improvise with officials from many walks of life. These officials seem to have succeeded in convincing at least some of the potentates of the Middle Kingdom that Russia was the true friend and best protector of China, despite the evidence that she was, on the contrary, the most expansive of outside countries. The Russians seem to have understood better the foibles of the Chinese officials of the Tsungli Yamen (Board of Foreign Relations) and its successor, the Waiwupu; the court and the eunuchs; and especially the Manchu clansmen. They seem to have grasped successfully the subtle relationship between central government and the viceroys in the provinces. Russian diplomats often saw long periods of continuous service in the east and had a good command of languages of the area. They were also skilful in adapting to the mores of the Chinese court. J. O. P. Bland, the experienced British commentator on things Chinese, wrote: 'The Russians pay their Chinese friends well not only for what they want but also to block our roads. They have the foremost men in the (Chinese) Empire in their employ and interest while we go on blundering in the dark, violating every principle of mandarin livelihood.'[18] This judgement doubtless reflects the distrust between Britain and Russia in coping with the problems of China and may therefore be unfair.[19] But it underlines the reputation which Russia had for maintaining good relations despite her inclination for racialism. One of the most effective experts was D. D. Pokotilov, the finance ministry man with special responsibility for the Russo-Chinese Bank and the Chinese Eastern Railway. Coming to China at the age of 22 in 1898, he acquired an unsurpassed knowledge of the Chinese language. His skill in handling Peking officials was outstanding; and the adherence of Li Hung-chang to the Russian cause was in large measure his doing. He was to become minister to China from 1905 to 1908.

JAPAN AND ASIAN POLICY

In Japan and Russia there were like and unlike elements. Unlike Russia, Japan was a constitutional state with a monarchy limited by the Meiji constitution of 1890. Like Russia, Japan reserved many prerogatives and autocratic powers to the emperor who for the period of this study was the Emperor Meiji (r. 1868–1912). By 1894 he had become an important ruler with abundant experience in seeing his country developing through years of rapid change. This did not mean that the emperor took an active part in state affairs. But at moments of crisis, he either convened an imperial conference or in other ways made clear his views. In foreign affairs he took a part in decision-making over Japan's part in the relief of the Peking legations in 1900, the signing of the Anglo-Japanese alliance in 1902 and in the decision to declare war on Russia. In general, he was able to hold up decisions while the substance was further studied. He did not tend in the second half of his reign to put up alternative policies of his own so much as to serve as a corrective or delaying force.

One example of the emperor's prerogatives was to refer issues to a body called the genro or elder statesmen. This was a group of cautious leaders, products of the Meiji restoration, and former prime ministers who were by the 1890s mainly in their late fifties. In foreign affairs these men were a counter-force to the political party leaders who were often fiery and belligerent. They restrained the more extreme groups and urged them to take account of the strengths of foreign powers. This body was extra-constitutional and depended on the exercise of the emperor's prerogatives. It has to be remembered that Japan was not stable politically in the 1890s and 1900s and the volatile members of political parties were often advocates of quite extravagant policies in foreign affairs. Only a senior body, backed by the emperor's authority, was in a position to keep them in check.

In Japan as in Russia, it is difficult to assess the exact weighting of those in the uppermost echelons of power. Because of the divinity ascribed to the Japanese emperor, it was difficult for commentators to estimate his role, though it was clear that he did not make the ultimate decisions as the tsar had to do. In order to find out who counted in Japan's decisions, it is sometimes necessary to look at the writings of foreign observers who were admitted to inner court circles. Such a person was Sir Claude MacDonald, the British diplomat who stayed in Japan for the first decade of this century. He wrote:

> I sat opposite to the Emperor at the lunch given to Admiral Noel and the officers of our Fleet. Besides plying a very healthy knife and fork, His Majesty chatted most amicably with everybody all around. The Imperial Princes, Arisugawa and Kanin who sat on either side, treated him with marked deference but Marquis Ito and Count Inouye (the latter sat next to me) seemed to speak on absolute terms of equality and cracked jokes which made this direct descendant of the Sun roar with laughter. It was a great revelation to me and one which pleased me very much for though a Mikado he seems very human.[20]

The high standing of the elder statesmen in the counsels of the Emperor Meiji comes out strongly from this passage which lifts the veil a little on the relationships between those at the top.

During the period covered by this study, Japan grew from being a regional power, able to gain ascendancy over Korea and China, to being a world power. From 1895 Japan set about a fundamental restructuring of her army and navy. It was to be completed within ten years and was to be funded by the large indemnity obtained from China after her victory over that country in war. Not only would both services be modernized but ordnance factories and shipyards would be developed so that Japan could speedily become self-sufficient in arms and naval shipbuilding. There was unquestionably a spirit of national pride in Japan's progress and achievement which began to show itself in nationalist rhetoric. All too often this was to be directed at Russia.

By contrast with Russia, the foreign ministry was young and small. But its bureaucracy was efficient and farsighted. The service became highly professional when the system of competitive entry by examination was instituted in 1894. Japanese diplomats were thereafter drawn from the elite of the university system; and even senior diplomats in the Japanese service were young by European standards.

The foreign minister was a junior, but important, member of the cabinet. By 1894 he was generally a career foreign ministry bureaucrat recalled from posting overseas to enter the cabinet. He had normally no political affiliation and to that extent did not count in the battles that the political parties were waging. The office holders changed often. Four of the foreign ministers in our period were strong characters who were able to hold sway by force of personality but not political clout: Mutsu (1892–96); Aoki (1898–1900); Katō (1900–1); Komura (1901–5). The foreign minister had to keep on good terms with the prime minister and through him with the genro if he was to steer through his policies. But serious disputes could arise among the ministers and between the anti-Russian foreign ministry and the pro-Russian genro.

As in the case of Russia, we must speak of 'many policies' rather than 'one policy'. Not only were there several policies in Tokyo (as we shall see as the study advances); but those on the frontier assumed that they had a certain degree of licence. Thus, consuls in China and Korea who often did not have a high opinion of the Chinese or the Koreans but tended to share the opinions of European diplomats, took certain liberties. They and the soldiers were often pursuing active policies of advance. The Russo-Japanese incident at Masampo in 1899 was a case where local officers tried to ensure that their own nation did not come off second best (probably without the knowledge of Tokyo). The time after 1895 was one of patriotism and confidence *vis-à-vis* Asian countries as expressed in the publications *Kokumin no tomo* and *Nipponshugi*.

There was already evidence of the divide between the army and the civilians which was to dog Japan's policies in the 1930s. That it did not unduly affect Japan's fortunes in the 1895–1905 period was due to the institution of the genro which put a brake on precipitate action by the army. But it was due even more to the fact that the genro contained within its membership both General Yamagata and General Ōyama, the military heroes of the Sino-Japanese war and the military leaders of the Chōshū clan from which the officer corps was in the main drawn. While the genro were often divided – and the tension between Yamagata the soldier and Itō the civilian politician was often considerable – it was generally possible to work for a consensus between any hard-line military position and more moderate lines of policy. Such was the contribution to Japan's international affairs of the genro, who had the personal confidence of the emperor and used it to intervene at crucial junctures in the interest of restraint.

The instrument for these consensual decisions was the imperial council (*gozen kaigi*) or council in the presence of the emperor. At these gatherings which were held irregularly, the senior members of the cabinet were summoned along with the genro to sit in front of the emperor to discuss policy. This procedure came to an end after the death of the Emperor Meiji in 1912. But, while it lasted, it kept an eye on the political and military hotheads and imposed some discipline over them.

The 1890s was a time when the political standing of the army and navy grew. The root of their power was the special position which the military held under the Meiji constitution of 1889–90. This recognized for the army the independence of the right of supreme command (*tōsuiken no dokuritsu*): there could be no civilian interference over the command and operation of forces. The army leaders had the right of direct access to the throne, the emperor being commander-in-chief. Even the cautious General Yamagata tried to use this right in 1894 against the wishes of Tokyo but was recalled from the field.

Japan had a remarkable knowledge of things Russian including culture and literature, in spite of being at a stage of development where she admired Europe and turned her back on Asia. The yearning of Japanese academics and intellectuals for the writings and social thought of Tolstoy, Gorky and Dostoievsky was immense. There were colleges in Tokyo for the study of the Russian language, both government-controlled and private. There were also many translations of the Russian nineteenth-century classics appearing in Japanese at the turn of the century.[21]

It would be misleading to judge the Japanese establishment by reference to the attitudes of Japan's progressive intelligentsia, which was in so many ways opposed to it. The establishment was much more taken up with the menace of Russia, seeing that country as the major threat to Japan's national security. As the interests of Russia and Japan came into conflict and their armed forces clashed from the 1850s onwards, there was published a substantial literature speculating about Russia's military and diplomatic objectives in the area of north-east Asia. After the confrontation of 1895 the Japanese government took positive steps through the army and navy to collect intelligence about

Russia and the vulnerability of the Russian Empire in Europe, especially Finland and Poland.[22] Thus, there was no shortage of information about Russia and her doings, even if it was largely hostile in tone.

There was no real counterpart to this in Russia. While there was academic instruction about things Japanese and while the Russians had built churches in Japan, even a cathedral (St Nikolai) in Tokyo, the Russian approach to Japan was similar to that towards other parts of east Asia, namely, superiority and a desire for assimilation.[23] It was understandable therefore if the majority of Japanese at the turn of the century looked on Russia as a menace, as a country whose interests and possessions impinged on their own and threatened to harm them.

EMPIRE OF CHINA

The two areas of north-east Asia which are the focus of this study are Korea and Manchuria, the latter a sparsely inhabited part of the Manchu empire of China. Korea had been historically a tributary state of China, though she had concluded commercial treaties with Japan and the western countries since the 1870s. After the appointment in 1883 of a vigorous Chinese viceroy, China regained some of the prestige she had lost but at the cost of antagonizing the Japanese. Increasingly the Korean king turned for protection towards Russia which saw this as a convenient opportunity. But the largest foreign community was the Japanese with 20,000 residents.[24]

Manchuria was one of the wealthier but under-populated parts of the Manchu empire which had reached its zenith in the eighteenth century. But the Manchus had more recently failed to come to terms with the challenge presented by western commercial states in their determination to stay in power. To be sure, they took steps towards consolidation and modernization; they created an army and navy with modern weapons; and they built factories. But, when a major test of strength came in the war with Japan of 1894–95, the Manchu institutions were found wanting and China came to be spoken of as 'the sick man of Asia'.

In the atmosphere of weakness which prevailed in China towards the end of the nineteenth century, the bureaucrats had to adapt their tactics accordingly. They were loyal to the dynasty in the main but they were also self-seeking. A bureaucrat like Li Hung-chang (1823–1901) was loyal to his monarch and to his country and to his family and friends. For him the survival of the dynasty was probably the prime priority, more important than the survival of the country. Li had a sense of national need as shown in his awareness of the need for a navy, for shipbuilding yards and ordnance factories. But he was at the same time not averse to feathering his own nest. From 1895 till his death he was the leader of the pro-Russian party at the Chinese court and received subventions from Russia for his services. 'Squeeze' was not, of course, purely a western importation; it was native to China. The Manchu court was heavily implicated in 'squeeze'. The leaders of the day had not a strong enough sense of nationalism to wage a campaign against these corrupt practices.

The illusion of 'sickness' was if anything increased by the uniqueness of the Chinese government system. This can be illustrated by remarks made by Sir Ernest Satow at the end of a six-year stint as British minister to China:

> China is not a centralized state of modern type, but rather a congeries of semi-autonomous satrapies, a confederacy of territories each possessing a separate financial, military, naval and judicial organization, in fact a sort of 'Home rule all round' system, presided over by a central committee for deciding questions referred to it by the provincial authorities.[25]

With this sprawling, amorphous, decentralized structure, China was unfamiliar to Europeans who had become used to the triumph of the centralized nation-state in the nineteenth century. To locate the focus of power in China was much more complicated. For foreigners the first point of access was to the Tsungli Yamen (Board of Foreign Relations) which possessed no real power. They reported to the grand council, a loose cabinet consisting of those who presided over the various boards. These had audiences daily with the empress dowager (1834–1908) who for most of our period was the dominant force. Behind her was the emperor who did not count especially after his attempts at reform in 1898. Then there was the legendary power of the two hundred or so palace eunuchs who exerted influence over the empress dowager. The independent authority of the provincial governors could be great as for instance at the time of the Boxer rebellion in 1900. Alongside them were the statesmen, some like Li Hung-chang himself who owed their position to successes achieved in the role of provincial governor. Li, who will be prominent in the early part of our story, and Prince Ching, a member of the imperial family who became prominent after Li's death, are the only two Chinese statesmen who can claim to have been world figures of any significance.

Manchuria was the name given to the territory known to the Chinese as the Three Eastern Provinces. It was divided for administrative purposes into the three provinces of Liaoning (Fengtien), Kirin and Heilungkiang. Of these Heilungkiang to the north was by far the largest while Liaoning was the smallest and most accessible. In the 1890s Manchuria had been regarded mainly as a place valuable for its strategic situation; but gradually, with the development of railway building in the area, it came to be recognized as a territory rich in agricultural, forestry and mineral resources. The railways attracted large numbers of Chinese labourers mainly from the province of Shantung and Hopei who stayed on in the north and, when the rail network was completed, impoverished Chinese farmers took advantage of it to establish themselves in the newly opened territory. So too did the Koreans who tried to set up farms across the Yalu river.

Our concern is largely with Liaoning and especially with its most southerly tip, the Liaotung peninsula. This possessed very special strategic significance, being so close to the approaches to the Chinese capital of Peking and commanding the Gulf of Chihli. It included, in particular, the naval base of Port Arthur (Lushun), the home port of the Chinese Northern (Peiyang) fleet. The dockyard there had been built at great cost by French contractors. The entrance to the harbour was a narrow one since the bay on which the town stood was shielded from the Yellow Sea by a vast peninsula, the Tiger's Tail. The harbour's east side had a depth of water of 9 metres while the west side was open to commercial traffic. Moreover its naturally strong position was improved by having the strongest fortress in China. Still it was basically a small place with a small population in 1894.

Talien, known to the Japanese as Dairen and to the Russians as Dalny, was in 1894 not much more than a fishing-village. The harbour was ice-free, like that of Port Arthur. It was intended by Witte to be an entrepôt for ordinary export items from Manchuria like soya beans, bean cake, coal etc.[26] In practice, however, it proved to be hard to attract trade to Talien. The Chinese merchants who were the dominant group in the coastal trade were not inclined to promote the growth of the port, while the foreign trading houses were content to work through existing channels. Like the rest of the Liaotung peninsula, Talien was a place of unmade roads and very primitive conditions, which were only redeemed by its accessibility to the sea. The coming of the railway age to this area was to bring about a transformation in its fortunes, as it became the headquarters of the new line.

A special part in our story will be played by Niuchuang (Newchwang), which was the only treaty port on Manchurian soil. There is some confusion about the proper terminology for this town. Niuchuang was about 30 miles up-country and not a port; it had seen its best days in the seventeenth century. On the Liao river was Yingkow, sometimes referred to as 'Port Newchwang', which was in fact the treaty port and the site of the foreign settlement. 'Newchwang' was the name used for it by foreigners, even though the official Chinese place-name was Yingkow. Yingkow was about fifteen miles from the mouth of the Liao river, which was navigable for 200 miles to beyond Mukden. Niuchuang had therefore great potential as a market for produce coming down from the Manchurian plain. Niuchuang was the place of settlement for foreigners, mainly Russians, Japanese, British and Americans, a community of 7,700 of which the Japanese made up 7,400. Opened as a treaty port in 1861, it had become a prosperous town by the 1890s with customs offices, consulates, warehouses of foreign merchants and the gunboat dock which gave a vestige of security in an area notorious for banditry. To the south, there was silting of the river at the bar. Additionally the river was frozen solid by ice in the mid-winter months. Yet, so long as Manchuria was opened by river, Niuchuang's position was assured. With the coming of railway venturers, however, there was the possibility that it might be passed by.[27]

THE RAILWAY AGE COMES TO NORTH CHINA

Until the final decade of the nineteenth century the string of Russian settlements which crossed Siberia were linked only by path and river. At the end of this chain was the port of Vladivostok, which was the focal point of Russia's naval power in the Pacific from 1871 onwards. Vladivostok was not ideal from the naval standpoint because of the serious icing problems in the winter.

Although an exceptionally powerful ice-breaker was available during these months, Russian ships still had to seek safe haven in ports to the south, including Japan.[28] And Russia could not secure a Korean port, for example, without inviting the resistance from one or other of the powers, as the Port Hamilton (Komondo) crisis had shown in 1885.

Could Vladivostok and the Russian colony around it be revived by opening up railway communication? The first rail survey across Siberia was conducted in 1887, though the idea had been talked of many times before by governors-general and military men. Now it was pursued. In February 1891 the committee which had been studying the matter came out in favour of building a line. The ministers adopted the proposal. Alexander III in his rescript of 29 March confirmed this decision to the world. His son, Nicholas Alexandrovich (later to be tsar as Nicholas II) was in the far east at the time and was ordered to perform the inauguration ceremony. In Vladivostok on 31 May the tsarevich laid the foundation stone for the station on the Ussuri section of the line.[29] The work had been started earlier on the track and, like the other sections scattered across Asia as far west as Cheliabinsk, made great progress. A special body called the Trans-Siberian railway committee was created towards the end of 1891 to deal with the problems of economic development and colonization of the area. New energy was infused into the scheme by Sergei Witte, who had been a railway specialist in the private sector before he became a minister. Although he had not been associated with this grandiose design from the outset, he soon made it his own. He had the expansive personality to cope with the large-scale problems which arose. It was a bond between him and the tsarevich, who was appointed chairman of the railway committee in 1893.[30]

The first stage of the enterprise was completed in 1897. The Ussuri line from Vladivostok to Khabarovsk was opened to traffic and passengers could travel between these towns in two days. This gave Vladivostok a new lease of life. In 1885 it had been a mean frontier town with a population estimated at 13,000, of which Russians made up 7,500 and Chinese, Koreans and Japanese 5,500. When the building of the line began, there was a great influx of labour for the railway, both Russians and others. By 1897 it had grown to 28,896 of which the Russians made up 16,265. The same rapid growth was to be found in other far-eastern cities like Khabarovsk and Blagovestchensk. It was assumed that these small communities would be expanded by migration when the complete route was in operation.[31]

The Trans-Siberian proper was built fast and expensively. It was built in sections using local contract labour – never a good way of effecting economies. On the other hand, it was to be a single-track line, built to minimum standards in order to ensure both cheapness and speed. The assumption was that it would take time for the traffic to pick up. Its construction was therefore seen as basic and experimental. The problem of passing Lake Baikal was not initially faced as the train was merely to be put on the ferry. It was not until 1904 that the Baikal loop was built to take the track round the cliffs at the southern end of the lake. It was in short a rough-and-ready enterprise, with the main emphasis placed on speed of construction.[32]

The great paradox was that Russia with her weak economy should have been so bold as to embark on this vast, uncertain and extravagant venture. The fact was that the Russian Empire had one of the weakest economies in Europe and there was a great discrepancy between that economy and her territorial aggrandizement in Asia. It was therefore a financial miracle that a country so retarded should have been able to contemplate building a railway on such a scale. It shows the extent of the imperialist drive. Since there could be no clear expectation of quick returns from a railway passing over an area so sparsely populated, Russia's investment in the Trans-Siberian was really an 'investment in potential'.

Russia could not have embarked on the Trans-Siberian railway project without enlisting the support of French capital. The availability of this was linked to the conclusion of, first, an entente (1891) and, later, an alliance between the two countries (1894). These arrangements offered political and defensive cooperation and smoothed the way for financial partnership.[33] It was not clear to contemporaries how far the military aspect of the alliance applied to the far east in those days of secret diplomacy. Certainly the Japanese thought it would and saw a proof of this in the three-power intervention of 1895. But it was generally held that the Franco-Russian alliance was confined to Europe, even if there were uncertainties on this point.[34]

The raising of French loans was one of the responsibilities of Witte.

By channelling the funds for the railway through his finance ministry, he ensured that he had a continuing control over the Trans-Siberian and related lines during their building phase. But he had a struggle and it was always doubtful how long his colleagues would permit his dominance. Witte originally had high hopes of the line being commercially viable and maintained this view in his memoirs.[35] He hoped to recoup the high expenses of rapid construction by the commercial profits of the line. But this optimistic assessment was soon dropped. Instead the railway came to justify itself more and more by strategic considerations. Firstly it offered the opportunity to step up the rate of colonization in Russia's eastern territories; and secondly it gave Russia the means to increase the number of her armed forces there at short notice. But the more that strategic considerations crept in, the more Witte had to share responsibility for railway decisions with the army and navy ministers who were more often than not his jealous rivals. This was to become true after 1898 and more so after 1900. This conflict of authority led to discord and, of course, as the prospects of profits receded, intrigue and attacks on Witte. Yet, to the outside observer, these disagreements were not obvious; and, as the various eastern lines were opened, there was great euphoria in Russia at a remarkable national achievement.

In Asiatic Russia the railway age went through three phases in our period. The first was the original Trans-Siberian line, which was intended to proceed by the Amur route (9,200 km), though the Amur line was not taken up till after 1905. The second was the shortened route from Lake Baikal through Tsitsihar and Harbin to Vladivostok (1,510 km). The third was the extension of the railway south from Harbin to Port Arthur (772 km). The second section became the 'Chinese Eastern Railway', while the third became known as the 'south Manchurian line'. Since this last line came south and west into territory of political and strategic significance, it was this as much as the Trans-Siberian railway which caught the imagination of neighbouring countries and raised their suspicions.

Let us remember that Russia saw her railways as having a *mission civilisatrice*. Indeed, Russian railways were regarded as uniquely civilizing. Thus, an early *Guide to the Great Siberian Railway,* published in 1900, states proudly:

> The civilizing policy of Russia in the East, which may be regarded as an exception to that of other countries, was guided by other principles and was directed to the mutual welfare of nations by the maintenance of peace throughout the immense extent of her dominions. The honour of having planted the flag of Christianity and civilization in Asia is due to Russia. The near future will show the results of the activity of our Government and of our civilizing enterprises, which will add to the glory and power of Russia and her Sovereign Chief.[36]

The railways also had the effect of changing the existing image of Siberia and the Maritime Provinces as a place of exile and of giving it social opportunities.[37]

China too had ambitions to build railways in the north of her territory. As early as 1878, Li Hung-chang had asked C. W. Kinder, a British engineer, to build a railway to Tangshan in order to carry coal from the Kaiping mines. By 1890 when the line to Kaiping had been completed, Li proposed that the line from Shanhaikuan should be extended through Mukden to Kirin and Hunchun, thus strengthening China's hold and preventing Russian influence from spreading in the area. To that end he set up the Imperial Chinese Railway Administration which took the line to Chinchow (Northern line) by the time the war with Japan began in 1894. When peace returned, Li wanted to enlist the financial and technical assistance of British interests. But the Hongkong-Shanghai Bank would not agree to raise a loan as the railway administration was heavily overdrawn. The Chinese made some headway and obtained major finance from British sources in 1898 to build the Northern Line Extension.

Since 1890 Japan, under the influence of General Yamagata, had been anxious to prevent the railways in Korea – both Seoul–Fusan and Seoul–Uiju – falling under Russian control.[38] She had been surveying the terrain between Seoul and Fusan to see whether she herself could build a line there. After the Sino-Japanese war, Russia which had gained influence throughout the peninsula objected to the building of the line unless it was in her hands. This only strengthened the Japanese resolve and a group of businessmen, led by Shibusawa Eiichi, raised enough capital to proceed with the line. When construction began, the Russians asked for the line to adopt the broad gauge that they used. The pace of building was speeded up in 1903 and most of the Seoul–Fusan line was completed before the Russo-Japanese war broke out, the remaining section being accomplished in January 1905.[39]

The significance of all this activity was that north-east Asia was for the first time experiencing the railway age. In these decades of imperialism railways were a means of one country expanding its territory. Russia and Japan – and most countries for that matter – were exerting pressure on the weak Chinese and Korean governments to obtain firm and exclusive railway privileges. The competition for these rail concessions excited serious international jealousies. It was clear that in the band of territory extending from Peking, through Chinchow and Port Arthur to Seoul, these concessions would be hotly contested. The vast railways of Russia excited the particular interest of military men in Japan who saw the security of their islands being threatened by them and concluded that Russia should be stopped before her railway network reached its full operating capacity. The deteriorating Russo-Japanese relationship which is the theme of this book has to be seen against the background of railway building.

REFERENCES AND NOTES

1.   Suematsu Kenchō, *The Risen Sun* (London 1905), p. x.
2.   Witte to Kuropatkin, 12 Mar. 1905, in *Krasnyi Arkhiv,* **19** (1927), no. 6, p. 140.
3.   Estimates of troop strength are very varied, being equally difficult to calculate on both sides. On the Japanese side, Itō Masanori, *Kokubōshi,* pp. 219–22; on the Russian, *Russko-Iapanskaia Voina* (Leningrad 1933).
4.   For example, Committee of Imperial Defence, *Official History of the Russo-Japanese War* (London 1910 (5 parts)); *Der Russisch-japanische Krieg* (Vienna, 1906). Attachés reports were also published by Germany and the United States.
5.   For example R. P. Dua, *The Impact of the Russo-Japanese War on Indian Politics* (Delhi 1966).
6.   Itō Masanori, op. cit., pp. 216–19, for Chief of General Staff's memorial of 1 Feb, 1904.
7.   G. A. Lensen, 'The attempt on the life of Nicholas II in Japan' in *Russian Review,* **20** (1961), pp. 232–53.
8.   Scott to Salisbury, 27 May 1898, Scott papers, 52297.
9.   G. P. Gooch and H. W. V. Temperley (eds), *British Documents on the Origins of the War, 1898–1914,* vol. 2, no. 282. (Hereafter cited as *BD.*)
10. M. H. Fisher and N. Rich (eds), *Holstein Papers: Correspondence,* iii, no. 480.
11. D. Abrikosov, *Revelations of a Russian Diplomat,* p. 88.
12. *Holstein,* iii, no. 480.
13. T. H. von Laue, *Sergei Witte and the Industrialization of Russia*, pp. 146–7.
14. I. I. Rostunov, *Istoriya Russko-Iaponskoi Voiny,* p. 35: 'Between 1892 and 1903 Witte laid down Russia's far eastern policy in the main.'
15. S. Iu. Witte, *Vospominaniya,* vol. 1, pp. 9 ff.
16. T. H. Sanderson to Cecil Spring-Rice, 2 Dec. 1903 in Spring-Rice papers (FO 800/241).
17. Witte to Kuropatkin, 12 Mar. 1905 in *Krasnyi Arkhiv,* **19** (1927), p. 140.
18. Bland to Burkill, 13 Apr. 1903 in J. O. P. Bland Papers, 3.
19. A. L. Galperin, *Anglo-Iaponskii Soiuz,* p. 31.
20. MacDonald to Lansdowne, 24 Oct. 1905 in Lansdowne papers (FO 800/134).
21. Nobori Shomu and Akamatsu Katsumaro, *The Russian Impact on Japan: Literature and Social Thought,* pp. 14–19.
22. Kurobane Shigeru, *Nichi-Ro Sensō to Akashi Kōsaku,* pp. 73–4.
23. A. I. Alekseyev, *Osvoenie russkimi lyudmi Dalnego Vostoka i Russkoi Ameriki,* pp. 158–9.
24. G. A. Lensen, *Balance of Intrigue* vol. 2, p. 804.
25. Satow to Grey, 31 Mar. 1906, in Grey papers (FO 800/89).
26. Witte, op. cit., vol. 1, ch. 9.
27. Bowra papers, 17, p. 63.
28. Alekseyev, op. cit., p. 145.
29. Harmon Tupper, *To the Great Ocean,* pp. 81–5.
30. Rostunov, op. cit., pp. 35–6.
31. Alekseyev, op. cit., pp. 144–6.

32. Tupper, op. cit., pp. 336–40.
33. V. I. Bovykin, 'The Franco-Russian Alliance' in *History*, **64** (1979), pp. 20–35.
34. Jordan (Seoul) to Morrison, 21 Jan. 1900, in Lo Hui-min (ed.), *The Correspondence of G. E. Morrison*, vol. 1, pp. 130–1.
35. Witte, op. cit., vol. 1, pp. 130–3.
36. A. I. Dmitriev-Mamonov and A. F. Zdziarskii (eds), *Guide to the Great Siberian Railway*, p. 51.
37. Ibid., pp. 51–2. 'The deliverance of Siberia from the sad lot of affording a refuge to the worthless elements of the Empire, was the logical result of that work of civilization which, giving social capacity and competency to that country, thereby strengthened its position as mediator in the great mission of Russia in the East for the introduction of the principles of Christian civilization into Asiatic life.'
38. Ōyama Azusa (ed.), *Yamagata Aritomo Ikensho*, pp. 175–80, 198–9.
39. Inouye Yūichi, 'Russo-Japanese Relations and railway construction in Korea, 1894–1904', pp. 95–6.

Chapter 1

THE FIRST RUSSO-JAPANESE CONFRONTATION (1894–97)

Our study must start with the Sino-Japanese war of 1894–95. The areas which come into contention between Russia and Japan and lead ultimately to the Russo-Japanese war – Korea, Manchuria and north-eastern China – were the battlefields of this war. While the war was fought between China and Japan, it attracted the close attention of the powers of Europe and in some cases affected their interests. It is therefore necessary to write of the campaigns of this war, the peace-making and its consequences, even though this can be done only briefly.

The Sino-Japanese war grew out of a dispute in Korea, which had traditionally been a tributary kingdom of China. In 1894 there had been serious civil disturbances in Korea, largely between the reformers supported by Japan and the more traditional court supported by China. When the Chinese reinforced their garrison in the peninsula by sending an expeditionary force, the cabinet of Marquis Itō Hirobumi, with the army chief of staff and his deputy present, decided on 2 June to augment its own garrison there. Three days later a general headquarters (Dai-hon'ei), the instrument for coordination between the commands of the army and navy, was set up, a sure indication that war was approaching. On 25 July encounters began with a naval battle in which Japan attacked a Chinese convoy carrying troops to Korea and sank the *Kowshing,* a British transport vessel under charter to the Chinese. Japan had won command of the seas and was able to send her troop transports to Korea freely. On 23 July Japanese troops entered the royal palace in Seoul and a few days later won the battle of Asan. This was followed by the official declaration of war on 1 August. The number of Chinese and Japanese troops was greatly stepped up. The Japanese pushed north and captured P'yongyang on 16 September, driving all Chinese troops out of Korea by the end of the month. Meanwhile Japan had signed with Korea an offensive and defensive alliance.

The Japanese entered Manchuria by crossing the Yalu river on 24 October. Another army group took advantage of the decisive defeat of the Chinese Peiyang squadron to stage a landing on the Liaotung peninsula itself. On 6 November it took possession of Talienwan and a fortnight later captured Port Arthur, the base of the Peiyang squadron. Meanwhile Marshal Yamagata Aritomo, commander of the 1st army, ordered his troops to move forward on Haicheng, an important strategic position, as a prelude to a crossing of the Liao river. But Prime Minister Itō in Tokyo was far from ready to contemplate Japanese troops entering Chihli province and obtained the approval of the emperor for the recall of Yamagata for the sake of recuperating from the illness from which he was then suffering.[1] Yamagata had shown himself inclined to follow a line independent of Tokyo. By this action, the prime minister prevented the army from pursuing any intention it may have had to march on Peking. When Yamagata returned to imperial headquarters at Hiroshima on 17 December, he presented a memorandum setting out the options open to the Japanese army and recommending that the army should be landed on the Shantung peninsula where conditions would be less severe than those it was suffering in Manchuria.[2]

While Yamagata had to resign his command, his policy recommendations were adopted. The Shantung peninsula was attacked in mid-January; and Weihaiwei fell to the Japanese after a naval battle on 12 February. Meanwhile in Manchuria the 1st and 2nd armies joined up and captured Liaoyang, Niuchuang and the port of Yingkow (6 March). Units crossed the Liao river two days later with tough fighting. It was another of Japan's objectives to obtain from China the island of Taiwan. In preparation for this, Japanese forces occupied the neighbouring Pescadores islands late in March and stayed there, awaiting the invasion of Taiwan.

By the spring the Japanese army and navy were in effective charge of a remarkably wide area of east Asia. The army commanders like Yamagata were heroes of the successful campaign which was popular with the people at large. Yet Japan's resources and manpower were strained and her commitments were dangerously dispersed.

PEACE-MAKING AT SHIMONOSEKI

The Chinese announced that they were sending Japan a peace delegation on 5 January 1895. The powers were genuinely anxious for the return of peace, partly out of sympathy for China, and partly out of their own self-interest. In order to overcome the uncertainty about the post-war far east, the Russians in particular wanted to learn Japan's peace terms.

On 27 January the Japanese leaders held an imperial conference (gozen kaigi) at the imperial headquarters in Hiroshima. In a lengthy report to the throne, Itō set out his strategy thus: 'If we are to announce

our peace terms, we cannot be sure that it will not encourage
interference from outside powers. That is almost inevitable but we
cannot predict what form it will take or give assurances to prevent it.'³
The conference was reconciled to the inevitability of outside
intervention without being quite sure from which quarter it would come.
In the Hiroshima prefectural office on 1 February the Japanese met the
Chinese peace delegates but found they did not possess sufficient
plenipotentiary powers. Negotiations failed and the Chinese returned
from Nagasaki to Shanghai on 12 February. In order to limit the degree
of foreign involvement, the Japanese decided that the next talks should
be held at Shimonoseki, a small port-town in west Japan not too far
from Hiroshima, the Imperial Headquarters for the war period.

On 20 March the first meeting took place between the Chinese
plenipotentiaries, Li Hung-chang and Li Ching-fong, and their
Japanese counterparts, Itō and Mutsu Munemitsu, the foreign minister.
After four days of negotiation Li Hung-chang, on his way back from the
conference to his ship, was seriously injured by a Japanese, and the
Japanese leaders agreed to grant a ceasefire, which was concluded on 30
March, and offered an armistice for twenty-one days, that is, till 20
April.⁴

On 17 April, just before the armistice was due to lapse, China
accepted the Treaty of Shimonoseki. Under article II China was to cede
to Japan the Island of Formosa together with all islands appertaining or
belonging thereto; and the Pescadores Group. For our purposes it is
more important to consider the details of the cession of Chinese territory
demanded by Japan:

> The southern portion of the Province of Feng-tien within the following
> boundaries: The line of demarcation begins at the mouth of the River
> Yalu and ascends that stream to the mouth of the River An-ping; from
> thence the line runs to Fen Huang; from thence to Haicheng, from
> thence to Ying Kow, forming a line which describes the southern portion
> of the territory. The places above named are included in the ceded
> territory. When the line reaches the River Liao at Ying Kow it follows
> the course of that stream to its mouth where it terminates. The mid-
> channel of the River Liao shall be taken as the line of demarcation. This
> cession also includes all Islands appertaining or belonging to the
> Province of Feng-tien situated in the eastern portion of the Bay of Liao-
> tung and in the northern part of the Yellow Sea.⁵

As map 2 shows, this represented a substantial territory from about 80
miles up the Yalu river in the east westward to Yingkow at the mouth of
the Liao river. With this as the northern limit, it contained a significant
part of the Liaotung peninsula and included all islands belonging to the
province. The territory included Lushun (Port Arthur), the base for
China's Northern (Peiyang) fleet. It should be pointed out that this was
to be handed over not as a lease but as an outright cession; that this was

the territory which the Japanese armies occupied at the time; and that it did not represent the maximum aspirations of the Japanese at the outset of the negotiations. It was an area of great strategic interest, both because its ports were ice-free during winter and because it was the natural gateway to Manchuria. But it was also in an extended sense the gateway to Peking.

From early in March, China's diplomats who were resisting concessions in the only way they knew, had been making representations against the Japanese terms by leaking them and seeking the support of those opposed to Japan. It stands to reason that the versions that they circulated tended to be the initial bargaining positions of Japan. The Japanese government was forced by these tactics to communicate its own versions of the terms, initially to Russia, the United States and Britain and later to France and Germany. During weeks of imprecise parleys and rumours, a grouping of powers took shape, including Russia, Germany and France but excluding Britain, the United States and Italy. In this development Russia appears to have been the ringleader, Germany the enthusiastic supporter and France the independent-minded and reluctant follower.

Japan had been aware of the possibility of outside intervention throughout the war and certainly from early in the negotiating process. Although she could not be sure in advance which of China's friends – and most of the world's powers seemed to fall in that category – would take part, she had to make contingency plans for such an emergency. Gradually it emerged that Russia, France and Germany were planning to urge her to renounce the possession of the Liaotung peninsula on the ground that it would be a constant menace to the capital of China. It was doubtful whether the three could fight Japan on land in the short run; but they could by assembling their combined naval strength cut off Japan's land armies in Manchuria. Japan, already overstretched as the result of her war efforts over six months, did not dare to risk challenging any joint move which was in contemplation. Her position was parlous enough for her to take steps in advance to forestall, if at all possible, the threatened intervention.

Strangely Japan, as part of her tactics for preventing the intervention which her leaders expected, had tried to probe Russia's intentions. On 14 February Foreign Minister Mutsu had met Russia's representative in Tokyo, M. A. Khitrovo, and confided to him, on the assumption that intervention would be by Britain and could best be prevented by gaining the trust of the Russians, that Japan would not include among her peace terms the cession of Chinese territory. Khitrovo replied that intervention by any of the powers would depend on what territory Japan wanted, Russia having no objection to Japan's taking Taiwan. After Mutsu had given an assurance that Japan had no intention of injuring any of Russia's interests, Khitrovo was prompted to say that Russia would not object unless Japan destroyed Korean independence.[6] The

Japanese appear to have attached too much importance to these casual and probably unauthorised remarks.

Ten days later the Russian minister passed over a message from his government, asking Japan to declare that it would recognize Korean independence as a prelude to peace. Mutsu had no hesitation in recognizing the independence of Korea and drew the conclusion that this was all that Russia cared about. Certainly there was a breakdown in communication and understanding between Russia and Japan at this time. At a meeting of the Special Committee at St Petersburg on 11 April, Lobanov, the foreign minister, presented a preparatory paper which argued:

> Among the Japanese peace terms is undoubtedly the occupation of the peninsula where Port Arthur is situated. This is objectionable, being a permanent threat to Peking and also Korea, whose independence the Japanese are supposed to have guaranteed. Such an occupation would also be very undesirable from the standpoint of Russian interests. But, if we were to ask Japan to give up this condition, what should we do if she turns down our request? Would we have to resort to force and would we be able to enlist the assistance of some other powers?[7]

During discussion at the meeting, the members were divided but, swayed by the arguments of Finance Minister Witte, ultimately concluded that their interests were sufficiently affected for them to resist by force in the last resort. It was decided:

> to advise Japan in a friendly way not to proceed with the occupation of the southern part of Manchuria which would interfere with our interests and offer a permanent threat to peace in the far east; and if Japan refuses outright to accept this advice, to declare to Japan that we reserved complete freedom of action and would act in accordance with our interests.[8]

The foreign ministry was to use this resolution as the basis of an official approach to other governments in Europe, though unofficial soundings had, of course, been proceeding at a frenzied pace during the previous ten days. Lobanov put the special committee's resolution before the tsar on 15 April and obtained his approval after a meeting of Witte, Lobanov, War Minister Vannovskii and Grand Duke Aleksei. This was a strong and determined line of policy and, though the possibility of a Russo-Japanese war was discussed, it was rather cursorily dismissed.[9] The proceedings do not show that it was the railway question which was the motive for Russia's action.

The Russians like the rest of the world had not expected that the war would be such a walk-over for the Japanese. Their approach was initially diplomatic and conciliatory. When in the autumn the Chinese army and navy had been trounced, Russia's posture changed. There were signs of her building up her far eastern squadron and her infantry units in Vladivostok. The value of this port as a base was enhanced by the use of ice-breaking plant so that it was not sealed off entirely by ice during the severe winter months. The Russian approach continued to be conciliatory into the spring of 1895. Inner military circles in Russia had doubts about their land forces in particular but seemed to be more confident about the effectiveness of the combined squadrons of Russia and France in east Asian waters – there was no mention of Germany. Despite their doubts, they were concerned about Japan's successful military action in taking Port Arthur and in concluding a treaty of alliance with Korea. It looked as if their own objectives in the area were being forestalled. There was of course an element of uncertainty about whether the Russians were amassing their naval strength in Chinese and Japanese coastal waters for war or merely for deterrent purposes.[10]

Despite the debate about Russia's true intentions, there was a considerable weight of evidence that she meant business. The Japanese, whose intelligence-gathering was devoted to this problem, clearly thought so. The Japanese estimate of Russia's strength in the area at the critical date, 23 April, was as follows:

> All Russian warships in Japanese ports were placed on the alert to set sail on 24 hours' notice. Each ship kept its boilers fed day and night and crews were confined to their vessels as if to indicate that hostilities were anticipated at any moment. In Vladivostok, men of all classes were called to the colours as the reserves were summoned for active duty. Fifty thousand active and reserve-duty men were mustered under the command of the governor-general of Eastern Siberia, and preparations are said to have been made to send them into battle on a moment's notice.[11]

THREE-POWER INTERVENTION

The ministers for Russia, France and Germany appeared at the foreign ministry on 23 April and presented their joint friendly advice. The notes took exception to the article of the Shimonoseki treaty dealing with the possession of the Liaotung peninsula which would be 'a constant menace' to the capital of China and to a lasting peace in the extreme east and asked Japan to renounce the definitive possession of the peninsula. It was Vice-minister Hayashi who was in charge of the ministry in Tokyo and had to receive the notes. This was because Prime Minister Itō was in Hiroshima after the conference to attend the emperor, while Foreign Minister Mutsu was at Maiko near Kobe because of illness.

Mutsu, well-known as a political strategist, argued from his sick-bed against the idea of an international conference which had been favoured by his colleagues. He was influenced in his thinking by the experience of the Congress of Berlin where (in his interpretation) powers who had acted as 'honest brokers' had also managed to take some of the pickings for themselves, and feared that this might be repeated in 1895. Since his colleagues accepted the logic of Mutsu's pleading, there was no choice but to accept certain of the recommendations of the three powers and look around for allies to support Japan against the Dreibund, the name which was given to the three-power partnership. At the same time Japan was determined not to let China escape scot-free and insisted on China proceeding with the ratification of the Shimonoseki treaty.[12]

The recommendations for a climb-down were taken from Maiko to Kyoto whither the cabinet's leading members had by this time moved. Their decision, duly ratified by the emperor, led to the announcement on 1 May that Japan agreed to renounce her possession of the Fengtien (Liaotung) peninsula, except for the region of Kinchow (Chinchow). This offer amounted to a willingness to return about seven-eighths of the peninsula and to retain only one-eighth, including the city of Port Arthur (Lushun), and was a considerable reduction of the strong strategic position she had obtained by the treaty. On the other hand, there was no doubt that Port Arthur was more valuable to her than the rest of the peninsula because of its good anchorage and its service in the past as the base for China's Peiyang fleet.

Whether Japan really hoped that the three powers would accept less than a complete evacuation is hard to tell. Mutsu's *Kenkenroku* suggests that it was a tactical move made without great hope of success.[13] In response, the three partners made military-naval preparations. Russia called reservists to the colours in the Trans-Baikal region and took similar steps in Vladivostok that were menacing. The three notified Japan that her compromise formula for the retention of Port Arthur and its environs only was unacceptable to them. The Japanese leaders held a crisis meeting in a Kyoto hotel on 4 May. They knew through intelligence of the joint naval activities of the three powers and had to bear in mind the advice of their naval experts who said that Japan might lose command of the Tsushima straits, thus suffering the separation of her armies on the continent from their home islands, and might suffer the bombardment of her coasts, while her own squadrons were mainly concentrated far away in the neighbourhood of the Pescadores. On Mutsu's recommendation, therefore, it was decided to tell the powers that Japan would renounce the whole of Liaotung, without being too specific about the terms for its return, the idea being that, while Japan would make concessions to the three powers, she would not make concessions to China. Japan's message was passed over to the representatives of the three powers in Tokyo on 5 May and accepted without delay.[14]

Ratifications were exchanged between Itō Miyoji, the Japanese plenipotentiary, and Wu Ting-fang, his Chinese counterpart, at Chefoo on 8 May in the presence of a Russian squadron. With this out of the way, the Japanese politicians turned to the problem of informing their people of the humiliation which they had suffered. A rescript in which the emperor notified his acceptance of the return of Liaotung was drawn up on 10 May and published in the official gazette (Kanpō) three days later. It was then carried in the newspapers.

Behind the scenes in Japan the weak response of the cabinet was resented and attacked. There was opposition from the soldiers and officers at the front and Yamagata had to be sent to cool things down on 7 May. Influential members of the Taigai Kōha (strong foreign policy group) called for a tough line when they met the prime minister in Kyoto. In the press Japan's weakness was condemned as a national humiliation which came on top of exaggerated praise for Japan's remarkable military victories. The prominent publicist, Tokutomi Sohō, pressed for the taking of Liaotung peninsula for security reasons, though he was much more anxious for Taiwan. He regarded the island as essential for Japan's expansion, whereas Manchuria was important as a shield against Russia: 'it is the fundamental principle of Japanese expansionism to defend the north and develop in the south'.[15]

Even among the advocates of fighting on, there was an awareness of the financial cost that would face Japan. The war which had lasted for just over six months had entailed expenditure which was double that of the pre-war budget. Most of the emergency expenditure had been financed by an issue of public bonds. If the Treaty of Shimonoseki came into being, Japan would at least be able to obtain an indemnity from China to defray her costs; but until the treaty was ratified the position was uncertain. So there were financial constraints on continuing the fighting.

In the end the need to withdraw exposed the shortcomings of the Japanese defence services. Japan's emotions had gone full cycle: from cool determination before taking on the Chinese in war; through euphoria over victories in all aspects of the war combined with concealment of reverses; to a sense of humiliation that she could not withstand pressure from the three world bullies. This led to a popular mood of determination to lie low and make sure by preparedness that this weakness would not be manifested again.

Russia, who had been in the van of the protesters, was the country which incurred most of the sullen resentment. It was Russia, whose naval strength in these waters was relatively well-known to the Japanese, that was regarded as the true menace rather than France and Germany who were unknown factors. The Russian squadron was in and out of Japanese treaty ports during the winter months; and the Japanese naval authorities concluded – probably rightly – that their own fleet was too dispersed in the Yellow Sea and, more especially, around Taiwan to cope with the expected challenge from Russia. They could not safely take into account that there was an element of bluff in the Russian challenge. So the Japanese capitulated, concentrating on maintaining their gains in Korea and setting out on an expansion of armaments. It would be wrong to imagine that the Japanese leadership had already resolved on a war of revenge with Russia ultimately; but it would be equally true that Japan in 1895 regarded Russia as the major obstacle on her path.[16]

The intervention of the three powers under the leadership of Russia was by no means at an end. There followed a long period of negotiation which lasted for six months and was supposed to be confined to Japanese and Chinese delegates. In reality, however, the Russians and their partners were breathing down the necks of the Chinese plenipotentiaries throughout the talks, so determined were they to secure an advantageous settlement over the return of Liaotung. Eventually the supplementary convention was signed on 8 November whereby within three months of China paying a supplementary indemnity of 30,000,000 taels the Japanese troops would evacuate Liaotung for Weihaiwei. China paid this amount (about £5 million) in London and Japanese forces were evacuated by 25 December. During the talks, the Japanese appear to have had uppermost in their minds the need to prevent the building of foreign railways in south Manchuria. To this end, Japan had inserted in the early drafts a clause to exclude any alienation of the Fengtien peninsula to another country. But Li Hung-chang was negotiating with the diplomats of the three powers prompting and prodding him. In declining to include any such guarantee in the treaty, the Chinese statesman admitted that the three governments did not like it and claimed that Russia took special umbrage because it implied that she was harbouring some sinister design. He promised to cover the issue by a diplomatic note. But this also was vetoed by the three powers. And Japan did not take up the cudgels with the Dreibund.

Opinion in Japan was furious with the government for failing to obtain a non-alienation agreement for Liaotung, either in the treaty or outside it. Military men and professors foresaw that only some non-alienation undertaking by China would prevent Russian ambitions in the future. Of course the government was not unaware of this possibility. Thus, Li Hung-chang was asked during the negotiating session on 4 November whether China had already given Russia permission to build her railways across Chinese territory and had sent her representatives to Liaotung to this end. Li denied both points. But strong suspicions remained.[17]

The three-power intervention which continued to affect Sino-Japanese affairs throughout 1895 created a new balance of forces in east Asia. While China would continue to be indebted to the three powers for saving her from her fate, Japan was likely to be in the opposition camp. Her leaders thought it had been a straightforward example of self-interested interference, backed by military threats, but recognized that Russia was already a force in north-east Asia – and one with which they were not inclined to enter into a dispute at this stage.[18]

RUSSIA TAKES COMPENSATION

After the crises of 1895 Russia improved her position in Manchuria and Korea, both by deliberation and by accident. She had not taken the lead in the Dreibund for disinterested reasons; and it was widely expected that she would take compensation. Having further assisted China by guaranteeing the loan wherewith to pay the first instalment of the indemnity to Japan, she felt herself to be entitled to state her price. There was moreover an atmosphere of expansion around the Russian capital at the end of 1895. The twelve months of court mourning following Alexander III's death were coming to an end; and the young tsar's coronation in Moscow was approaching as the ice of winter made way for a season more suited to elaborate royal ceremonial.

Rumours abounded that Russia would ask for railway concessions in China. On 5 December the Russko-Kitaiskii (Russo-Chinese) Bank was set up in the Russian embassy in Paris by its French subscribers.[19] Almost immediately there was talk of Russia seeking means of shortening the existing Trans-Siberian route as planned by pushing the line through the north of Manchuria, a proposal which had the support of Sergei Witte as finance minister. But the view did not go unchallenged. Count Kapnist, speaking for the foreign ministry, deplored the idea of placing so great a length of track in someone else's territory, a hostage to fortune in an unstable land. Others like the governor of the Amur region criticized it because it would weaken the railway as an instrument of colonization. He claimed, rightly as it would appear, that to build the line through Chinese territory would not assist colonization or military consolidation along the Amur river. As any Russification of Manchuria could not be contemplated in the short term, a line around the Amur river which would be under Russian control would be preferable from a military point of view. As this demonstrates, the idea of a Trans-Manchurian railway was not without its critics. But the cards were stacked in favour of Witte's views. Nicholas gave his assent. The minister in Peking was instructed to introduce the proposal to the reluctant Chinese.[20]

A critical point in our story is how the Russians obtained special rights in Manchuria, due largely to the attendance of Li Hung-chang at the coronation of Emperor Nicholas II. Li, though out of favour in China since the Japanese war whose disasters were held to be his fault, was the emissary favoured by Russia. He was appointed on 16 February 1896 and reached Moscow on 30 April. Before Li's arrival, the Russian minister at Peking, Count Cassini, gave the Chinese some proposals for a 'Trans-Manchurian railway', arguing forcefully that it would help Russia to protect China against possible trouble with Japan. But the Yamen would not concede the point and stressed that it would not allow any concessions to any of the powers.

Li had discussions with Lobanov and, more especially, with Witte over the twin issues of Manchurian railways and a treaty of protection for China. Although anxious for a protective alliance, Li was not easily convinced over the railway and, knowing the extent of opposition to it in Peking, was by no means a 'push-over' in discussions with the Russians. But eventually Russian determination won the day and the terms of a draft convention were communicated to China on 16 May. Telegrams sped to Peking where special precautions were taken for them to be deciphered at the highest level in order to prevent leaks for which the Chinese bureaucracy was renowned. On 3 June Li attached his seal to the secret agreement while he was in Moscow with Lobanov and Witte. It was to last for fifteen years and to cover the following points: mutual assistance in the event of Japanese aggression; no separate peace with the enemy without joint agreement in advance: the use of Chinese ports by Russian warships in emergencies; the construction by Russia of a railway through Heilungkiang and Kirin to Vladivostok, the line to be used by Russia in transporting troops and supplies. The ratification of this agreement was to depend on the signing of a railway contract in implementation of the last of these items.

For three months after Li's departure from Russia, there were heated debates in Peking over participation in the Russo-Chinese Bank, to which the railway concessions would be given. Russia's further intention to build a line from the Trans-Manchurian to some port on the Yellow Sea was also mooted; but it was lost in the debate over whether the new line should be built on the Chinese or the broad Russian gauge. The Chinese could not afford to hold out; and the two agreements for the bank and the railway were completed. Ratification of the alliance followed on 28 September.[21]

After visits to Berlin, Paris, London and Washington where he was accorded the status of an international statesman, Li reached Tientsin again on 3 October. What would his future be? Some like the empress dowager respected his resilience; others like the emperor blamed him for China's failure in war. What seems clear is that France and Russia exerted themselves on Li's behalf. Li seemed to be Russia's man; and Russia wanted him to stay at his post so as to have someone in high places. This was not the balanced response which the Yamen favoured but there was no one of equal stature or ability to march Li. In October, therefore, an edict was issued, appointing Li to the Yamen, where he immediately assumed the leadership.[22]

The fact that the Li–Lobanov treaty was secret and not properly disclosed till 1922 led to infinite speculation in the years that followed. Li's conversations were more far-reaching than the treaty itself. And, of course, Lobanov died just as Li was leaving the Russian capital. The fact that a secret convention was in existence created all sorts of doubts on the part of those who were worried about Sino-Russian relations, notably the country which was the 'contemplated enemy', Japan. This was of course a common enough experience in a generation of secret treaties. But a great deal of Russophobia in Japan focused on these various treaties where it was widely believed that China was thereafter Russia's puppet.

Moreover there were real doubts about how widely the text of these secret treaties was known and understood in China herself. Speaking of the 'Li–Lobanov treaty', a later Russian minister observed that it was 'a treaty of which neither Prince Ching nor the Empress-Dowager nor the Grand Council knew anything'.[23] Certainly there had not been adequate consultation between Li in Russia and those in Peking over the nature of his discussions. When some years later the Russians insisted on the setting up of a Chinese customs house at Dalny, they pointed out that the 1896 agreements laid down that the customs there would be under exclusively Russian management. One of the senior Maritime Customs officials wrote in despair: 'The way seems blocked at every turn by some secret treaty with Russia, of which no one, not even the highest officials of the [Chinese] empire, has any knowledge. I wonder if this agreement received Imperial sanction.'[24] Certainly the vagueness and secrecy allowed Russia leverage to capitalize on the rights she had acquired.

RUSSIA ASCENDANT IN KOREA

In 1896 there was an unexpected upset in the strong position which Japan had gained in Korea. For the duration of the Sino-Japanese war, Korea had been under the protection of Japanese troops by a treaty of alliance signed at Seoul on 26 August 1894. Although the independence of Korea was recognized by both parties to the treaty of Shimonoseki, Japan in practice acquired paramount influence there after the war. She was opposed by an anti-Japanese faction which enjoyed the favour of the queen. In October 1895 Queen Min was brutally murdered; and a Japanese minister was implicated in the plot. After legal proceedings Japanese officials were acquitted. Meanwhile the king lived out a precarious existence in his own palace, swayed by conflicting Japanese and Russian parties. In February of the following year Russia landed at Chemulpo a force of marines which marched on Seoul and led to a *coup d'état*. With the seals of office, the king fled from the palace to take refuge in the Russian legation. Partly this was due to the congenial personality of the senior Russian representative, Karl Weber (Waeber), who had been in Korea since 1885 and had cultivated the goodwill of the Korean court, especially the deceased queen. Partly it was due to the Russians appearing to be less interfering in the faction-ridden court than the Japanese. As hosts to the king, the Russians naturally became an important force in Korean politics. There could not be any doubt that the king's was an anti-Japanese move. From the protection of the

Russian legation, he dismissed pro-Japanese officials, replaced some Japanese, including military instructors, and passed down punishments on Japanese for misdemeanours. He also gave privileges to Russian businessmen and took steps to appoint Russian advisers.

These events ended the period of Japanese ascendancy and left the Russians triumphant. Not unnaturally the Japanese wanted the king to return to his palace from this partisan environment. But such was the latter's accumulated suspicion of Japan that he wished to stay on under Russian protection indefinitely. Anxious to steer clear of too great involvement in domestic disputes and avoid a clash with Japan, Russia professed that she wanted to be rid of the king but had to leave the decision to his free will. Whatever their public professions, the Russians knew they held a trump card.[25]

After this blow Japan sent the trustworthy diplomat, Komura Jūtarō, to Korea as minister. His mandate was to call for a return to complete independence in Korea as had been prescribed in the treaty of Shimonoseki. His discussions with Minister Weber turned on the separation of the various military forces in the peninsula and especially on the withdrawal of Japanese and Russian troops (apart from the legation guards). The Seoul protocol that resulted, sometimes referred to as 'the Weber–Komura agreement', was drawn up by the diplomats on the spot with a view to assisting a more senior mission to Russia which was to be conducted by General Yamagata Aritomo. For some time Japan had wanted to send a leading statesman to Russia to negotiate at the highest level. Now an opportunity was offered by the celebrations for the coronation of Tsar Nicholas II. The Weber–Komura agreement was completed on 14 May just as Yamagata reached Russia after being fêted in the United States and in European capitals.[26]

On 26 May Yamagata had his first discussions with Foreign Minister Lobanov-Rostovskii in which there was some measure of agreement to the terms drafted by Japan. When the statesmen discussed dividing the peninsula into a Russian zone to the north and a Japanese zone to the south, they apparently looked at each other and smiled. At their next meeting Lobanov announced that Russia had agreed to train the personal bodyguard of the Korean king who was afraid of the Japanese and would only return to his palace if he had a Russian guard. For a while the Japanese plenipotentiary thought that it would be wiser to defer the treaty but Lobanov made a minor modification and this led to the initialling of the Yamagata–Lobanov protocol on 28 May. The terms, which spoke of Korean independence and the need for reform, were anodyne enough. But there were two clauses which were kept secret, dealing with the arrangements for keeping equal numbers of troops in the peninsula. The open clauses together with the Weber–Komura agreement were published in 1898. The new protocol seemed to recognize equal rights for both Russia and Japan in the peninsula.

Yamagata's reception in Russia had been rather muted. Nor were his negotiations wholly successful. Perhaps Japan had been over-optimistic in hoping to cash in on the generosity of spirit which was assumed to exist in Russia at the time of the coronation. But Lobanov and the other Russian officials showed little sign of being accommodating to the Japanese. On two particular points, Yamagata did not succeed. First, he failed to secure the return of the Korean king to his palace. True, the Russians said that they were not detaining him and wanted him to leave their legation. But the fact remains that it was of great advantage to Russia to have such an honoured guest. For the remainder of his time in Russian protection, he offered Russia many concessions including the grant of forest rights for twenty years on the Korean side of the Yalu and Tumen rivers as well as mining concessions on the coast of Tumenking and other privileges on Dagelet island. Eventually it took a vigorous move by anti-Russian Koreans themselves to induce the king to return to his palace on 20 February 1897, after a year's absence.[27]

Second, there was Japan's disappointment over the Russian military advisers. The Japanese government protested against the employment of so many Russian military instructors but was told that Russia had promised to provide these advisers prior to the negotiations and was bound by that promise. Thus during July 1897 three Russian officers and ten non-commissioned officers arrived in Korea to train her soldiers for three years. While a picture of reciprocity and equal rights was presented by the letter of the Yamagata–Lobanov protocol, that spirit was violated in practice. Russia continued to have the predominant voice. So the balance of power which Yamagata had sought eluded him. The 'pushy' Aleksei de Speyer who was appointed to Seoul as chargé (1896–97), was quick to secure one-sided privileges for Russia. In return for the undertaking to employ only Russian advisers, Russia promised to recognize the Korean king as emperor. She then secured the appointment of Kir Alekseyevich Alekseyev as chief commissioner of Korean customs in place of the British national, John McLeavy Brown, who, however, refused to resign. Meanwhile there were manoeuvres for the opening of a Russo-Korean bank. In November Korea's finances were placed under Russian control. So the work of expansionist officials on the spot undid the earlier protocols and placed Russia in a strong position of ascendancy.[28]

REFERENCES AND NOTES

1. Fujimura Michio, *Nisshin sensō*, pp. 129–31.
2. R. F. Hackett, *Yamagata Aritomo in the Rise of Modern Japan,* p. 163.
3. Itō to emperor, 27 Jan. 1895 in *Nihon Gaikō* Bunsho (hereafter *NGB*), vol. 28.

4. I. H. Nish, 'The Three-power intervention of 1895', pp. 208–11.
5. *Nihon Gaikō Nempyō narabi ni Shūyō Bunsho,* vol. 1, pp. 165–7 (hereafter *NGNB*).
6. Mutsu Munemitsu, *Kenkenroku:,* pp. 136–7.
7. Lobanov paper of 6 April 1895 in *Krasnyi Arkhiv* ('Pervye shagi russkogo imperializma na Dalnem Vostoke, 1888–1903'), **52** (1932), pp. 74–5.
8. Ibid, pp. 78–83.
9. Ibid, p. 78.
10. Mutsu Munemitsu, op. cit., pp. 136–7.
11. A. Malozemoff, *Russian Far Eastern Policy,* p. 244.
12. Mutsu Munemitsu, op. cit., p. 217: Japan was 'to continue standing firm against the Chinese'.
13. Ibid, pp. 215–17.
14. Ibid., pp. 218–20.
15. For similar views from the Taigai kōha, and the views of the new political parties, see Mutsu Munemitsu, op. cit., pp. 145–6.
16. Russia appears to have recognized this, see Rostunov, *Istoriya Russko-Iaponskoi Voiny,* pp. 38–9.
17. Kajima Marinosuke, *The Diplomacy of Japan,* vol. 1, pp. 379–81.
18. Professor Fujimura in the sub-title of his standard history of the Sino-Japanese war, *Nisshin Sensō,* describes it as a turning-point in the modern history of east Asia.
19. R. Quested, *The Russo-Chinese Bank,* pp. 1–4.
20. The so-called 'Cassini Convention' between China and Russia was reported by the Shanghai correspondent of *The Times* on 8 Dec, 1896.
21. Rostunov, op. cit., pp. 38–9. The agreement between China and the Russo-Chinese Bank, concluded at Berlin on 8 Sept. 1896 is found in O. K. Smirnova (ed.) *Sbornik dokumentov po istorii SSSR: Period imperializma,* pp. 126–9.
22. J. K. Fairbank *et al.* (eds), *The I.G. in Peking,* vol. 2, nos. 1036–40.
23. Ernest M. Satow, *Korea and Manchuria between Russia and Japan,* p. 193. 21 Mar. 1903.
24. A. Hippisley (Shanghai) to Rockhill, 30 Jan. 1903, in Rockhill papers.
25. Kajima, vol. 1, pp. 425–31.
26. *NGNB,* vol. 1, pp. 174–5.
27. Hackett, op. cit., p. 174; Kajima, vol. 1, pp. 448–50.
28. G. A. Lensen, *Balance of Intrigue,* vol. 1, pp. 676—9.

Chapter 2

THE FAR EASTERN CRISIS
(1897–98)

Russia had acquired specified rights and unspecified privileges in both Manchuria and Korea. She was to build on these in company with her partners of 1895 during the crisis in east Asia at the end of 1897 and the beginning of 1898. These events, like all events in history, were affected by the personalities of the politicians involved and the struggles between them. It is desirable, therefore, that we should first take a look at some of the domestic changes which had taken place in Russia and Japan.

Tsarist government, unlike that of Japan, was not subject to the quick change of its cabinets. It was, however, swayed by changes in the tsar's advisers. After the sudden death of Prince Lobanov-Rostovskii in August 1896, there was no candidate available who was acceptable to all the parties as foreign minister or at all comparable in personality to the dominating Lobanov. In April 1897 the choice fell on Count Mikhail Muraviev, who had been counsellor at the Berlin embassy (1884–93) until he had fallen out with the kaiser and had then been posted as ambassador to the small but influential court at Copenhagen (1893–97). The new arrangement was that he should hold office along with Count Vladimir Lamsdorf as deputy minister. Lamsdorf had been the anchorman at the ministry under Lobanov and M. N. de Giers before him, and was renowned as a conscientious, devoted but self-effacing official. Muraviev had little direct knowledge of east Asia and had to play himself in. Lamsdorf for his part also knew little of the east but had long experience at the ministry and had a reputation for following moderate policies in the light of international opinion.[1] If anything, there was an inclination on the part of both to look at the far east in terms of European 'higher diplomacy', in which they were more experienced.

The new partnership came to power at a time when Sergei Witte, the self-confident finance minister (1892–1903), was in the ascendant. For the diplomats, this aggravated the problem of where the writ of the finance ministry ended and that of the foreign ministry began. That dividing line was particularly hard to establish in east Asia where railway diplomacy was the primary activity. This led to ups and downs in relations between Muraviev and Witte and numerous attempts by one to out-manoeuvre the other. Though Muraviev was a comparative newcomer to the St Petersburg scene, he was well known to the court and had good relations with the tsar. Thus, he was sometimes able to carry policies against the opposition of Witte, even in the far eastern field. Muraviev was not universally regarded as being up to his new office and, inexperienced as he was, he was probably unsure of himself and jealous of rival influences. Earlier in his career he had had a reputation for being a *bon viveur;* but after he became foreign minister he seems to have moved much less in society.[2]

Muraviev had inherited a diplomatic team in the east who were ambitious for Russia. From an earlier generation, Count Cassini, minister in Peking from 1891 to 1898, was appointed ambassador to Washington. His place was taken as chargé by Aleksandr Ivanovich Pavlov, a former naval officer who had acted as Cassini's private secretary. Weber, who had for ten years been head of legation at Seoul, stayed on alongside Aleksei de Speyer because of the unexpected turn of fortune which had brought the Korean king to the haven of the Russian legation. Although he had served off and on for a long time in Tokyo, Speyer was anxious to leave no stone unturned to improve Russia's position in Korea. The move of two younger men to the eye of the storm did affect Russia's approach to the courts of Peking and Seoul and certainly marked a tougher attitude at the periphery.

The place of the tough-minded Khitrovo in Tokyo was taken by Roman Rosen. He had served in Tokyo from 1877 to 1883 and was appointed from a post in Belgrade in June 1897, reaching Tokyo in August. On appointment he prepared for Muraviev a note in which he warned Russia with the 'heaviest and most unanswerable arguments' against the possibility of war breaking out with Japan. His criticisms were directed at the war ministry and its policy of encroachments, especially in Korea. Rosen claims to have persuaded Muraviev to his views and ensured that the memorandum was presented to the tsar. Perhaps this is a sign that Muraviev was coming round to a policy of concentration on Manchuria rather than Korea.[3]

Japan's reaction to the crisis was determined by the state of disarray in which her domestic politics were during the winter of 1897–98. At every stage of the oncoming crisis the ministries were so preoccupied with internal argument and financial crises that they could not seriously consider intervening in international affairs either by themselves or in company with others. Since 1896 a coalition cabinet had been presided over by the experienced elder statesman, Matsukata Masayoshi. He had difficulties with both his coalition partners, the Shimpōtō (Progressive party) and Jiyūtō (Liberal party), and positively lost the support of the latter in November 1897. When the Diet met in the following month, the opposition put forward a motion of no confidence and the Diet had to be suspended. The ministry resigned on 25 December but a new cabinet could not be formed till 12 January 1898. The choice fell on the elder statesman, Itō Hirobumi, who was expected to offer strong leadership. But the new prime minister devoted his main attention to preparing for the general election which was scheduled for 15 March. It will be clear that this was not a time when the government could be expected to take important initiatives abroad, though it had of course to attend to the sentiments of a noisy public opinion.

The foreign minister of the day was Nishi Tokujirō, a Russian linguist and former student of the University of St Petersburg. From 1886 he had acted as minister to Russia for ten years and witnessed a series of crises at first hand. As an accomplished diplomat, he served as foreign minister at the end of Matsukata's term and succeeded into Itō's. While he could not be described as pro-Russian, he was more sympathetic to Russia than the majority of Japanese. He was deeply disillusioned about the state of Japanese politics. His feeling was that, until Japan sorted herself out economically and politically, there was little scope for her to aspire to a high profile in world affairs: hence this was not a time of active initiatives abroad.[4] Japan became an unobtrusive observer rather than the spearhead of action that she had been three years before.

RUSSO-GERMAN SQUABBLE

In the aftermath of the Triple Intervention, Germany had been planning to establish a coaling station in east Asia. Surveys had been made and proposals were first put to the Chinese government in December 1896. It seems that the Germans had decided tentatively on Kiaochow bay. The problem was that the Russians were thought to have 'priorité de mouiller' (priority of anchorage) there; that the Russian fleet had used it in the winter months; and that – but this was rumoured only – a port there had been promised by China to Russia. With these factors in mind, the German emperor went to St Petersburg for discussions in August 1897 and obtained an impression that the young tsar had told him that Russia's interest at Kiaochow would only last until she acquired a port somewhere to the north and that he would not stand in Germany's way. Other accounts suggest that the tsar made no secret of the fact in private conversation that 'if the Kaiser had desired to make himself unpopular at Petersburg he had been very successful'. This seems to imply that there had been some unwelcome browbeating by the kaiser of his cousin and that the tsar had resisted, knowing the kaiser's unpopularity in Russia. When Nicholas next met the kaiser at Darmstadt and Wiesbaden on 18–19 October, the kaiser again broached the matter and thought he had obtained even more positive approval.

The German fleet was instructed to proceed to Kiaochow on 6 November, using as a pretext the fact that two German Catholic missionaries had been recently murdered in Boxer troubles. When Nicholas was asked for his formal sanction, he replied on the following day that he could neither approve nor disapprove, since the harbour had only been Russia's temporarily in 1895–96. The German action had been taken without advance approval and before this damaging message was received. It appears that behind the scenes the Russians were furious, feeling that they had been hoodwinked and let down. Muraviev protested vigorously and concocted a claim to Kiaochow, based on the use Russia had made of the anchorage in 1895–96. He added menacingly that the commander of the Pacific squadron would send his ships into Kiaochow if Germany sent her squadron thither. Germany was appalled by the 'insolent tone' Muraviev had adopted; but the disagreement was slowly patched over.[5]

On 14 November the German squadron entered Kiaochow bay. China reacted to Germany's action in the only way she knew, by calling on Russia to neutralize and discourage the Germans. When news reached Peking that the Germans had landed at Kiaochow, Li Hung-chang issued under the Russo-Chinese alliance of 1896 a direct invitation to Russia to occupy temporarily a Chinese port as a counter-measure to the German action. When Muraviev received this information from Pavlov, he prepared a lengthy memorandum in which he advocated accepting the Chinese invitation but disapproved of taking the port of Fusan, recommended by the navy, and suggested the acquisition of a port on the Liaotung peninsula, preferably Talienwan or Port Arthur (Lushun). When this was sent to the tsar on 23 November, he replied that the ice-free port chosen should be either on the Liaotung peninsula or in the north-east corner of the Bay of Korea. By this time Muraviev had conceded Kiaochow to Germany.[6]

The tsar quite properly convened a conference of affected ministers to discuss the various proposals which were in the air. At the meeting on 26 November, Muraviev developed his arguments but found he was opposed by the finance and navy ministers. Witte opposed the recommendation to take compensation for Kiaochow on the ground that it would be improper for Russia, which had undertaken to defend China's integrity against Japan, now to appropriate Chinese territory. Expressing the naval line, Admiral Pavel Tyrtov, the director of the navy ministry, was doubtful whether Port Arthur would satisfy the needs of the Pacific squadron and still considered the ports of southern Korea more suitable, while realizing that it was not an appropriate time to acquire them. He therefore counselled that no action be taken. Though supported by war minister Petr Vannovskii, Muraviev had been opposed by the giants. The conference decided not to occupy Port Arthur or any other port. The tsar accordingly accepted this recommendation.[7]

Muraviev thought that a great opportunity had been lost. He reverted to the matter in conversation with the tsar, informing him that British ships were operating near Talienwan and Port Arthur and suggesting that Russia should seize the ports before Britain did. The Chinese had allegedly warned him of this danger. Senior army officers were in favour of occupying them. The tsar therefore gave his sanction. On 11 December Muraviev informed the Chinese that Russia would accept the Chinese invitation and send a squadron of ships to Port Arthur. This represented a clear change of plan. Witte was highly incensed with the foreign minister and the tsar and, as was his wont when his advice was not taken, spoke indiscreetly to foreign diplomats. His world-view of the Russian railway had been rejected in a short-sighted gesture. He predicted dire consequences would result from this action. The Russian squadron reached Port Arthur on 19 December. The kaiser was quick to offer his congratulations, thus indicating that German–Russian tensions had been resolved without recourse to war. Moreover, from the Russian side, their public communications were modest and full of good intent. The conduct of the naval commander at Port Arthur, who insisted on not landing his troops, suggested that the Russian presence at the port was purely 'temporary'.[8]

Because of the vagueness of Russian intentions, it was hard for other powers to make any response. The British sent ships to Chemulpo and Port Arthur in ways that Russia found to be menacing; the Japanese did likewise. But Lord Salisbury, the British foreign secretary, gave the assurance that the British ships had not received orders from home and would be withdrawn shortly. Britain and Japan were content with an observer role. The Japanese troops over the water at Weihaiwei were viewing the Russian movements vigilantly – and the German movements equally and at close quarters. Japan had upwards of 4,000 troops in Shantung who were legally entitled to stay there so long as the indemnity due her by China remained unpaid. The Japanese fleet was moreover on alert at Tsushima. Thus, Japan was not without bargaining counters in her dealings with Russia.

The proceedings of Germany and Russia caused a great deal of excitement in Japan. With her armies in Weihaiwei, she did not welcome the German move at Tsingtao. But the Russian action at Port Arthur was several degrees more objectionable to Japan, because it menaced the territory which she had been forced to evacuate under Russian pressure three years before. Had the strength of public opinion been the sole factor, she might have protested. But Russia, in a message of 17 December, stated that her ships had anchored in Port Arthur with China's permission purely in order to resist the earlier German action. Foreign Minister Nishi took note of the statement and made no protest. But this was illusory. The Japanese army and navy leaders were not prepared to accept a diplomatic apologia over a port which had formerly been theirs. Also we know from the Japanese documents that the Japanese were highly suspicious. From Chefoo where they had a consulate, from Weihaiwei where they had troops and from the legation in Peking where Minister Yano was skilful at probing for information, Japan kept Russian actions under close scrutiny and appears to have been well informed about the goings-on at Port Arthur and Talien.[9] Reports also told of the progress at Harbin where the headquarters of the Chinese Eastern Railway was being set up.

By the end of the year the Chinese were aware that their ploy of setting one barbarian off against another had failed. Some among them – the so-called Anglo-Japanese-American party – were hopeful of enlisting the support of Britain and Japan against Russia and Germany. The Yangtse viceroys, Chang Chih-tung and Liu Kun-i, were the sponsors of this tactic. But it held out few attractions for Britain because of European considerations; and Japan would not act on her own, though she was a force to be reckoned with.[10]

RUSSIAN LOANS AND LEASES

It would be easier for Muraviev to achieve some settlement over Liaotung if China were given a loan and paid off the final instalment of the indemnity due to Japan under the Shimonoseki treaty. This raised the question of the financial links between powers and their international rivalries. After hot competition the first payment had been made to China from a Franco-Russian loan for £16 million in June–July 1895. The funds were mainly raised in France and guaranteed by Russia; they were secured on the Chinese customs revenues and yielded 4 per cent interest; China undertook not to conclude a further loan for a period of six months. British banks and, more especially, German banks, which felt betrayed by Germany's Dreibund partners, opposed the Russian-organized loan unsuccessfully. But in March of the following year an Anglo-German combination arranged a second loan for a similar amount, again secured on the Chinese customs.

It became clear during December 1897 that China would need a further loan before the indemnity could be fully paid and the Japanese occupation armies could be removed from Weihaiwei. Intense lobbying developed between supporters of the Franco-Russian and Anglo-German groups. Although they were not involved in the financial struggle, the Japanese needed the money desperately for their reconstruction programmes and welcomed the prospect of the immense payment being made on time. One might say that, in order to resist the expected trouble from Russia and her friends, they wanted the indemnity funds more urgently than a base like Weihaiwei in the Yellow Sea. So far as the other powers were concerned, the existence of these delicate loan negotiations had its influence on any demands for Chinese territory. Until the Chinese leaders had decided in favour of one group or the other, it was inopportune for Russia, Germany and the others to make explicit demands from China for leases or concessions. There was therefore a period around New Year when political developments were held up, pending the outcome of financial negotiations.

When Li made the initial approach to Russia, he found the leaders divided. During the loan negotiations in December it was brought home to Muraviev that in matters financial he had to take a back seat to the ministry of finance and Witte. Witte agreed to take on the loan provided that Russia would have exclusive rights of railway building, etc. in Manchuria and would be given the right to build a port. Li Hung-chang, however, would not relinquish Manchuria to Russian hands nor would he offer Port Arthur, the port which he imagined Russia to have in mind. He had no hesitation in approaching the rival loan consortium. It was necessary, therefore, for Russia not to put a foot wrong and for the purpose behind the squadron wintering at Port Arthur to be left vague and uncertain. Hence Li was given an ambiguous assurance on 4 January that Russia had no immediate intention of making any territorial acquisition but relied on China's friendship to be offered a suitable port in the area and a railway linking the Russian lines to Chinchow. This statement was intended to be reassuring to the Chinese; but with the Russian squadron already at Port Arthur it was hardly the expression of Russia's intention to withdraw as Malozemoff implies.[11] The statement may have been framed with a view to reassuring China of Russia's peaceful intentions; but it was hardly likely to strike China's statesmen that way.

Russia's appeal for continued solidarity with the Germans and French had also fallen on deaf ears. While the French were presumably prepared to back the China loan if Witte had successfully negotiated it, the Germans were disillusioned with Muraviev. Instead the German bankers continued the cooperation with the British bankers who had operated together in the China loan field since 1895.

China, confronted by tough terms from both groups of creditors, asked Japan on 2 February to agree to the postponement of the final instalment of the indemnity. But Japan immediately refused. It has to be assumed that she was not sufficiently worried by a possible Russian presence in Port Arthur for her to retain her garrison in Weihaiwei: she needed the money more than a garrison in the area of conflict. The Anglo-German loan agreement which had been initialled on 21 February was finally concluded in March, thereby ensuring that the funds were made available for Japan, whose forces were withdrawn in May when the territory was transferred by lease to Britain.

The way was now clear for Russian action. The German lease of Kiaochow was concluded on 6 March for ninety nine years and consummated with the visit to China of Admiral Prince Henry of

Prussia in April. Early in March, therefore, the Russians asked pointedly for the lease of Port Arthur and its environs, about which they had been hinting for some months through Hsu Ching-cheng in St Petersburg and others. Russian military operations cleared Port Arthur and Talienwan of Chinese soldiers and sailors on 16 March. They asked for the same terms as Germany had received. Eventually China signed a treaty on 27 March after daily negotiations at the Yamen. It conferred on Russia the lease of the harbours of Port Arthur and Talienwan for twenty-five years (less than had been granted to Germany), with a neutral zone along the frontier of the leased territory. Port Arthur was to be an exclusively naval port closed to the vessels of other nations, while Talienwan (except for an inner harbour to be reserved for naval use) was designated as a trading port, a free and open port which was less convenient to trading countries than a treaty port. (By article VI it was laid down that a customs house be opened under Russian management at Talienwan.) The treaty extended the concession granted to the Chinese Eastern Railway Company in 1896 to permit the construction of a branch line from that line to the leased territory. China was to retain sovereignty over the lease, though civil and military administration was to be in Russian hands. Li had to overcome opposition from the empress dowager and others over these concessions and was, it is alleged, induced to do so by reason of a substantial bribe from Russia.

An Additional Agreement of 7 May 1898 set out the boundaries of the lease and its neutral zone. The terminus of the new branch railway was to be at Port Arthur or Talienwan and at no other port in the peninsula. Various other provisions prevented any other national from acquiring rights or privileges. In other words, Russia by the second treaty obtained something approaching monopoly rights in the southern half of Manchuria.[12]

The position in the neighbourhood of Port Arthur was defined in two further treaties. On 6 July the Chinese Eastern railway entered into an agreement with China for the construction and operation of the line contemplated from Harbin to the leased territory. On 11 August 1899 the tsar announced the building of a modern port at Talienwan to be called Dalny (lit., 'far away') and confirmed that it was to be free and open. Clearly Russia had procured the ice-free port that she sought.

These changes were significant and of course unpopular in the rest of the world. Sir Robert Hart of the Chinese Customs, who was no mean observer, said that the Ching government was in effect under a Russian protectorate and that the concessions obtained by other powers paled into insignificance by comparison with the terms which Russia had extracted.[13] The other powers reacted in the weakest way possible by making demands from China, rather than opposing Russia directly. True enough, there had been a battle over the loan to China; but over the concession there was no overt action, though a certain amount of covert pressure was placed on the Yamen. Without positive promises of foreign support there was little resistance that the Chinese could make. At a popular level too there was evidence of hostility and jealousy abroad. Thus on 11 June in Nagasaki there was a set-to between Russian and Japanese seamen, which was thought to derive from popular emotions over the Liaotung peninsula and Russia's actions there.

Successful as Muraviev's bid for the Star of Empire was,[14] it was by no means unopposed in Russia. There were indeed several options open to Russia and at the conferences held over the winter months to find a consensus to put before the emperor there were frequent debates over whether to take a lease (which was deemed to mean territorial annexation) or merely extract railway privileges. Each course was equally imperialistic. In fact, Muraviev went ahead in the face of hostility from Witte, from the admiralty who probably wanted Masampo but were indecisive, and possibly even the army and General Kuropatkin. By March the others rallied to Muraviev's lead when they saw that the Chinese had obtained their loan elsewhere. But they were later to remind Muraviev of his 'folly' in insisting on Port Arthur.[15]

KOREAN OPPORTUNITY

Russia realized that Japan had a strong sense of grievance over her acquisition of Port Arthur. Naturally she tried to insulate herself against Japanese 'opposition' until the lease had been clinched with China, so that Japan could not pull strings at the Chinese court. Rosen, the minister in Tokyo, felt that Russia's purpose could be achieved by making concessions to Japan in Korea. Muraviev may also have favoured this view and been prepared to cut down Russia's commitments in the peninsula; but his *bona fides* cannot be satisfactorily tested. At all events the two external powers in Korea began to negotiate early in the new year.

Fortunately for Russia, the government in power, presided over by Marquis Itō, was probably more inclined to find a peaceful solution with Russia than any which held office in our period. It would be unfair to call Itō – as some Japanese were inclined to do – pro-Russian: but he and his foreign minister, Nishi, had a great fear or respect for Russia and were more ready to trust her word than most Japanese leaders. It was also fortunate for Russia that Itō's bureaucratic cabinet was squabbling with the up-and-coming party politicians over a wide range of issues, political and financial. This meant that Itō was anxious to avoid the sort of adventurist policy which had been adopted in 1894–95 when the issue of Korea and Manchuria had come up before. The watchword was 'safety first'. The Japanese, though they hated what was going on in Port Arthur, were not prepared to act alone against Russia and, though they explored possibilities, could not find any country willing to act with them over an issue limited to north-east Asia.

Outwardly the Japanese did not oppose Speyer or K. A. Alekseyev. Despite China's pleas, Japan had made no serious complaint about Russia's intentions over Port Arthur either. From St Petersburg the Japanese minister, Hayashi Tadasu, who had only reached there in May 1897, urged that this was a good opportunity for Japan to consolidate her position in Korea by obtaining Russia's recognition for it. Muraviev had asked him on 7 January whether they could reach some arrangement to avoid complications there. Foreign Minister Nishi agreed to enter into a new treaty over Korea. On 16 February Hayashi gave the Russians an outline for a new agreement. A month later, Muraviev returned a counterdraft, promising that Russia would not intervene in Korea or interfere in Korea's domestic concerns.[16] This was a considerable *volte-face* from the forward policy being currently pursued in the peninsula by the Russian minister, Speyer. But Russia was not sufficiently interested in Korea to sustain the ambitions of the man on the spot. Instead Muraviev, who had no knowledge of east Asia, was content to treat Korea merely as a pawn on an international chess-board, dominated by European kings. Accordingly the military instructors to which Yamagata had taken such exception and the financial adviser, Alekseyev, against whom the Japanese had made no protest, were withdrawn in March. The Russo-Korean bank which had been set up with a flourish the previous autumn held over its operations. Evidently Muraviev was pursuing his 'Port Arthur first' policy and was prepared to sacrifice the forward policy in Korea to that end.

Naturally the Russian position was a surprise to the Japanese leaders. But it accorded so well with Itō's own hopes that it was taken seriously. At all events, Russia's moderation over Korea was one among several factors preventing Japan from intervening over Port Arthur. It was not the sole one. Itō's cabinet was unstable and, even after the general election on 15 March had given it victory, it was still prepared to turn a blind eye to Port Arthur.

The Japanese initiative appeared to get lost in February. To be sure, it was taken up by Russia but without much enthusiasm or speed. When it arrived on 17 March, the Russian counterdraft suggested that Russia was not really in such a placatory mood, but was more concerned with winning time. Nonetheless, despite its election victory, the Itō ministry was inclined to do a deal with Russia. Itō's thinking was that Korea had always been a stumbling-block between the two countries so long as Russia was searching for an ice-free port; but Russia's penchant for Port Arthur was welcome in so far as it might remove a formidable cause of friction between them. It was at this time that Japan first formulated the doctrine of Man-Kan kōkan (exchange of Manchuria for Korea). On 19 March, therefore, Foreign Minister Nishi handed over the following note to the Russian minister:

> The Japanese government is not unwilling to conclude a self-restraining understanding with the Russian government. That is, it would not be unwilling to undertake mutually to recognize the autonomy and independence of Korea and not to interfere directly in the internal affairs of that government. But the case may arise when Korea will need the advice and assistance of foreign countries. If one or other of the two governments does not give it, Korea will inevitably ask some third country. This is basically undesirable in the interests of our two countries. Accordingly the Japanese government is of the opinion that *the obligation of giving advice and assistance should most appropriately be borne by Japan, considering her territorial propinquity to Korea and her present interests there.* If the Russian government agrees with this view, the Japanese government will recognize Manchuria and its coastline as being beyond the sphere of Japan's interests.[17] [my italics]

This was an offer based on a modified form of Man-Kan kōkan: while Japan promised to 'disinterest' herself in Manchuria, Russia was not to be required to 'disinterest' herself in Korea. It was equivalent to applying a policy of spheres of interest to north-east Asia. While Muraviev with his 'Port Arthur first' doctrine may have been favourably inclined, the Russian military was opposed to making any concessions over Korea for fear of the effects on the security of the Maritime Provinces. The Russian reply was therefore a polite refusal.

The sphere-of-influence formula clearly did not appeal to Russia. Once the lease of Port Arthur and Talienwan was in the bag on 27 March, the Russians became distinctly less forthcoming in their assurances to the Japanese. Nishi was told of the lease by Minister Rosen on 29 March. Soon after on 2 April Rosen reported to Nishi that his government could not agree to exclude Russian power completely from Korea, though it was delighted to hear that Japan considered Manchuria and its littoral to lie outside her sphere of interests. Nishi, we are told, heard this reply with a wry smile.[18]

This presented the Japanese cabinet with a dilemma. A lengthy session of the cabinet was held that day to discuss whether to pursue negotiations with the Russians now that Man-Kan kōkan had been rejected. It decided that Japan had no option but to pursue the necessary steps for what she could dredge from them. But they had to consider some of the contrary views that had been coming in, like those of Hayashi. On 26 March Minister Katō in London had sent on an elaborate memorandum attacking Russia's southern advances and the notion of a Russo-Japanese understanding, even if one could be reached. Instead he appealed for serious consideration to be given to an alliance with Britain as a counterpoise to Russian expansion.[19] It was rejected at the cabinet on 2 April. But it may have had an effect on the other decision taken on the request of Britain for Japan's agreement to Britain applying for a lease on Weihaiwei when Japan pulled out her troops thence after she had received her indemnity payment from China.

The Itō cabinet duly gave its blessing to this proposal. Japan's decisions on that day represented an attempt to balance her approaches to Russia and Britain.[20]

Despite her disappointment, Japan persisted with her negotiations on the Russian terms and clinched an agreement with Rosen in Tokyo. The Nishi–Rosen protocol which was signed on 25 April 1898 is so important that it is reproduced in full (apart from the preamble):–

1. Japan and Russia confirm the sovereignty and complete independence of Korea, and agree to abstain from interfering in the internal affairs of that country;
2. Japan and Russia, in the event Korea should request either Japan or Russia for counsel and assistance, shall not take any measure regarding the appointment of military instructors or financial advisers without having first arrived at a mutual understanding on the subject;
3. Recognizing Japan's predominant and developing commercial and industrial enterprises in Korea, as well as the large number of her nationals residing in that country, the Imperial Russian Government agrees not to obstruct the development of the commercial and industrial relations between Japan and Korea.

The new protocol which made no mention of Manchuria aimed at reaffirming the balance between Japanese and Russian rights in Korea. It therefore improved the standing of Japan against that which she had in practice enjoyed over the past two years and which had been laid down in the Weber–Komura and Yamagata–Lobanov protocols. It could not of course be interpreted as a Russian pull-out. But it suited the thinking of Prime Minister Itō who wanted to avoid any confrontation with the Russians – a view which was shared in essentials by Foreign Minister Nishi. So Japan had to be content with the practical concessions given in clause 3, which gave the green light to Japanese companies desiring to develop their enterprises in Korea. It was an example of low-posture diplomacy on the part of Japan. Considering that Russia had embarked on the talks in a mood of offering compensation for her gains at Port Arthur, she did not greatly diminish her position in Korea. To that extent it amounted to a negotiating victory for Muraviev. But the talks were shrouded in secrecy and only insiders on both sides knew the details of the protocol.[21]

Taking together developments in Manchuria and Korea, Russia had gained and Japan had lost. There were various defences which the Itō ministry put up against the attacks it received for mishandling the crisis. One was that Japan had originally received enticing promises from Muraviev and Rosen. W. L. Langer justifies Muraviev's action in a typically *realpolitik* way by saying that the Russian foreign minister 'embarked boldly upon the only sound procedure, buying off the Japanese [over Port Arthur] by making concessions in Korea'.[22] But, as soon as he reaped his reward in China, Muraviev appeared to the Japanese to have gone back on his word. Russia had come forward with no real concessions for Japan in the Nishi–Rosen protocol, while she herself emerged with substantial strategic, political and commercial gains from the spring crisis. Bearing in mind the humiliation Russia had inflicted on Japan in 1895 over the tip of south Manchuria, the conduct of Russia's ministers in 1898 was very insensitive.

The other defence of Itō's position was that he was taking the long view. Japan could not, he believed, defeat Russia in arms so Japan's primary aim should be to keep the peace as long as possible. The new feature of the 1898 crisis was Itō's conversion to Man-Kan kōkan, a doctrine very different from the course of action which Japan had adopted in 1894 and 1895. Under it Itō was not going to make a fuss over leases which Russia acquired at Port Arthur and elsewhere, provided Russia gave similar undertakings over Korea. In 1898 Russia would not admit any intention of disinteresting herself in the Korean peninsula. But it was still open to Japan in later years to raise the formula with Russia, even though it had been rejected in 1898. Itō and a number of diplomats like Tsuzuki Keiroku and Kurino Shinichirō were enthusiastic supporters of this doctrine. But it was a minority view; and the army and many in the foreign ministry were opposed. It is doubtful whether Japan would have declared indefinitely in the future that she was 'disinterested' in Manchuria or accepted compensation for turning a blind eye on events in Manchuria by improving her position in Korea. Still, in the state of Japan's defences in 1898, and her political chaos, there was something to be said for Man-Kan kōkan.[23]

REFERENCES AND NOTES

1. *Dnevnik V. N. Lamsdorf* (Moscow 1926 and 1934).
2. Scott to Salisbury, 27 May 1898, Scott papers 52,297: Muraviev 'is evidently not regarded in influential circles, or even by many of his subordinates, as being as yet quite "à la hauteur de la situation".'
3. R. Rosen, *Forty Years of Diplomacy,* vol. 1, pp. 145–6 (hereafter cited as *Forty Years*).
4. Nishi to Katō (London), 18 Feb. 1898, *NGB* 31/I, no. 338: 'Since things are all going badly in the political and economic fields here, I have hardly any strength left to deal with affairs abroad.'
5. N. Rich and M. H. Fisher (eds), *Holstein Papers,* iii, nos. 636 and 639; Malozemoff, *Russian Far Eastern Policy 1881–1904*, pp. 97–8.
6. Malozemoff, op. cit., p. 99.
7. Ibid., pp. 100–1.
8. Ibid., pp. 101–2; S. Iu. Witte, *Vospominanya,* vol. 1, pp. 120–4.
9. Taguri to Komura, 4 Jan. 1898, *NGB* 31/I, no. 195.

10. G. E. Morrison, who was an acute commentator, thought that Japan could take on not just Russia but France and Germany as well.
11. Malozemoff, op. cit., p. 103.
12. Ibid., pp. 104–5.
13. Hart, in J. K. Fairbank *et al.* (eds), *The I. G. in Peking*, vol. 2, no. 1112.
14. Hart to J D. Campbell, 5 Dec. 1897, in J. K. Fairbank *et al.* (eds), *The I. G. in Peking,* vol. 2, no. 1090:''The Star of Empire' glittering in the *East* is distinctly Russian.'
15. Scott to T. H. Sanderson, 30 June 1900, Scott papers, 52305; Witte, *Vospominanya,* vol. 1, pp. 131–3.
16. *NGNB,* vol. 1, p. 186.
17. *NGB* 31/I, no. 583.
18. G. A. Lensen, *Balance of Intrigue,* vol. 2, p. 809.
19. Katō, 'Teikoku seifu no hōshin taidō', 26 Mar. 1898, in Itō Masanori, *Katō Takaaki,* vol. 1, Tokyo 1934, pp. 292 ff.
20. I. H. Nish, 'Japan and China: the case of Weihaiwei, 1894–1906', pp. 29–35.
21. Rosen described the protocol as 'lame and pointless'. *Forty Years*, vol. 1, p. 159.
22. W. L. Langer, *Diplomacy of Imperialism 1890–1902,* New York 1951, p. 471.
23. Itō, *Katō*, vol. 1, p. 29: 'The crumbling of Japan's foreign policy-making is accounted for by four flawed pillars: party controversy; financial problems; the Russophil views of the Elder Statesmen; and Itō's penchant for extreme caution.'

Chapter 3

THE ROAD TO THE OPEN DOOR (1898–1900)

The last chapter covered a series of leases, concessions, and acquisitions of railway rights in east Asia. These events set in train in China a process which to the journalist went by the name of 'slicing the melon'. More technically, it was an acquisition of spheres of interest by the various powers. 'Spheres of interest' in China were rather vaguely drawn zones spreading from a lease on the coastline into the hinterland where the acquiring power tried to claim, and seemed likely to exercise, monopolistic powers and commercially exclusive rights. These spheres were liable to injure the competitors of the 'monopolist' and thus break down the conceptions of free trade in China; they were also liable to injure her political integrity. While each of the spheres was a challenge to China's integrity, it was widely believed that there was nothing more injurious to the survival of China than Russia's sphere of interest in Manchuria, since it came so close to the Chinese capital itself.

The Chinese and their friends tried to limit the effectiveness of these spheres. Within the Chinese élite the pro-Russian group and the pro-western group tried to resolve this problem by setting one imperialist country off against the other. Thus, when Germany extracted Tsingtao and Russia Lushun (Port Arthur), Britain appears to have been offered Weihaiwei as a deliberate act, in the hope of offsetting these earlier leases. China's friends too – including those of the Imperial Maritime Customs like Robert Hart and Alfred Hippisley – were also lobbying to neutralize and limit Russian expansion. Our concern in this chapter is, however, with the ways adopted by the powers to neutralize Russia's acquisitions in Manchuria before it was too late. It is perhaps too early yet to speak of an anti-Russian front in the far east. But those opposed to Russia acted, partly by separate, partly by coordinated, moves to that end, without making a frontal assault upon her.

JAPAN'S DISCREET ADVANCES

Itō's non-party ministry may have been persuaded to follow a low-posture foreign policy because of the political strife and financial difficulties it was facing. In the general election in March the Liberals (Jiyūtō) and Progressives (Shimpōtō) gained substantial support. The Itō ministry was unable to reach the necessary political alliance with these parties which attacked its land tax bill in June. The government suspended the Diet; and the opposition parties retaliated by combining to form the Kenseitō. Itō thought it opportune to resign and leave the inexperienced party politicians to take office in what was to be the first truly party cabinet. Although his 'safety first' attitude in foreign affairs was notorious, Itō had before his resignation secured Japan's position in China during the scramble for concessions there. On 22 April Japan had asked China through her minister there, Yano Fumio, for a non-alienation agreement for the province of Fukien, which lay opposite the Japanese colony of Taiwan. The Tsungli Yamen promised not to alienate the territory and thus consented to its becoming virtually a Japanese sphere of interest.[1]

Ōkuma Shigenobu presided over a short-lived cabinet (June–October 1898), combining the offices of prime and foreign minister. Ōkuma's standpoint on Chinese affairs was different from Itō's. He was less prepared to forgive Russia and seek accommodation with her. For the present he confined himself to a policy of 'assurances'. After the Japanese troops had been withdrawn from Weihaiwei in June, the last remnant of the force left as a result of the peace settlement in 1895, Ōkuma consolidated Japan's position by seeking rights in foreign settlements at Hankow (16 July), Shashih (18 August) and Tientsin (29 August). These were followed subsequently by similar agreements with China relating to Fuchow (28 April 1899) and Amoy (25 October 1899).

Ōkuma also wanted to place China under Japan's guidance as a way of ousting the Russians at the Chinese court. This may have been one of the reasons for the visit paid to China by the former prime minister, Marquis Itō. This coincided with the Hundred Days of Reform. But within three months, the Chinese emperor and the reform party were crushed by the conservatives. Ōkuma granted the reformer K'ang Yu-wei and other liberals full protection if they sought asylum in Japan.[2]

Yamagata, whom we have last seen as the Japanese emissary to Russia in 1896, took over as prime minister in October 1898. He appointed as his foreign minister Aoki Shūzō, who was an experienced diplomat and a former foreign minister. While Aoki was well known for his anti-Russian sentiments, Yamagata was a man of caution who was by no means certain of the best approach to Russia.

In November, Yamagata managed to attain one of his prime objectives. Taking advantage of the political crises of 1898 in east Asia, he succeeded in getting his military-naval budget through the Diet. He was assisted in this by strong nationalist influences which were at work in the country. November had seen the inauguration of the To-A Dōbunkai (a cultural society for east Asia) under the presidency of the prominent aristocrat, Prince Konoe Atsumaro. Basically it was dissatisfied with Japan's record since 1895 and wanted her to acquire territories in the way that the imperial powers had done. While Japan's oligarchic rulers were by no means persuaded of the need for violent action, they realized that they had time on their side, provided they kept up their national strength.

Japan was developing her commercial and industrial stake in Korea, which Russia had granted in the Nishi–Rosen protocol. The number of Japanese living there increased; Japanese language newspapers were developed.[3] Between 1898 and 1900 there was a great expansion of trade: Japan was strongest in Korea's export trade and less strong in the import trade where she took second place to the Chinese merchants. Japan also acquired railway rights, first for the short Seoul–Chemulpo railway and then for the Seoul–Fusan railway. Some Japanese thought they should go easy with the construction because of possible Russian objections, but Yamagata and his war minister, General Katsura, believed that strategic priorities were more important than political niceties.[4] Capital for investment abroad being short, the group of entrepreneurs led by Shibusawa were slow to take up both surveys and proceed with the actual construction.

BRITAIN'S INVOLVEMENT IN NORTHERN RAILWAYS

In April 1898, one month after China had granted Russia the lease of Liaotung, the Chinese Railway Administration asked the Hong Kong and Shanghai Banking Corporation for a loan to fund the extension of the Northern line to Hsinmintung and Niuchuang. These negotiations led to a preliminary agreement early in June. On the insistence of Witte, Chargé d'affaires Pavlov complained bitterly to China about the loan on the grounds that it ran counter to the Additional Treaty which he had just signed whereby no line close to the Chinese Eastern Railway should be built by any country but Russia. Nonetheless the preliminary details of the loan were worked out on 15 June. In reply to Russian protests the Chinese stated that the proposed line would come under the control of China and not of Britain and that the railway itself would not become a mortgage for the loan. Pavlov repeatedly protested that the railway property should be held by the Chinese and not be allowed to pass into the hands of another country.[5] Since an impasse had been reached, it became necessary for the British government to discuss the matter with the Russians. Britain gave the firm assurance that China should have control of the railway which should not become the mortgage of a foreign country. This merely reiterated what Pavlov had earlier been told in Peking; but, coming from London and the British government, the statement had greater force.

Despite Russian objections, the negotiations were able to proceed haltingly in September on a more general basis. Some Russians had claimed since 1895 that Britain had been trying to strengthen her economic and commercial hegemony in China with the help of the Japanese. They were therefore highly suspicious of British interference in Manchuria, especially when it had railway implications.[6] The British ambassador, Sir Charles Scott, diagnosed the anti-British lobby as follows:

Any difficulties in settling the Chinese railway difficulties come not from the Government but from the old evil of Balkan days, non-official Russia – in this case the Hebrew financiers on the Board of the Russo-Chinese Bank who have very great power in the Russian money market and of whose services the Finance Department has often need ... Of the President of the Board Ouchtomsky [sic] he [Muraviev] made very light and treated as a myth the idea of his having any political weight in the Emperor's Councils but a Jewish banker named Rothstein had to be reckoned with.[7]

But the government itself may not have been as reconciled to British activities as this assessment suggests.

Meanwhile in October the British and Chinese Corporation entered into a formal agreement with China to extend the Peking–Shanhaikuan railway to Hsinmintung. This involved Britain in lending China the sum of £2,300,000 repayable over forty-five years. The new agreement covered also the construction of a branch line to Yingkow (Niuchuang) and provided that the chief engineer would remain a British national, namely Claude Kinder, who had been responsible for the line within the Great Wall.[8]

Even though the Russians had a guarantee that the mortgage would extend only to the Shanhaikuan–Tientsin section of the line, they were still filled with distrust. Their fear was that the 'Chinese line' would be a feint; that these would in fact be British railways, operating under the disguise of formal Chinese control; and that Britain would thereby acquire political interests in the trans-Liao part of Manchuria to the north of the Great Wall. Even if the British government gave specific assurances, private interests would subvert them. Moreover, were British activities not the thin end of the wedge? Would they not be followed by Japanese and American entrepreneurs, if Russia showed any sign of weakness towards the British? The Northern Extension itself – and any other railways that followed it – would break the Russian monopoly of trade in the area and upset the calculations on which Witte sought to recoup the colossal expenditure made on the Russian railways in the east.

During the talks on the Northern Railway Extension, Russia had proposed that the two countries reach some understanding over China. The chargé d'affaires in London, P. M. Lessar, who is later to play an important part in our story as Russian minister to China (1901–5), proposed a reciprocal agreement whereby Russia would not interfere with British railway interests in the Yangtse area while Britain would not interfere with Russian railway developments in Manchuria. The Russians were informed on 15 August that Britain would be required to enter upon a self-denying ordinance in Manchuria apart from the Northern Railway Extension as the price for holding her more valuable interests along the Yangtse.

While the idea secured the agreement of Muraviev and Lamsdorf, it met with resistance from Witte whose finance ministry was most closely concerned in the enterprise. The British ambassador, Sir Charles Scott, put the proposition to Witte in November thus:

> [Britain's aim was] to retain, for our trade and enterprise in China, equal opportunities, with a fair field and no favour, and the object of the proposed Agreement was to prevent the development of the commerce and enterprise of both countries being blocked by the exercise of foreign diplomatic influence at Peking, in opposing the grant of railway concessions or loans for their construction, or by the creation of artificial barriers such as differential treatment or preferential railway rates in favour of any particular nation.[9]

This bears a resemblance to what later became the Open Door doctrine for China and anticipated the American initiative over Manchuria. Though Witte was reassuring that Russia was now content and was not aiming at further expansion, he was not favourable to the suggested terms of an Anglo-Russian agreement. His own proposals for a general agreement were regarded by the British ministers as derisory.

The delayed Russian proposals were not handed over until 8 February 1899 and then reverted to the simple idea of an exchange of notes rather than a formal agreement by treaty. By February Muraviev was satisfied with the Niuchuang Railway loan and the assurances that the security did not give the British bank control of lines north of the Great Wall. Witte was also pacified but took a different view over the 'main' line to Hsinmintung which featured in the prospectus of the Northern Extension line, saying that he could not possibly acquiesce in any recognition of this part of the line, as it would seriously impair the commercial value of the Russian line.[10] Hsinmintung was some 200 miles from Mukden, the central point of the Russian extension plans, and a line to that point could arguably be used by foreign interests or the Chinese as a challenge to Russia. This last-minute dissension on the

Russian side was overcome and Muraviev was able to hand over the text of the identic notes in virtually final form.

Patience prevailed. On 28 April the Anglo-Russian Railway (or Scott–Muraviev) Notes were signed in St Petersburg. Their substance, which is relevant to us, must be given here:

1. Russia engages not to seek for herself or on behalf of Russian subjects or others railway concessions in the Yangtse basin, and not to place obstacles either directly or indirectly in the way of railway enterprises in that region supported by the British Government.
2. Similar engagement, *mutatis mutandis*, by Great Britain with regard to railway concessions north of the Great Wall.

Supplementary notes were also exchanged, providing that the above general arrangement was not to infringe in any way the rights acquired by the British and Chinese Corporation under their loan contract in regard to the Shanhaikuan–Niuchuang line, and

> that the Chinese Government may appoint an English engineer and a European accountant to supervise the construction of the line and the expenditure of the money appropriated to it ... As regards the extension to [Hsinmintung] from the point where the line branches off to Niuchuang, it is further agreed that it is to be constructed by China, who may permit European, not necessarily British, engineers to periodically inspect it and certify that the work is being properly executed.[11]

AMERICAN ATTEMPTS TO RESTRAIN RUSSIA: THE OPEN DOOR DOCTRINE

The story of the Open Door notes is already known from the varied works on the subject. Without repeating the story, we here wish to argue that the United States, in canvassing the support of foreign governments for the Open Door, was primarily aiming at restraining Russian activities in Manchuria.[12]

It is broadly accepted that Open Door ideas developed in the brains of Alfred Hippisley, one of the senior officials of the Chinese Imperial Maritime Customs, and William W. Rockhill, a junior of John Hay at the State Department in Washington. Earlier in his career as a diplomat, Rockhill had been secretary of legation in Peking in the 1880s, when he had met Hippisley. Hippisley had a wife from New England and so commonly spent part of his furlough in the United States. It appears that he sojourned there on his way to Britain in 1899. Before going on leave, Hippisley had been serving in Peking as relief for the chief secretary. He had therefore been close to Sir Robert Hart; but there is no evidence that he had a mandate to speak for him since Hart had the reputation of having no confidants in China. Yet in what Hippisley said he was reflecting Hart's rather gloomy thinking at that time, particularly that the division of China into spheres would be the death of that country. He had written on 3 April 1898: 'What I always feared is slowly but surely approaching, a Russian protectorate [over China]'.[13]

It appears that Rockhill engineered a meeting between Hippisley and John Hay, who had assumed office as secretary of state on 30 September 1898. Evidently Hippisley argued that those powers which had laid claim to a sphere of interest in China would soon impose a preferential tariff on merchandise passing through it and should be prevented from doing so. His friend, Rockhill, clearly favoured some sort of American initiative. Urged to develop his ideas by letter, Hippisley wrote in detail:

> Spheres of interest – euphemistically termed 'the economic and geographical gravitation of certain portions of the Chinese Empire' – have now been recognized and must be treated as existing facts. So far, however, the special rights and privileges claimed by each Power in its own sphere, consist only of preferential or exclusive rights to construct railroads and exploit mines in it. They have not as yet been extended to a claim to impose a differential tariff on merchandise consumed in or passing through it; but how soon such a claim may be advanced no one can say.[14]

While this was an attack on spheres of influence and their long-term effects, it was couched in general terms and not explicitly directed at Russia. In passing this to Hay with his strong commendation, Rockhill replied to Hippisley at Lenox, Massachusetts:

> I would like to see [the United States] make a declaration in some form or other, which would be understood by China as *a pledge on our part to assist in maintaining the integrity of the Empire.* I fear, however, that home politics and next year's elections will interfere with this adoption of a policy advocated by England.[15] [my italics]

There is no evidence that Hippisley was urged by the British government to make his proposals, only that the Hippisley–Rockhill idea reflected existing British practice. Hay urged Rockhill to go ahead: he was 'more than ready to act' but thought 'the very vague assurances given by Great Britain, Russia and the other Powers should be expressed in much stronger terms'.[16]

It was primarily Russia which provoked the new American initiative. In a letter which crossed with the above, Hippisley passed on the latest news he had received from Peking: 'the activity of the Russians in Manchuria is simply wonderful.... The Russification of Peking and of North China will proceed as rapidly as has that of Manchuria.'[17] These are precisely the districts which are great consumers of American textile fabrics, Hippisley added. American exports tended to be concentrated by coincidence in Russian and, to a lesser extent, German spheres of interest. If Manchuria were to be closed, some of America's trade would be lost. In other words, an essential part of Hippisley's advocacy was that a new dimension had to be taken into account – Russian activities in Manchuria, the need to guarantee the integrity of the Ching empire, and the damage which might be sustained by United States trade. In coming round to support Hippisley's views, Rockhill had of course to think of a much wider range of grounds for American action, but the danger of Russia was an essential one for him also. When Hay received Rockhill's note of 18 August, he agreed that it was a good starting-point for obtaining a declaration of intentions from the powers on the basis of American leadership. The notes in which both Hippisley and Rockhill had a hand were prepared and issued on 6 September. They took the form of identic notes, inviting various governments to adhere to the principle of equal commercial opportunity in China. More specifically the notes added that, while the United States accepted the existence of spheres of influence in China, it called for the elimination of discriminatory practices over rail tariffs, harbour dues, etc. in these spheres. While the American notes appealed to the sense of national commercial advantage on the part of the recipients, they also contained a broader implication of 'moral diplomacy', an attempt to shame the expansive powers into committing themselves against monopolistic spheres against their will.

On 13 October Rockhill wrote that 'much depends on what the Russian Government may say'. This re-emphasizes the point that it was Russia which was the focus of American attention and her action in Manchuria which led the Americans to launch the Open Door policy. Did the Russians interpret the notes in this way? Professor Langer writes 'We know that Muraviev was enraged by the American démarche and determined to make no reply. When the French deserted them and replied, the Russians were obliged to crawl out as best they could.'[18] The Rockhill papers tell another story: Russia was, to be sure, deliberately dilatory; but Rockhill had a conversation with Count Cassini, the Russian ambassador in Washington and formerly minister in Peking, on 24 November in the company of Pavlov, the chargé d'affaires in Korea. Cassini had visited Paris around 19 October when Foreign Minister Muraviev was received by President Loubet. He reported that Muraviev did not seem to know anything about the Open Door notes because he did not refer to them. It may be that Muraviev had left the Russian capital in the company of the tsar before the Hay note had been studied.[19] But ignorance was a pose which he often adopted and was by no means untypical of his lackadaisical approach. Since the court was to continue on tour while the tsar went on a state visit to Britain, Cassini was asked to handle the negotiations arising out of the Open Door notes in Washington.

Cassini took up with Rockhill the question of the leased territory in China and of the conventions recently concluded with Britain concerning their exclusive rights over railways and mines in their area north of the Great Wall. All of these had to be protected. Referring to Liaotung, he said that his government could not bind itself to give any pledges concerning it; that for the term of the lease it was an integral part of the Russian Empire and under Russian law. Neither could it bind itself to maintain the port of Dalny for the whole period of the lease as either an open port or a free port, but that for the time being, of course, everybody was ensured 'the same enjoyments' in it as Russian subjects. Pavlov, who was present as the local expert, said not too accurately that the organization of the customs service in Manchuria had not yet been formed; that it was still a question whether the duties would be levied by the Chinese customs service or a Russian service acting for them. Rockhill drew the inference that Russia's policy would be to give preferential rights to her subjects located in the leased territory (apart from Dalny which the tsar's ukase of 30 July 1899 declared to be a free port). It is clear too that the Russians had drawn far-reaching conclusions about their leases and the rights they had derived from the Anglo-Russian agreement.[20]

Cassini's negotiations in Washington led eventually to the preparation of a delphic note. Muraviev replied to Hay on 30 December:

> [Russia] has already demonstrated its firm intention to follow the policy of the open door by creating Dalny (Talienwan) a free port; and if at some future time that port, although remaining free itself, should be separated by a customs limit from other portions of the territory in question, the customs duties would be levied, in the zone subject to the tariff, upon all foreign merchandise, without distinction as to nationality.[21]

The artful Russian note referred to one part of the lease and not to spheres of interest. Rockhill commented that 'the acceptance of Russia is not as complete as I would like it; it has ... a string attached to it'.[22] Though Rockhill was not the mouthpiece of the State Department, it was evidently unhappy with the response also. Japan too was highly suspicious about the Russian reply. What, for example, did it mean to say that Dalny might at some 'future time be separated by a customs limit from other portions of the territory in question'? It seemed to imply that, though Dalny might become an open port and a free port, the Russians had different ideas for the rest of 'Manchuria'.

When the United States had made her move, the Yamagata cabinet was delighted. Japan was not one of the countries approached in the first instance, presumably because she was not thought to have a 'sphere of interest'. She asked, however, to be invited to subscribe to the note in view of her existing interests in China. It was not until 20 December that the Hay proposals were put to Japan; and she adhered without reservations shortly after. In the spring of 1900 she was, however, to demand a non-alienation agreement for the province of Fukien in south

China, which was on the mainland opposite her colony of Taiwan.[23]

It was on 20 April 1900 that the American secretary of state disseminated the text of the various powers' replies. They were a disparate bunch. Yet the president expressed gratification at the successful outcome of the negotiations. While the European powers kept their own counsel, Japan was surprisingly the country which tried to prick the bubble of American complacency. On 29 May Aoki stated what was incontrovertible: 'These answers are no more than declarations of the intention of these Powers to apply the m.f.n. treatment to all nations and cannot be construed as categorical replies to the three propositions contained in the original American proposals.'[24] In particular, the responses of Germany, Russia and France were little more than assurances about the application of most favoured nation principles. On 30 July John Hay replied that he 'did not seek to obtain replies [from the powers] couched in identical terms', desiring only statements of the policy they proposed pursuing in China as regards foreign trade. He was satisfied that the various governments intended to maintain 'liberty of trade and equality of treatment for all the world within the territory in China over which they exercise control or influence'.[25] By this admittedly limp response Hay was trying to apply Open Door doctrine both to leases and to spheres of influence. By giving the maximum of publicity to the replies of the powers, he hoped to put them on their honour and thus achieve what was important for the United States, the preservation of her trade interests in China as far as possible.

In many ways, the Open Door notes fell short. Japan looked in vain to them for a positive guarantee of action in restraint of great-power expansion in the area. Since the United States was content with such evasive replies, Japan could not regard the first Hay note as a major breakthrough. It did nothing to stay the hand of those who seemed to be set on expansion in China, notably Russia in Manchuria. Rockhill as one of the architects of the Open Door, nonetheless, claimed that there were some international merits in the whole operation. Hereafter, he argued, the United States holds the balance of power in China: 'the success of these negotiations places in the hands of the U.S. great power for doing good in the east; I only hope that they will use it to good advantage'.[26] Would this offer the Chinese American protection against inroads by foreigners?

Whatever else happened, Washington became a factor in the unfolding drama in the far east. To Russia the United States had become a partisan, one of the powers seeking to delimit her activities. It was true that there was not much threat of American military involvement: her land forces in the area, stationed in the Philippines, were too few; and her China squadron was relatively small and had no base in China. Nor did America's policy of avoiding entanglements with foreign powers suggest that she would align herself too closely in the area. Yet she had become the spokesman for what was generally regarded as a British policy. The historian can say that Britain did not put Hay up to the issue of his notes and, while Hippisley had his importance in the formulation of the doctrine, his ideas were meshed into many others coming from other quarters. Moreover Hippisley did not speak with the tongue of Whitehall, of Sir Robert Hart or the British mercantile community in China.

The importance of the episode is that the United States had decided that her national interest in relation to Russia's activities in Manchuria made it opportune for her to seize the initiative. By taking this initiative, she took also the leadership in the crisis and, despite the weakness of the initiative, she could not extricate herself later from the Manchurian problem. America was committed also to the defence of the territorial integrity of China and therefore Manchuria, at least on paper and in the rhetoric of public pronouncements. Of course, like Britain in her Anglo-Russian agreement, she was not prepared to confront Russia directly and openly but sought to ensure her own position by means other than force and to defend the interests of her merchant community.[29]

KOREAN TENSIONS

Meanwhile the Russians were as active as ever outside China. A. I. Pavlov, the Russian chargé in Peking since Cassini had left because of ill health, moved in August 1898 to Seoul and was replaced by M. N. de Giers. In China Pavlov had been the diplomatic instrument for Russia's expansive policies and, even by the standards of these imperialist times, he was tough-minded, unyielding and conspiratorial. Now he applied the tactics of Peking to the situation in Seoul. For Russia to expand her sphere there was a need to ignore the Nishi–Rosen protocol, for, even if that had not called for Russia to withdraw from the peninsula, it had at least implied that there should henceforth be a balance between Japan and Russia. Instead Pavlov and his consuls became active in the south at places like Masampo, Mokpo and Kojedo. In pursuit of Russian privileges at these points he was overbearing and tried to capitalize on Korea's goodwill towards Russia for services in the past.

This can best be illustrated by the case of Masampo, one of the finest harbours in east Asia, though still only a fishing-village. This port particularly interested the Japanese, being just west of Fusan, the starting-point of Japan's railway project in Korea. In October 1898 Ōkuma, during his brief period as foreign minister, had authorized his consul-general in Seoul to purchase for strategic purposes certain areas at Masampo.[28] Certainly both the army and navy were actively reconnoitring the area. Japan's leading expert on the subject, Professor

Yamawaki Shigeo, identifies the central figure in this to have been Colonel (later Major-general) Tamura Iyozō, who expressed the view in June 1899 that 'if Russia gets her hands on Masampo, Japan must become useless'.[29] Tamura is later to play an important part in the run-up to Japan's war with Russia.

In May 1899 the Russian navy tried to obtain a piece of ground for its own use at Masampo. Tamura immediately took steps to take possession of landing facilities there for the Japanese army. The problem, of course, was that if in any war in the neighbourhood of the Tsushima Straits Japan did not have command of the seas, she ought to have facilities for urgent landing.

In November, in the electric atmosphere of Fusan, there was a local disturbance involving Russian and Japanese seamen which greatly annoyed the tsar. So ugly did the confrontation become that the press speculated whether a collision might not take place between Japan and Russia. Itō, now in opposition, wrote to Admiral Yamamoto, the navy minister, on 1 December that there was talk in the Russian capital of Japanese preparations for war. If nothing were done about it, Russia would reinforce her garrisons in the far east even further and increase her fleet. Japan must therefore take steps to clear away Russian misunderstandings.[30]

By February 1900 the rumour circulated that Pavlov on return from overseas was demanding a lease of land for military-naval use at Mokpo or Masampo. A large Russian squadron including the battleships *Rossiya, Donskoi,* and *Rurik* sailed from Port Arthur and weighed anchor at Masampo threateningly. The Japanese cabinet, while not proposing to intervene to prevent any action, laid down that Russia should not acquire any site which would command the harbours of Kojedo island. Her minister at Seoul was asked to ensure that the Russian lease should be selected inside the harbour of Masampo or its immediate vicinity. Japan also appealed to Muraviev to this effect. Japan argued that Korea should inform the Russians that there was already an understanding between Japan and Korea over Kojedo; 'if any money is necessary to secure such an answer it will be remitted by me'.[31] Whether this was really done is not easy to discover.

Agreement was reached between Korea and Russia regarding the lease in Masampo open port on 12 April. It turned out, however, that some of the lots transferred were already the property of Japanese landowners who had purchased them privately during the scramble for concessions of the previous year. It was decided that the lots should be exchanged amicably for others. This was finally accomplished in September. And Russia acquired a concession at Pankumi, Masampo. A secret agreement between Russia and Japan laid down that Russia would not seek a lease of Koje island (Kargodo) and Korea in turn would not alienate it to any other power. When this leaked out, the Japanese decided not to press on with one of their ambitions, a lease of

Koje, which could in the new circumstances only be acquired at the risk of war. Could Russia's promise not to take Koje island be trusted? Many in Japan had no confidence in it. They believed that Russia's long-term intention was to command the Tsushima straits and that this must be resisted at all costs. That was why, when the Russo-Korean agreement was nearing completion, Japan placed her fleet on a war footing.

Masampo had been the focus of a war scare. But this passed with the coming of the Boxer disturbances in China in June. The Masampo quarrel was forgotten but it was by no means resolved. It was a symptom of the continuing *malaise* between Russia and Japan over Korea. A well-informed commentator like Dr Ernest Morrison predicted that a rupture would not come in 1900 but it would take place sooner or later.[32] For the present the Japanese leaders were cautious. As their representative in St Petersburg said on 22 July, 'the Korean question is to be settled between Japan and Russia independently of the other Powers which take no serious interest in Korea'.[33] Japan, in other words, was not prepared to entertain an international solution to the problem. Nor was she ready for a head-on clash with Russia.

Japan's caution over Russia may be illustrated by a story of Admiral Yamamoto, Japan's navy minister in the Yamagata cabinet (1898–1900). Late in 1899 the Japanese naval attaché in Russia, Commander Nomoto, reported that Russia, which had hitherto allowed him to inspect navy-yards, had withdrawn that privilege because equivalent facilities had not been given to the Russian naval attaché in Tokyo. It was alleged that preparations for mobilization were being hurried forward in these navy-yards, hence the withdrawal of the reciprocal privileges. When it came before the cabinet, Prime Minister Yamagata was very worried. Outside the cabinet the elder statesman, Itō, was similarly alarmed and wrote specially to Yamamoto. As a result, Admiral Yamamoto sought an interview with the Russian minister, Rosen, who said that naval matters were reported by the attaché, Captain Chagin, direct to the tsar. It was not therefore a matter under his jurisdiction. Yamamoto nevertheless explained that he had told Chagin that he would be given permission to witness the review of the fleet but would not be allowed to see naval manoeuvres; this was not only to suit the convenience of the Japanese but was also universal practice. He told Rosen that the notion that Japanese navy-yards were being worked to death in preparations for mobilization was a complete misunderstanding. Rosen went on to discuss the suspicious movements of a Japanese called Hidaka at Masampo where he seemed to be spying on Russia's coal stocks at that port. Again Yamamoto gave mild reassurances which Baron Rosen undertook to report to St Petersburg. Before long the privileges of the naval attachés were restored in both capitals.[34]

It was possible to improve Russo-Japanese relations on *ad hoc* problems by using personal contacts. But there was a deep-seated unease, especially among men on the frontier, say, in Seoul or Masampo.

RUSSIA IN THE EAST ON THE EVE OF THE BOXERS

The early Soviet historians of the *Krasnyi Arkhiv* assembled under the title 'Tsarskaya diplomatiya o zadachakh Rossii na Vostoke v 1900' a number of memoranda by the tsar's closest advisers in the early part of 1900. These throw important light on the motives of those in European Russia over the affairs of Manchuria and Korea. These memoranda are not primarily concerned with the far east, but with 'the east', by which they mean all territories from the Maritime Provinces and Korea to Iran and even Africa.[35] Foreign Minister Muraviev prepared a memorandum in order to reach a consensus with his colleagues on the shape which Russian policies should take at this time of high imperialism. It was written in the light of two events: the south African war which had broken out in the autumn of 1899 and was to hold Russia's arch-rival, Britain, in its clutches for three years; and the Hague peace conference which owed much to the initiative of the tsar himself. In the masterly way typical of this period of high imperialism, Muraviev discussed Russia's problems, beginning with Africa, Turkey, and Persia, before turning to Afghanistan and the far east. The argument reflected Muraviev's prime interest in Europe or at least with the near east. While he argued in favour of taking advantage of Britain's preoccupation to improve Russia's position in Afghanistan, Persia and Turkey, even to the extent of acquiring the Bosphorus, he gave a negative answer on whether she should 'take compensation of some sort in the far east'. While in recent years all the aspirations of Russia had been focused on her search in the far east, it was desirable at this time to wait for the completion of the Trans-Siberian railway. He declared himself against taking a naval station on the southern coastline of Korea, which would only excite the opposition of Japan and involve Russia in serious expenditure. Muraviev's three conclusions pertaining to the far east which he regarded as 'undoubtedly necessary for the purpose of protecting our paramount interests' in the area were:

1. to proceed with bringing the forces of the Priamur military zone and those on the Kuantung peninsula to a state of warlike preparedness as was initiated by the War Minister in the previous year;
2. to attend to the speediest possible equipment of Port Arthur and the construction of the railway lines on the Kuantung peninsula, which would join that peninsula to the Siberian 'mainline'.

3. not to forget that, for the sake of holding Russia's power in the Pacific ocean at an appropriate level, a prime condition is *to maintain a squadron which is strong and provided with supplies for all eventualities.* [Muraviev's emphasis][36]

While professing to agree with the findings of their 'Dear Colleague', the other ministers had considerable reservations to make. As befitted the finance minister, Witte opposed the three points above on the ground that the Russian budget was already burdened by heavy outlay on railways and other projects in the far east and would not be able to stand up to opposition from Japan and Britain. Kuropatkin was more concerned with central Asia. It was the navy minister who concentrated on far eastern problems. Admiral Tyrtov on 27 February in a rather muddled and contradictory letter wrote that it was indispensable for the Pacific fleet to have a coaling station in southern Korea, in view of the traffic plying between Vladivostok and Port Arthur, which were 1,100 miles apart. His conclusion was that:

> Russia has no need for territorial seizures of any kind, as is accurately explained in your [Muraviev's] memorandum; and we shall not follow aggressive policies in the far east. But we can only keep Japan in check by the threat of effective force. For this peaceful objective the tsar has established a particular credit for the construction of a fleet which will be 30% larger than the Japanese in the Pacific ocean; for this objective it is necessary to have also a port in southern Korea, which is envisaged as being in Mozampo [sic] bay with the island of Kargodo adjacent to it. If the occupation of such a port cannot be realized at the present time for the sound reasons set out in the memorandum, it is necessary to proceed with the acquisition of it gradually by diplomatic methods and by purchase and to achieve our goal, to which we must press on unswervingly. Regrettably, however, the case last year where proper respect was not shown by Korea for our rights in Mozampo [sic] indicated that the influence of Japan is evidently greater in Korea than is ours.[37]

While Muraviev, Witte and Kuropatkin were more concerned about railways with their destination in Manchuria, Tyrtov reflected the preoccupation of the far eastern fleet with Korea. His object was not merely to obtain a base for its own sake but also to hold Japan in check. Allowing for the fact that Tyrtov was probably playing down his views to make them more palatable to his colleagues and the tsar, it does seem that he comes close to advocating an 'aggressive policy', despite Malozemoff's disclaimer on this point.[38]

Muraviev then summarized the views of his correspondents for the tsar and in some cases modified his recommendations. It would appear that these were seen by the tsar on 13 March without his making any comment on them. It is an interesting example of a Russian perspective on Asian policy, a sort of St Petersburg view of the world. They were evidently not entirely up to date in their information about railway progress. Nor were they in line with the thinking which their juniors in Korea, Manchuria and China shared. If there was a general will to go slow in the area and allow moderation to prevail among the leaders of the tsarist government, M. N. Pokrovskii in his editorial note to these documents writes of the awareness of the three departments of state of the necessity to leave the decision on these paramount problems to the exercise of diplomatic skills or face 'the cost of a decisive European war'.[39]

Although the tsar's advisers were content to tread water, Russia's fortunes in the far east had made great headway over the previous five years due to the energies of the men on the spot. Firstly, the Russian railways were making rapid progress. No sooner had the concession for the Chinese Eastern Railway Extension been granted than construction was undertaken in sections, beginning in south Manchuria. From April 1899, steamer after steamer, laden with railway material, came into the various ports and, by arrangement with the Chinese, were cleared free of duty. The result was that by the end of the year the railway from Port Arthur and Talienwan as far north as Mukden, a distance of some 300 miles, was opened. The rails had been laid down but they were only spiked to the sleepers. Permanent bridges were not completed and so it was not possible for regular traffic yet to pass along it. It was, however, possible to proceed by engine and observation car along its length, as also along the line from Niuchuang to the junction point with the main line at Tashihchao. By June 1900 the line north to Harbin had come into use on this basis. It was not only the Russians who had made great strides. So too had their rivals on the Anglo-Chinese line. The furthest point to which the Northern Extension was open to traffic was Chunghouso, though it was also possible in that case to travel up further by trolley.

Apart from railways, the Russians were putting down roots in many areas. The banks were establishing themselves in this frontier situation. Vladivostok and Port Arthur were being developed as naval bases for a large-scale and expanding building programme. Russian consular and customs representatives were becoming more numerous on the scene. All in all, the Russians had good grounds for taking pride in their achievement and the speed of their accomplishment. As a corollary there was no little jealousy on the part of the other powers.[40]

The jealousies tended to be worked out not in Port Arthur or Dalny which were already Russian preserves but in the more developed – and more international – treaty port of Niuchuang. There the new Russian consul, Ostroverkov, who arrived in July 1899, acted as though he was in full control straight away. The Russians, using the plausible excuse that an outbreak of bubonic plague which had led to the death of six Chinese during the summer might spread up the railway line, tried to take over the port. They devised a scheme for a Sanitary Board, which would consist mainly of Russian officials and Russian doctors, in whom the sanitary and police control of the town – in effect its administration – was to be vested. This ploy was opposed by the consular body who successfully argued that the new board must be a Chinese one with the Taotai, the chief Chinese figure in the area, at its head. This illustrates that long before the military measures which Russia took in 1900 there was bitterness and tension between her and the other powers over the treaty port of Niuchuang and that Russia, despite the strength of her position, did not always emerge successful.

There was no shortage of international incidents. Increasingly Russia came to be faced by Japan in association with Britain and the United States as the countries most opposed to Russian expansion. Their attitude to the Russians was often a 'bitter-sweet' one. We may quote the case of Niuchuang again. Since small foreign communities at treaty ports were always vulnerable to the actions of the Chinese, there were advantages in having the Russians around in strength. There was a Russian gunboat, generally the *Otvajnii,* in the river; and its sailors patrolled the settlement every night. On the other hand, jealousy grew like wildfire. As soon as the *Otvajnii* seemed to be permanently installed, the Japanese in July 1900 sent their gunboat the *Tatsuta,* while the British followed suit by sending HMS *Fame,* commanded by Lieutenant Roger Keyes. Any action which was not warranted by existing treaty rights was immediately challenged by the consular body.[41]

Wherever one went in north-east Asia there was evidence of resistance to the current wave of Russian expansion. The Russians clearly thought it unreasonable. They also held rightly that there was likely (in the climate of the south African war which had begun in 1899) to be little resistance from Britain. If therefore diplomatic activity was necessary, it should be directed at the Japanese. Since Russia was inclined to go slow and adopt conciliatory tactics, she wanted to employ her negotiating skills. To this end Muraviev sent his most highly regarded diplomat, Aleksander Petrovich Izvolskii, as minister to Tokyo in June 1900. He relieved Rosen who had been in Tokyo since August 1897. The popular Rosen commented that Izvolskii would have a difficult job. But he hoped his successor, who was a clever man, would have some success. Others thought that it was a panic measure: 'The Russian Government became alarmed and sent Izvolskii who was regarded as their best diplomatist to Tokyo in order to keep the peace for a few more years till the railway was completed. In this they were successful.'[42] Certainly Rosen had had his full stint and was due for re-posting but Izvolskii was a new face and not immediately popular. Sir Claude MacDonald, the British minister, described him as 'a very slippery customer but most plausible and pleasant withal'.[43] In discussing Russian representation in the Japanese capital, the anti-Russian foreign minister, Aoki, described Rosen as 'a nice fellow to deal with but the Russians are always trying to grab something'.[44] When it was suggested that Rosen's recall was connected with Masampo, Aoki replied that Rosen had asked for a change: anyhow, even if Izvolskii were the active personage he was represented to be, that would not matter, just as in the case of Khitrovo, whom they had not found difficult to deal with.[45]

This chapter has covered the aftermath of the scramble for concessions in China in so far as it was relevant to the ever-growing tension between Japan and Russia. The Russians were surprisingly uncertain about their priorities but in east Asia had no realistic option other than to proceed with their railways in which a great national investment had been made and considerable progress was manifest in surveys and construction. Naturally they had no wish to embark on war for which they were in any case ill-prepared in the area. They were therefore in a mood of consolidation and negotiation, in which they had great expectations from Izvolskii's appointment to Tokyo. From the Japanese side also, there was no wish for outright confrontation. In the crisis over Port Arthur, Japan had been discreetly silent, largely because of the cautious viewpoint of Marquis Itō. Instead she tried to negotiate with Russia a 'package deal' linking Manchuria with Korea, the so-called Man-Kan kōkan formula. Although the Russians would not accept a deal on this basis, the Nishi–Rosen protocol which emerged was serviceable for the role which the Japanese envisaged for themselves, that of peaceful economic penetration of the peninsula. But behind the diplomatic niceties of the Nishi–Rosen protocol there was incessant squabbling in the ports on the southern tip of Korea, notably at Masampo. Japan was not alone in trying to keep Russia at arm's length. The powers were also taking action in restraint of Russia: Britain in the Anglo-Russian Agreement on Manchurian railways; and the United States in the Open Door diplomacy which they had launched. As a result Japan was becoming part of a group of anti-Russian powers which was being formed and whose course of action in the future was far from clear. While suspicion of Russia's east Asian activities was everywhere to be seen, it was still on a modest scale compared with what emerged when China herself took a hand in events with the outbreak of the Boxer disturbances.

REFERENCES AND NOTES

1. *NGNB*, vol. 1, p. 185.
2. Miyazaki Tōten, *My 33 Years' Dream*, ch. 19.
3. FO 46/453, Lowther to Salisbury, enclosing Gubbins, 10 July 1895.
4. Inouye Yūichi, 'Russo-Japanese relations and railway construction in Korea', pp. 92–4.
5. *BD*, vol. i, p. 1.

6. A. L. Galperin, *Anglo-Iaponskii Soiuz,* p. 39.
7. Scott to Salisbury, 8 Sept. 1898, Scott papers, 52,297.
8. *BD,* vol. 1, p. 1.
9. *BD,* vol. 1, no. 59.
10. Scott to T. H. Sanderson, 6 Apr. 1899, Scott papers 52,303.
11. Ambassador Scott reported 'The Vedemosti, Prince Ouchtomsky's paper (he, you know, is a Director of the Russo-Chinese Bank) violently attacks the agreement with England and the Russian press is far from enthusiastic about it' (Scott to Bertie, 18 May 1899, Scott Papers 52303; *BD,* vol. 1, no. 61.)
12. See M. H. Hunt. *The Making of a Special Relationship,* for a bibliographical note containing an up-to-date review of American studies on the Open Door.
13. J. K. Fairbank *et al.* (eds) *The I.G. in Peking,* vol. 1, no. 1102.
14. Hippisley to Rockhill, 25 July 1899, Rockhill letterbook.
15. Rockhill to Hippisley, 3 Aug. 1899, ibid.
16. Rockhill to Hippisley, 18 Aug. 1899, ibid.
17. Hippisley to Rockhill, 16 Aug. 1899, ibid.
18. W. L. Langer, *Diplomacy of Imperialism 1890–1902,* New York 1951, p. 687.
19. *Documents Diplomatiques Français, 1870–1914,* 1st series, vol. 15 for 1899, no. 286. (Hereafter cited as *'DDF'.*)
20. Rockhill to Hay, 24 Nov. 1899, Rockhill notebook Q; A. Malozemoff, *Russian Far Eastern Policy,* pp. 117–18.
21. Malozemoff, op. cit., p. 118.
22. Rockhill to Hippisley, 16 Jan. 1900, Rockhill notebook Q.
23. I. H. Nish, *The Anglo-Japanese Alliance, 1894–1907,* pp. 75–6.
24. A slightly different version of this message is in *NGB* 33, no. 30.
25. *NGB* 33, no. 32.
26. Rockhill to Hippisley, 16 Jan. 1900, Rockhill notetook Q.
27. On American policy, see Akira Iriye, *From Nationalism to Internationalism: U.S. Foreign Policy to 1914,* London 1977, p. 165.
28. Yamawaki Shigeo, 'Masampo Jihen' (3 parts) in *Tōhoku Daigaku Bungakubu Kenkyū,* 1959–60.
29. Ibid., part 1, pp. 7–13.
30. Japanese navy microfilm.
31. *NGB* 33, nos. 148–56 and 168.
32. Morrison to V. Chirol, 10 April 1900, in Lo Hui-min (ed.), *The correspondence of G. E. Morrison,* vol. 1, no. 78.
33. *NGB* 33, no. 221.
34. Japan, Navy Ministry, *Yamamoto to kaigun,* pp. 105–7. See also I. H. Nish, 'Korea, focus of Russo-Japanese diplomacy, 1898–1903' in *Asian Studies,* Manila, **4** (1966), pp. 70–83.
35. *Krasnyi Arkhiv,* **18** (1926), pp. 3–29.
36. Ibid., p. 20.
37. Ibid., p. 21.
38. Malozemoff, op. cit., p. 122.
39. *Krasnyi Arkhiv.* **18** (1926), pp. 2–3.
40. A. Hosie (Niuchuang) to Salisbury, 14 Feb. 1900.
41. See (Admiral) Roger Keyes, *Papers,* pp. 1–3.

42. C. Hardinge, *Old Diplomacy,* p. 71. Among Izvolskii's strongest sponsors was Nicholas II's mother.
43. MacDonald to Hardinge, 30 June 1904, Hardinge papers 3.
44. Satow to Salisbury, 12 Oct. 1899, E. M. Satow, *Korea and Manchuria between Russia and Japan,* p. 95.
45. See Satow to Salisbury, 25 Jan. 1900, in Scott Papers, 52,302: 'The chief cause of ill-feeling was a row at Fusan [?] between some Russian man of war's men and the Japanese, which had come to the knowledge of the Emperor Nicholas. The latter then had instructions sent out to Rosen [Nov. 1899] to express his deep *personal displeasure.*'

Chapter 4

CONFUSION IN CHINA (1900)

The summer months of 1900 saw a mighty transformation of the east Asian scene. By the autumn the armies of the powers were in control of the provinces around Peking, while the armies of Russia had moved in in great strength to occupy strategic points in China's three eastern provinces. This was in retaliation for the actions of the Boxers in north China culminating in the siege of the foreign legations in Peking from 4 June to 15 August (which will be discussed briefly in this chapter) and for the slightly later outbreaks in Manchuria (which will be considered in more detail in the next chapter). The Russian occupation of Manchuria was to drag on for year after year and be a major cause of the Russo-Japanese war.

The Boxer turmoil which afflicted China in 1900 was the culmination of a series of incidents which had been taking place since 1898 over a wide area of China north of the Yangtse. These incidents, given by foreigners the sinister name 'Boxer' (because of their association with secret societies of that name), were the result of peasant uprisings, brought on by food shortages and droughts, but they developed momentum also against missionaries and foreign nationals. Since the successes of Christian missions and the foreign inroads of 1898 were blamed on the weakness of the Chinese court, the 'Boxers' also became anti-dynastic. The empress dowager and her acolytes, who had come to power after the failure of the Hundred Days' Reform two years earlier, appear eventually to have succeeded in turning the thrust of the Boxers' energies away from themselves and directing it against the foreign communities. Nowhere could these energies be more effectively employed than around the imperial capital; and the Boxers had since August 1899 been converging there.

On his arrival in St Petersburg in May, the new Japanese minister, Komura Jūtarō, observed how surprised he was to find the Russian foreign minister able to take a remarkably sanguine view of the situation in China. We know from Russian sources that Muraviev took the view that there was a special relationship between Russia and China and that

Russia's position there was different from, and more favourable than, that of other powers. The tsarist government's great concern was that the powers, in attempting to suppress the Boxers, would intervene in China's domestic affairs to such an extent as to bring down the regime of the empress dowager, who, in the Russian view, represented the stable element in Chinese society. The fact that the empress dowager and Li Hung-chang were also in Russia's pocket and should not be disturbed was a major ingredient in her thinking. This was the basis for Russia's softly, softly approach. The Russian minister in China, Mikhail (de) Giers (1898–1901), was a past master of this approach. In the diplomatic body in Peking, Giers was heartily disliked and distrusted for going his own way. But then the Peking diplomats failed to see either the 'special relationship' or indeed any special generosity of spirit on Russia's part towards China.[1]

As the Boxers were approaching Peking, the Russians took their own stand. When the Peking diplomatic body called on the Tsungli Yamen at the end of January to suppress the 'anti-foreign societies', Giers refused to join it. When its members agreed to petition their home governments on 10 March for a naval demonstration to be made in northern Chinese waters with a view to bringing pressure to bear on the Manchu government to put down the Boxers, Giers again refused to join and even tried to persuade some of the ministers to change their minds. It was, therefore, possible for the others to argue later that, if the Russians had only joined in showing solidarity at this stage, the situation would not have deteriorated as it later did. In the event, the European governments did not agree to take the kind of gunboat action recommended. When in May they did make a naval demonstration, Russian vessels were present but did not take an active part.[2]

What factors lay behind this individualistic and more sympathetic approach to China? Japan's new minister was quick to make his own diagnosis: Russian officials were specialists in European and near eastern questions and were generally weak in understanding the far eastern situation; when they received information from north China, they could not understand the place-names; it was, therefore, difficult for them to assess the realities of the situation. Many foreign ministry bureaucrats asked Komura to help them in assessing this information; and he alleges that he had a backstairs influence in this way, being able to pick up much information about Russian attitudes which he was able to convey to Tokyo.[3]

A second aspect was that the Russians claimed that they were not the target of the anti-missionary zeal of the Boxers. They held that, though Russia was a deeply Christian country, she had taken no part in missionary work in China. Though the Russian Orthodox Church did pursue missionary activities elsewhere in the world, it had not looked to China proper as a mission field, as the French, British, Italians, Americans and Germans had done. The tsar was moreover critical of the actions of other countries' missionaries, saying that they cloaked their shameless enterprises in the saintly name of Christ.[4]

A third factor was that Russia's prime concern was not with China proper but with Manchuria and her railway there. Not only did Russia have a long indefensible frontier with China but she also had a railway on Chinese territory which was not readily defensible. The fact was that the constructors of the Chinese Eastern railway had all along been meeting with attacks on their workers and on the Russian guards by Chinese (call them 'Boxers' if you will). These were being kept secret but were a source of great anxiety. In keeping with the increased tempo of disturbances in the Peking area, the attacks in Manchuria increased. It was not that Russia could not in the long term cope with the situation because she could mobilize about 160,000 reservists in the area. But many of these were west of Lake Baikal and, by the time they were on the spot, the Russians would be fully stretched in keeping control of the line. In this sense, Manchuria was Russia's top priority; and Peking only secondary.

Only when Russian interests suffered did Giers join the others. On 28 May the diplomats at Peking called for reinforcements from naval vessels off Taku; and a small force of 350 men reached Peking. After disjointed disturbances in north China, they reported to their governments a week later their fear that they might be besieged in Peking and asked for an expeditionary force to be sent. Russia's minister endorsed the request; and Admiral Sir Edward Seymour, commander-in-chief of the British far eastern squadron, set off from Taku on 11 June at the head of an allied force of some 2,000 men including Russians from Port Arthur; but, finding his way barred by Boxer forces around Peking, he was forced to retreat to Tientsin. Unaware of the fate of these forces, Sugiyama Akira, shokishi (chancellor or senior clerk) of the Japanese legation, was sent to make enquiries at the Yamen but he was killed and decapitated by Chinese. This forced the Japanese cabinet to consider intervention in an enterprise which was only marginally of interest to their people. There was no reason why Japan should support the various contingents of the European powers or associate herself with the missionary cause. Moreover, the Japanese had no illusions about the opposition they would face if they sent a large-scale expedition to the Peking area. Prime Minister Yamagata's interim decision was that it was unwise to send a large force on its own and sensible to wait for an invitation from the powers.[5]

PEKING HOSTAGES AND THEIR LIBERATION

The news from China suggested the existence of a horrific emergency. On 13 June the Boxers entered Peking after the court had given orders for any allied force to be resisted. The allied vessels seized the north and south forts at Taku, led by Japanese marines with great spirit. In retaliation for this 'invasion', the Chinese court decided to make war on the allies and raised no objection to a siege of the legation quarter in Peking. In the gruelling circumstances, the German minister, Baron von Ketteler, decided to protest to the Tsungli Yamen in person and was killed by the Boxers on 20 June.

On 21 June, at the height of the crisis, Count Muraviev died suddenly. Because there was an ugly wound on his left temple at the time of death, there were persistent rumours that he had committed suicide on the ground that he had contributed to the trouble in China and to a deterioration of his country's position there. The night before his death he had dined till 1 a.m. with Witte and Kuropatkin on the Islands. It appears that there had been acrimonious political discussion during the course of which Witte had laid a good deal of the blame for the crisis in China on Muraviev's insistence in 1898 on taking Port Arthur (against Witte's advice). Whether such harsh criticism from the blunt Witte would have led Muraviev to commit suicide is hard to say. Certainly the official government announcement asserted that, after rising late, he had merely slipped in his study and grazed his temple on the sharp side of a bureau; death had been immediate. But Witte felt some remorse at the reproaches he had made against Muraviev's policy the night before he died.[6]

Muraviev's death left the foreign ministry numb. Lamsdorf, for long his close associate and sole confidant, took over as acting minister in the interim. But it was not expected that he would succeed ultimately, since he was highly strung at the best of times and suffered from palpitations of the heart. It was impossible to predict where the succession might come to rest: and it was possible that a new man might be found among the strong group which disapproved of the 'peaceful' approach which Muraviev had followed.[7] *Le Temps,* which had the ear of St Petersburg society, was bold enough to announce the appointment of Izvolskii, then minister in Tokyo, to the vacancy. But Komura, while admitting that there was such an intention in court, did not think it likely that one who was unable to see eye to eye with Muraviev should be appointed. Eventually Lamsdorf was approved as acting minister on 7 August, and this was confirmed six months later. But Muraviev's state funeral and its aftermath disrupted affairs at the height of the China crisis.

Meanwhile in Tokyo Yamagata convened an emergency meeting of his cabinet on 15 June and, after consultation with Itō, the 'opposition' leader, agreed to send two infantry divisions to China under Major-general Fukushima, one of the Japanese army's Russian experts. In London the cabinet felt especially powerless, with the main force of the British army employed in south Africa. Despite moves to take the lead in asking Japan to intervene, it was not until 22 June that it agreed to send British reinforcements and seek support in Europe for Japan to send an emergency force to China of (say) 25–30,000 men. Knowing the financial difficulties of the Yamagata government, Britain offered the sum of one million pounds towards the cost of the expedition. The Japanese declined this and insisted that the main consideration with them was not money but support of the powers. In other words, they wished to be sure that there would not be a repetition of 1895, that is, that Japan's intervention would not be faced by a hostile three-power coalition of Russia, Germany and France. Certainly there was much talk in the press and in diplomatic circles about the 'revival of the Shimonoseki Treaty Triad' in the interest of preserving China's territorial integrity. The result was that Britain for the rest of the month had to argue persuasively for a major role to be given to Japan in the relief of the legations.

The European powers did have suspicions of Britain and Japan. Britain's attempt to 'sponsor' Japan was regarded with grave suspicion. It was considered to be Britain's way of compensating for her international powerlessness during the south African war by calling in the Japanese. Moreover, it was regarded as Britain's way of forestalling Russia in any plans she had. These suspicions were of course by no means groundless. The Russians therefore stalled, pretending to misunderstand Salisbury's intentions and raising matters of little substance. European countries were suspicious also of Japan, arguing along lines already made familiar by the kaiser, namely that Japan was working for the solidarity of the yellow race. Certainly France was anxious to take advantage of every crisis to breathe new life into her alliance with Russia and Delcassé offered to go to St Petersburg.[8]

The military position of the allies was uncertain. On 17 June they had landed a force to capture the Taku forts, with Japanese and Russian participation. Russia was in a position to supply 8,000 men from Port Arthur (so Kuropatkin estimated), while retaining 4,000 for the defence of that port. But she was awaiting reinforcements from Siberia. Admiral Alekseyev, the Russian commander, agreed that without substantial reinforcement the allies could not advance beyond Tientsin. On the Japanese side, they had agreed on 26 June to mobilize some 10,000 additional men who would not be transported to China until replies from the powers. Their estimate of the number of troops needed for the retaking of Peking was 70,000, because the maize was standing high in the fields, roads were non-existent and the Chinese had opened the sluices on the Pei-ho, thereby stopping river-craft sailing up to Peking. Though not everyone accepted this pessimistic estimate, it did serve to illustrate how perilous and difficult an operation to relieve the legations would be.

In this emergency, the European powers could not afford to delay their approval. The Russians, though still opposed to any mandate being given to Japan for the despatch to China of a massive army, would not interfere with her freedom of action to send troops of her own volition provided she acted in conjunction with the other powers. Izvolskii's reply to Japan was rather curt and tepid but Russia was not going to stand in the way of Japanese participation. Since Germany's troops were still on the high seas, she and her partners were not inclined to give the Japanese too much encouragement but did not object. Using this authority, the Japanese cabinet on 6 July agreed to mobilize the fifth division for service in China; and arrangements for its transportation were completed immediately.[9]

The allied armies had some success with the occupation of Tientsin on 14 July – a significant victory which demoralized the ill-disciplined Boxer forces. The Japanese fifth division reached there a week later. But there was still a wide gulf between the military commanders of the various countries about the size of force which would be needed to relieve the legations. Many commanders, including the Japanese, wanted to defer the attack until the number of troops available exceeded 50,000 men. Two things made a decision more urgent: one was the indication that those in the legations were still alive whereas previously they had been thought dead; the other was that the intensity of the siege was stepped up from 28 July onwards and the capacity of the foreigners for survival was less certain. The commanders took the plunge and moved west early in August and on the 14th freed the foreigners from the eight-week siege.[10]

Even as this advance on Peking was being made, a strange diplomatic exchange was taking place among the powers involved. For some time the issue of whether there should be an overall commander for the expeditionary force had been discussed. The Russians had not approved of Admiral Seymour, while others had not liked Admiral Alekseyev. Now that victory was in sight, the need for a peace-time general as commander-in-chief became an issue. On 6 August the German emperor asked the tsar: 'Is it your special wish that a Russian should be commander in chief? Or would you eventually like one of my generals? In the latter case, I place Field-marshal Count Waldersee at your disposal' [English original]. The tsar replied, quite privately, that he had no objection in principle. The kaiser then approached other monarchs, saying that the tsar was sponsoring the name of Waldersee and that he would set out from Europe very soon. Britain refused to act as sponsor; Japan was keenly hurt; and France was very annoyed at the breakdown of consultation with Russia.[11]

How does one explain the Russian action? Was it the inept act of a tsar who could be easily browbeaten? Certainly there were Russian generals who were ambitious for the post. General Kuropatkin and Admiral Alekseyev are two that were mentioned. Moreover, Russia's ally, France, was strongly in favour of a Russian general becoming allied commander-in-chief and was reluctant to have a German. Certainly, Waldersee (1832–1904) was not an ideal choice. High as was his reputation as a strategist, he had never been in tropical climes or had any experience of military operations there. Moreover he was largely a court general – and one in his late sixties to boot.[12]

Perhaps Russia's attitude during the episode has to be interpreted in the light of her desire to have limited commitment to operations in the Peking area. She was prepared to join the other powers for the relief of Russian nationals in Peking and her legation there. But her commitment to international action was not a wholehearted one. Moreover there were likely to be difficulties with China and between the allies if Peking was relieved.[13] The effect of Waldersee's appointment would therefore be to immerse Germany in many of the unwelcome problems of north China for some time to come. Nor was the appointment of Waldersee likely to be so catastrophic. He was appointed for operations in Chihli only; and this would not affect the autonomy of the generals of other forces acting elsewhere. Moreover he would not reach the scene for some two months, by which time the situation was likely to be radically changed.

The fact that the appointment of a German commander-in-chief had been made over the head of a Japanese general did not enter into Russian thinking. None the less it was a slight to Japan that the elderly Waldersee should be appointed rather than the Japanese divisional commander-in-the-field, Lieutenant-General Yamaguchi. But the Japanese swallowed the affront without protest.

RUSSO-JAPANESE EVACUATION OF PEKING

History is full of surprises. When the siege of the legations had been broken, there were in the Peking-Tientsin area substantial foreign contingents, all with a sense of triumph and each with its own national ambitions in mind. Moreover the German force, though still on the high seas, had been seen off by the kaiser with a speech which was bloodthirsty and revengeful. There was the prospect, therefore, of the province of Chihli being overrun by foreign troops in order to stamp out the Boxers. They had, of course, not been defeated or disarmed but only demoralized; those in the immediate vicinity of Peking had been most seriously affected.

To the surprise of all, the Russians on 25 August announced that they would withdraw their legation and troops from Peking to Tientsin. We now know that the tsar had been furious that Russian troops under General Linievich had taken such a prominent part in the attack on Peking and had been (as the Russians imagined, though each general claimed it for his own) the first troops to enter the Chinese capital. The tsar's reaction was part of the softly softly approach and was intended to hasten the return to the capital of the Chinese court which had gone into hiding at Sian, and also to prepare the way for the return to Peking of Li Hung-chang, Russia's ally in China. Russia pinned her hopes on Li's readiness to believe that she was more reliable than the other powers.

The orders for withdrawal were sent to Minister Giers and General Linievich on 25 August. The army there was seriously dissatisfied with the prospect of withdrawing from Chihli and the railway zone, suspecting that it had been designed as part of a weak-kneed policy towards Britain. Indeed, Linievich had earlier announced that Russian troops were to winter in Peking and the province of Chihli in the present strength of 15,000 men. France was also doubtful of the wisdom of the new Russian policy, stating that her objections were mainly over 'timing and conditions'.[14] But Russia went ahead with the recall, even if it was not followed by any of the other powers.

Gradually the reservations, internal and international, were overcome and the evacuation took place. Perhaps because of talks between Delcassé and Witte in Paris around 5 September, the French came over to the Russian position. They agreed to act together over Tientsin. Russian troops began to evacuate Peking on 13 September. By the 29th they had been pulled out, leaving only an enhanced guard at the legation. They then undertook an overland march by 5,000 men towards Shanhaikuan of which we shall have more to say in the next chapter. Minister Giers was reluctant to evacuate Peking and adjourned his departure several times before he withdrew on the 29th. Though the senior diplomat, he was absent from the decisions of the diplomatic body as it faced the whole range of post-Boxer problems, punishment of pro-Boxer officials, demand for an indemnity, reparations for atrocities, etc. But his absence proved to be a temporary one and by the end of October he was back in Peking for diplomatic conferences.

The search for Russian motives is a difficult one. They seem to have been a mixture of idealism and self-interest. The decision to recall forces was technically the responsibility of the war minister. Kuropatkin put it on record that 'the aim is to stop all military measures in China as soon as possible, as once Russian troops are loosed on the warpath, they cannot be easily kept in hand, and seem to care little for the political complications which their action may cause.'[15] But the military on the spot was not inclined to pull out too soon. Indeed Kuropatkin, during the emergency, had earlier been an advocate of vigorous action around Peking. In order to prevent any evasion of the responsibility for withdrawal, Lamsdorf asked the emperor to specify in an irreversible form that the military would evacuate all Chinese territory. This suggests a basic suspicion between the civilians and the military as well as between the command at St Petersburg and at the front. When the emperor stood firm for withdrawal, it was not challenged by Kuropatkin.[16]

The thinking of Lamsdorf and the emperor was that the recapture of Peking so soon had been unfortunate in its effects. The joint expedition had been too successful in relieving the legations so quickly; but the allies had had to pay the price when the imperial family was evacuated to Sian, leaving no legally constituted government to deal with the incoming armies. The sheer success of the military action, brought about by a sense of rivalry between the military commanders of the various powers, had caused the Chinese court to panic and might cause the emperor to abdicate.

Russia's objective was to keep Peking as the centre of Chinese administration and to ensure the safe return of the emperor and empress dowager to their capital as soon as possible. It was Lamsdorf's fear that, if they did not return and did not negotiate, the powers as a body would be forced to assume some responsibility for 'occupying' the territory, that is, at the very least, for governing and policing this country of over 400 million. This was a recipe for disaster and was quite alien to the thinking of the tsarist government.

Of course, Russia's views were not disinterested. She did not want the decentralization of power in China proper and in particular the passing of authority from Peking to the viceroys. If central authority were to pass to the Yangtse viceroys, then Russia would be the prime sufferer. Moreover there was the dilemma of Li Hung-chang, still returning to the north from Canton. It was in Russia's interest to re-establish him in power and to return to the status quo ante. This would be easiest if Russia were to be inconspicuous in the imperial capital and were widely seen to be so.

Just as Russia was withdrawing in order to further her interests in Manchuria, Japan was considering which interests she should be pursuing at this juncture. Within a week of the entry into Peking, the cabinet instructed General Kodama, the governor-general of Taiwan, to land a force at Amoy where there was an international settlement. At least one of the objects of the expedition was to give the Chinese inhabitants a stern warning against 'riotous movements threatening the safety of the foreign residents and [especially] the burning of a Japanese temple'.[17] Japan's action was immediately followed by jealous foreign powers. Before the expedition had achieved anything, it was called off from Tokyo. No one knows why but it would appear from the coincidence of dates that the cabinet thought that Russia's withdrawal from Peking presaged a crisis in the north and it would be dangerous for Japan's forces to be embroiled in a southern adventure.

After that brief episode where the international gamekeepers curbed the activities of the Japanese poacher, the Japanese, who had the largest forces in China proper, proceeded to withdraw them as speedily as possible. Such a sizeable expedition had been a substantial drain on the Japanese exchequer. The ninth brigade was withdrawn in October and other units progressively in the following months.

While the China crisis was coming to a head, Japan was considering her long-term role in east Asia. She seemed to have a choice between expansion in the south where she would not seriously ruffle the other powers – the line of lesser resistance – and in the north where she was bound to run into trouble from Russia. Was it a good moment to move into Korea when the Russians were accumulating great strength in Manchuria? There had been desultory negotiations over Korea. Firstly Izvolskii had presented a neutrality plan for solving the Korean issue but Japan responded that to discuss Korea during the Boxer troubles was liable to drag in third parties and this would not suit those directly involved. She preferred to stick to the Nishi–Rosen protocol.[18] Meanwhile in St Petersburg the Japanese minister, Komura, had been discussing the orient unofficially, putting forward the hypothesis that Korea might be allotted to Japan, while Manchuria was allotted to Russia; and neither side would challenge the other's rights. This Man-Kan kōkan proposal did not interest the Russian side which was not inclined to abandon its stake in Korea, even if it was now greatly inferior to what she was acquiring in Manchuria. The Japanese therefore considered invading Korea, as many pressure groups were demanding, but decided as a preliminary to consult the Germans. They delayed their reply until a cabinet crisis in Japan made such an expedition impossible.[19]

The Russian withdrawal from Peking led to a far-reaching re-examination of policy in Japan. Among the various ministers who contributed memoranda on what the country should do in the autumn, Prime Minister Yamagata prepared one which argued that Japan should *not* use the present crisis in north-east Asia to consolidate her position in Korea before it was too late. He took the view that the Japanese were not yet prepared to challenge the might of Russia and would be sensible not to bring up the question of opportunities in Korea for the time being. His line of argument was as follows:

> Even if Britain privately agreed to it and the United States raised no objections, Russia, Germany and France would join together and oppose [Japan's taking Korea]. In the event of war, would Britain still help us with her military-naval forces? If we cannot rely with confidence on Britain allying with us, we will be forced to fight alone against a threefold enemy?[20]

Yamagata's memorandum seems to indicate that he was ready to take some advantage of the conditions of chaos in China – and the expectation that the European powers would capitalize on the presence of their forces there – by acquiring either territory or a sphere of influence. The greatest constraint on such actions was that the Dreibund of 1895 would re-emerge. It would take a fresh form but, with the armies of Germany and Russia so strong in north and north-east China, it would be clearly advisable for Japan to avoid any advance in that area which would lead in all likelihood to a confrontation. The prime minister was inclined therefore to give his preference to an advance in the provinces of Chekiang and Fukien, opposite the Japanese colony of Taiwan. Japan's fear of an adverse French reaction to a forward move in the neighbourhood of Taiwan was obviously less than the real fear of a hostile Russian reaction if Japan advanced in Korea. In either event, there is the feeling that Japan would not take steps on her own. She looked to Britain for defence against the Dreibund but did not have confidence that much help would be forthcoming. While Japan was as calculating as the other powers in the crisis of 1900, she was less determined and more cautious.

THE GREAT DIVIDE OVER CHINA

The Chinese court had meanwhile moved to the safe distance of Sian, fearing retribution and punishment for some of the princes who had inclined to cooperation with the Boxers. They left their corner to be argued by Li Hung-chang, the former viceroy of Kwantung. On 14 September Li set off by English ship from Shanghai. From Taku he came under the protection of the Russian forces. He reached Tientsin on 20 September and finally returned to Peking on 11 October. One observer describes him as a prisoner of the Russian troops,[21] though Li as always had his own corner to defend. Certainly the Russians were not inclined to sacrifice the investment they had made in Li over the decade of the 1890s. The British minister, Sir Ernest Satow, who had recently reached Peking, commented that his diplomatic colleagues resented de Giers's 'somewhat dictatorial manners in our conferences and his apparent desire to pose as the friend of China. They suspect him of communicating to Li the details of our conferences.'[22] But how much of Russia's 'special relationship' still held good in the autumn?

In a way the Russians had had some success. They had manoeuvred back to Peking their ally among the Chinese leaders. They had tried to give the Chinese the impression of conciliating the court and the empress dowager. The Chinese had responded to this by the telegram of thanks which the emperor had sent to Tsar Nicholas for having removed his troops.[23] They had ensured their influence in Peking. There were, however, contradictions in Russian policy. The doubt persisted that Russia proposed to annex Chinese territory in Manchuria, despite the tsar's explicit declaration against any annexation of territory. But for the present their action in Manchuria was presented as a temporary occupation, while they were posing as the protector of the dynasty (so they claimed) against internal rebellion.

With that scant regard for international crisis which afflicted Russian leaders, the tsar set off for his shooting lodge in Poland in August. He proceeded thence to Livadia in the Crimea to avoid the unpleasant autumn temperatures of the Russian capital and the empress fell ill with abdominal typhus.[24] Early in October Lamsdorf set off to join his sovereign at Yalta. He worked there throughout the autumn, only returning to St Petersburg on 12 January. The foreign affairs of the country were conducted in the very special secrecy of the Crimea and were the despair, needless to say, of the idle diplomats at St Petersburg.

Meanwhile the Japanese minister, Komura, had been chosen to represent his country in Peking. This was a signal honour for him as the problems which China faced were serious ones and demanded the services of a competent official able to take part in international negotiation. The mandate reached him on 23 October. In order to conform to the conventions of the Russian court, he had to proceed to the Crimea to announce at an audience with the emperor the end of his mission. There he met Lamsdorf, Witte and Kuropatkin and also the Chinese minister to Russia, Yang Yu, who, despite the opposition of the Russian officials, had accompanied the court to the south. He had been told not to neglect any opportunity to influence the Russian court and stuck doggedly to his task.[25]

Komura set off for Peking on 8 November via London and the United States: he showed no interest in returning by the Trans-Siberian railway. While he was staying in New York he prepared a memorandum on the situation, especially his reflections on the problems of China, Britain and Russia in the east. This is an extract from the document:

> With the recent sudden ending of the China affair, I am returning home and shall go immediately to Peking. It is in fact no time since I went to Russia and there were many things that I wanted to study. But there is an anxiety that, if we lose the present opportunity, the agony which we have suffered up to now over the problem of China will burst like a bubble (i.e. will be in vain). Japan's fundamental object is China. For the problem of China the forthcoming Peking conference will be vital. Since my experience hitherto has primarily been with China, it will undoubtedly be a marvellous opportunity to tackle it again ...
>
> Before leaving Russia recently, I went to the Crimea to have an audience with the tsar, and saw quite a bit of southern Russia at the same time. I observed the condition of the Russian peasants in the countryside. It is rather similar to that in Korea or China. I examined the situation of troops which Russia sends to the east from Odessa where transportation is very difficult. It would be difficult enough if they were only sending some thousands of soldiers; but there would undoubtedly be special difficulties in despatching tens of thousands of troops to the east. To this would have to be added the problems over horses and provisions. But now that Russia is pursuing the building of the Siberian railway, it looks as though she is determined to establish her base in the east.[26]

Komura returned to Tokyo on 19 December and set off for China forthwith. He is to play an important part in our story; and his sojourn in Russia gave him a rare experience and insight.

REFERENCES AND NOTES

1. Hardinge to T. H. Sanderson, 4 Oct. 1900, Hardinge Papers 3.
2. I. I. Rostunov, *Istoriya Russko-Iaponskoi Voiny,* p. 40; B. A. Romanov, *Russia in Manchuria,* pp. 178–9.
3. Japan, Foreign Ministry, *Komura Gaikō shi,* vol. 1, pp. 150–1.
4. Romanov, op. cit., p. 179, records that the tsar believed that the Boxers were fighting against '*west European* missionaries', i.e. not against the Russian Orthodox Church.
5. Tokutomi Iichirō, *Kō shaku Yamagata Aritomo den,* vol. 2, Tokyo 1933, pp. 410–11.
6. Scott to Sanderson, 30 June 1900, in Scott papers, 52,303.
7. Scott to Salisbury, 28 June 1900, in Scott papers, 52,303.
8. I. H. Nish, *The Anglo-Japanese Alliance,* pp. 83–6.
9. Ibid., pp. 86–7.
10. Ibid., pp. 86–8.
11. William II to Nicholas II and reply, 6 August 1900, in *Willy–Nicky Correspondence,* no. 23.
12. Nish, op. cit., pp. 88–9.
13. Before his death, Muraviev had written that Russia should not become leader of an international force. *Krasnyi Arkhiv,* **18** (1926), pp. 14–15.
14. *DDF,* 1st series, vol. 16 (1900), no. 285.
15. Romanov, op. cit., pp. 185–6.
16. A. Malozemoff, *Russian Far Eastern Policy,* p. 135.
17. I. H. Nish, 'Japan's indecision during the Boxer disturbances', *Journal of Asian Studies,* **20** (1961), pp. 451–5.
18. Izvolskii to Lamsdorf, 23 Mar. 1901, in *Krasnyi Arkhiv,* **63** (1934).
19. *NGB* 33, no. 522.
20. I. H. Nish, 'Boxer disturbances', *Journal of Asian Studies,* **20** (1961), pp. 451–5.
21. *Komura Gaikō shi,* vol. 1, p. 168.
22. Satow to Salisbury, 1 Nov. 1900, Satow Papers 11.
23. Hardinge to Sanderson, 4 Oct. 1900, Hardinge Papers 3. Hardinge thought Russia's object was 'to make the Chinese believe that Russia was the Power which prevented the partition of China.'
24. Hardinge to Sanderson, 15 Nov. 1900, Hardinge Papers 3.
25. *Komura Gaikō shi,* vol. 1, p. 151; Hardinge to Sanderson, 7 Nov. 1900, Hardinge Papers 3.
26. *Komura Gaikō shi,* vol. 1, pp. 151–3.

Chapter 5

MANCHURIA UNDER BOXERS AND RUSSIANS (1900–1901)

When the Russian troops were pulled out of China proper, they were soon actively engaged against the Boxers in Manchuria. While the defection of the Russian force from the allied expedition was an international disappointment, especially to the German force which had just reached China, it made good sense from Russia's national viewpoint. The number of Russian residents in China proper was small, probably less than 500, while her trade and interests were correspondingly much smaller than those of many other countries. In Manchuria her investment in the Chinese Eastern railway and its ancillary enterprises was vast; her people were the most numerous foreign community; and it was vital to protect her trade prospects.

Boxer activities in their various manifestations spread to Manchuria later than to the rest of China. Partly this was due to the 60,000 or so workers on the railway, many of whom were strong-bodied immigrants from Shantung. This province had seen anti-Christian movements and Boxer activities in 1899 but had been held effectively in check during the major outbreaks of 1900. It was natural therefore that Boxer ideas should burst out in Manchuria even if the majority of railway workers themselves did not come out in their support.

The position in the three eastern provinces – Fengtien, Kirin and Heilungkiang – differed. Towards the end of June meetings became more frequent and the anti-foreign campaign was launched. The Fengtien military governor, General Tseng-ch'i, ignored the empress dowager's instructions to take up arms against the foreign community and concentrated on keeping the peace. His subordinates, however, took the opposite view and forced him to promulgate the order. Early in July a Catholic church in Mukden was set alight with the murder of five French missionaries. In the Liaotung peninsula where railway building had progressed farthest, large sections were destroyed or damaged, the track being thrown into rivers or disposed of in other ways. Mukden and Liaoyang junction stations were occupied and damaged.

The military governor of Kirin was less affected. He managed to control the Boxers and avoided major trouble with the Russians. The governor of Heilungkiang, General Shou-shan, was less fortunate. This arose from the massacre of Blagovestchensk, a town on the Amur river. The Russians, despite earlier assurances, asked the Chinese population to leave by crossing the Amur river. In the charged atmosphere, they were shot at both by the Chinese from the south bank and the Russians from the north. After this massacre on 14 July the Russians occupied towns on the Chinese side of the river, from which it was expected that new offensives would be launched by China. In doing this, they sustained very substantial losses. The governor resisted and it was only after a month of fighting that the provincial capital of Tsitsihar fell to the Russians. Unlike the other governors, Shou-shan had to commit suicide on 29 August.[1]

The Russians, civil and military alike, were caught unprepared by these anti-foreign outbreaks. The fact was that there was inadequate financial provision for security for the Chinese Eastern railway in its building phase. There were estimated to be 3,000 troops – what were called 'Matilda's guards' after the name of Witte's wife. When disturbances took place in the summer, they were found to be in the wrong places and lacking in discipline. In order to relieve this inadequate force, it was necessary to get reinforcements urgently. Witte, shattered by accounts of the sheer vandalism to his beloved line, sanctioned the cost of a large force. 'It is better to lose money rather than prestige,' he wrote on 7 July.[2] As a first step he opened a credit for each of the three military governors if they could stifle the Boxer activities in their provinces. This had only a limited effect. Thereafter he had to make over the operation to the minister for war, a reversal of his earlier policy. This ended for good the monopolistic control of the finance ministry which he had exercised over this Manchurian railway operation. Since Kuropatkin could not divert troops from Liaotung or from the Peking campaign, he had to undertake a mobilization in the Priamur and Siberian military districts.[3]

Kuropatkin authorized his troops to invade Manchuria on 9 July. Those in the north were to come under General Grodekov while those in the south would be under Admiral Alekseyev's command. In the north they managed to save Harbin from the siege on 2 August and to complete the recapture of the Eastern railway mainline by the beginning of September – a colossal task covering vast distances and inhospitable countryside. The next points which it was indispensable to seize were the seats of the two military governors, Tsitsihar and Kirin. When these were taken, only the southern spur of the Eastern railway from Harbin to Port Arthur remained to be repossessed.

Because there was a civil war of sorts going on in Fengtien, the military situation there was rather intractable. General Tseng brought off an anti-Boxer coup in August; but late in September he was faced with the return of pro-Boxer groups led by his subordinates. He found it expedient to evacuate Mukden. On 1 October the Russian force under General Subbotich entered the city and the Chinese soldiery fled. With this act, the Russians became masters of the situation. But the fact remained that, militarily, the Boxers and their supporters had not been defeated but had merely gone to ground – a position similar to that obtaining in Chihli province in China. While the troops at the disposal of the Russian commanders were considerable, they still fell far short of the numbers needed to patrol and secure the vast railway network. With this uncertainty, the Russians embarked on their 'occupation' of Manchuria. They would occupy the principal points of strategic value and undertake measures necessary for pacification. But they would seek to work with Chinese officials and Generals Tseng and Chang-shun (of Kirin) continued to hold their posts.[4]

Even allowing for the fact that Russia was taken by surprise, she had not been shown to advantage in the months of the Boxer crisis. All sorts of shortcomings had been revealed: squandering of military expenditure; the lack of readiness to transport great numbers; defectiveness of provisions; and shortcomings in arms, guncarriages and rolling stock. All these hampered the numbers of Russian troops available in the east.[5] In St Petersburg the government departments were thought to be in a state of panic. Most prominently the finance ministry with its immense investment in the railways and its urgent need to recoup the expenditure was anxious but impotent. Clearly the whole project had been set back by about two years and there would have to be considerable retrenchment in all parts of the administration before it could return to normal.

Naturally such a crisis generated recrimination about the past and disagreements about the future. The war ministry accused Witte on several counts: he had been too penny-pinching with the result that there was too little rolling-stock to carry reinforcements and provisions so that they had to be sent by sea; he had relied too much on the so-called 'Matilda's guards' for the protection of the railway line and had neglected the broader security aspects of Manchuria as a whole.[6] It was a standard complaint of Kuropatkin that Russia's strategic interests differed from her railway interests. Clearly this brought into the open a fundamental division between the army and the civilian government. Kuropatkin was anxious to exploit the crisis to alter the balance in his favour. He asked Witte for an extraordinary credit for 12 months to cover the expenditure needed for mobilization; but the finance minister only agreed with ill grace to a six-month credit. The truth was that there were divided counsels among the tsar's intimate advisers; and that the peacetime domination of the railway project by Witte had given rise to serious weaknesses which his many enemies were not slow to disclose.[7]

THE TREATY PORT OF NIUCHUANG

In the Russian view the events in Manchuria proper had been an aberration – a misunderstanding between Chinese and Russians in which the outside powers had no standing. As a corollary, the Russians did not believe that the outside powers had any role in the resolution of the problem. As an extension, they did not want the outside powers, whose representatives were preparing in the autumn to collaborate in what became known as the Peking Conference to deal comprehensively with the settlement of Chinese affairs, to intervene in any way with the settlement in Manchuria.[8]

This argument, which was certainly not accepted by Japan, Britain or the United States, broke down over the settlement of Niuchuang. Niuchuang with its own port of Yingkow, a town of some 80,000 inhabitants fifteen miles up the Liao River, had been recognized as a treaty port for four decades. It had a foreign settlement with an array of foreign consuls and a scattering of foreign businessmen. While the Russians claimed at times that the port was a bilateral issue between the Chinese and themselves, it was in law an international issue where the outside powers had treaty rights.[9] Niuchuang was the meeting-point between two rail systems – the Chinese Northern Extension through Chinchow approaching from the west and the south Manchurian line of the Chinese Eastern railway which had built a spur from the east. As such it was a natural point of tension.

Niuchuang was sufficiently close to the events of northern China to reflect occurrences there. Boxer outbursts were on the cards from the middle of June onwards. The Russian gunboats, *Gremiastchii* and *Otvajnii,* were, therefore, anchored off the Bund for the summer months. The Japanese, for whom this was an important trading port, responded by sending two of their gunboats also, one being the *Tatsuta.* They were clearly not prepared to regard this port as one to be policed by Russia alone. The Japanese consul, Tanabe, who was head of the consular body, was told to be vigilant about Russia's actions there and reported in detail to his government.[10]

From the end of June Niuchuang had become a haven for refugees, missionaries and railwaymen from the Three Eastern provinces. The railway line to the west towards Chinchow and east to the Chinese Eastern railway had been attacked and damaged in many places. Russian troops took over the Chinese barracks on 26 July. Early in August about 3,000 further troops arrived in transports. Taking advantage of an attack on the Foreign Settlement, they advanced on the Chinese town and, because of the 'prehistoric' arms being used by the Boxers, had no difficulty in capturing it. Hitherto the Chinese Taotai in Niuchuang had been doing his best to keep the Boxers quiet, despite orders from the Tartar Taotai at Mukden to the contrary. Now he had to flee and the Russian flag was hoisted over the main building in the town, the Imperial Maritime Customs headquarters. It looked as though the Russians were, in retaliation for the destruction of their railway and the murder of their citizens, starting a policy of seizing the whole of Manchuria and adding it to the Russian Empire.[11] Admiral E. I. Alekseyev, commander-in-chief of naval and military forces, arrived from Port Arthur to take the surrender of the Boxers.

But Niuchuang, unlike the rest of Manchuria, was not an exclusively Sino-Russian matter. The 'treaty powers' had rights which they, disappointed with Russia's performance at Peking, were determined to insist on. Alekseyev insisted that the customs should come under Russian control pending rendition of the port to China. He insisted that the temporary administration would act in the interest of Russians as well as foreigners and Chinese and would not infringe treaty rights. He appointed Ostroverkhov as administrator and Protassiev as co-commissioner of customs (this being a compromise solution). In September the civil administration asked the consular body to nominate someone for the municipal council; but, after consulting their governments, the consuls declined to put forward any name. On 6 October the Russian flag was hoisted over the buildings of the Shanhaikuan railway but it was on the orders of the Russian military authorities allegedly to prevent the destruction of the terminal by the rebels. The new situation at Niuchuang was disheartening both to Chinese and foreigners who were however impotent.[12]

CHINESE NORTHERN RAILWAYS

The third part of Russia's Manchurian problem related to China's Northern railway to the west of the Liao river. It was partly a railway problem over which Britain and Russia had been negotiating since 1898 and partly a political problem because Russia thought that, if she were to maintain a semblance of military influence with the Chinese authorities, she must be strong along the Tientsin–Shanhaikuan route and beyond. But how fare this was a well-constructed strategy and how far a response to a developing military situation is hard to say. Russia had just evacuated her armies from Peking and they were engaged in a long march towards the Great Wall in a mood not particularly friendly to the central government in St Petersburg. They had to hold the passage where the Wall comes down to the sea to prevent further penetration by the Boxers to the north, while attempting to restore the railway to working order.

At the start of the Boxer emergency, the construction of China's Northern Extension railway had reached Niuchuang (Yinkow), while the main line to Hsinmintung was under construction. The line was Chinese, though the actual line to Shanhaikuan was mortgaged to British bondholders and the rolling-stock and earnings of the line to Niuchuang acted as their security. But the Russian engineers found these lines to be in need of repair and protection against further Boxer assaults. At the height of the campaign, Russia took under her wing the section from Taku to Tientsin and Peking, relieving the British engineer, Kinder, and his staff. Britain, the United States and Japan protested but had to be content with Russia's assurances – which they did not believe – that she would return the section to China after the disturbances ended. There followed a battle for Shanhaikuan. Early in September Britain contemplated recovering the town herself but decided not to risk a clash with Russia. As a result, the line from Taku to Shanhaikuan was occupied by Russian troops 'by right of conquest' and they denied Britain's rights over the railway under the Anglo-Russian railway agreement. The high-handedness of the Russian military authorities whose attitude over the return of the lines was markedly different from that of St Petersburg suggested that they thought they were there to stay.

This would have been a difficult enough legal issue in peacetime; but during the mopping up campaign when tempers were frayed it was doubly complicated. A special role had to be played by Field Marshal Waldersee, who arrived as commander-in-chief on 17 October and had to decide the issue on overall strategic considerations. His writ, however, only ran to the Great Wall. He entered into a railway agreement with the Russians whereby Russian military control of the Peking–Shanhaikuan line should be ended when they had completed the bulk of the repair work. On 25 January 1901 Russia eventually handed over to Waldersee the section from Yangtsun to Shanhaikuan but retained the section from there to Niuchuang until she had been recompensed for her expenses for repair of the whole length. It was left to China and Britain to recover the first of these sections from Waldersee; but the latter could not guarantee the section beyond the Great Wall because it went beyond the sphere of control of the allied forces which he commanded.[13]

Although Japan was not directly affected by this railway diplomacy, she looked on with great vigilance. Waldersee confirmed his order about the Peking–Shanhaikuan line, just two days after the signature of the Anglo-German agreement of 16 October. From the British point of view, this treaty was an attempt to win German support against Russia in an issue of this kind, the Peking–Shanhaikuan line. But the Germans saw it as primarily an agreement about the Yangtse area and would not accept anti-Russian commitments north of the Great Wall. The Japanese adhered to this agreement with alacrity because they saw it as a break in the Dreibund of 1895 whose resurgence they were always expecting. In the event, the agreement collapsed, Bülow announcing this in March 1901. It suggested to Japan that there was still an element of collusion between Germany and Russia over the latter's expansionist activities at this time.

AFTERMATH IN MANCHURIA

The fall of Mukden did not ease the problem of the occupation or the pacification of Manchuria. The Taotai left Mukden and was not available. The Boxers disappeared into thin air; identification and punishment were difficult, if not impossible. According to one estimate, the force which Kuropatkin had built up in Manchuria ran to 4,000 officers and 173,000 troops. Clearly such a force could not be afforded or indeed supplied for long, because the crops had gone unharvested in the wartime conditions. So a scheme for demobilization was drawn up and put into effect to a limited extent.[14]

That it did not proceed at a faster pace was due to several factors. Firstly, the Boxers may have disappeared; but the bandits (*hunghutze* or redbeards) took their place, making up for famine conditions by pillaging. The Russian troops were needed over a wide area to protect foreign nationals. Secondly, by the time this problem had subsided, the means of transport for an extensive evacuation were not available. The railway tracks were not yet mended; and steamers could not ply on the Sungari and Amur rivers because they were frozen. The result was that by the end of the year 28 of the 42 infantry battalions were left and stayed on till the spring.[15] This was a sizeable force, if it were merely to be applied to police duties. The Russians were glad to keep out of the administration of the occupied territories and concentrated on garrison duties in the major towns. They tried to exercise control over the Taotai by appointing advisers, but this was not an easy task for a serving officer to perform.

As the Blagovestchensk incident has reminded us, one consideration which had to be taken into account in framing Russian policy was that it was difficult to exercise control over the Russian army from St Petersburg. An attempt was made in a letter from the leading British businessman in Niuchuang, H. J. Bush, to *The Times* of London, to explain the local situation: the Siberian army was composed of the dregs of her population and discipline was an unknown quantity; the trouble was that, when roused, the Cossacks, though fine troops in some ways, could be barbarous and unscrupulous; and their officers were almost as bad.[16] It was difficult to get through to these uneducated troops the notion that the purpose of the Russians was to withdraw from Manchuria. It was equally difficult to persuade the Chinese who came into contact with such an army that the Russian purpose was conciliatory. The Russian military authorities on the spot had gone far (over the Blagovestchensk massacre, for example) to convince the Chinese that they were in Manchuria to stay and would be ferocious if resisted.

This factor was readily admitted in St Petersburg, openly in the foreign ministry and tacitly in the war ministry. It was the consequence of the commanders being given *carte blanche* and more generally of officers on the frontier becoming accustomed during the period of tsarist expansion in Asia to exercise too much latitude and being praised for local initiatives. There was a genuine fear in the capital of the army abroad.

General N. I. Grodekov, commander in the northern region of Manchuria, asked Kuropatkin on 24 August for advice on long-term objectives. He received guidance from the tsar that he was not to annex any portion of Chinese territory, in order to reconstitute the relations of friendship and neighbourliness which had persisted with China.[17]

As if in confirmation of this, Kuropatkin told the French with whom the Russians shared many of their worries that, once pacification had been accomplished overall, Russia could revert quietly to the original plan, which was to hold the Chinese Eastern railway line by some military posts, assisted by '*gardes-voie*' (railway guards). This guard system was the system which was organized militarily along all the Trans-Siberian railway at that time and consisted of a special corps of workers made up of army reservists.[18] What was serving Russia's purposes on the main route ought to be well suited to the Eastern railway, even though it passed through foreign territory.

Russia's defence of the railway guards always mentioned the need for 'withdrawal of troops'. But suspicious foreign observers felt that they saw through this railway guard system. Thus, Charles Hardinge, the British chargé d'affaires in St Petersburg, commented:

> Now it is proposed to very largely increase this force and in order to keep up the fiction of withdrawal of Russian troops from Manchuria they are still to be called railway guards and to be nominally under Witte, but the officers are to be officers of the regular army, and in this way the forces though nominally under the control of the Minister of Finance will be practically under the control of the Minister of War who will be able to place them in strategic positions.[19]

How far these suspicions were justified is hard to say. It was a natural thing for the Russians to make use of their demobilized and jobless soldiery for this purpose. On the other hand, merely to transform the soldiers into railway guards came close to being a sleight of hand. To that extent, Hardinge has grounds for writing of the 'fiction of withdrawal'.

This is only one aspect of a broader problem – the problem of double talk among the Russian leaders. While they spoke innocently and plausibly about withdrawal and pulling out, this only took place partially and gradually. What was the cause of the delay? Witte in his *Vospominaniya* makes clear the role of the army in this. So too did Lamsdorf in this conversation with Sir Charles Scott, the British ambassador:

> Lamsdorf told me that one of his most serious embarrassments in conducting foreign relations was the entire inability of the military party, particularly in distant parts of the Empire, to understand the necessity of taking the rights or interests of other powers into consideration if they saw their opportunity for laying their hands on anything they wanted, or thought would strengthen the military position. He said I must have observed this in course of our recent difficulties in China ... Kuropatkin was equally unable to understand this necessity, or indifferent to the consequences of ignoring it.
>
> Lamsdorf said that, although it was true that he had had an occasional standup fight with the Minister of War he found in him a loyal and good colleague, always amenable to reason and ready to respect diplomatic considerations when clearly explained to him, but he must warn me that this was not the general case in all military quarters, and that he believed a great deal of his difficulties originated in the fact that military Authorities in distant parts of the Empire often acted under the mistaken impression that they would earn credit with the Minister of War by some spirited action initiated on their own responsibility.[20]

TSENG–ALEKSEYEV DRAFT AGREEMENT

It will be recalled that at the end of October, the retiring Japanese minister, Komura, had been in the Crimea to present his greetings to the tsar on giving up his post, and had there found the Chinese minister, Yang Ju, who was in his opinion making a nuisance of himself with Lamsdorf and the other officials. After much persuasion, Yang obtained from them the undertaking that Russia was ready to return to China the Three Eastern provinces provided Russian troops continued to protect the railway. When Li Hung-chang heard this, he took the approval of the court and authorized the generals of Kirin and Fengtien (Mukden) to commence negotiations with the Russians for the return of their respective provinces. The Fengtien general, Tseng-ch'i, had already sent one of his underlings who claimed to have skill in negotiating with Russia to consult I. Ia. Korostovets who represented the Russians in Port Arthur. Things moved slowly and it was not till 19 November that the 'plenipotentiary' returned thence to Hsinmin, bearing the agreement which he had concluded with Korostovets on 10 November. Tseng thought it unwise to report his action officially. He was not anxious to invite an official rebuke for nominating (without authority) a 'plenipotentiary' and choosing one who was in any case discredited and retired. On the other hand, Tseng was desperate to return to his seat of authority in Mukden.

The draft contained clauses which were unacceptable to Tseng. But Alekseyev insisted that it had to be accepted before the general could be permitted by Russian troops to return to Mukden. On the assurance that the terms were provisional and subject to ratification, Tseng signed the agreement with strict reservations, pointing out that he did not have plenipotentiary powers. When the signature had been given on 30 November, Tseng was able to go back and thus obtained greater freedom of movement; but it was not on the scale that he had been led to expect.

The text of the draft agreement gradually leaked out to the court at Peking, which was furious and ordered that Tseng-ch'i should be punished. But, when Giers insisted in Peking that the dismissal of Tseng would prejudice future negotiations with Russia regarding Manchuria, he was reluctantly reinstated as Taotai in March 1901 and served at Mukden till 1905. Alekseyev fared little better. Though he had commanded the Russian far east squadron during the Sino-Japanese war and again during the Boxer expeditionary force, he seems to have lacked political muscle to carry the day with the tsar and his immediate advisers. He had not taken the trouble to refer 'the treaty' to Minister Giers in Peking. The result was that he was not supported by his home government. Thus, while the provisional agreement was a shrewd move from the standpoint of both Alekseyev and Tseng, enabling both to return to normal relations in some respects, their governments, realizing that it was a political hot potato, declined to ratify it. In consequence the 'treaty' lapsed in January 1901.[21]

The Tseng–Alekseyev agreement was the subject of a journalist scoop by Dr George Ernest Morrison, Peking correspondent of *The Times* of London. Morrison's scoop lay not in procuring a copy which was in any case available to all the legations in Peking around the end of December. His genius lay in taking the risk of telegraphing the text to London and ensuring that it was carried in the paper. The diplomats had taken the more cautious and financially prudent course of sending the text by sea. The result was that the text appeared in the paper on 3 January and became known to the British, Japanese and possibly other governments from journalistic sources rather than from the diplomats in the first place.[22]

Morrison's message stated that 'the Agreement will necessarily be followed by similar agreements with respect to the other two provinces [Kirin and Heilungkiang] and then Manchuria will be a *de facto* Russian protectorate'. Morrison had for some time been sending anti-Russian telegrams from Peking, showing that the Russians had no intention of giving up Manchurian territory. This assessment was based on personal observations he had made during journeys to the area; now the situation on the ground was going to be crystallized in a legal form. Despite some exaggeration, this caused a furore. Naturally the thought of a *de facto* protectorate resulting from the Boxer crisis over such a vast and potentially rich area was objectionable to most of the powers. While the other powers were engaged in the multi national Peking conference, which was giving rise to tensions enough of its own, the idea that the Russians were trying to enter into a separate peace with China behind the backs of their 'allies' was the last straw. It was widely condemned.[23]

In their first trial the Open Door powers – United States, Britain and Japan – had failed. Russia had moved into Manchuria and, despite honeyed words and unspecific assurances, she evidently intended to stay. Of course, time alone would tell. Other powers also had troops which they intended to keep in China while the emergency lasted. But the Open Door powers were annoyed and frustrated by their own impotence. They were unwilling – and probably unable – to dislodge the Russians by force from Manchuria and were having no success in extracting any definite guarantees of withdrawal from them by diplomatic means.

REFERENCES AND NOTES

1. The most detailed accounts are in G. A. Lensen, *The Russo-Chinese War*, and R. Quested, 'A fresh look at the Sino-Russian conflict of 1900 in Manchuria'.
2. Witte to D. S. Sipiagin, 7 July 1900, in *Krasnyi Avkhiv*, **18** (1926), p. 32. Hardinge to Francis Bertie, 20 Sept. 1900, Hardinge Papers 3: 'Before the recent disturbances there were 2–3,000 troops (some say 10,000) to guard the line. These were not under the Minister of War but the Minister of Finance and were frivolously nick-named "Matilda's Guards". Matilda being the *petit nom* of Mme de Witte, a lady of acknowledged notoriety in the past.'
3. A. Malozemoff, *Russian Far Eastern Policy*, pp. 136–7.
4. Lensen, op. cit., pp. 160–3.
5. Scott to T. H. Sanderson, 25 July 1900, Scott Papers 52,303.
6. Malozemoff, op. cit., p. 131.
7. Scott to Sanderson, 8 Aug. 1900, Scott Papers 52,303.
8. R. Quested, *'Matey' Imperialists?*, ch. 2.
9. Lensen, op. cit., p. 55.
10. A very detailed treatment is in *NGB* 33 supplements.
11. Bowra Papers 17, pp. 73f.
12. Bowra Papers 17, pp. 83f.
13. *BD*, vol. 2, pp. 1–2.
14. Quested, op. cit., pp. 53–4.
15. Malozemoff, op. cit., p. 144.
16. Lensen, op. cit., p. 253.
17. Ibid., p. 252.

18. *DDF,* 1st series, vol. 16 (1900), no. 294.
19. Hardinge to Bertie, 20 Sept. 1900, Hardinge Papers 3.
20. Scott to Lansdowne, 6 Feb. 1902, Scott Papers 52,304. Kuropatkin told Witte that this would give Russia an excuse for seizing Manchuria and turning it into a second Bokhara.
21. R. Quested, 'An introduction to the enigmatic career of Chou Mien'. It was described by Lamsdorf not as a treaty but as 'a modus vivendi' between the Russian military authorities and Chinese civil authorities to prevent further disturbances in Manchuria.
22. *The Times,* 3 Jan. 1901.
23. Morrison Papers 312/65, diary for 9 Aug. 1905, tells how Morrison met Korostovets at the Portsmouth Conference: 'He said my action in giving such wide publicity to what was an innocent procedure was deplorable for Russia. It was Li Hung Chang who was to blame. He advised the signature of a purely temporary military non-political agreement and then Admiral Alexieff made the mistake of not getting from Li Hung Chang his approval in writing of such a procedure. When Mr K. signed with Chou Mien, Li Hung Chang left him in the lurch.'

Chapter 6

JAPAN RESISTS OVER MANCHURIA (OCTOBER 1900 –JUNE 1901)

The Yamagata ministry which had presided with caution over the Boxer emergency was replaced on 19 October by Yamagata's rival, the experienced Marquis Itō. Some wanted Itō himself to assume the portfolio of foreign minister, while others wanted him to appoint Hara. The genro, Matsukata, suggested Katō Takaaki for this office, because of their Mitsubishi connection. Certainly Katō was not unqualified because of his service as minister to Britain from 1895 onwards. Moreover, he had made a success of his diplomacy in London, which was then the major diplomatic capital in the world in Japanese eyes. But, at forty years of age, he was young; he lacked diplomatic experience at the Tokyo end; and he had also been consistent in taking a moderately anti-Russian line. This need not have been important in itself; but his appointment was something of a paradox because Itō was renowned for his soft line towards Russia and for seeking detente with her. This led Katō into inevitable disagreements with the prime minister.

Itō became prime minister as president of the newly-founded Rikken Seiyūkai. Indeed it was probably to give the new party a baptism of fire that Yamagata, who was fundamentally opposed to political parties, suddenly resigned on 26 September and recommended that Itō should be invited to form a cabinet. It was therefore a time of great political excitement. From December through to March the Diet was in session; and the battles between the parties kept up the political temperature.

Another factor in the charged atmosphere of the day was the creation of new and often right-wing political groupings. In January 1901 the Kokuryūkai (or Amur river society) was set up and in February the Sanshi club. More significant for the time being was the formation of the Kokumin Dōmeikai on 24 September with Prince Konoe Atsumaro, scion of the Fujiwara clan, as president. Konoe was an unusual political phenomenon in Japan, a person of aristocratic origins, who was president of the House of Peers, head of Gakushūin College, and the head of the second family of the realm next to the emperor, but who espoused radical causes and opposed the clan-based establishment. He was a believer in cementing good relations with Asia and especially China. In June 1898 he had founded the Tō-A Dōbunkai, of which he became the active president. This was to become one of the main constituents of the Kokumin Dōmeikai (sometimes known as the 'Tai-Ro Kokumin Dōmeikai' – or Anti-Russian National League).[1] Other constituents included political parties, journalists, professors, political associates of Konoe and the Genyōsha, a radical association which developed an interest in continental expansion. In general it stood for the preservation of the integrity of China and the protection of Korea. More specifically it was set up to prevent the Russian occupation of Manchuria and to consider how Japan could become involved in railway building and the acquisition of rights in Korea and Manchuria. Clearly it was founded as a counterpoise to Russia's occupation of Manchuria. It launched itself by a National Convention in October and followed up with speaking tours around the country. In essence the Dōmeikai was a super-party, linking many of the opposition groups of diverse hues. Early in the new year, differences developed between the factions in the lobby and from April onwards its activities were greatly reduced. It lingered on till 27 April 1902 when it was disbanded after the Chinese and Russians signed a treaty for the evacuation of Russian troops from Manchuria.

Although it was short-lived, the Dōmeikai was unquestionably significant. With its wide range of constituents it created quite a stir and focused the attention of the people on the Manchurian and Korean issues. Both directly and indirectly it put pressure on the government. As we shall see, its effect was to give comfort to those in the cabinet who were more militant against Russia. Having said that, it would be hard to trace any direct link between Dōmeikai actions and government policies. Indirectly it criticized the Itō ministry at a time when it faced widespread opposition in the Lower House.

No one was more worried by these activities than Minister Izvolskii. He interpreted them as maligning his country but also as spoiling his own diplomatic initiatives. The Dōmeikai maligned his country by dwelling on Russia's acquisitive motives in Manchuria but also by saying that Russia could never be satisfied with an independent Korea over the border but would in due course want to acquire that also. In short, Russia's activities in Manchuria posed a danger to Korea. It spoilt his diplomatic initiatives in the sense that Izvolskii wanted to turn a blind eye to Manchuria and to focus his diplomacy on a scheme for neutralizing Korea.[2] The Dōmeikai condemned the government for lack of resolution at the end of the Boxer crisis and was by no means prepared to turn a blind eye to Manchuria or to accept a neutralization scheme for Korea, which in its view must inevitably lead to a deterioration in Japan's existing position there. Indeed the Dōmeikai in its propaganda was inclined to dwell on the old Dōbunkai idea of Japan's civilizing mission in China and Korea.

What worried Izvolskii and puzzled others was the anomalous position of Prince Konoe. He held of course the official position of president of the House of Peers and yet he behaved in a most independent, not to say idiosyncratic, way by coming out against a central part of the new prime minister's position. Moreover he won a good measure of support for his arguments. Konoe was within his rights in what he did; but it was out of line with what was expected of him. Certainly his presence within this super-lobby of discordant opposition groups gave it a respectability which it would not otherwise have had.[3]

Under Dōmeikai influence, the policies which were being canvassed were to take a less submissive line towards Russia and, as part of this, to use the occasion of Russia's concentration in Manchuria to seek an agreement with her which would give Japan a similar predominance in Korea.

During this rough political baptism, the Seiyūkai suffered and its new president most of all. Itō, the reluctant prime minister, who had been under great stress during the formation of his cabinet, retired to his country residence at Ōiso on 28 October, soon after accepting office, on the pretext of illness, leaving Saionji as interim prime minister and relying on his juniors to carry on as best they could. For recuperation Itō went to Atami and, after a month at that resort, came back to Ōiso. He returned briefly to duty on 10 December to face the new Diet. But recurring troubles forced him to retire again to his country residence. Indeed the whole life of his ministry was affected by his bouts of illness; and it was this that convinced the leaders of Japan that they must seek younger men as prime minister in future.[4]

Not that there were no factors that favoured Itō's more conciliatory line. Firstly, his ministry had to face serious crises of domestic politics, especially with the local government of Tokyo city. Secondly, the Japanese expedition for the siege of Peking had been a substantial drain on finances; and it was unlikely that anything could be done by way of large military operations. Here was the classic scenario for a split in the ministry, with the prime minister and finance ministers aligned against the foreign, army and navy ministers. All in all it seems to have been hard for Itō to gain the upper hand over dissentient party members. There is probably some truth in Izvolskii's assessment that 'parliamentary events have unfortunately considerably weakened the authority of this statesman which was recently so great'.[5]

KOREAN NEUTRALIZATION NEGOTIATIONS

After the relief of the Peking legations, Izvolskii felt that the time was ripe for positive negotiations with Japan. He had been in Tokyo since

1900 and no one doubted that he was one of his country's top-level diplomats with a promising career ahead. He was pleasant, suave, accomplished. But he was also slightly distrusted by other members of the diplomatic body. Moreover, he does not seem to have hit it off with the Japanese as Rosen had before him. His communications with St Petersburg leave the impression that he was not really happy in Tokyo and was conscious of his inability to win the trust of the Japanese (though this was not easy for Russian diplomats at any time after 1900).[6]

With surprising disregard for Japan's preoccupation with Manchuria, Izvolskii concentrated his diplomacy on Korea. It was his judgement (and that of Russia) that the anti-foreign movement in China would spread into Korea and in all likelihood Russia and Japan might find it necessary to send troops to the peninsula in order to restore order. There had earlier been various exchanges of view between Izvolskii and Foreign Minister Aoki, who had left office in October, and it had been arranged that, before troops were sent to Korea, there would be conversations in order to work out the spheres within which the two countries would operate. When Katō took up office, he confirmed on his audience day on 15 November that he would abide by the arrangements of his predecessor. Happily the disturbances from China (and Manchuria) did not spread to Korea; and the need to send expeditions of troops did not arise. But, as the risk of instability in the peninsula subsided, the Japanese recognized that their security perimeter, which they had long regarded as including Korea, had become much weaker since the Russians had taken over as an occupying force beyond the Yalu.

Soon after taking office, Itō, according to Izvolskii, gave him an assurance of 'his readiness to enter into a discussion of conditions under which the neutrality of Korea might be established'. It was therefore distinctly inconvenient for the Russian minister that Itō was so often ill and out of town. The Koreans in power for the time being were thought to be in favour of some such solution. Hayashi Gonsuke from the Japanese legation there reported on the fitful talks he had been holding from the summer of 1900 onwards, though he was not personally in favour of the proposal. The Korean foreign minister also visited Japan and gained the impression that Itō was inclined towards international recognition of Korea's neutrality, while Katō and the foreign ministry were generally not.[7]

Izvolskii proposed the neutralization of Korea under international guarantee, that is, by Japan and Russia. But Katō, who had a firm idea that this was not St Petersburg's proposal but Izvolskii's own, insisted on seeing evidence that the Russian envoy did in fact have direct and positive instructions from his government before embarking on conversations. After a time instructions were received and discussions did take place. Katō reacted by insisting on linking Korean neutralization with Russian evacuation from Manchuria: Japan would not discuss Korea's neutrality until the Russians took steps to move their armies out of the three eastern provinces.[8] It is hard to say whether this was just a method of fobbing off Izvolskii by imposing conditions which Russia was most unlikely to consider, far less to concede. But Japan had nothing to lose. From her point of view, 'neutralization' meant the sacrifice of a position in the peninsula – as it did also for Russia. But, whereas Russia was making Manchuria into a sphere of influence and was gaining overall, Japan was the only loser. It was politically undesirable in view of the actions of Kokumin Dōmeikai and others to be seen to make concessions when the situation in north-east Asia was so fluid.

There were grounds for some scepticism about Izvolskii's authorization. He had not lost the confidence of the tsar or his sponsor, the Dowager Empress Marie; but he was not thought to be on good terms with the ministry or to have the sympathy of the bureaucrats. This had been known to the Japanese since Komura had represented them at the Russian capital.[9] In the autumn things were not easy for Izvolskii at the Russian end. Not only were members of the tsar's inner cabinet in the Crimea so that, as one foreign diplomat observed, 'we are practically at present without a responsible government at St Petersburg'[10] but also, as we have already seen, the tsar was badly incapacitated. The empress was suffering from typhoid fever; and the emperor, who frequently reflected his wife's moods, had lost his stamina. The rumour had it that 'General Friedricks, the Minister of the Household, is the only one who has any access to the Emperor during his illness and M. Witte says that under no circumstances will he leave Livadia as long as any of the other three Ministers (War, Foreign Affairs, and Home) remain there.'[11] The consequence of this was that, with all the problems of the far east mounting up and waiting for a decision, Lamsdorf was unable to see the tsar for a month at a stretch. There was therefore a distinct lack of a clear policy line; and the result was to leave the decision-making to the men on the frontier, either the military-naval men in Manchuria or the diplomats who were all inclined to take advantage. It is probably true that the tsar with the advice of his ministers recognized this and was genuinely afraid of leaving so many decisions to others.

On 7 January Izvolskii asked Katō for his views on the Russian neutralization proposals. Katō reserved his judgement and finally replied through the new Japanese minister to St Petersburg, Chinda, that Japan could not take up the programme for neutralization of Korea until after the withdrawal of the Russian army from Manchuria. In communicating this to Izvolskii subsequently, Katō admitted that the existing arrangement between the two countries through the Nishi–Rosen agreement of 1898 was satisfactory to the Japanese.[12] Nothing further was heard of the proposal for the present.

Izvolskii was insulted by Katō's tactics. By replying through the Japanese minister to Russia, Katō had by-passed him. He was quick to complain to his diplomatic colleagues that he had lost face with his government. The probability is that Izvolskii had less authority to make his neutralization proposals than he liked to think. The relations between Katō and Izvolskii continued to be very strained.[13] Yet Izvolskii reported the Japanese position fairly enough. In the middle of February he analysed the Japanese standpoint thus:

> Japan is willing to risk facing what is an established fact, namely that Russia has appreciably increased her sphere of influence, and this explains the Japanese government's frantic attempts to prepare the way beforehand so as to reap suitable rewards. I have already had occasion to point out that the only place where Japan can look for such rewards is in Korea, for every acquisition at the expense of China is very unpopular here and contrary to the spirit of the latest Japanese policy. When in its last communication the Japanese government asserts that the last Russo-Japanese agreement with regard to Korea remains in force ... this only proves that it considers it immature and contrary to its interests to bind itself by entering into a new agreement in this matter until the fate of Manchuria has been finally decided.[14]

MANCHURIAN NEGOTIATIONS

Korea was a separate problem, though it had its connections with the chaos in China. The problems of China proper were being ironed out by the 'allies', that is, those who had taken part in the allied expeditionary force at what (for want of a better name) might be called 'the Peking conference'. It was the assumption of those attending that they were together dealing with the aftermath of the Boxer disturbances wherever they occurred, that is, the so-called 'collective approach'. Among the most active sponsors of the collective approach was France who was most hard-working in the preparation of drafts for dealing with the problems of punishment, indemnity and the treatment of the Chinese court. Russia refused on principle to allow the subject of Manchuria to appear on the agenda of the Peking conference: it was, she argued, a bilateral issue between herself and China and no other power had the right to a voice in its solution. This was an example of the 'individual approach'. The Chinese, of course, did not share the Russian interpretation on this point. The majority of China's leaders were hoping to play off Russia against the powers and the powers against Russia; and this tactic could best be employed at a conference. But neither China nor the powers were able to bring the issue of Manchuria before the Peking conference.[15]

In the search for a bilateral solution, the Chinese were divided. Li Hung-chang was ready to compromise with Russia though he was anxious – and optimistic – about acquiring Manchuria again. The Yangtse viceroys were less ready to compromise and were already approaching the seaward powers – Britain, the United States and Japan – for aid against the Russians. On the Russian side too there were divisions. In the Crimea Kuropatkin, Witte and Lamsdorf laid down the guidelines for Russian government control of Manchuria. Kuropatkin drew up the substance and Witte only amended it in order to ensure that his own railway empire was not squeezed out when Manchuria became an army preserve. The guidelines were eventually approved by the tsar on 17 December.

But action had to be held over until the return of the tsar's court to the capital in January. The inside story suggests that there were intense disagreements between the decision-makers in St Petersburg. Kuropatkin and Witte, the ministers most closely involved in Manchuria – and in a sense rivals in that quarter – wanted to proceed with some form of treaty with China which would affirm and possibly consolidate the gains made by Russia in the Tseng–Alekseyev agreement, that is, the local arrangement which was never ratified by either central government. Lamsdorf, who was less involved but had to bear in mind the strong storm of indignation to which the abortive Tseng–Alekseyev treaty had given rise abroad, feared a repetition of this external interference. He therefore advised that the terms should be modified from the harsh conditions which his two partners were inclined to impose. He further argued that it might not be very worth while to negotiate with a Chinese government which was so weak and with a court which was in exile, and contended that Chinese statesmen thought of inconvenient western treaties as mere scraps of paper which had to be evaded. But the main ministers could not wait and met Lamsdorf only to the extent of modifying their demands.[16] Their main change was to ask for further economic concessions in Manchuria instead of an indemnity, though they did agree not to stick out for the right to run the Manchurian customs, thus avoiding a clash with the powers.

After a great deal of final polishing, the Russian draft was ready. Witte's draft had been altered several times and Lamsdorf had worked on it, obtaining the approval of his colleagues on 8 February. By the time that it was passed over on 20 February to Yang Ju, the Chinese minister at St Petersburg, it was in greatly modified form. Since Lamsdorf had the final hand in it, it was likely to stand scrutiny if and when the terms of the note were leaked to the powers. Almost immediately the diplomats in Peking (excepting those of France and Belgium) protested over any individual settlement between China and Russia.[17]

It was one thing for the powers to protest to China, quite another for them to protest to Russia. Li Hung-chang who had to deal with the Russian ultimatum, remarked that the western countries would not stand up to Russia but 'only wag their tongues at us'.[18] There were no promises of armed support so he recommended the court to yield. But the Yangtse viceroys wanted to mobilize world opinion against Russia in the name of the Open Door, that is, by promising the United States, Britain, Germany, etc. equal commercial rights in Manchuria. Open Door countries like Japan and Britain did try to obtain information direct from Russia. But after several attempts in March, all they received was the statement that there was no reason in international law why Russia should reveal the treaty before it was concluded.

A notable absentee from criticism of Russia was Germany. On 14 March her chancellor took the opportunity to state that the Anglo-German agreement concluded in October 1900 was not considered by Germany to apply to Manchuria. Thus, Germany was not proposing to challenge Russia's draft treaty. This was a great disappointment to Japan who had specially adhered to that treaty under the strict understanding that it did apply to Manchuria. Katō was furious. Until this time, he said, the German chargé d'affaires in Tokyo had boasted of the protests which his country had been making in Peking over Manchuria; but after this he suddenly made a complete *volte-face*. taking the line that Manchuria was nothing to the Germans, though it meant much to Japan. Not sympathetic to Germany by nature, Katō drew the conclusion that the Germans were merely trying to get Japan involved in fighting Russia over Manchuria. The *Japan Times,* often the instrument for the views of the foreign ministry, denounced the German statement but conceded eventually that European powers had few interests in Manchuria and could not be expected to oppose Russia, but that Japan was in a different position, having life-and-death interests there.[19]

Our especial concern is with the reaction of the Japanese government. Hitherto it had been cautious, only sending troops to China when invited, and withdrawing the bulk of them when the crisis was over. Now the ministers were divided over their attitudes to Russia. Prime Minister Itō told the Belgian minister in February:

> Russia has considerable interests in Manchuria, and it is legitimate for
> her to protect them. During last year's troubles, she was the only one to
> send troops and maintain order in this part of China. She thereby helped
> the other Powers, limiting the area where their troops had to intervene.
> If she continues to maintain order in North China without hindering the
> commercial development of other nations, Japan will be able to
> safeguard her interests, in spite of the presence of military forces.[20]

This was a remarkably broad-minded view to take and was out of line with Kokumin Dōmeikai propaganda. There are suggestions that it was not representative of the government's attitude. There is evidence that the Japanese minister in Peking, by this time Komura, was the first to protest to China against signing the draft Russian treaty. The implication is that Japan was prepared to take a strong line regardless of the actions of other powers. In short, Japan was prepared to take a lead over Manchurian affairs in advance of other world powers.

Following the circulation of a lengthy historical note prepared by Katō, the Manchurian problem was before the Japanese ministers for almost a week from 14 March. Finally on the 20th Japan urged China not to agree to Russia's demands; and on the 25th Chinda, the minister to St Petersburg, gave Lamsdorf Japan's tactful protest which urged on Russia improvement of the existing draft treaty. The Russian however stuck to his line that this was purely a matter between Russia and China and declined to accept the protest note. Katō then proposed to his colleagues that Japan should reply that this attitude was totally unacceptable. But the prime minister would not agree, saying that it would be dangerous to pick a fight with Russia over this and too early to take up such a strong position. So the Japanese cabinet confined itself to telling Russia that it could regretfully not agree with Lamsdorf's statement.[21]

The fever pitch which the Manchurian issue had reached has to be seen against the background of the Itō government's troubles with the Diet. The government had asked for an increase in taxes because funds were required urgently *inter alia* for maintaining Japan's forces in China. On 25 February the Upper House (kizokuin) failed to pass the tax bill which had earlier been approved by the House of Representatives. The cabinet therefore suspended the Upper House, first for ten, then for a further five, days. Meanwhile ferocious lobbying went on in which most of the genro were drafted in to support the budget; Yamagata, Saigō, Inoue and Matsukata joined the fray by persuading their political supporters. Eventually the emperor was forced to intervene by issuing an imperial proclamation (shochoku) to the members of the Upper House, instructing them to pass the budget on 12 March. Four days later they complied through their president, Prince Konoe. It was a desperate move for Itō to call the emperor into the political arena in this way; and the Lower House condemned the government for it. A motion of censure against the government was defeated by a very narrow margin. The immediate storm had passed; but Itō had unquestionably lost some of the authority which he had had in former times.

In his report, the Russian minister took the view that the closure of the Diet session would relieve the government and save it from having to answer delicate questions about foreign policy until it reopened in the autumn. He admitted quite generously that the Itō government 'had succeeded in preserving a fairly mild tone in all its answers and generally in keeping the agitation in the Diet on the Manchurian issue within bounds. The agitation will, however, continue in the form of newspaper articles, addresses to meetings etc. and it may yet cause the cabinet some difficulty.'[22]

On 5 April Lamsdorf was able to announce in an official communiqué that Russia gave up her demands, withdrew the terms under negotiation and intended to stay on in Manchuria for the time being. China had not kept the deadline for negotiation by enlisting the support of others. It left Russia with no choice but to cancel the talks. What had Russia to lose? With the railway coming close to completion, time was on her side; she could afford to wait. True, international protests were a nuisance. But she had been internationally unpopular before and there seemed to be no pressing reason for withdrawing from the territory merely because a world-wide campaign of complaint had been organized against her.

Russia's decision to break off the talks with China could not in the circumstances be recorded as a victory for those like Japan and Britain who had tried to lodge formal protests. Indeed, the protests had been received in a most cordial and inoffensive spirit. In the case of Britain, Lamsdorf had argued that his final terms had been 'quite innocuous' and had seemed to suggest that the objectionable articles should be attributed to 'the machinations of Russians like Prince Uchtomsky (Uktomskii) and other rabid politicians of the forward school in China, into whose wine Lamsdorf and finally the emperor have been putting as much water as they can'.[23] Presumably one of the reasons for representing the Russian approach as sweet reasonableness was to divide the opposition. In particular, it was in Russia's interest to divide Japan and Britain, the only two of the Open Door powers who were likely to take positive action, and ensure that the two did not act together over Manchuria. On the British side, this was the time for a special mission led by the Duke of Abercorn to announce to the Russian emperor the accession of Edward VII. The tsar had gone out of his way to show the mission his enthusiasm for the most friendly relations with Britain. On 18 April Ambassador Scott reported that Lamsdorf's remarks struck him 'as a decided attempt at an overture or the renewal of the attempt to come to an understanding about China, prompted by the Emperor's sincere wish in that direction ... It is also very likely that they are not a little alarmed here about the feeling in Japan and the possibility of our entering into any engagements to support her in active resistance to Russia.'[24] Lansdowne replied that he would not reject an overture; but none came.

JAPAN'S RESISTANCE DEFUSED

How close had Japan been to war? It is hard for the historian to say. He can more easily answer the question: how did it appear to contemporaries? First we should quote Katō's remark to MacDonald at the height of the crisis on 21 March: Japan had quite given up all idea of offering China any material assistance in opposing the demands of

Russia but had decided to warn her of the consequences of signing any such agreement as was contemplated.[25]

But it did not necessarily appear so to outside observers. d'Anethan, writing in late March, took the view: 'I do not say that war is imminent, but it is far from improbable.' The Belgian minister attributed this to the army and navy who were seeking to persuade the government to take a firmer attitude towards Russia: within the cabinet the ministers of war and navy pushed for energetic action and were controlled with difficulty by Itō and Katō; the military element were pushing for an aggressive policy and had the country behind them and demagogues like Count Ōkuma were asking the government to deal a decisive blow to Russia in Manchuria or lose all prestige in China.[26]

Similar were the views of the diplomatic body, and most importantly of Izvolskii. He reported that:

> the most dangerous and hot-headed member of the cabinet is Naval Minister Admiral Yamamoto; ... the navy is in almost full fighting order and is already distributed among the south-western ports lying nearest to the area of possible hostilities. With the arrival of the last battleship but one ordered from England, Japan's programme of naval armament can be regarded as almost completed ... The War Ministry has not made any special preparations and would require one year to come to a state of readiness.[27]

The opinion of his active military and naval attachés was that war was an unlikely possibility, though Izvolskii was clearly much alarmed at the strength of anti-Russian feeling which was almost universal in Japan. He was inclined to predict that Japan's immediate aim was 'a break with Russia' and she would only be satisfied with an unconditional withdrawal from the Manchurian area. Izvolskii's pessimism was not accepted by the ministers; but his assessment of the intensity of Japanese popular feeling may not have been too wide of the mark.

Some of the conjectures of d'Anethan and Izvolskii cannot be substantiated. We now know something of the opinions in senior military-naval quarters in Japan. Thus at a meeting on 1 April Yamamoto, the navy minister who is spoken of by Izvolskii as being the most extreme, supported Itō's cautious line and took pains to pacify Katō, while Kodama, the war minister, remained neutral.[28] Kodama may in this have been reflecting the attitude of the more senior and influential general, Field Marshal Yamagata. Although we do not know Yamagata's advice at the crisis of April Fool's day, we do have his seminal memorandum which was eventually completed on 24 April. He there argued that 'relations between Japan and Russia have not yet suffered a major upset but sooner or later a serious collision is inevitable ... If we are to prevent war, we must secure the help of other powers to arrest Russia's southward advance.'[29] He seems to imply that Japan was not strong enough militarily to take on Russia and must for the present adopt a cautious stance, his 'shinchōron', (doctrine of circumspection). So the army was relatively restrained. Moreover the matter was fully and officially discussed. Thus the matter went to the cabinet and was referred to the supreme military council (gensuifu) where it was discussed by Prince Komatsu, Marshal Yamagata, Admirals Saitō and Itō under the personal chairmanship of the emperor. The subject went again to the cabinet who instructed the foreign minister to make a second – milk and water – protest to the Russians. By the time this was done on 8 April, the Sino-Russian parleys were at an end; and the polite protest was fruitless.

While the Japanese military felt themselves unready to resist by force Russia's activities in Manchuria which they so much detested, the Russian military were taking a line which did not entirely accord with Lamsdorf's. In response to the complaints of the powers, Lamsdorf had been firm but deceptively ingratiating. The language of the Russian military was different. After the finance ministry's monopoly over the railways collapsed in 1900, a new role was thrust on Kuropatkin, the war minister, who seems to have oscillated a good deal in his attitude. He had started off by hailing the Boxer disturbances as a great opportunity for Russia, but he was not insensitive to world opinion. No one was more involved with military operations in Manchuria itself than Admiral Alekseyev, by this time with a mandate running from the Liaotung peninsula throughout the south and centre of Manchuria. His attitude is best revealed in a private letter he wrote to Kuropatkin:

> The protest of the powers against our intention to hold on to Manchuria must be seen as complaining against an accomplished fact, which should have been clear to them for some time past. In our agreement with China for building the Chinese Eastern railway, they should have marked our right to defend it with the means which most suited our purpose. Whether this was to be by troops or guards was an internal matter of a strategic and technical nature to which they could not reasonably object.[30]

Alekseyev went on to urge Kuropatkin to stick it out, not to withdraw the Russian troops and to ignore the protests of outside powers who would soon lose interest. Perhaps Japan, with her considerable stake in Manchurian trade based on Niuchuang, was most likely to persist but she could be bought off by offering her an agreement which would give her what she wanted in Korea, while Russia obtained full freedom of action in Manchuria.

One factor which served to defuse the situation was the precipitate resignation of the Itō ministry. It arose out of the disagreement between Finance Minister Watanabe Kunio and the cabinet over the public debt, which developed around the end of March. Itō eventually resigned on the ground of cabinet disunity on 2 May, Watanabe being the only member who refused to resign. The succession was offered to the only genro who had never been prime minister, Inoue Kaoru; but he declined. General Katsura, the war minister in the retiring cabinet, was recommended for the post. After the assistance of his patron, Yamagata, Katsura managed to form a cabinet with the navy's cooperation and announced it on 2 June after a month-long political crisis.

The post of foreign minister was given to Komura Jūtarō on the understanding that he would not leave his present post at Peking until the peace treaty between the allies and China was signed. For the time being the berth was filled by Sone Arasuke, who was the finance minister. But he avoided all initiatives on the ground that things should be left for Komura's arrival. In due course the Peking protocol was signed on 7 September and Komura was able to leave for Tokyo. He already knew much about the problems of Manchuria and Korea. In these intervening months, Japan was finding her feet with a new and inexperienced ministry while Russia was glad to have re-established the status quo in Manchuria. Even the pessimistic Izvolskii was able to report that the relationship had been restored to a happy equilibrium.[31]

Komura returned from Peking on 19 September but in unorthodox fashion. He had left the Chinese capital on 9 September and embarked on the cruiser *Chitose* at Taku, sailing with her across to Chefoo. Without informing Tokyo, he visited Korea, landing at Chemulpo and Masampo, and had an audience with the Korean emperor and his officials. He had been minister in Korea in 1895–96 and knew the ministers there well. He had taken the opportunity of first-hand observation of an area which was in his view vital to Japan's security and a major impediment to good relations with Russia.[32]

Komura returned to a lame duck ministry which had endured four months of interregnum under Sone, who had been fully employed at the ministry of finance. He took over as foreign minister on 21 September at the age of forty-seven. He was well known for his strong-mindedness, not to say obstinacy, and was to some extent a committed man. While still in Peking, he had been consulted by the Katsura government about the approach being made to Britain and had given his approval. Moreover he had worked hard with W. W. Rockhill, the American plenipotentiary at the Peking Conference, and Sir Ernest Satow against the Russians at the conference. Though this had not endeared him to the Russians, he gave the impression in Tokyo of beginning his ministry with an open mind.

On 11 October Izvolskii conveyed the impression of his first meeting with Komura who was still inclined to keep his options open. He thought the new foreign minister, who had seen service in St Petersburg, was not a Japanese who had a leaning towards any particular European country; he seemed quite sincere in his desire for a rapprochement with Russia. He formed the impression that Komura was already informed of the negotiations on which Lessar, the new Russian minister in Peking, and Li Hung-chang were embarked and possibly had an inkling of the terms. Komura, it was thought, would not make a positive move until he had examined the terms and seen that they were in accord with the evacuation announcement.[33]

There were probably no victors in the Russo-Japanese brinkmanship of the spring of 1901. Russia came out with dignity *vis-à-vis* China without reducing her terms of withdrawal. She came out, however, with a tarnished image *vis-à-vis* the rest of the world. Her mishandling of the situation had caused an international hullaballoo, in the face of which Lamsdorf had appeared to act shiftily. There seemed to be no concordance between the military policy and the St Petersburg line. So most concluded that Russia was following a dual diplomacy. The crisis was not an unmitigated disaster for China. Her leaders saw that most of the world was opposed to the Russian military protectorate over part of their territory and knew that they could rely on this recurring if later terms were equally unsatisfactory. They still had the skill to play off one barbarian against the other. But the Russian armies were still there. So China still had to negotiate in the future and could only hope that her foreign supporters would secure for her better terms.

It was also something of a turning-point for the Japanese. They had been the focal point of the international opposition. Lamsdorf had taken the view that, if Russia took over Manchuria, there would be no resistance offered. It was typical of his Eurocentric views that he could not conceive of opposition being offered except by a great (that is, a European) power. So he was surprised when Japan resisted so stoutly. The Russian reaction was generally one of astonishment that she should embark on such a reckless course as to challenge Russia. Certainly it was a new experience for Japan. But the fact was that Manchuria and Korea were part of the national cause. In ventilating it, the government was reflecting popular sentiment. Professor Tsunoda writes of it as a 'coming of age'. She had not flinched at taking the lead but, having exposed herself, she had acted circumspectly.[34]

REFERENCES AND NOTES

1. Marius Jansen, 'Konoe Atsumaro' in A. Iriye (ed.), *The Chinese and the Japanese,* pp. 107–23.
2. 'Nakanune Russko-Iaponskoi Voiny' in *Krasnyi Arkhiv,* **63** (1934), 3–54. Translated in *Chinese Social and Political Science Review* as 'On the Eve of the Russo-Japanese War' in vols 18–19 (1934–36). (Hereafter referred to as 'Eve of War'.)
3. Jansen, op. cit., p. 109.
4. *Kōshaku Itō Hirobumi-den*, vol. 3, Tokyo 1943, pp. 480–8.
5. Izvolskii to Lamsdorf, 14 Mar. 1901, 'Eve of War', p. 587.

6. *d'Anethan Dispatches,* pp. 154–5.
7. Tsunoda Jun, *Manshū Mondai to Kokubō Hōshin,* pp. 38–44.
8. Katō, vol. 1, pp. 434–7; *NGB* 34, no. 174.
9. Japan, Foreign Ministry, *Komura Gaikōshi,* vol. 1, p. 149.
10. Scott to Sanderson, 13 Dec, 1900, in Scott Papers 52,304.
11. Scott to Lansdowne, 29 Nov. 1900, in Scott Papers 52,304.
12. Chinda to Lamsdorf, 22 Jan. 1901, 'Eve of War', pp. 574–5.
13. MacDonald to Lansdowne, 21 Mar. 1901, FO 46/539.
14. Izvolskii to Lamsdorf, 22 Feb. 1901, 'Eve of War', p. 582.
15. I. H. Nish, *The Anglo-Japanese Alliance,* pp. 111–16.
16. A. Malozemoff, *Russian Far Eastern Policy,* pp. 156–60.
17. The whole document, consisting of 14 articles, is in B. A. Romanov, *Russia in Manchuria,* pp. 297–9.
18. M. H. Hunt, *Frontier Defence and the Open Door,* pp. 18–19.
19. Nish, op. cit., pp. 104–11.
20. *d'Anethan Dispatches,* p. 146.
21. Tsunoda Jun, op. cit., pp. 61–4.
22. Izvolskii to Lamsdorf, 14 Mar. 1901, 'Eve of War', p. 591.
23. Scott to Lansdowne, 4 Apr. 1901, Scott Papers, 52,304.
24. Scott to Lansdowne, 18 Apr. 1901, Scott Papers 52,304; W. L. Langer, *Diplomacy of Imperialism, 1890–1902,* New York 1951, pp. 741–2.
25. MacDonald to Lansdowne, 21 Mar. 1901, FO 46/539.
26. *d'Anethan Dispatches,* pp. 148–50.
27. Izvolskii to Lamsdorf, 5 Apr. 1901, 'Eve of War', pp. 130–1.
28. Japan, Navy Ministry, *Yamamoto Gombei to Kaigun* gives no indication of Yamamoto as being anxious for war or conflict with Russia.
29. Yamagata, 'Tōyō Dōmeiron', *Yamagata-den,* vol. 3, pp. 494–6.
30. G. A. Lensen, *The Russo-Chinese War,* pp. 253–4.
31. Izvolskii to Lamsdorf, 30 July 1901, 'Eve of War', p. 139.
32. *Komura Gaikōshi,* vol. 1, p. 200.
33. Izvolskii to Lamsdorf, 7 Aug. and 10 Oct. 1901, 'Eve of War', pp. 240–1.
34. Tsunoda, op. cit., pp. 71f.

Chapter 7

AFTER THE PEKING PROTOCOL (JULY–DECEMBER 1901)

The Peking protocol was signed on 7 September. In accordance with it, the allied troops evacuated the Forbidden City ten days later. Within a month the Chinese court left Sian in order to return to Peking. These factors all seemed to foreshadow a new attitude on the part of the Chinese. The move to Sian had been presented as a visit of inspection to one of the provinces; while the court was there, it made frequent calls for 'no surrender'. For it to have accepted the protocol and to have embarked on the homeward journey so quickly seemed to be a hopeful sign. In fact, however, the court took its time over the return in the manner of a medieval circuit and did not reach the capital till 7 January 1902.[1]

The need to restore the normal situation was urgent in the eyes of the Russians. Where the powers as a whole had been able to make peace with the Chinese for the province of Chihli, Russia should be able to make a new approach to the Chinese leaders over Manchuria on a bilateral basis. It was necessary to test the likely response of China after the Peking protocol.

Russia had modified her position during the summer. Witte, who had long taken the categorical position that the annexation of Manchuria by Russia would be no solution to the problem, devised a phasing for the evacuation of troops from the area on 24 June. This was a breakthrough from previous negotiations and was to anticipate the formulae which Russia would henceforth put forward. But would a formula on these lines commend itself to Kuropatkin, the minister of war who was most affected by the Manchuria débâcle? Witte expected the support of Lamsdorf who had been a fairly consistent ally until then. A conference was held on 11 July at which the chief of the general staff, Witte and Lamsdorf were all agreed that it would be preferable from their own standpoints (whether political, military or financial) to restore the Shanhaikuan-Yingkow railway to the Chinese owners and withdraw Russian troops from the west of the Liao. The verdict of the three ministries was approved by the tsar on 18 July.[2] As the next step,

Lamsdorf asked his colleagues whether Russia should retain the rest of Manchuria or merely hold one of its provinces. He also asked Izvolskii and Giers on 30 July what would be the effect on China and Japan of 'an official announcement by Russia that she intended to add Manchuria to her possessions'. In a supplement two days later, he added that Russia had no intention of repudiating the promises given earlier that she would withdraw her troops from Manchuria as soon as normality returned to China, provided the actions of the other powers or China did not obstruct her. There were certainly elements of uncertainty and prevarication in the statements which Lamsdorf was making. His representatives on the spot tended to confirm that Russia should evacuate her troops though without making it absolutely clear from how much of Manchuria. On 7 August Izvolskii warned that Japan would go to war if Russia should annex Manchuria but she would in time grow accustomed to 'an established fact' though occasional periodic outbursts in favour of war and joint protests with other powers were only to be expected.[3]

On 1 August Lamsdorf wrote to the other ministers:

> The presence of our troops in Manchuria and the numerous measures that have to be taken by the War Ministry in evacuating that country, connected with the guarding and fortification of certain coastal and frontier stations, and by the Finance Ministry with regard to various questions connected with the construction of the railway, so complicate the general situation that at the slightest lack of caution on the part of the local Russian authorities, one may expect Japan at any time to take active measures ... If our military and naval position in the Far East is considerably weaker than that of Japan, it would be extremely advisable to take steps to bring the forces of the pri-Amur district gradually and cautiously into full readiness for emergencies ... The best way out of present difficulties would be as soon as possible to carry out the tsar's will and prepare to evacuate Manchuria before international pressure forces that course upon us.[4]

The response of his colleagues was guarded. Witte considered that a complete administrative and military evacuation was essential and that railway guards would be enough to ensure the railway's security. This was a solution which suited his own ministry and was a return to the pre-Boxer situation. Kuropatkin, however, urged neither annexation nor complete withdrawal of troops. He argued that the Amur river was an unsatisfactory frontier against China's inroads because roads were lacking and inadequate for defence and that Russia should create from northern Manchuria either an independent state or a province nominally subject to China but in practice under her influence on the same lines as the state of Bokhara. In order to avert international opposition to such a step, he recommended the immediate restoration of Mukden (Fengtien) province and part of Kirin province while holding on temporarily to the north. This course was supported neither by

Witte, who never welcomed counter-proposals, nor by Lamsdorf who, like the chairman he so often was, did not make clear where his own views lay. He tended to preside as a neutral between two strong-minded ministers who were deeply involved in the Manchurian situation.[5]

Witte had meanwhile evolved a new scheme for dealing with the evacuation of Manchuria. While there should be official negotiations between Russia and China for the restoration of the provinces, there should also be indirect negotiations between the Chinese government and Pozdneyev, the representative of the Russo-Chinese bank in Peking and a staunch ally of Witte. In return for concessions over evacuation, China would give the Russo-Chinese bank large-scale mining concessions in Manchuria. This would enable Witte to balance his budget over the Manchurian railway through the private enterprise of the bank which was in his control. But he reckoned without Chinese hostility.[6]

JAPAN, UNITED STATES AND BRITAIN STAND TOGETHER.

The position on the spot bore little resemblance to the debates going on in St Petersburg. Whereas the triumvirate were all agreed on some programme of evacuation, this message had not penetrated through to the men on the frontier. For example, at the treaty port of Niuchuang (Yingkow), where the triumvirate were agreed that it should be restored to China and Russian troops evacuated, there was no sign of this in the reports of the foreign consuls. The port was in effect in Russian occupation. This was a paradox because the Russians had handed over the government of other towns in Manchuria to the Chinese but continued to hold (of all things) a treaty port under a Russian civil administrator. So far as customs duty at the adjoining port of Yingkow was concerned, it had to be collected by Russia for the time being; and this seems to have applied to Chinese transit dues like li-kin. Admiral Alekseyev had worked out an ambiguous arrangement with Sir Robert Hart (for the Imperial Maritime Customs) whereby the commissioner would conduct the customs business, while the Russo-Chinese Bank would accept the moneys in trust for the Chinese government of the day.[7] Duty payments were to be made to the Russo-Chinese bank which had become the bank of the civil administration and the Manchu governor-general of Mukden was encouraged to have dealings with that bank for his administration. Extensive quarters were being constructed adjoining the terminus of the Shanhaikuan-Niuchuang railway for the use of Russian troops. The Russian flag flew over the forts and public buildings; and the Russian customs flag flew over the customs buildings and other craft.

It was the conclusion of the Japanese, the British and the Americans that the Russians intended to hold on to the administration for some time to come. This is not to say that the administrator was unaccommodating to foreign interests; he recognized that foreign countries had treaty rights which he undertook to uphold; but there was no sign of any willingness to depart or expectation of evacuation. It was clear to all outsiders that Russia was not acting in accordance with the Peking protocol and had no intention of doing so. In accordance with the complaints of British merchants at that port, the senior British naval officer at Taku authorized the gunboat *Algerine* on 27 October to stay at Niuchuang. The admiralty had strong objections to leaving a ship there for the winter on the ground that it was wasteful to tie up a vessel for a prolonged period. The government was inclined to agree but felt it had to be done.[8] The Russians were furious and the new Russian minister at Peking, Pavel Lessar, at the request of Admiral Alekseyev, lodged a complaint on 8 November with the British authorities in Peking, on the ground that the presence of a British vessel would cause embarrassment and force the Russians to keep a vessel there for the winter too. Naturally Britain replied that Niuchuang was a treaty port and there was nothing strange in keeping a gunboat there in accordance with her rights. When this reached London, Lord Salisbury, the prime minister, wrote an important minute:

> In view of what happened four years ago [1898], I do not think that after Russia's message we can safely remove the vessel. The commercial public opinion on the Chinese littoral is very mendacious and very malignant and we must count on their misrepresenting and distorting anything that we do ... The objections of the Admiralty are professional and of little value. They always have an objection to placing British vessels in any place where the F.O. wants them.[9]

After this uncharacteristic intervention, orders were given to send the *Algerine* to Niuchuang on 15 November for the winter and the views of the admiralty were overruled. Immediate action was necessary because navigation was about to close at the port because of icing up and it was essential to get the vessel in position. On 28 November the USS *Vicksburg* was sent by the Americans to winter there also and the Japanese acted likewise. This drew together the three Open Door powers and forced the Russians to be more sensitive over the treaty rights of other powers. The three ships were lodged in dry docks dug in the river bank in the Russian railway settlement. It was an expensive gesture; but the Open Door powers were determined to prevent Russian possession of Niuchuang.

The motives for this strong line were various. From the standpoint of the Japanese, the major traders in the area, the port of Niuchuang was the point of entry for her goods and it was essential that it be kept open and not subject to the obstacles and hindrances which might arise if the

Russians established a monopoly over the port facilities. From the standpoint of the European powers, the key factor was the reopening of the Shanhaikuan-Niuchuang line to passenger traffic in April 1901. From this point the main route between Europe and Peking followed the Trans-Siberian and Chinese Eastern railways, then the line from Harbin to Niuchuang, changing on to the Chinese line to Peking. If this route was to thrive, it was necessary that Niuchuang's status as a treaty port should be reaffirmed. Since the Russians showed no willingness to do so, men-of-war of the powers visited Niuchuang all summer in the hope of forcing home the message that there was going to be serious opposition to their permanent possession of the Three Eastern provinces. When, as was thought to be imminent, Sino-Russian negotiations were reopened, it was essential that both sides should understand that most of the world's powers had an interest in the place and that it was not a port purely of interest to Russia and China. If any Russian forward move was to be effectively challenged, some sacrifice had to be made. Hence the British, the Americans and the Japanese simultaneously but independently decided that their men-of-war should winter in the port, while conceding that it was a costly operation of doubtful effectiveness.

This came as no surprise to the Russians. Alekseyev had been reporting on intelligence he had been collecting about increased British activity in the sector Taku-Chinwangtao–Niuchuang. Indeed he had come across a rumour that Britain was arranging for the landing of a Japanese force around Chinwangtao. There is no confirmation of this in other documents; and it is only mentioned here to show the rumours which were circulating.[10]

RUSSO-CHINESE NEGOTIATIONS RESUMED

When the Peking protocol was signed, talks began between Chinese and Russian delegates at Peking. On the Russian side it was left to Lessar to conduct the talks. He had reached Peking in twenty-one days from Moscow by the Trans-Siberian, Chinese Eastern and Chinese Extension (Niuchuang) lines on 12 September. Lessar was for some years to be counted among the most distinguished diplomats in the far east and had a much broader outlook than most Peking diplomats who were set in the table-thumping imperialist mould. As an official at the London embassy, he had been instrumental in bringing about the Anglo-Russian railway agreement in 1899. Dr Morrison, who rarely indulged in flattery, committed to his letters this assessment: 'He is infinitely superior to de Giers. The combination of Lessar, Kroupensky, Pokotilov, de Wogack and Baron Gunsburg is one very difficult to compete with. Lessar is indeed very clever.'[11] Lessar brought to his new post negotiating skill and knowledge of far eastern problems.

The Russian terms were considerably reduced. To meet the objections of the powers, they no longer claimed a concession for a branch line to the Great Wall at Shanhaikuan. To meet the demands of the Chinese, they were ready to discuss a phased withdrawal. In discussion Li Hung-chang asked for further concessions over troop numbers. Elaborate arrangements had been made for appropriate remuneration to be provided for Li who was regarded as the most amenable of the Chinese officials. Yet Li fought his corner tenaciously enough. The St Petersburg desire to evacuate primarily for financial considerations was not shared by Russians on the spot. The army, the railway officials and the bankers on the whole reported their belief that, if evacuation was carried out, the railway guards left would not be able to deal with attacks on the line from Chinese quarters. The other problem was that the longer the negotiations took, the more difficult would it be physically to carry out any pledge to withdraw troops according to a time-limit.

As in the previous case, the draft Russo-Chinese agreement reached Tokyo and London in umpteen versions from umpteen sources, each of which claimed to be 'authoritative'. Towards the end of October there was a strong indication that signature was imminent. Lamsdorf hedged and would not communicate a text to any foreign government while it was under negotiation, claiming indeed that the Chinese had come to him for a settlement, not he to the Chinese. Hence the only course of action left was for the powers to protest to the Chinese against the inclusion of any stipulations which were opposed to treaty rights. Since the Chinese were opposed to a revised banking agreement, they took advantage of the interest shown by the outside powers.

It was a less urgent crisis than had afflicted Katō in the spring. In the first place, the Russian terms seemed from the leaked versions to be more moderate. Secondly there seemed to be some evidence that the Russians were feeling the financial pinch of keeping so many troops tied down in Manchuria. There was therefore a notion that a moderate treaty was in Russia's long-term interest. But Witte wanted some banking agreement as a *quid pro quo* for the phased withdrawal of Russian troops. On the other side, it was already known in Peking that Li Hung-chang was seriously ill. In irreverent mood, Francis Bertie wrote: 'Li Hung Chang is dying, peace be to his pigtail! But I suppose that some other subservient but not equally able servant of the Russian Government will be forthcoming in High Places in China.'[12] This illustrates the consciousness of Li's strong commitment to Russia, but at the same time the strong respect for his abilities. In fact, he died on 7 November, working to the end. With him the existing negotiations over Manchuria lapsed. His successor was Prince Ching (I-k'uang) who was a lesser figure and had little claim to being a world statesman as Li was. Ching stayed away from the capital to make sure that negotiations dropped and, as he busied himself with the return to Peking of the Chinese court from Sian, he was not available for further talks.

Li Hung-chang has been an important figure in this study and his death was an important turning-point. He had received bribes from the special Li Fund and had more recently become the apostle of the reluctant acceptance of the Russian protectorate over Manchuria.[13] His death was a great loss to the Russian interest; and he left no strong pro-Russian official as a successor. He had been at his desk up to thirty hours before his death, completely determined, as he had always been, not to let anyone else dabble in affairs while he was still able to cope. This is not to support the contemporary foreign view that he was merely a Russian stooge. Li was a formidable negotiator who recognized the weakness of the hand he had to play. It was his task to make the best of a bad job.

The breakdown in the Russo-Chinese talks was only a temporary one. When it occurred, the Russians announced boldly that, until there was a treaty, their occupation would be prolonged. In fact, however, things were moving adversely against them. On the one hand, even with the railways coming increasingly into operation, the provisioning of their troops scattered over a vast area was a major headache, especially when weather conditions were bad. On the other, there were the budgetary considerations which were the concern of Witte: it was desirable to reduce the cost of the Manchurian operation. In December, therefore, Prince Ching agreed to resume the negotiations with Russia. With the approaching return of the Court to the capital, it was desirable to regularize the position in the north-east and 'normalize' the situation there. The Russians still persisted with the demand for a banking agreement which held things up. Ching positively refused to countenance any such agreement and the issue was allowed to slip out of the discussions in January 1902.[14]

ITŌ'S TALKS WITH RUSSIA

One of the most important events in the run-up to the Russo-Japanese war is the visit of Marquis Itō to Russia in November–December 1901. But Itō's journey to the major cities of the United States and Europe was on a vast scale and is part of global history. In this study we have for reasons of space to confine our attention to the visit to St Petersburg alone and the Russian reaction to the exclusion of other aspects of the trip.

Towards the end of August Itō announced his intention of visiting the United States in order to help him recuperate. When another of the genro, Inoue, heard this, he urged Itō to travel to Russia for conversations and sought to get the prime minister's approval for this. Katsura only promised to convene meetings of the cabinet and genro.

At a meeting of the genro on 13 September, there was a rumpus between Itō and Yamagata who reminded him that, if he went to Russia, he must report to Tokyo and not run ahead to negotiate on his own. This was clear evidence of the widespread distrust of Itō's 'soft' views on Russia so far as they were known. So he did not receive any mandate from the government, though he was not discouraged from going. He set off on 18 September from Yokohama and travelled through the United States until he sailed from New York to Boulogne and finally reached Paris on 4 November. He was there paid every courtesy by the French government.[15]

Before his departure Itō had met Izvolskii who was overjoyed when he heard that Itō proposed to visit St Petersburg. Izvolskii had long held that, if there were to be negotiations, they were most likely to succeed with Marquis Itō. Itō's resignation as prime minister had been a bitter disappointment to him. Now that an initiative had evidently been taken from the Japanese side, Izvolskii's dreams were revived. The Russian foreign minister was similarly excited and sought the aid of his ally, the French.[16] But it has to be remembered that the day after the elder statesman set sail, the new foreign minister, Komura, arrived and took office, uncommitted to whatever had been arranged with Itō.

With the British negotiations so far advanced, the Japanese leaders had to decide how to proceed with Itō's approach to Russia. On 20 November Katsura asked the elder statesman to go to the Russian capital without delay, thus reversing his earlier stand. Itō accordingly speeded up his itinerary and reached St Petersburg on the 25th. But he felt that some clarification was still necessary, in view of the requests he had received from the London legation to confine himself to 'a pleasure trip' or 'an informal exchange of views' in the light of the progress which had been made with the British alliance. Did Katsura share this view? In a message which reached Russia on 27 November, the prime minister asked Itō to confine himself to an off-the-record (*zatsudan teki*) exchange of views. Such language could only be rarely used to a genro. This suggests that Katsura was putting a partial damper on Itō's activities in St Petersburg.[17]

On the following day Itō was received most cordially by the tsar at Tsarskoye Selo. He was presented with the Gold Cordon of St Alexander Nevsky and urged by the tsar to return to Japan by the Trans-Siberian route. Lamsdorf also gave a state reception for Itō who could not have had warmer hospitality. But, in the absence of any clarification from Katsura, he deliberately delayed fulfilling the political purpose of his visit. He knew from telegrams received that his fellow-genro, Inoue, was arguing that Japan should only go ahead with Britain after Itō had found out how far Russia would give way over Korea; but that Katsura, Komura and Hayashi felt that this course was dishonourable. At all events, he declined to have political talks until some points were clarified.

Itō may also have become vigilant after an encounter he had with Major Tanaka Giichi, later to play an influential role in the 1903 crisis. Tanaka had been living in St Petersburg since 1898, not as an attaché but as a ryūgakusei, a student abroad. Since, however, he was aged thirty-eight and had the rank of major, it was likely that he was engaged in intelligence work. He describes himself at this period as 'rambō' (rowdy, violent, lawless) and 'hōju' (self-indulgent). As a clansman of Itō, he felt bold enough to offer him his advice and, as one of Japan's few Russian experts, suggested that Itō drop his idea about 'Man-Kan kōkan' which would only play into Russia's hands.[18]

We have full accounts of the meetings on 2–3 December when Itō had his conversations with Lamsdorf and Witte in both the Russian and Japanese versions. Itō was not attended by anyone from the Japanese legation. Presumably the reason was that he did not want his conversations to be regarded as 'official' or authorized, while the legation had in any case been instructed to keep its distance. Instead Itō was accompanied by Tsuzuki Keiroku, who had earlier escorted Yamagata in 1896 and was described on this occasion as Itō's interpreter. Though Tsuzuki was not a professional interpreter, he spoke French and German. But it seems odd that Tsuzuki and Lamsdorf should not have carried on a perfectly good conversation in French, in which they were both proficient. But, whatever the difficulties in communication, the records of the two sides match quite well.

Lamsdorf was cautious, well-prepared and deflatory. His was the voice of a man who thought that time was on the side of his country because of the railway and there was no need to make concessions to the Japanese. Russia was content with the existing Nishi–Rosen note which conferred reciprocal rights in Korea. Hence the earlier roles had been reversed: this time Japan was seeking change and an improvement in terms, while Russia was content with the status quo. At all events, Lamsdorf, though he poured a douche of iced water on Itō's ideas in conversation, asked for a statement of his demands in writing, to which Itō agreed cordially enough.

In marked contrast Witte was expansive and typically forthcoming. Russia sought nothing in Korea, he said, and was quite content to give Japan her head there. He mentioned that Russia had just declared that she would withdraw from Manchuria without fail: 'In Russia as in Japan there are those who declare that we must capture the whole world. In our army and navy those who have such ambitions are especially numerous. But our Government and Emperor do not think thus.'[19] In his bluff and hearty way Witte had highlighted one of the factors which Japan and Russia had in common: the difficulty of controlling the views and activities of the military abroad. Witte left the parleys to see Lamsdorf who had just had his weekly audience with the tsar. There was abundant consultation about Itō's ideas.

The nub of Itō's proposals which were written in English is the clause calling on Russia to recognize 'Japan's freedom of action in its *political,* industrial and commercial aspects and her *exclusive* right to help Korea by giving her advice . . . and military aid' (my emphasis). His terms were entirely about Japan's demands in Korea and made no mention of Manchuria. Contrary to what might have been expected, there was no specific suggestion of Man-Kan kōkan. There can be several explanations for this: perhaps Itō was influenced by Tanaka and refused to put in writing Japan's true feelings about Manchuria; perhaps Itō, the experienced negotiator, set forth only Japan's initial bargaining position. Itō's concentration on Korea seemed to confirm the Russians in their existing view that Japan's objections were confined to that peninsula. So Lamsdorf in his preliminary reaction and later in his formal reply deals cursorily with Manchuria but emphasizes Korea and Russia's desire to share privileges there. Russia was not prepared to allow Japan political or exclusive rights there.

Conversation turned to how Russia's response could reach Itō. He was due to leave St Petersburg immediately after the meeting in accordance with his (for some reason not entirely clear) inflexible schedule. The elder statesman proposed that letters might be addressed to him in Berlin where he would be staying for 10–14 days. Lamsdorf asked how it would suit if he arranged further discussions in Paris. There then followed (in the Japanese account) what was in retrospect an interesting fragment of conversation:

> Itō: That would make it too late.
> Lamsdorf: Is this matter as urgent as all that?

Despite this hint, Russia's foreign minister did not glean that it was a matter of now or never for him.[20]

Itō left Russia empty-handed and disappointed. He had no mission but he had a purpose that had been frustrated. He had however clearly exceeded the request of Katsura who wanted his trip to Russia to be the occasion of a casual exchange of views and not for the passing over of a set of written terms.

Acting by Russian standards with great dispatch, Lamsdorf obtained the views of Witte, Kuropatkin and the navy and passed them together to the tsar on 13 December. Kuropatkin made his detailed comments on 10 December and actually redrafted the agreement to bring it into line with military and, to some extent, naval thinking. His ideas are constructive:

> We have decided to evacuate our troops from Manchuria . . . Even if we keep the Northern parts of Manchuria in a certain state of dependence, we have every reason to believe that a break with Japan will be avoided.
> Consequently our new agreement with Japan ought not to be bought at too high a price. Complete renunciation of Korea by conceding her to Japan is too high a price . . . we should use every means to hinder Japanese forces being moved to Korea and stationed there permanently.[21]

But basically the army minister and the navy minister when his remarks eventually came in were favourable to an agreement with Japan, albeit a fairly unyielding one.

Lamsdorf obtained the tsar's approval to a counter-draft which was largely his own and sent off his reply on 14 December. It was carried by special messenger accompanying the crown prince to Germany to ensure secrecy and handed over by the Russian ambassador in Berlin on 17 December. It covered:

1. Mutual guarantee of Korean independence.
2. Joint agreement (or Japan agrees) not to use Korean territory or any portion of it for military objectives.
3. Joint agreement that military installations of a kind to menace the complete freedom of passage through the Korean straits would not be placed on the Korean coastline (or Japan agrees . . .).
4. Russia admits the following items to Japan: (a) that Japan possesses freedom of action in Korea in respect of industrial and commercial connections; (b) that Japan after prior consultations with Russia has superior rights to help Korea by active support and thus make her conscious of obligations inseparable from better government; (c) Russia includes in the above military help if necessary to quell disturbances prejudicing peaceful relations between Korea and Japan.
5. Former agreements are completely cancelled by this agreement.
6. Japan acknowledges Russia's superior rights in that part of the territory of the Chinese Empire adjoining the Russian border and undertakes not to infringe Russia's freedom of action in that area.
7. On the occasions prescribed in article 4 Japan undertakes not to send forces beyond the number which the situation dictates and to recall troops immediately the mission has been achieved and agrees that having fixed clearly in advance the area of a zone adjoining the Russian frontier, the Japanese army will never cross that boundary.[22]

If Lamsdorf had been unconciliatory in conversation, this draft was even more limiting. It met the needs of Kuropatkin over restricting Japan's military operations and Shishkin for the freedom of passage for vessels moving between Vladivostok and Port Arthur. Clause 7 was a provision formulated by the Russian military authorities. But the final version was basically the work of Lamsdorf with Witte assisting, and Lamsdorf succeeded in persuading the tsar to overturn some of Kuropatkin's more extreme suggestions.

In his explanatory letter to Itō, Lamsdorf first declared Russia's enthusiasm for a permanent agreement with Japan in order to prevent misunderstandings arising. But Russia required assurances, first, regarding Manchuria and second, over zones of Korea adjoining the Russian frontier. Moreover Lamsdorf asked for 'some slight compensation for all the important rights which Russia is to grant to

Japan in Korea'. This was to take the form of Japan's recognition of Russia's preferential rights – not exclusive rights – in Manchuria. Since this was the most that Russia would give Japan in Korea, there was only a slight degree of reciprocity.[23]

In looking at Lamsdorf's terms, we see that they were mainly concerned with Korea where Russia had no intention of *désintéressement*. But by clause 6 Japan was asked to recognize Russia's preferential rights in all regions of the Chinese Empire bordering on her frontiers and undertake not to infringe Russia's freedom of action in that area. This clause was evidently intended not to apply to all Manchuria, though this is of course doubtful. It presumably referred to the railway lands of North Manchuria on which Kuropatkin and his associates had set their hearts at this stage. This was of course Russia's preliminary bargaining position. But there was no sign here of substantially reducing her claims in Korea. It was not therefore the Man-Kan kōkan for which Itō was hoping.

How did Itō, now spending a fortnight in former haunts in Berlin, and receiving honours and attention from the kaiser, view this message? Almost as soon as he had reached Berlin, he had telegraphed on 6 December that he found the Russian leaders ready to accept the following as a basis for discussions:

> If Japan and Russia will guarantee jointly the independence of Korea, desisting from using Korean territory or any portion of it for any purpose of military strategy, and will not construct fortifications such as gun emplacements on the Korean coastline so as to menace the free passage of the Straits of Tsushima, Russia will acknowledge Japan's special freedom of action in Korea in matters industrial, commercial and political and in such military measures as are needed for the suppression of civil disturbances and the like.[24]

Basically an honest, if optimistic, account of Russia's position. In conclusion he stated: 'today presents a suitable chance of making an agreement with the only other country in the world which has interests in Korea. I heartily recommend an amicable agreement with Russia, which will become impossible after the conclusion of the British agreement.'

TOKYO REACTS TO ITŌ'S OVERTURE

Itō's logic did not appeal to those in Tokyo who had Britain's final draft of the Japanese alliance burning a hole in their green-topped tables. Cabinet, genro and emperor agreed that they could not disregard or delay the British draft in the light of such uncertain gestures by Russia and notified Itō accordingly on 13 December.[25] This was understandable enough because even Itō's enthusiasm for some form of settlement with Russia had suffered a considerable setback.

When, eventually, the Japanese statesman received the written counter-proposals through the Russian ambassador in Berlin, he found that from Japan's standpoint they were some degrees less favourable than the impression he had earlier formed. Just before he left the German capital for Brussels, he told Katsura: 'Lamsdorf volunteered that, using this draft as a basis, formal negotiations might be opened in Tokyo ... If we miss this opportunity, I fear that such a favourable opportunity will perhaps not recur in the near future.'[26]

Itō again supported the continuation of negotiations in Tokyo. On 21 December Katsura replied in a strong, almost brutal, telegram in which he argued that, if Japan were to make a treaty in order to deprive Russia of her privileges in Korea, Japan would have to conclude an agreement which would be inconsistent with her former professions over Manchuria: 'Since the crisis in Manchuria developed we have undertaken responsibilities to various foreign powers. Such responsibilities certainly cannot be neglected if Japanese honour is to be respected in the world. This policy started during your Ministry; and I inherited it and have consistently valued it as a wise policy.'[27]

He went on to explain that in February as a result of combined representations by the various powers Japan brought to nothing the Manchurian convention which was being negotiated between Russia and China.

Moving on to the above-quoted phrase in Itō's telegram, Katsura commented that Russia's position in Manchuria had been recognized in Nishi's memorandum of 1898 and Komura's proposals of 1900: 'Our policy has changed on this with the march of events ... We used to ask that Russia's position in Manchuria might be equivalent to Japan's in Korea. But our current proposals must on this occasion discard such a basis.'[28]

This was of course the moment of truth. Katsura was saying that, because of the events of 1901 in Manchuria, Japan could not 'disinterest' herself there any longer. This implied that for the Katsura cabinet at least Man-Kan kōkan was no longer an acceptable basis. Itō could legitimately counter that he should have been told this in September rather than in December after his negotiations in Russia. Instead he complained that Katsura was misjudging his objectives by looking at Lamsdorf's counterdraft: 'My aim is to create circumstances more favourable to Japan than an agreement on a reciprocal basis but, if absolutely necessary as a final concession, to yield even a reciprocal agreement.'[29] In other words, Itō was hoping for more than Man-Kan kōkan but was prepared in the last resort to fall back on that position, thinking that Russia would, on account of her political difficulties and her financial position, accept his stipulations: 'Even though we conclude an agreement with Britain either to change or to maintain the status quo in Korea, we will not benefit Japan in the slightest unless we on our part reach the milepost of a Russo-Japanese Agreement on the same problems.'

With this indignant blast, Itō set off from Brussels to London. Soon after his arrival he received two lengthy telegrams from Katsura of a suitably placatory kind. While he argued that there was after all no great difference between his view and Itō's on suitable concessions from Japan to Russia, 'you must get Russia to concede that she has no alternative to withdrawing from Manchuria and must not use any part of her territory there for military purposes. In short, the reciprocal principle should confine Russian military activity in Manchuria to suppression of disorder or revolt or protection of railways.' Japan must try to solve the Manchurian problem on a basis that she could accept for Korea – a modification of Man-Kan kōkan.[30] In the second telegram Katsura expressed the hope that Russia would make a binding agreement not to hinder the linking of the Korean railway with the Russian Chinese Eastern railway and the Anglo-Chinese railway between Shanhaikuan and Niuchuang. Probably this was further than Itō himself would have gone but it showed that Katsura – and behind him presumably the Japanese army and Komura – had considerable ambitions for his country in Manchuria and was not prepared to give any promise of detachment. (Lamsdorf may of course have had suspicions along these lines on the basis of Izvolskii's reporting.)

Katsura's views arrived long after Itō had already replied to the Russians from Brussels. He had been unable to do so before his departure from Berlin in detail but had taken a week to study the matter amid a heavy schedule of engagements in the Belgian capital. His reply was that he did not doubt the conciliatory spirit of Russian statesmen but from the counter-proposals could not yet see much prospect of the countries easily reaching an agreement of any permanence. Over Manchuria, Itō commented, Russia's counter-demand was both sweeping and unrealistic and lost its meaning by its vagueness: 'Firstly I am anxious to know definitely what policy and measures it is the genuine intention of the Russian government to apply in that region and secondly I cannot obtain any definite impression about the precise zones in which Russia wishes to exercise her power.' Over Korea, he replied that Russia's counter-proposals 'return to the former view that Japan should act as a sort of custodian and be relegated to the status of a party carrying out ordinances on which both countries had previously agreed. Japan's special freedom of action under our former agreement is incompatible with and opposed in principle to conferring beforehand about her actions'.[31] Itō confessed that he was doubtful about the advantage of referring the Russian draft to his government as a basis for future negotiations and asked for further time to study Lamsdorf's proposals. He declined Witte's invitation to travel back to Japan by the Trans-Siberian railway.

At this point Itō must have been forlorn. He had not received the expected encouragement from Russia. Even if he had, he never intended to go back to St Petersburg for further negotiations. More serious for his peace of mind, his advice on the British alliance had been rejected by the authorities in Tokyo. He told Katsura on 12 December that Japan's freedom of independent action should not be in any way impaired so that she might, at some favourable opportunity, come to an agreement with Russia at least on the Korean question.[32] But in response to a conciliatory but firm telegraphic reply from Katsura, he replied from Berlin the following day in a mood of resignation:

> Even if we join in an alliance of a defensive character with Britain, on which you have already embarked, there would still be room for us simultaneously to come to terms with Russia over Korea, that is to say, we must reserve the right of independent action to reach an agreement with Russia, even though it involves perhaps inevitably considerable concessions (say) in Manchuria.[33]

Even if his schemes had failed on both points, Itō took comfort from the above idea and proceeded with his journey to London. His activities there have been discussed in detail elsewhere and need not be repeated here. In conversations with Lord Lansdowne, he said that he was not himself opposed to the British alliance and asked whether Britain had any objection to Japan's seeking an agreement with Russia over Korea. To everyone's surprise, Lansdowne agreed provided it was not incompatible with the British alliance. Itō did not see why this should be so. In a deeply ironic way, therefore, the major success of Itō's European journey was achieved in Britain.[34]

RUSSIA AFTER ITŌ

How did Lamsdorf and the Russians react to the cool response from Itō in Brussels? We know only indirectly. Lamsdorf was optimistic but had one worry. This was connected with Itō's announced intention to return to Paris *en route* for his steamer at Naples. It was probable, he thought, that the question of an understanding between Japan and Russia would come up for discussion between Delcassé and Itō. Lamsdorf, perhaps rather fearing Delcassé's brokerage, instructed his ambassador to put the foreign minister in the picture about the discussions which had taken place:

> Marquis Itō has presented quite unofficially a notice containing four points and making clear the solution which Japan would like to see given

to the Korean question. Count Lamsdorf, after examining this notice, observed to Itō that it only included very large demands for concessions in favour of Japan, while all agreements presuppose the stipulation of advantages equal or equivalent for both contracting parties. Itō having recognized the justice of this remark, the notice was revised and completed by the insertion of conditions on which the Russian cabinet agreed to negotiate; these conditions were as follows:

1. Independence of Korea; 2. Prohibition of using Korean territory for a strategic object; 3. Liberty of the Korean Straits.

... Itō's notice, modified in this way, was sent to him in Berlin in order to serve as the basis for the conclusion of a Russo-Japanese accord.

Shortly after, Itō acknowledged receipt to Lamsdorf by a letter sent from Brussels, in which, while making reservations as regards the Russian cabinet's proposals, he added that he would give a final reply after studying the question deeply. This attitude on the part of Itō leads one to suppose that he does not wish to decide before assessing the chances of success which his mission could have in concluding a loan for Japan in Europe.[35]

There is no reason to believe that this was not a genuine summary of the position as Russia saw it. She saw France as the likely donor of financial aid to Japan and expected therefore that Delcassé would have some leverage with Itō. In our interpretation, the conclusion of a loan did not enter Itō's calculations and so Russia's appreciation of the situation was seriously distorted.

Lamsdorf comes out of the incident as perplexed as Itō. In February 1902 the British and Japanese representatives were to give him notice of their new alliance. The French ambassador reported that Lamsdorf was greatly affected by this news 'so absolutely unexpected by him'. Evidently he excused himself on the ground that Izvolskii had not in any way prepared him for such a disaster. He was too bowled over to attempt an immediate appreciation of the treaty.[36] Lamsdorf must have asked himself whether the counter-proposals which he had sent to Itō had been so unacceptable to the Japanese that they had gone over to the British side. He may have assumed that Itō, in his disappointment, had authorized the clinching of the alliance when he was in London. Such was the common perception of the powers that the elder statesmen had in those days. In fact, it had not happened that way at all. Itō had not taken a large part in bringing about the British alliance, though he had had talks with Lord Lansdowne. He was thinking in a much broader perspective: of talks with Russia under the umbrella of the Anglo-Japanese alliance.

We have seen in this chapter an important series of negotiations between Japan and Russia governing the future of north-east Asia. From the Japanese side, it might be described as personal, unofficial and exploratory. Its results were disappointing to those who wanted a settlement with Russia and expected by those who did not. It was an endeavour of one of the political groupings within Japan with doubtful authorization. From the Russian side, there were difficulties about assessing the Itō mission but, granted that, her statesmen were not very conciliatory. Knowing, as we now do, the general consensus about the need for a substantial withdrawal from at least southern Manchuria, they need not have been so rigid in their approach. This was, however, to be the prototype for later negotiations between the two sides in 1903, just as it was the follow-up to the Man-Kan kōkan diplomacy, which had led to the Nishi–Rosen protocol of 1898.

REFERENCES AND NOTES

1. C. C. Tan, *The Boxer Catastrophe*, p. 236.
2. Lamsdorf to Kuropatkin and Witte, 1 Aug. 1901, 'Eve of War', pp. 234–5.
3. Lamsdorf to Giers and Izvolskii, 30 July 1901 and replies, 'Eve of War', pp. 234, 240.
4. Lamsdorf to colleagues, 1 Aug. 1901, 'Eve of War', pp. 234–8.
5. A. Malozemoff, *Russian Far Eastern Policy*, pp. 168–9.
6. Ibid., pp. 168–70.
7. Hart to Hioki, 2 Aug. 1901, *NGB* 33, Supp. no. 1858.
8. Tyrrell to Hardinge, 20 Nov. 1901, Hardinge Papers 3.
9. Salisbury to Lansdowne, 9 Nov. 1901, FO China 1510.
10. B. A. Romanov, *Russia in Manchuria*, p. 436, fn. 155, quoting Alekseyev telegram of 30 June 1901.
11. Morrison to V. Chirol, 7 July 1902, Morrison Correspondence, vol. 1, p. 195.
12. Bertie to Hardinge, 5 Nov. 1901, Hardinge Papers 3.
13. G. A. Lensen, *Balance of Intrigue*, pp. 508–13.
14. E. M. Satow, *Korea and Manchuria between Russia and Japan*, pp. 163–8.
15. For greater detail of Itō's Russian trip, see I. H. Nish, 'Itō in St Petersburg', pp. 90–5.
16. Izvolskii to Lamsdorf, 16 Sept. 1901, and Lamsdorf to Nicholas II, 6 Nov. 1901, 'Eve of War', pp. 241, 247–51.
17. *Itō Hirobumi Hiroku*, Telegrams from Itō's journey, nos. 19–23 (hereafter cited as *Itō Hiroku*); Japan, Foreign Ministry, *Gaimushō no 100-nen*, vol. 1, p. 420.
18. *Tanaka Giichi Denki*, vol. 1, pp. 175–6.
19. *Itō Hiroku*, no. 27.
20. *Itō Hiroku*, no. 30.
21. Kuropatkin to Lamsdorf, 10 Dec. 1901, 'Eve of War', pp. 260–1.
22. Taken from the translation of the Japanese version in *Itō Hiroku*, no. 52.
23. *Itō Hiroku*, no. 51.
24. *Itō Hiroku*, no. 34.
25. *Itō Hiroku*, nos. 45–6.
26. *Itō Hiroku*, no. 53.
27. *Itō Hiroku*, no. 58.
28. Ibid.
29. *Itō Hiroku*, no. 60.
30. *Itō Hiroku*, no. 61.

31. *Itō Hiroku,* no. 60.
32. *Itō Hiroku,* no. 43.
33. *Itō Hiroku,* no. 48.
34. I. H. Nish, *The Anglo-Japanese Alliance,* pp. 201–3.
35. Ouroussoff to Delcassé, 4 Jan. 1902, *DDF,* 2nd series, vol. 2 (1902), no. 4.
36. Montebello to Delcassé, 13 Feb. 1902, *DDF,* 2nd series, vol. 2 (1902), no. 84.

Chapter 8

KURINO, KOMURA AND KOREA (1902–3)

The drama of Itō's visit to St Petersburg concealed what must be described as the first Russo-Japanese top-level talks. Although the talks were a disappointment to both sides, they were an earnest that both sides wanted to preserve the peace and realized that there was a risk of its being broken. The Russians emerged from the talks unsure of themselves and, when the Anglo-Japanese alliance was announced, rather bruised. They chose to interpret Itō's visit as part of the Japanese 'alliance strategy' – which it was not – rather than the action of one of the opinion-forming groups off its own bat – which it was. Itō was displeased with the Russians who had not conceded the Japanese case over Korea and also with Katsura in Tokyo who had begun to take a new and tougher line over Manchuria while Itō was in Europe. But he was a wise enough statesman to know that he could not expect to attain his object at his first attempt.

The historian, seeing a broader spectrum of events, is able to say that Itō's visit did accomplish important results. By obtaining from Britain the assurance that there would be no objection to Japan negotiating directly with Russia despite the existence of the Anglo-Japanese alliance, he had opened the way to a second round of exploratory talks with Russia without any risk of a charge of duplicity on the part of Britain. In this sense, Itō's 'off the record' talks were followed up on an official level; and the respective positions of the two countries on Manchuria and Korea were further explored, as this chapter will show.

KURINO AT ST PETERSBURG

Kurino Shinichirō (1851–1937), one of Japan's senior diplomats, returned to Paris in mid-December. A protégé of Itō, he arrived there in time to meet the elder statesman, who was on the rebound from London and on his way back to Japan via Italy. Kurino heard from Itō on 7 January for the first time that negotiations for an alliance with Britain had made great headway in London. This made him so disgusted that he thought seriously of resigning from the foreign service.[1]

Kurino had seen service in the United States where he had been an acquaintance of Theodore Roosevelt. In 1897 he was appointed as minister to Paris, where he won a reputation as one who wanted to bring about reconciliation between his country and Russia.[2] After something of a fracas with the Japanese foreign minister, he returned home in October 1900 and awaited reposting. On the day following Komura's appointment as foreign minister, Kurino was asked whether he would agree to be posted to St Petersburg. He claims to have replied that, if the Japanese government decided to consolidate its policy towards Russia on the lines that he wanted and conclude a treaty which had a positive character, he would accept this special assignment. He drew up a long memorandum giving his views; and Prime Minister Katsura on 16 October gave a party at his official residence where he, Komura and Kurino exchanged views about it. As a result, Kurino finally agreed to accept the new posting. His memorandum was an important argument for Man-Kan kōkan and stressed Japan's claims for freedom of action in Korea – in short, they were views very close to Itō's.[3]

It was depressing for Kurino to hear from Itō that a British alliance was at such an advanced state. At Itō's suggestion he enquired whether Tokyo's attitude had changed and passed on his findings to Itō in Naples: 'Katsura and Komura desire to come to an arrangement with Russia on Korea. But, while assenting to views set out in my memorandum, they do not propose to give final orders to conclude a [Russian] agreement but rather instruct me to try when I reach my new post to seek out the basis for an agreement.'[4] Kurino thought that this was rather a shifty approach. But it was also cautious and not out of line with Britain's thinking.

One of Kurino's first tasks when he moved to the Russian capital was to inform Lamsdorf about the conclusion of the British alliance on 30 January. He reported that the Russian foreign minister received it with utter astonishment since he had apparently been blinded by the Itō mission and failed to recognize the secret diplomacy which had been proceeding in London. Lamsdorf acknowledged – and it was widely admitted in the press – that this was a signal failure of Russian diplomacy.[5]

The clauses of the British alliance which are relevant to this study were those which offered a guarantee of independence and territorial integrity for Korea and China (and by extension Manchuria). Regarding Korea, it was stated that Japan was interested in a peculiar degree '*politically* as well as commercially and industrially' there and that it was admissible for her to safeguard those interests if they were threatened. By this Japan had been conceded points which Itō had failed to win in St

Petersburg. By implication, the whole alliance gave Japan *inter alia* protection against aggressive action by a third power in east Asia, which could only be Russia.

Like any treaty, the alliance did not represent a complete meeting of minds. Britain had some reservations about Japan's willingness in the longer term to permit Korea's territorial integrity. Moreover, though the alliance had sprung from the Manchurian dilemma, Britain and Japan had separate interests there. Under the Scott–Muraviev agreement (1899), Britain had recognized Manchuria as a Russian sphere of interest, safeguarding only the Northern Extension railway from Peking to Mukden and the interests of British bondholders therein. Japan had no such commitments and was divided over how much leverage Russia should be allowed in Manchuria and what action the Japanese should take if she overstepped the mark. Moreover the alliance made no provision for military cooperation, though a separate note covered naval cooperation. Only in the months before the war with Russia broke out was the looseness of some of the terminology of the alliance revealed.

The other relevant consideration is whether the Anglo-Japanese alliance encouraged Japan to go to war. This was to be a common accusation in Russia which became strongly Anglophobe in 1904. This view was to be echoed by Russian historians later. B. A. Romanov, writing in 1928, speaks of Japan as Britain's infantryman, that is, that Japan would fight Britain's battles for her. Later A. L. Galperin also speaks of Britain egging Japan on to make war on Russia in east Asia.[6] I have argued elsewhere against such views, stating that Britain had made it clear during negotiations that she did not discourage Japan from entering into practical discussions with Russia. The effect of the alliance treaty was not to egg Japan on but rather to strengthen Japan's hand if she decided to proceed with negotiations with Russia and, in the last resort, to strengthen Japan's hand if she decided to make war.[7]

The British cabinet generally accepted the cogency of the arguments Itō put before them during his visit to London. Itō's account of these read:

> I am myself not one of those who distrust the Anglo-Japanese
> negotiations and am generally in favour of their success. ... I realize that
> for Britain to engage in war with Russia on behalf of Manchuria is
> something she would not relish under any circumstances. Before my
> departure Japan seemed to be trying to oppose absolutely any Russian
> move to push her interests into Manchuria. There is an agreement [of
> 1898] in being between Russia and Japan regarding Korea; and Japan is
> on that account much restrained at present but cannot revoke it. This
> agreement is something which Japan has borne long enough and cannot
> allow to continue. I have no thought of pursuing a two-headed policy
> towards Russia and Britain nor do I support a Russo-Japanese alliance. I

only desire by the most peaceful methods to reach a complete agreement with Russia by moving the milepost of our existing Russo-Japanese agreement just a bit forward in order to protect our interests in Korea.[8]

Britain having accepted this, Japan was free to make her approaches to St Petersburg. This is a reminder that the alliance did not turn Japan into a fief of Britain but, on the contrary, increased Japan's capacity for independent action and thinking without placing her under an elaborate obligation to have advance consultations. To cite an example, Japan refused to accept the provisions of the Anglo-Chinese commercial treaty of 1902 (the Mackay treaty) as the basis of her trading with China.

While Britain in good conscience could justify her action as not provoking war in the east, she had, of course, embarked on a risky course. There was a definite risk of war if Russia was not conciliatory towards Japan. But there was the hope that war could be localized, firstly to the 'extreme east' to which the alliance was limited, and secondly to the two powers directly involved. Lansdowne, who, more than any other, was responsible for the alliance on the British side, wrote reflectively to the king:

The Anglo-Japanese Alliance, although not intended to encourage the Japanese Government to resort to extremities, had, and was sure to have, the effect of making Japan feel that she might try conclusions with her great rival in the Far East – free from all risk of a European coalition such as that which had on a previous occasion deprived her of the fruits of victory [the coalition of Russia, France and Germany in 1895].[9]

Lansdowne's reference to the Dreibund reminds us that Japan had some old scores to settle with the Russians: the humiliation of 1895 by the Dreibund intervention; the seizure and leasing of Port Arthur in 1898. The desire for a showdown with Russia was present in the minds of some Japanese well before the alliance came into being. The alliance could offer a naval protective shield if Japan had grounds of her own volition to go to war; but it was not itself the motive force for going to war.

The alliance was aimed not just at Russia but also by implication at the Franco-Russian alliance in east Asia. It was not unnatural, therefore, that there should be some Franco-Russian response. In a way the alliance might have been a blessing for Russia by inducing France to go further with Russia in east Asia – to extend the Dual Alliance to the east. But France was not ready to become involved in north-east Asia and generally stalled discussion. When Lamsdorf raised the matter of responding to the alliance, the two could only agree on a 'milk-and-water' agreement, signed on 16 March 1902. It stated that the Anglo-Japanese convention had given them much satisfaction since it reaffirmed the essential principles which France and Russia had always accepted and which remained the basis of their present policy. They reserved to themselves eventually to take steps to assure the integrity and free development of China, in the event of the aggressive action of a third power or new troubles there threatening their own interests.[10] This applied the alliance to a modest extent to the East: but France almost immediately began to consider her obligations of a military kind under the Russian alignment and, as a way out, veered more and more towards some understanding with Britain. Although the two sides had initially stood together, it has to be said that in 1902 the Anglo-Japanese alliance tested the effectiveness of the Franco-Russian alliance in the east and found it wanting.[11] The British foreign office did not see the new measure as specially significant:

> The Franco-Russian agreement seems anodyne enough. Just as we were pushed to terms with Japan in order to avoid her running wild, it is natural that the French and the Russians should wish to be assured that neither party will put the other in a hole over Chinese questions without previous consultations.[12]

KOREAN NEGOTIATIONS

As we saw, Komura gave instructions to Kurino that, as soon as he took up office in St Petersburg, he should examine ways of resolving the Korean question, satisfactorily from Japan's point of view, and secretly take preliminary steps to open formal discussions in future. Pursuing these enquiries, Kurino was told by Lamsdorf on 24 February that, if the Japanese government genuinely wanted a friendly understanding with Russia with a view to securing peaceful relations and upholding the mutual interests of the two countries and if article IV of the Anglo-Japanese treaty did not prevent it, it would be possible to conclude a separate treaty (*betsuyaku*) between Japan and Russia. To this, the Japanese foreign minister replied on 12 March that the Japanese government earnestly hoped to reach an understanding with Russia on the question of Korea and there was nothing in the British treaty to prevent such a thing. The problem was to find an acceptable basis for the negotiations and an appropriate time to open them. Komura told Kurino that he must be careful that the success of the negotiations was not put at risk because there was internal confusion in the Russian government. On the following day Izvolskii told Komura in Tokyo that he had heard from Itō in detail about the exchange of views he had had with Lamsdorf. He wanted to know what the cabinet's reaction was. Komura, stating only his own personal opinion, assured him that the Japanese government had in the past always wanted an understanding with Russia over Korea and there was no change of any kind in its attitude at present.[13]

By July Komura thought that the power of the military party in Russia that had attacked Witte and Lamsdorf over the conclusion of the Anglo-Japanese treaty was gradually weakening and the strength of the civilian party was being restored. Assuming that it would be opportune to open negotiations as soon as possible, Komura on 7 July instructed Kurino to look into the effect on possible Russo-Japanese talks of the Franco-Russian declaration and President Loubet's visit to the Russian capital to give substance to the Franco-Russian alliance, to analyse whether they had changed the opinion of the Russian government on this issue, and what thoughts the Russian government had about the basis for negotiations. On 23 July Kurino on the basis of these instructions exchanged opinions with Lamsdorf on his individual responsibility and was told that since there was no objection from the side of the Anglo-Japanese alliance, there would be none from the side of Russia; and Itō's exchanges with Lamsdorf could form the basis for negotiation.[14] According to Russian accounts, Lamsdorf revealed on 4 August that Japan had suggested to Russia that the previous Russo-Japanese agreements be annulled and a new agreement formulated on the basis of recognition of Japan's paramount interests in Korea in return for Japan's recognition of Russia's paramount interests in Manchuria. On 14 September Kurino saw Lamsdorf and had a further private discussion on the basis of Itō's earlier talks. The Russian foreign minister was cordial and said that they could get down to business on the basis of balancing the rights and interests of Russia and Japan in Manchuria and Korea. He added, however, that he had to accompany the tsar on his autumn holiday to Livadia in the Crimea and would not return till the second half of December. The matter could not be pursued in this period.[15] Since the views of the Russian side had been clarified in such a positive manner, Komura passed over to Kurino what he wanted to be the nub of the talks, though it had not been considered by the government (1 November). Kurino appears to have reformulated them into a personal draft of five points (*shian*); but Komura asked Kurino to defer action since he disagreed with the formulation. It seems likely that Kurino, the ally of Itō, had erred too much towards Man-Kan kōkan for Komura's liking. 'Negotiations' were therefore held in suspense.[16]

Lamsdorf was obviously viewing these talks *sub specie aeternitatis* because he mentioned that Russia was about to appoint Rosen who was *persona grata* to Japan as minister to Tokyo. The implication was that Rosen might be able to push forward these overtures which had just been launched. But Rosen was not expected to arrive in Japan from Munich until April 1903 so there cannot have been a high priority in Lamsdorf's mind. The unexpected return of Rosen was due to the fact that Izvolskii had asked for family reasons to be transferred to some European posting. This became possible through the appointment of Count Benckendorff as ambassador to London, which left the Copenhagen legation empty. Izvolskii had not been a great success in

Tokyo, appearing to the Japanese to be brusque and stand-offish.[17] It may therefore be that there was a strong desire for his transfer after three years in Tokyo. Izvolskii records that, on his arrival at the Russian capital, he was received coldly by the tsar and the advice that he tried to give on far eastern affairs – and Japan in particular – was systematically disregarded. It suggests that the climate of the imperial court in the spring of 1903 was such that Izvolskii appeared to be far too conciliatory to the Japanese.[18]

Rosen, for his part, was happy to return to Japan where he had had a rich diplomatic experience. He was a believer in the expansion of the Russian empire in Asia and in the development of her Siberian empire. Yet he was neither authoritarian nor conservative. Rosen admits that there was a hiccough over his appointment in 1903. It appears that in a memorandum, presented after his reappointment to Japan had been announced, he had expressed views which were unwelcome to Witte and Lamsdorf:

> I held the scheme of the 'pacific conquest' of Manchuria, through 'pacific penetration' by means of railways, banks etc., to be impracticable; that, therefore, the huge expenditure incurred in the pursuit of such a scheme did not seem to me to have been justifiable; but that now we were bound in duty to defend the vast interests acquired and created by us in Manchuria at such onerous cost to the State.

These were in fact very trenchant criticisms of Witte's enterprise in Siberia and Manchuria. They were reflections on the Asian scene from the distant standpoint of Europe which were salutary. But, according to Rosen, he had unwittingly incurred the bitter enmity of the two statesmen who tried unsuccessfully 'to cause the Emperor to revoke my appointment'.[19]

Japan improved her position in Korea during 1902. The policy of the Japanese which became perceptibly stiffer, even if it remained cautious, was one of political and economic consolidation. Politically they placed their advisers at the Korean court and tried to build up a nucleus of pro-Japanese Korean politicians. But a permanent improvement in Japan's standing depended on economic penetration. Although it was difficult to procure supplies of suitable emigrants, the number of Japanese who went to settle in south-east Korea grew rapidly in 1903 to 30,000. Moreover, despite a shortage of Japanese capital for use overseas, Japan gradually assumed control of mines, posts and telegraphs. The Japanese-controlled Daiichi Bank was beginning to secure financial control as great as that of a central bank, issuing the only currency notes available and making loans to the Korean court. Steps were also taken to raise funds for the construction of the railway between Fusan and Seoul for which a lease had been granted in 1898 but on which work had been held up. Clearly, if the Korean peninsula was to be opened up to Japanese commerce, this rail artery was indispensable. A foreign loan for the purpose was raised in London in 1902, while the Japanese cabinet decided to vote almost two million yen towards specified projects in Korea in 1903, of which the building of the Seoul–Fusan railway had the top priority. Thus, Japanese enterprise in Korea was becoming notably more dynamic; and the government was becoming increasingly drawn in.[20]

This activity was motivated by hostility to Russia's entrenched position; and public opinion in Japan was intensely anti-Russian. But in other areas 1902 was not a bad year for Russo-Japanese relations. Thus the arrangement for fisheries around Sakhalin was renewed. Baron Matsukata on a round-the-world trip received a warm welcome in St Petersburg. In Tokyo a Russo-Japanese society was founded under Itō and Inoue in order to improve relations and foster good-neighbourly links. It attracted many adherents and held its inaugural meeting at the end of the year under prestigious auspices. So Izvolskii had not been inactive.[21]

RUSSO-KOREAN INITIATIVE

The Korean court in the autumn reverted to the proposal made two years earlier for an international guarantee for Korea. This was a device for ensuring that the present emperor and his family stayed in power and that the state was not submerged by the two competing giants, Japan and Russia. Not surprisingly the Koreans were supported in their endeavours – or, some would say, were fed with the idea – by some Russians. Most notable of these was Pavlov, who had been chargé at Seoul since 1898. In September he went on leave and was replaced by Weber who returned to his place of former glory to attend the fortieth anniversary celebrations of the Korean emperor's accession to his throne (which was in any case postponed). In Tokyo Pavlov paid calls on Izvolskii and rumours grew that he was active also in Paris when he took up the issue with Cassini on his way to Washington as Russian ambassador. For a proposal of this kind to succeed, American support was important because the most practical outcome was for Korea to be neutralized under the guarantee of the powers most involved, in this case, the United States, Russia and Japan. Rumours of Pavlov's activities were carried in the Tokyo newspapers. Japan, therefore, made it clear that it would be impossible for her to 'accede to any arrangement which might impair the actual position of Japan in Korea.' Since Japan was by this time in a dominant position, though not necessarily an unchallenged one, she saw the proposal as one hostile to herself. John Hay under the guidance of Minister Horace Allen appears to have been non-committal. When, therefore, the Japanese minister enquired about

135

Washington's reactions, Hay could honestly say that no proposal had been put to the United States government. Within a matter of months this particular proposal had been overshadowed by events in Manchuria. The Koreans, as we shall see, revived it in August 1903, as the prospect of war grew stronger. But Japan persisted in discarding the concept of international guarantee. For her 'the powers' were never disinterested. She wanted the peninsula for herself.[22]

Even if Japan offered a united front on this matter, there was in fact dissension just below the surface. Hayashi Gonsuke told the British minister in Seoul that Itō was not disinclined to the idea of Korean neutralization, presumably on the grounds that it would contribute to a peaceful solution for a troublesome area. Foreign Minister Komura, he said, would not hear of such a thing. Hayashi himself appears to have thought that Japan might be 'disposed to entertain the proposal if Russia carried out a *bona fide* evacuation of Manchuria but the mere concentration of Russian forces along the railway line would not satisfy Japan'.[23] In other words, some Japanese were prepared to treat Korean neutralization as a *quid pro quo*. But the reins were in the hands of Komura who would not entertain encroachments on Japan's power in the peninsula and was thoroughly suspicious of all formulae put forward by the Koreans. He saw the latter as acting as puppets for sinister Russian intentions. He was successful in steering the suggestion away from the meeting-table where it could be advocated by Itō. As the French minister remarked with some prescience, 'whenever the question of Korea is brought up in conversation, Japanese statesmen slip away and become silent'.[24]

REFERENCES AND NOTES

1. Hiratsuka Atsushi, *Shishaku Kurino Shinichirō den.*
2. *DDF,* 1st series, vol. 16 (1900), no. 198.
3. *Japanese Weekly Times,* 23 Nov. 1901.
4. Kurino to Itō, 20 Jan. 1902, *Itō Hiroku,* no. 71.
5. *DDF,* 2nd series, vol. 2 (1902), no. 84.
6. A. L. Galperin, *Anglo-Iaponskii Soiuz,* pp. 160, 177.
7. I. H. Nish, *The Anglo-Japanese Alliance,* pp. 202–3.
8. *Itō Hiroku,* no. 48.
9. Lansdowne to Edward VII, 18 Apr. 1904, [British] Royal Archives R/42; Newton, *Lord Lansdowne: A Biography,* London 1929, and Magnus, *King Edward VII,* London 1964, pp. 308–9, use 'condition' instead of 'coalition', I believe mistakenly.
10. *DDF,* 2nd series, vol. 2 (1902), no. 84.
11. Lamsdorf also proposed that the Dreibund of 1895 should be reconstituted with Russia and Germany and France; but Berlin did not respond. B. A. Romanov, *Russia in Manchuria,* pp. 249–50.

12. T. H. Sanderson to Scott, 26 Mar. 1902, Scott Papers 52,299.
13. Japan, Foreign Ministry, *Komura Gaikōshi*, vol. 1, pp. 297–300.
14. Ibid., p. 298.
15. A. Malozemoff, *Russian Far Eastern Policy*, p. 202.
16. *Komura Gaikōshi*, vol. 1, p. 300; *Nichi-Ro Kōshōshi*, Tokyo 1944.
17. *d'Anethan Dispatches*, pp. 154–5.
18. *The Memoirs of Alexander Iswolski*, London 1920 p. 21; Scott to T. H. Sanderson, 6 Aug. 1903, Scott Papers 52,304: 'Izvolsky is, I am told, under a cloud at present at the Foreign Office – he tried to air his views of the Far East at Lamsdorf's dinner and was pulled up roughly by Witte each time and so mercilessly snubbed by him that he finally shut up. When he talked of China's future, Witte asked him how he could possibly know anything about the future.'
19. Rosen, *Forty Years*, vol. 1, pp. 205–7, 208–9.
20. The Seoul–Suwon sector was opened in Oct. 1903.
21. The Society was founded by Nakata Keigi in July 1902 and the name of the politician Hara Kei was associated with it.
22. Kajima Morinosuke, *Nihon Gaikōshi*, vol. 6, pp. 187–204.
23. Jordan to Francis Bertie, 8 Nov. 1902 in Jordan Papers 3.
24. *NGB* 36/1, nos. 694–700; *DDF*, 2nd series, vol. 2 (1902), no. 409.

Chapter 9

RUSSO-CHINESE CONVENTION AND ITS AFTERMATH (1902–3)

Attitudes and actions were moulded by the exciting new development: the approaching completion of the Chinese Eastern railway. As we saw, the new Russian minister to Peking had travelled from Russia by rail in September 1901 to take up his post. He had reached Niuchuang from St Petersburg in fifteen days and, after transferring to the Peking–Hsinmintung line, had arrived at his destination in twenty-one days. This was a trial run for a rather special passenger. The construction teams had been forced to open certain parts of the track, even before their work was completed. The railway therefore opened in part for passenger express traffic, and in part for slow traffic, intended for freight, for the military and for government needs. The railway had been conceived of from its origins as a carrier of goods in transit from ports on the Pacific Ocean to Russia and the reverse. The sooner the commercial viability of the Chinese Eastern route could be tested, the better from Witte's point of view.

Quite apart from the teething troubles of the new railway, there were the financial problems. The construction costs had soared well beyond the original estimates. The actual construction with the teams making the long journey by sea to Vladivostok and Port Arthur, the heavy expenses for security purposes during the Boxer troubles and the interest payments were a major anxiety for Finance Minister Witte. It was for this reason that the desperate remedy of opening the line, even at the cost of interfering with some of the construction work, was adopted. The railway enterprises were a major drain on Witte's budgets. One of the jobs which absorbed much of the time in the British embassy around this time was the study of these budgets in order to see how Witte masked the large losses which the world thought he was incurring on these railway gambles. By adroitness, he did conceal the main problems in such a way that when the Chinese Eastern opened on 1 July 1903, there was a general mood of excitement and achievement in Russia.[1]

In the case of the much vaster Trans-Siberian route also, the railway was not really open until the summer of 1903 except for the carrying of special passengers. Even then there were considerable shortcomings. Some of the tunnels were not workable; the railway workshops were not completed; and work on the improvement of the single track still remained to be done. Needless to say, the greatest shortcoming was around Lake Baikal. It was decided that work on the track around the lake would have to be deferred till 1905 at the earliest. This meant that the whole Trans-Siberian system was subject to the vicissitudes of the weather there, especially during the winter period. During 1902 the ferry broke down and disrupted the system for a fortnight.[2] To sum up, the Siberian railway was a spectacular Russian achievement, which had been accomplished at great speed in inhospitable climatic conditions. It had great consequences for Manchuria and for Russian policy throughout the east. But there were still many rough edges to be smoothed; and many of these raised in Russia the hotly disputed aspect of cost. Then there was the greatest of all question-marks: would the railway perform well in an emergency, say for the mobilization and movement of troops in a war? Probably Russia had no advance plan for transporting her armies, it being left to the improvising genius of the Russian people to achieve this.

The railways encouraged the Russian leaders to travel and see for themselves. As the narrative unfolds, we find that Witte went east along the tracks; that Kuropatkin conducted an elaborate inspection of the east; and that Bezobrazov, whose role is described below, paid several visits to Manchuria and Korea. The consequence was that some of those who had a role to play in decision-making in the run-up to the war knew the terrain and the political situation for which they were prescribing.

RUSSO-CHINESE CONVENTION

For reasons of communication and finance, Manchuria was an important and ever-present problem for the Russian leaders. They wanted a permanent settlement, which could not be with the Tartar generals but must be concluded with the Peking authorities. They genuinely wanted evacuation of their garrisoning troops because it was very expensive to maintain an army of occupation and Russia's financial situation was a constant source of worry for Witte. Moreover they wanted to concentrate on the main enterprise, the running of both the Trans-Siberian and Chinese Eastern railways on profitable lines, and spend less time in diplomatic bickering.

Thinking back to the palmy days which she thought had existed after 1895, Russia again wanted to be popular with China and had a hankering after her former role as protector. She regarded Manchuria as exclusively the problem of Russia and China and was furious that China insisted on dragging other powers into the Manchurian negotiations by leakages. In other words, the Chinese no longer looked to Russia as a friend and wanted to set one barbarian off against another, while Russia mistakenly believed that she could win back Chinese goodwill.

But Russia could not make even a partial withdrawal without obtaining guarantees. The first negotiations had lapsed in the international crisis of April 1901. But, as soon as the Peking protocol was concluded between China and the powers in September, the Russians resumed the negotiations with a fresh draft which in due course leaked out from the Tsungli Yamen. Japan, Britain and the United States were as active in the spring as they had been in the autumn in opposing the settlement which the Russians were (in their eyes) imposing on China.

Li Hung-chang's successor at the Wai Wu Pu, as the Tsungli Yamen had become, was Prince Ching. Ching (I-kuang) was a Manchu prince; Manchuria was his homeland; he was surrounded by Manchu lobbies and regarded himself as an instrument of the Manchu dynasty. Unlike Li, he was not able to look at the Russian occupation of Manchuria as something of academic interest or merely a debating point. He was bolder in resisting the Russians, though he was in the last resort weak and unable to hold out against pressure. The Japanese regarded him as a 'nonentity' but this judgement may have been influenced by the fact that he did not often accept their advice. It was Ching who at the end of 1901 passed the new Russian drafts to Japan and the other powers.

The instructions given to Lessar were to get China to agree to a convention with the Russo-Chinese bank. Witte's idea was that the bank, a subsidiary of the Russian Ministry of Finance, should be granted fresh financial concessions in Manchuria, while a separate convention – a sort of *quid pro quo* – would provide for Russian forces to evacuate the three provinces. Negotiations for the first were broken off by the Chinese on account of Japanese and American protests in February 1902. When Prince Ching returned his counterdraft on 15 February, he asked for the Russian evacuation to be undertaken within twelve months rather than the eighteen months mentioned in the Russian draft.[3] The Russian choice of dates had reflected the expected date of operation of the railway and the immense climatic difficulties which made the evacuation of troops from remote areas where communications were poor a nightmare. Russia wanted to ensure that the pull-out of troops did not imply a pull-out of interests. Eventually the Russians conceded on this point; and the Japanese urged China's leaders to settle without delay on the existing terms which were probably the best available. On 8 April the Chinese signed the evacuation agreement from which the salient terms are given:–

II. The Russian Government, *provided that no disturbances arise and that the action of other Powers should not prevent it,* to withdraw gradually all its forces from within the limits of Manchuria:

    a. within six months from the signature of the Agreement to clear the south-western portion of the Province of Mukden up to the River Liao-che of Russian troops, and to hand the railways over to China

    b. within further six months to clear the remainder of the Province of Mukden and the Province of Kirin of Imperial troops

    c. within the six months following to remove the remaining Imperial Russian troops from the Province of Hei-lung-chiang.

IV.   The Russian Government agrees to restore to the owners the Railway Shanhaikwan-Newchwang-Sinminting which since the end of September 1900 has been occupied and guarded by Russian troops. In view of this, the Chinese Government binds itself:

1.   In case protection of the a.m. line should be necessary, that obligation shall fall exclusively on the Chinese Government which shall not invite other Powers to participate in its protection, construction or working nor allow other Powers to occupy the territory evacuated by the Russians;

2.   The completion and working of the a.m. line shall be conducted in strict accordance with the Agreement between Russia and England of 16 April 1899, and the Agreement with the private Corporation respecting the loan for the construction of the line. And furthermore the Corporation shall observe its obligations not to enter into possession of or in any way to administer the Shanhaikwan-Newchwang-Sinminting line.

Clause II included Witte's suggestion for a let-out clause (in italics), which would give Russia grounds for keeping her troops in Manchuria. Clause IV gave evidence of Russia's distrust of the British syndicate involved in the Niuchuang line. Moreover Minister Lessar handed over separately from the convention a note stipulating that the 'surrender' of the civil government of Niuchuang into the hands of a Chinese administration would take place only after the withdrawal thence of foreign forces and landing parties and the restoration to the Chinese of the then internationally administered city of Tientsin.[4]

Japan – and Britain for that matter – hailed the Manchurian agreement as a triumph for the alliance or for the Open Door powers. At long last Russia's resolve had been worn down and she had become desperate to settle the Manchurian occupation by evacuation of her troops. The new treaty was described as 'reassuring'.

But the negative can also be argued: it was not so much the threat of the Anglo-Japanese alliance as the persistence of China that was rewarded; there was no guarantee that evacuation of troops would be followed by an open door. Indeed the eighteen-month interval allowed to the Russians would enable them to take steps to close the door against foreigners of whatever nationality. Even the troop withdrawal was by no means straightforward since Witte had successfully included the condition that 'if disturbances should occur, the troops might be kept on'. In any case, though the troops might be removed, there was provision for civil guards or railway guards to replace them and these were intended to be veterans. Almost as soon as the treaty was signed, there was dissatisfaction in Russia and a call for extensive amendments had to be made. Because of the safeguard clause the foreign ministry accepted that the treaty was negotiable and could be altered or augmented. Kuropatkin insisted, for example, in August that the Chinese should be asked to promise not to use Japanese military instructors in Manchuria.[5]

On another front, Witte made himself active in seeking arrangements not with the central Chinese government but with the provincial ones in Manchuria where the real power lay. The Russo-Chinese Bank, the instrument for Witte's planning, tried through its agents to obtain concessions of various kinds. Though Pokotilov, its Peking manager, was active, the scheme ran into problems from the Chinese and from Russian officials themselves who were often resentful of Witte's activities and of the Bank in particular. By the end of 1902 the Bank had achieved only modest successes, causing some to question whether it was the best agency for Russian expansion.[6]

MANCHURIAN EVACUATION

Japan and the other powers had played a part in the formulation of the Russo-Chinese treaty, though Lamsdorf of course would have denied this. Now that the treaty was accomplished, it was left to China and these interfering outsiders to monitor Russia's phased withdrawal. This task was performed with differing degrees of commitment by Japan, the United States and Britain – the so-called Open Door powers in Manchuria.

It is doubtful whether the Russians ever seriously thought of fulfilling the three stages to the letter. Since their withdrawal was conditional on no disturbances arising and banditry was endemic in the area, they had a valid excuse for not observing the treaty too strictly. But, quite apart from that, Witte was to admit in 1904, when he was no longer the tsar's minister and was to a degree in the huff, that there had never been any serious intention of carrying out the evacuation treaty.[7] A close British observer of the scene disputed whether the Russian empire regarded itself as committed to long-term treaty commitments of this sort. He wrote: 'When inconvenient to Russia she simply cancels [agreements]; because, as she says, can you expect to bind the will of our great Emperor or to criticize his actions? The Empire is above the law as well as morality, and I am sure this most estimable Monarch here thinks so.'[8]

In any case, the enforcement of the treaty lay not in the hands of St Petersburg but in those of the frontiersmen, that is, the army and the railway bosses in Manchuria; and this was always the kind of situation which Lamsdorf and even Witte found it hardest to control. W. J. Oudendyk, the Dutch diplomat, and Dr G. E. Morrison of *The Times* visited Manchuria in the autumn of 1902. Their ears heard from the Russian officials on the spot that they were preparing to withdraw though their eyes did not suggest that there was much substance in such promises. At the same time, these travellers observed that the Russian occupation was a military one, superficial and still far from affecting the economy deeply. Further it was not really punitive and undertook much progressive, humanitarian work. Indeed, Morrison wrote an article for his newspaper on the 'Results of the Occupation' along these lines.[9]

During 1902 China was approached by the Open Door powers, then recognized to be Britain, the United States and Japan. Following the settlement of outstanding political questions by the Peking protocol, they sought to negotiate a commercial settlement. Britain led the way by sending Sir James Mackay to Shanghai to conduct the negotiations ending with the Anglo-Chinese commercial treaty of 5 September 1902. This allowed the Chinese an increase in customs duty in return for assurances governing the abolition of likin, and the introduction of a national coinage. Since Japan did not favour the increase in customs duty which this allowed, she followed suit by opening her own negotiations. The treaty that resulted a year later (of which more will be said anon) emphasized – in case emphasis was needed – that Japan regarded Manchuria as part of China and as a part where she would stand up for her treaty rights and commercial privileges.

Meanwhile Japan was developing her stake in the Three Eastern provinces. The number of immigrants may have been small. By December 1903 there were only 2,806 Japanese residents who stayed mainly in the ports, engaged as workmen, shopkeepers and small businessmen. But the Japanese controlled most of the seaborne trade through Niuchuang and were worried about the future prospects it had in comparison with the rival port of Dalny which Witte was determined to build up and which benefited from the direct link with the Chinese Eastern railway. So long as Russian troops occupied the south of Manchuria, there was little practical likelihood of the Open Door being fully observed and a distinct possibility of privileges being given to Russians. Hence the Japanese added their voice to the Chinese in calling for speedy Russian evacuation from Manchuria.

The first stage of evacuation of land west of the Liao river was satisfactorily concluded by October 1902. This excluded Niuchuang, a place where the powers enjoyed treaty rights and were especially vigilant, it being the junction between the Chinese Eastern and Chinese Northern Extension railways. To show that they were not prepared to lose their privileges without protest, Britain, Japan and the United

States again sent gunboats to Niuchuang for the winter. In response the Russians tried to establish their own customs house and post office at the port.

WITTE IN THE FAR EAST

Diplomatically the year 1902 came to an uneventful end in Russia. Due to the tsarina's miscarriage, there was an unusual calm at court which announced that it would stay on until Christmas at its Crimean retreat, the Italian Renaissance palace at Livadia about a mile from Yalta, and remain in strict seclusion. Lamsdorf, who had to be in attendance on the tsar in October, had used the pretext of his approaching trip to cancel regular audiences at St Petersburg before he set off. This led to considerable dislocation of normal diplomacy in the last quarter of the year. One diplomat wrote that after the foreign minister's departure 'there will only be a kind of living letterbox at the Foreign Office for our communications, as Count Lamsdorf will continue to transact all business of the Department from Yalta until near Christmas'.[10]

It is relevant to our study to note that, with the death of Home Minister D. S. Sipiagin by assassination in April 1902, Witte had received a severe setback. A most formidable attack on the finance minister's power was directed against the expenditure on the Siberian and other railways in which there seemed to have been great unaccountable losses while the indisputable domestic needs of Russia herself had been neglected. This had given rise to widespread discontent. Whereas Sipiagin had been a great friend of Witte and had submitted to what he accepted as Witte's superior statesmanship, his successor, V. K. Plehve, would not accept second place. Within the tsarist autocracy the minister of the interior had to be a dominant force in the emperor's councils. The system which Witte had painstakingly moulded had altered this tradition and concentrated power in the hands of the finance ministry, dangerous as that could be during the ill-understood industrialization process. It became clear that, once Plehve had found his feet, Witte's power would be seriously challenged.[11]

In August 1902 the tsar asked Witte to make a tour of inspection to Manchuria. He spent about two months mainly in Harbin but with side-trips to Dalny, Port Arthur and Niuchuang (15 October). He seems to have been engaged in dealing with practical problems, relating to railway building and operation. On his return he presented an extensive report which, among other things, expressed the view that withdrawal from Manchuria was essential because Russia had problems enough in colonizing Siberia and that evacuation was the only way of overcoming international opposition and domestic hostility towards Russia's actions. Concerned about the security of his railway – and his investment – at the hands of marauding bandits, he felt that a reinforcement (to 25,000) of the railway guards by whom he had been impressed would guarantee adequate safety.[12] Like most of Witte's writings the report was bold, opinionated and boastful. It took a strong line though it recognized that many views were possible on the subject of the evacuation of Manchuria. This aspect was not one which found favour with the tsar and his court. The whole thrust of Witte's argument in the report was in defence of his own view in the past. For the future he emphasized the necessity for the railway guards to occupy all the principal cities of Manchuria including Kirin.

The report reached the tsar during his extended vacation in the Crimea. He convened a meeting of Witte, Kuropatkin, Lamsdorf and Plehve to discuss the situation in Manchuria. There seems to have been unanimous agreement that Manchuria should in the future be annexed to Russia and made dependent upon her. The conclusion was on the whole evasive on the main issues and considerably less forthcoming than Witte himself. This implied that the finance minister's views had not found favour with his colleagues.

That the emperor himself was less than satisfied with them seems clear from the fact that A. M. Bezobrazov, who had been staying at Livadia, was despatched to Manchuria on a personal errand from the tsar at the end of November with a substantial subvention from the Treasury. Romanov thinks that Witte avoided dismissal by a hair's breadth on 1 January 1903 by agreeing to this.[13] This was the first major sign of imperial favour for Bezobrazov, the entrepreneur whose views on Russian enterprises in Manchuria and Korea came into the ascendant at this time as Witte's fortunes declined. He will feature increasingly among the decision-makers in 1903.

When the court returned to St Petersburg for the Russian new year, Lamsdorf convened a conference of diplomats at the ministry on 24 January 1903. Lessar from Peking was at home for medical treatment; Pavlov, the minister from Seoul, was already on leave; and Roman Rosen, who was on his way back to Japan on appointment as Izvolskii's replacement at Tokyo, also attended. The diplomats and Lamsdorf maintained the view that the evacuation agreement with China should be honoured but held that the implementation of the next phase might be delayed until China accepted fresh conditions, drawn up by Lessar. Korea was brought up in the context of Witte's proposal for an immediate agreement with Japan even if it entailed conceding Korea to her. But all three diplomats felt that such a price was too high.[14]

This was a preliminary to the special conference on 7 February where the four who had taken part in the earlier meeting were joined by the ministers chiefly involved, Witte, Kuropatkin and Admiral Tyrtov. They eventually accepted Witte's suggestion that some agreement with Japan would be desirable, and that the most pressing need was for some decision on a clearly defined policy toward Korea, and for 'complete unanimity' in the standpoints taken by all ministries, their local representatives and agents. It was further accepted that it would be best if Russia were to wait for Japan to reopen the negotiations even on the unfavourable terms set out in the note of 4 August. There was general support for talks with the Japanese, even if there was to be delay. One dissenting voice was that of Kuropatkin who found no solution other than to absorb northern Manchuria, that is, all of Heilungkiang province and most of Kirin province, while southern Manchuria might be given up. In the end, the result was that Lessar's terms were accepted. The second phase of the evacuation was to be delayed (according to Kuropatkin) until better climatic conditions since winter was difficult for troop movements.[15] While unanimity was expressed, there were wide gaps between the views of the various ministers and diplomats. Romanov is justified in writing: 'A refurbished programme for the "imperial" policy was put together that buttressed the outward unity of the "cabinet" but did not settle a single one of the questions set for discussions. Imperial diplomacy made a decision that irrevocably committed it to a course of delays, remaining for the most part inexplicable.'[16]

PRECONDITIONS FOR EVACUATION

It took an extraordinary time for these terms to be communicated to the Chinese. The St Petersburg conference had approved them early in February and the tsar endorsed them without delay. They were then sent to Grigorii Antonovich Planson, who had been despatched to deputize for the ailing Lessar and was a protégé of the Grand Duke Alexis, Alekseyev and the war party. Planson returned his modified version on 26 March. Lamsdorf gave him the go-ahead on 15 April. The chargé presented the seven demands to Prince Ching on 18 April as follows:

1. No free port to be opened or consulate of other powers to be established in the district evacuated;
2. No nationals other than Russians to be employed in the north;
3. Same arrangements as regards administration as during the occupation;
4. Niuchuang customs revenue to be paid into the Russo-Chinese Bank;
5. Niuchuang sanitary regulations to be managed by the Russians;
6. Russia to have the right to use Chinese telegraph poles in Manchuria for Russian wires;
7. No portion of the Three Eastern provinces to be ever alienated to any foreign power.

It would appear that Planson had presented the demands in very strong language and with suggestions of more authority than he in fact possessed. Japan urged China to refuse and, when enquiries were made in Russia, Lamsdorf rebutted them by saying that any delay in carrying out the evacuation was due to the natural necessity for obtaining assurances that China was fulfilling her obligations 'which could be better ascertained by the Russian minister who was about to return to Peking, than by a Secretary temporarily in charge of the Legation'. Lamsdorf seemed to be hinting that Planson did not have his full confidence and that matters should rest till Lessar in whom he did have full confidence returned from Europe.[17] Planson, who had been diplomatic secretary to Alekseyev in Port Arthur before acting at Peking in Lessar's absence, reflected the more forceful approach of the men on the spot rather than the cautious line of St Petersburg.

The big question was whether in the light of this the Russians would withdraw in April in accordance with their treaty obligations. They were due to withdraw troops from the province of Mukden east of the Liao river and from the whole of Kirin. While there were of course logistic difficulties in undertaking the evacuation in these areas, they were not insuperable. It should have been possible to evacuate in March–April when the ground was still frozen. Later in April the thaw would set in; and tracks would be passable only with difficulty. Dust storms from the Gobi desert were commonly a great problem from March onwards. But the districts in question were remote from the Gobi and were probably little affected by dust. It would seem that the reasons for Russian hesitation and inconsistency were political rather than geographical and climatic. While the three leaders who dominated Russia's policy-making in the east – Witte, Kuropatkin and Lamsdorf – agreed to move their troops out of Mukden province, they were not agreeable, or at least unanimous, to move out of Kirin to the north.

The practical outcome was an extraordinary one. It was reported that Russian troops evacuated Niuchuang barracks on 8 April and Mukden a few days before. But instead of leaving these areas they reoccupied them. In Mukden the number of Russian troops was reduced to a hundred, who acted as guards at the Commissaire, the consulate and the Russo-Chinese bank. There were another forty troops attached to the railway outside Mukden. Barracks for railway guards were being built with accommodation for a large number but they were proceeding very slowly. Some put the failure of the Russians to fulfil the treaty down to an incident on the Yalu river side of the province between Russians and Japanese. Others explained it by the need to force the Chinese to accept supplementary terms for Niuchuang.[18] In the railway zone outside the immediate area of Mukden, Liaoyang, forty miles to the south, was still held in force. In the rest of Mukden and Kirin provinces there were few foreign observers; and it is very hard to make an accurate estimate of the percentage of troops who retired from their positions at this time. The explanation could be that most of the local commanders felt that the evacuation convention had been badly drawn up and needed redefinition. They may also have shared the view of Kuropatkin that it was the duty of the army to ensure the security of the trunkline of the Chinese Eastern railway from Manchouli to Nikolsk-Ussuri and that this could only be done by holding a cordon sanitaire to the south. This might run from the junction of the Nonni and Sungari rivers to the Pacific ocean at the Tumen river and might take in Kirin city and Changchun.

It was in Niuchuang, which should have been evacuated in the first phase in October 1902, where most reluctance was observed on Russia's part. The Russian administration claimed that it was willing to retire but that the obstacle was the need for the sanitary control of the port and town in the interest of the foreign community. As a precondition for evacuation the Russians wanted to establish a sanitary board, consisting of Russian and Chinese officials. The Chinese, however, appealed to other powers who saw in this a device for Russia to retain influence in the port and also a means of imposing vexatious sanitary requirements which could possibly impose difficulties on shipping, other than Russian. The Russians claimed that the danger of infection being imported into Manchuria and thence into Russia along the railways was very great. They would not give up the administration of the town until the Chinese agreed to the setting up of a sanitary board. For the present the town continued under the administration of Consul Grosse.

Since Niuchuang was a treaty port, there arose also the question of customs revenue and the role (if any) of the Chinese Imperial Maritime Customs Organization. Despite professions to the contrary, the Russians clearly wanted to take over the Manchurian customs administration from China. In March the British-born inspector-general of the Chinese customs service, Sir Robert Hart, as a result of much Russian pressure, agreed to appoint from the ranks of the customs service itself a Russian as acting commissioner at Niuchuang. He was N. A. Konovalov. Hart wrote: 'There will be an Anglo-American-Japanese howl over this. Coming, however, from myself as a mere service movement ... and without any promise to always station a Russian there, it will be less harmful than an appointment wrested from China as a condition to rendition and perpetualized.'[19]

Hart's move was ineffective in ensuring the rendition of the port. The customs duty collected by the Russians was paid into the Russo-Chinese Bank. Accounts were presented to Hart and the Chinese government; but, despite the considerable balance accumulated, the Chinese were not permitted to draw on it. It was in effect reserved for Russian purposes. Since the customs duty was to a large extent levied on Japanese and, to a lesser extent, British trade and since Niuchuang was a treaty port, outside parties were hostile and resentful of the Russian regime there.

The powers thought that Hart had been innocent, not to say naïve.

The Japanese doubted the wisdom of appeasement tactics towards Russia. They conjectured that Russia's acquisition of the Niuchuang customs would not be short-lived. But Hart, probably quite rightly, insisted that he was the servant of the Chinese government and had no greater powers than it. He was not under instructions from the foreign diplomats or from foreign governments and had the right to make decisions which did not appeal to them for political reasons. But the end result was that Russia had gained political and customs control of Niuchuang, from which she would not be readily dislodged.[20]

Some four days after presentation of the Planson demands, the Chinese gave their official rejection of these terms, refusing to discuss the matter until the evacuation of Manchuria had been completed. On 26 April, at another of the special conferences at which these matters were discussed in St Petersburg, all parties agreed to continue the occupation of northern Manchuria. Even Witte and Lamsdorf who had previously seemed to be favourable to early evacuation, now came round to the more severe views of the other ministers. But this internal decision was not conveyed to the Chinese and the world. Instead a smokescreen of conflicting views arose from the Russian ministers. Even if there was now a united front on this point, Russian policy generated a great deal of confusion.[21]

While the Russians were being tough towards China, they were trying to be lenient towards the powers with interests in Manchuria. In formal assurances given on 11 July they stated:

> Whatever may be the result of the negotiations which are pending between Russia and China, and bear exclusively upon the protection of Russian interests of the first importance in the occupied province, [Russia has] no intention of opposing the gradual opening by China, as commercial relations develop, of some towns in Manchuria to foreign commerce, excluding, however, the right to establish 'Settlements'. This declaration does not apply to Harbin. The town in question being within the limits of the Concession for the Eastern Chinese Railway, and not unrestrictedly subject to the Chinese Government, the establishment there of foreign Consulates must therefore depend upon the consent of the Russian Government.[22]

This message was designed to meet the anxieties and complaints of Japan and the United States in the first place and also Britain and the other powers. But it was in vague terms and contained no guarantees as to timing.

The exact status of Planson's demands to China was a matter of dispute at the time and has been a matter of mystification to historians ever since. Planson asked for no new ports or towns in Manchuria to be opened to foreign commerce and apparently told the Chinese that, if assurances were given along these lines, the Russian military party would be appeased and evacuation would be carried out without difficulty. When further enquiries and protests were made by diplomats in St Petersburg, Lamsdorf gave the most positive assurances that no 'demands' whatever had been formulated by the Russian government and presented to China. It is hard to accept these statements as being more than half-truths. The Japanese ambassador in Washington after discussion at the State Department expressed the opinion that 'Russian diplomats are devoid of authority in their action although it remains to be seen how far the Russian Government support it when they succeed', and that the present Planson demands were only 'tentative measures to test how far other Powers will act'. Japan reluctantly took the view that the inexperienced Planson was *not* acting under instructions from his home government. But Lamsdorf's pronouncements had been as bewildering as had been his statements in 1901.[23]

Embarrassed by the storm of international protest, Lamsdorf went further and described Planson privately as stupid. He informed the powers that the matter would be held in abeyance until Lessar, the minister to Peking, returned to his post from sick leave in Russia. It was expected that, as Lessar was a Lamsdorf supporter and an experienced diplomat, he would adopt a less obtrusive style. In the event the approach to China was delayed until September because Lessar was involved in other policy-making meetings after his return to the Chinese capital. He was moreover awaiting death from an incurable disease.[24] Russia's intentions about evacuation remained a mystery to the outside world all this time. Shrouded in the mists of mystery, the Russian troops stayed on in Manchuria.

REFERENCES AND NOTES

1. The last rail was laid in Manchuria on 3 Nov. 1901, ten years after the start of the railway project.
2. H. Tupper, *To the Great Ocean,* pp. 228–30. Claud Russel, 2nd secretary at the British legation at Peking (1902–4), recounted his experiences: 'Anyone can go to Irkutsk but after that there is complete disorganisation. The Passport from the Ministry of Interior was condemned as valueless by the Commandant at the Manchurian frontier. The journey took me 35 days from Moscow to Pekin – so I did not save much on the sea journey. There is a great deal of sleeping on the floor and very little washing – the last 14 days I did not get any clothes off. I cannot recommend the route as things are.' Russel to Scott, 10 Feb. 1902, Scott Papers 52,302.
3. B. A. Romanov, *Russia in Manchuria,* pp. 243–4.
4. Ibid., p. 246.
5. Hardinge to Lansdowne, 30 June 1904, Hardinge Papers 46.
6. R. Quested, *The Russo-Chinese Bank,* Birmingham 1977, pp. 57–60.

7.   *BD,* vol. 2, no. 281.
8.   S. Gwynn (ed.), *The Letters and Friendships of Sir Cecil Spring-Rice,* vol. 2, p. 377; S. Iu. Witte, *Vospominaniya,* vol. 1, pp. 335–6
9.   *The Times,* 22 Oct. 1902; W. J. Oudendyk, *Ways and By-ways in Diplomacy,* p. 124; Lo Hui-min (ed.), *The Correspondence of G. E. Morrison,* vol. 1, pp. 196–7.
10. Scott to Lansdowne, 2 Oct. 1902, Scott Papers 52,304.
11. B. A. Romanov, *Rossiya v Manchzhurii,* pp. 369–70; A. Malozemoff, *Russian Far Eastern Policy,* p. 196.
12. Romanov, *Rossiya,* pp. 379, 412–14.
13. Romanov, *Russia in Manchuria,* p. 281.
14. *Krasnyi Arkhiv,* **52** (1932), pp. 110–11.
15. Ibid., pp. 111–24.
16. Romanov, *Russia in Manchuria,* p. 291.
17. 'Planson' is the Russian version of Georges A. de Plançon de Rigny, generally known in Peking as 'de Plançon'. He served as diplomatic secretary to Alekseyev in Port Arthur before coming to Peking in Lessar's absence and afterwards. See J. K. Fairbank *et al.* (eds), *The I. G. in Peking,* vol. 2, no. 1257.
18. Ibid., no. 1277.
19. Ibid., no. 1275.
20. Konovalov continued as acting commissioner at Niuchuang until July 1904, just before the Japanese attack on the port.
21. Malozemoff, op. cit., pp. 205–7.
22. Lansdowne to Scott, 11 July 1903, FO 46/564.
23. *NGB* 36/1, nos. 128, 150.
24. Fairbank *et al.,* op. cit., vol. 2, no. 1302.

Chapter 10

JAPAN'S SEARCH FOR CONSENSUS (1903)

The problems of Korea and Manchuria were matters of primary concern in Japan. But the Katsura cabinet which had been formed to counter the activities of the political parties was in serious political difficulties and faced bitter opposition whenever the Diet was in session. We are not arguing that Japan in her stiff resistance to Russia was puffing up an artificial issue in order to divert the attention of politicians and people from domestic, and especially parliamentary, disputes. But domestic politics did put pressures on the government as it considered whether to embark on negotiations with Russia – the subject of the present chapter.

The focus of opposition between the parties and the non-party ministry was the budget which contained proposals for the continuation of the unpopular land tax. This had led in December 1902 to the dissolution of the Diet. It was still an issue in May 1903 when the house of representatives met after elections in which government supporters were seriously outnumbered. If the Katsura ministry was to survive, it had to cultivate the goodwill of Itō Hirobumi, who was the leader of the Seiyūkai. He was both political opponent and elder statesman. In the latter capacity, he had to take into account national, as against purely party, interests and to try to prevent the collapse of the ministry. While this weakened Itō's position and popularity as a party leader, it gave him great strength in his bargaining with the government, especially over relations with Russia, where his viewpoint differed substantially from that of the Katsura government. In the mid summer sitting the Diet approved the bill providing for naval expansion. Admiral Yamamoto steered through an eleven-year programme covering the building of 3 first-class battleships, 3 first-class cruisers and 2 second-class cruisers. But the Land Tax bill was thrown out. This did not deprive the ministry of funds because the budget for 1902–3 continued in force. But it was a defeat for the government and, while it did not resign, it brought the session to a speedy close on 4 June.

As we have seen, Russia defaulted on her promise to withdraw her troops. Uchida Yasuya, Japan's minister in Peking, reported on

Russia's failure to evacuate and on her fresh demands and asked for instructions on how to proceed.[1] It so happened that several of the cabinet were in Kansai district for the fifth Domestic Industrial Exhibition (Naikoku Kangyō Hakurankai). It was therefore opportune to have a meeting at Murin'an, Yamagata's country villa at Kyoto, on 21 April. Itō and Yamagata had already had a preliminary endeavour at a meeting of minds on 15 March when there was a gathering of genro, which reached the conclusion that: 'Russia seemed to wish no immediate clash with Japan over Korea; therefore Japan should endeavour to maintain the status quo and, should an opportunity arise, negotiate with Russia to reach an agreement on Korean independence and to prevent the Korean problem from becoming a cause for war between Japan and Russia.'[2] This is quoted from Itō's account and may be over-optimistic. On this occasion Katsura and Komura from the government side met Itō and Yamagata from the genro side and agreed to the following propositions:

1. When Russia fails to honour her Manchurian Evacuation agreement and does not withdraw her troops from Manchuria, Japan should protest to Russia;
2. Using the Manchurian problem as an opportunity, we should begin negotiations with Russia and resolve the Korean question;
3. Over Korea Japan should obtain the recognition of her predominant rights (Yūetsuken) and make no concessions of any sort to Russia;
4. Over Manchuria we should recognize Russia's predominant rights and on this occasion settle Korea once and for all (komponteki ni).[3]

Thus Katsura and Komura took their initial steps towards opening negotiations with Russia in full anticipation of, or even determination for, war.

Already means of influencing public opinion were emerging. On the one hand, the Russo-Japanese Society had been founded in the autumn of 1902 under the patronage of Marquis Itō and Count Inoue and, though it was running out of steam by mid 1903, it had done something to improve neighbourly relations. On the other, there had been set up in 1901 the Kokuryūkai, literally the Black Dragon society, because 'Kokuryū' represents the Chinese title for the Amur river. The intention of the society was to drive the Russians to the Amur river, then the frontier between Manchuria and Siberia. The implication was that Japan should be prepared to go to war for this purpose. Together with the Tai Ro Dōshikai and Tai Gaikō Dōshikai, which have already been discussed, it constituted a formidable lobby and exerted a continuing pressure on governments of the day.[4]

There were other pressures of a less political kind. On a more secret level there was the activity of the seven professors who at the end of May 1903 were assembled by Konoe Atsumaro and his associates to make representations to government leaders to adopt forceful measures against the continued Russian occupation of Manchuria. They did this by calling on government leaders individually and arranged to have a statement submitted to Katsura, Komura, Yamamoto and War Minister Terauchi on 10 June (and later to Kodama, then governor-general of Taiwan) critical of their policy of drift and neglect. It was finally made public on 24 June and sharpened the case for war.[5] In Japan at the time it was incredibly bold for civilians to pontificate on defence policy which was regarded as the professional preserve of certain clans. Six of the professors were professors of law at Tokyo Imperial University, one came from Gakushūin. By a strange irony the Law Faculty was the place where the young diplomats for recruitment to the foreign ministry were trained. One of these, Yoshida Shigeru of the graduating class of 1906, studied under one of the jingoist professors, the professor of constitutional law. This was what gave Yoshida his distaste later for academics and their interventions in politics.[6]

Another group which emerged in May 1903 was the Kogetsukai, really only a dining club which met at the Kogetsu restaurant in Tokyo. Though its membership was flexible and secret, it appears that it consisted of members of the army general staff (in the majority), the navy general staff, and the foreign ministry. They constituted a discussion group which tried to formulate a programme for lobbying their superiors. As in the case of the professors, divergent views probably emerged. But the common ground seems to have been a conviction that 'war with Russia was ultimately inevitable and that the sooner the war started, the more favourable the military situation would be for Japan'. The Kogetsukai decided to carry their ideas to the cabinet and genro individually and sought to persuade them to adopt an attitude in favour of war at an early date.[7]

The Kogetsukai views had a varied reception among the top political leaders. But they seem to have commanded some support among the middle reaches of the bureaucracy where it was solidly based. The elder statesmen were congenitally suspicious of lobbies of this kind, consisting of younger men with their rash schemes to quicken the pace which the genro wanted to set. Evidently Katsura as prime minister and Yamamoto as navy minister were not ready to be propelled into war and resisted their approaches. Those within the cabinet who proved to be more amenable were the foreign minister, Komura, who was less cautious and circumspect in his dealings with the Kogetsukai, Terauchi, the war minister who doubtless saw the strategic advantages of taking on the Russians without delay, and General Kodama, the home minister who with his Taiwan experience had ideas of Japan as a colonial power.

The middle months of 1903 saw a crisis in Japanese decision-making. It was in this context of dithering and uncertainty that these lobbies, each in its own way, tried to influence opinion among those placed at strategic points in bureaucracy and government.

KOREAN CRISIS ON THE YALU

These various lobbies did not differentiate between the thrust of Russia's expansion in Manchuria and Korea, since they were primarily interested in the expansion of Russian railways and Russian armies. Early in 1903 there seemed to be signs of a 'new' Russian interest in Korea. In February Russia asked Korea that a concession for the construction of a railway from Seoul to Uiju should be granted to Baron Ginzburg, a Russian entrepreneur with official blessing, whose name has appeared before. The concession had been given before to the French and, when that concession had lapsed, to Koreans with French specialist advisers. But work had been suspended for many months. It was now renewed by application from the Russians. The Japanese, who were engaged in the Seoul to Fusan line, objected, even though they had no plan to build from Seoul to Uiju at that stage. A railway battle was in the offing between Russia and Japan.

In April and May the Japanese received reports of a Russian settlement being established at Yongampo 15 miles from the mouth of the Yalu on the east bank to the south of Uiju. The Russian minister told the Koreans that it was necessary as a site from which to ship the timber cut in a concession granted in 1896. Originally belonging to a Russian trader, Briner, the concessions had been bought in 1898 by the court on the recommendation of Bezobrazov. Apart from the commercial motive of making a profit, the enterprise had the political motive of holding Russia's position in Korea and limiting the operations of other countries there. This enterprise drew fire from writers who argued that it should come under the commercial umbrella of the finance ministry and Witte and not be in the form proposed. After the Boxer episode, Bezobrazov had returned to the attack, suggesting that Russia should not be so obsessed by Manchuria that she neglected Korea and promoting again the interests of the timber concession. It was this timber company (or companies) which brought on the crisis in the east, but underlying it was a crisis between Witte, the Russo-Chinese Bank and the Bezobrazov and Grand Ducal interests.[8]

It was hard to obtain reliable information about the happenings in such a remote part of the Korean firmament. Laporte, the collector of customs at Chemulpo, the port of Seoul, was accordingly sent as a neutral observer to the area. His report stated that at Yongampo he had seen about sixty Russians in ordinary dress who had obtained possession of 50 acres of land for timber concessions. Moreover,

Shahotzu, on the Chinese side of the Yalu, was held by Russian troops, who had two steam launches operating on the river and had installed the telegraph from the Chinese side. The companies were evidently engaged in exploiting the timber resources on the Chinese and Korean banks of the river which they were hoping to ship from Yongampo. Bezobrazov had visited the site in the spring and had evidently won the attention of the tsar and the Grand Duke Alex Mikhailovich, who was one of his confidants and an important figure behind the throne.

While the Russians were positively entrenched on the site, intense diplomatic activity was taking place in the excitable diplomatic atmosphere of Seoul. The Japanese saw the Yongampo activities as an unwarranted intrusion into Korea, claimed to be a Japanese sphere of interest, and as the thin end of the wedge. Her supporters in the Open Door group were also seriously disturbed by this development. They suggested that Russia was not observing the Open Door for Korea and was not likely to do so for Manchuria, as she had so often proclaimed. The three therefore proposed that the Korean government should open the Yalu river to all traffic in accordance with the Open Door. But Minister Pavlov in Seoul opposed this idea successfully and played on the basically anti-Japanese sentiment of the Korean court. By an agreement of 20 July, the original concession of 1896 was confirmed and supplemented.[9]

Just as the Russian actions on the Korean frontier were not reported to, or fully known to, the authorities at home, being known only to the men on the frontier, so the detection of the Russian actions was largely a matter for the Japanese military on the frontier. This was the responsibility of military attachés overseas who reported to the war ministry and the general staff. Early in May Major Nozu, the attaché at Seoul, telegraphed to Chief of Staff Ōyama that, according to his subordinates, Russian forces had occupied the district of Yongampo in the north of Korea and were engaged in building-works. The general staff set about examining Russia's enterprises in northern Korea and prepared an appreciation of her actions. Since there were details in the draft which were disadvantageous to the group which favoured an early war with Russia, the appreciation was amended by several middle-ranking officers including General Iguchi Shogo and Major Tanaka Giichi whom we have earlier seen in St Petersburg and who had since returned to join the general staff. In its final form, it reached the conclusion that Russia was aiming not simply at preserving her interests but at occupying both banks of the Yalu, at invading northern Korea and at making preparations for war against Japan. Such was the appreciation of Russian activities which Ōyama presented to the throne on 22 May.[10]

As against that, Komura received on 15 May a telegram from Consul Segawa at Niuchuang, saying that the real purpose of Russia's actions in Manchuria and Korea was not to make preparations for war but to obtain mining and forestry rights in every part of Manchuria and on the banks of the Yalu.[11] The foreign ministry had confidence in Segawa who was a Russian linguist of distinction and believed in his observations which were sent to the emperor and all departments of state. They took, it goes without saying, a much more moderate view of Russian intentions than was to be found in the army staff appreciation.

This clash of opinions came to a head at a meeting within the general staff on 8 June. In the memorandum circulated beforehand by General Iguchi, who must be regarded as one of the leaders of the pro-war party, he set forth the army's views systematically. Basically he considered Russia to be in a mood of expansion to west and east and south and expressed the opinion that she was devoting all her strength to expansion in Manchuria and Korea and should be resisted on both. After comparing the army and navy strengths in the far east, the memorandum suggested that an early war would be of advantage to Japan. The following points were adopted as the conclusions of the conference:

1. Russia's failure to complete the withdrawal of troops from Manchuria must give rise to grave alarm in Japan for the future and must not therefore be allowed to pass unnoticed;
2. In order to avoid disasters in the future, Japan should act together with Britain and the United States, demand from Russia the open and public (kōzen) withdrawal of her troops and secure firm guarantees about permanent peace in the far east. If Britain and the United States will not join us in this, Japan should open official discussions with Russia for herself;
3. If by any chance these discussions break down and Russia does not respond to our demands as a means of [safeguarding the] peace, Japan should achieve her objects by armed force.

   The present is the most favourable time for this purpose, bearing in mind the superiority of our forces over Russia, the fact that the Trans-Siberian is incomplete, the existence of the Anglo-Japanese alliance, the hostility of the Chinese people etc. If we let to-day's favourable opportunity slip by, it will never come again.[12]

This was not a unanimous stance; but it was backed by a sufficiently vocal and influential majority among middle-rank army officers that it could not be disregarded. General Ōyama to whom it was addressed was far from convinced of its logic and regretted that it appeared to reject Man-Kan kōkan. None the less he allowed it to form the basis for the general staff memorandum of 17 June which we shall discuss later.

While the upper echelons of the defence staff were discussing war preparations, they received a visit from General Kuropatkin. On 22 March Kurino in Russia had been told by the war minister of his plans to travel to the east and conduct a tour of inspection of Vladivostok and Port Arthur and his hope of visiting Japan. He asked his government to extend the necessary invitation; and Tokyo showed no hesitation. By 3 April Kuropatkin was able to report that the tsar had consented to his journey to Japan. He set off from St Petersburg at the end of the month but, because of problems with his timetable, his original plan to spend a week in Tokyo had to be reduced to four days. He arrived at Shimonoseki in western Japan on 12 June and travelled by rail to Tokyo with a large retinue. He was treated as a state guest and accommodated at Shiba Palace. Since he carried with him a letter from the tsar, he was received in audience by the Japanese emperor. He had substantive discussions with Katsura and Komura.[13] But for the rest, he was the guest of the Japanese army, inspecting units and assessing the infantry, cavalry and the officer corps. Before his visit to Tokyo was complete, he received a telegram from Russia, inviting him to stay on in Japan since there was no point in reaching Port Arthur for the forthcoming conference before Bezobrazov arrived. Kuropatkin had no choice but to pass time in the Kansai area before boarding the cruiser *Askold* at Kobe. This carried him through the Inland Sea to Nagasaki whence he travelled on 28 June to Port Arthur.

Naturally Kuropatkin's visit was surrounded by all manner of rumours about his having a 'mission'. Some newspapers were bold enough to print the treaty which he was supposed to have signed in Tokyo. While there had been long and penetrating discussions between the Russian war minister and his Japanese opposite number and also with Katsura and Komura, there is no evidence that anything in the nature of a treaty was envisaged. The various accounts we have of the talks suggest that they were revelatory, that is, that Kuropatkin explained Russia's up-to-date attitudes on Manchuria and her railways there, while the Japanese expressed their worries about Korea. The attitudes were cordial; the talking was tough. It was certainly a bonus for the Japanese leaders to have met the Russian war minister face to face. Likewise Kuropatkin was favourably impressed by what he saw of the Japanese army and reported accordingly when he spoke at the Port Arthur conference.[14]

DISCORD IN TOKYO

No sooner had Kuropatkin left by the back door than talks began to see if Japan could reach consensus on a policy towards Russia. The initiative came from the army which prepared a draft memorandum for circulation on 17 June. The army, having foreknowledge that Admiral Itō, the chief of naval staff, and Admiral Ijūin, the deputy chief, were in favour of its line (that Korea was a basic lifeline for Japan's security), hoped that its memorandum would secure also the approval of the naval general staff. But the Satsuma-based naval leaders would not give their assent without the approval of Admiral Yamamoto, the navy minister. He, however, dismissed the army memorandum, asking 'what if Korea is lost to Japan? It will suffice if Japan secures her own island territories.' This interesting clash of views prevented the two services joining in a united front, and the memorandum 'on settling the Korean question' went forward to the emperor on 22 June as the opinion of the army only.[15]

Meanwhile Katsura and Komura were pushing ahead with obtaining approval for a moderate civilian line which advocated opening negotiations with Russia. In preparation for an imperial council which was due to be held on 23 June, Komura drew up a document arguing his ministry's case at length, the standard practice in Japan when a major issue of state was to be considered. It included some echoes of the army's phraseology: 'Korea is like a dagger pointing at Japan's heart and she could never endure its possession by a foreign power. Russia's activities in Manchuria and Korea are leading eventually to her domination over Korea.... In order to ensure Korean security, Japan should limit Russia's activities in Manchuria to those permitted under existing treaties.'[16] As always the Korean and Manchurian issues were inextricably linked. Komura proposed a basis for negotiations but added as a postscript: 'it will be very hard to get Russia to agree to such a deal so it is essential that, before embarking on negotiations, we are fully determined to secure our objectives regardless of the ultimate sacrifice.'

A council in the presence of the emperor was held on 23 June. Among the elder statesmen in attendance, Itō and Inoue favoured a more moderate and circumspect line than that of the cabinet. A compromise resolution setting out the conditions for an approach to Russia was finally passed:

1. In case Russia does not withdraw her forces from Manchuria, especially from Liaotung, in contravention of her promises, such a situation should be turned to Japan's advantage in order to resolve the Korean problem which had been unsolved for years;
2. In solving this Korean problem, Korea should be requested not to cede to Russia any part of her territory for any reason whatever;
3. In Manchuria, however, in view of the superior position already held by Russia, some concession to her may be allowed.[17]

This formula seemed to tilt towards the Itō line of Man-Kan kōkan once again and to represent a slight climb-down by the cabinet and the army. These guidelines were of course for internal reference. It was left to the government, and the foreign ministry in particular, to formulate the terms to be laid before the Russians.

The foreign ministry lost no time in informing Britain of its intentions, inviting a full and frank exchange of views and asking

Britain's blessing on its intended independent initiative. In reply Britain suggested that Japan should approach Washington over the action she proposed to take. From this the Japanese deduced that Britain was inclined to propose a joint approach to Russia on behalf of the Open Door powers and hastened to ask Britain not to think of taking part in any such approach. They gave the assurance that their negotiations would not prejudice their obligations under the alliance. In conveying Japan's thinking, the British minister reported:

> They intend to alone approach the Russian Government with certain friendly proposals, as the project does not, in their opinion, lend itself to joint or parallel action. As common action thus forms no part of the scheme of the Imperial Government, and as its strict secrecy is of the utmost importance at this juncture, they can see no advantage in communicating with United States Government on the subject.[18]

It appears, therefore, that consultation with the United States which was notorious for leaks and indiscretions to journalists, was not on the Japanese agenda. The Japanese wanted a free hand and no intrusion from friendly powers. It further appears that Britain, who had been consulted as a friendly gesture because of the alliance, did not consider herself sufficiently committed to get involved in this issue and thought that the United States was the outside power with the prime interest in Korea and Manchuria.

At all events Britain's suggestion for combined action found no responsive chord in Japan. Since the Japanese may have been hopeful of securing for themselves acceptable concessions from Russia, they naturally did not want others to share in the concessions or monitor them. So far as we know, no approach was made to the United States. It is perhaps worth remarking that the Japanese historian, Kajima, who is not generally critical of Japanese tactics, writes: 'The author believes that, in order to have averted the war, it would have been absolutely necessary for Japan to have conducted negotiations hand in hand with Britain and the United States, because the Russian Government, particularly the Czar, felt it humiliating to conclude a treaty with Japan on the basis of reciprocity.'[19] We have no way of knowing on what evidence Kajima offers this opinion but he often had access to confidential sources.

Another factor which may have dissuaded Japan from a shared initiative was the extent of disagreement within Japan itself. Itō went around making no secret of these divisions. He told MacDonald that Manchuria was really no longer a part of China and should realistically be allowed to be taken by Russia, provided Japan was compensated in Korea. He may have hoped that he was feeding London with an indication of Japan's long-term intentions. MacDonald initially reported on the basis of this conversation that 'it is not improbable that the nature of the arrangement with Russia would be a free hand for

Japan in Corea with equal facilities for Russia in Manchuria on the part of Japan'.[20] In other words, Itō purported to suggest that the Man-Kan kōkan formula had been adopted at the various top-level meetings.

MacDonald received hostile reaction when he told the foreign minister on the following day of that conversation. He reported that 'Komura exhibited very considerable annoyance when I told him what had occurred at my meeting and when I informed him that I had communicated Itō's words to London.' He asked that the impression should very speedily be corrected and himself authorized Hayashi to put the record straight. Komura's account was that Japan's proposal

> would be based on the principle of maintenance of integrity of China and Corea and of the open door and commercial equality for all. He said that views expressed by Itō were his own personal ones and were not shared in by the Cabinet. The principle of the proposed arrangement had been drawn up by the Cabinet, approved of by the great majority of elder statesmen and had been sanctioned by the Emperor.[21]

The significance of this is to reinforce the point that the Japanese leaders had not proposed to go ahead with negotiations purely on the basis of Man-Kan kōkan as Itō wanted. The majority were opposed to a trade-off between Korea and Manchuria. In other words they did not want complete *désintéressement* of Japan in Manchuria, the position that had been taken by Itō in Russia in 1901. Secondly it indicates that the genro view was no longer automatically adopted or even respected; that statesmen like Komura had to steer decisions away from genro views that they did not like. MacDonald like many foreigners at the time thought that what Itō said would call the tune; but it was not so.

Since the government's defeat and the suspension of the Diet sittings on 4 June, Prime Minister Katsura regarded himself as a dead duck prime minister. He was between a belligerent army, which by the end of July was raring for war, and the top policy-making body, the imperial council – where the cautious voices of Itō and Inoue carried (as he thought) disproportionate weight. In the midst of jockeying for position, Katsura, claiming ill-health, resigned and asked that the genro should choose his successor from among themselves as had been the earlier practice. By this ploy Katsura was complaining about Itō's excessive influence in policy-making in his dual capacity as genro and president of the majority Seiyūkai party. He retired to his seaside villa, leaving the navy minister to lead the cabinet. The crisis was only resolved when the emperor, on the recommendation of Yamagata who was Itō's rival, issued a rescript on 6 July appointing Itō as president of the privy council, an office he could not hold jointly with the leadership of a political party. Katsura was then commanded by the emperor to return to his duties as prime minister and went back to Tokyo, miraculously restored in health. It had been a protest against the genro and their powers of interference. It was Katsura's attempt to put Itō in his place. It did not entirely succeed because Itō was too experienced to be overlooked and too important to be ignored. It was, however, a shot across his bows, a warning that he could not expect to get his way as he had for four years, when his view was a minority one.[22]

On 28 July Komura informed Russia that Japan wished to exchange views over their respective interests in Korea and Manchuria. Count Lamsdorf agreed three days later to the opening of discussions. Komura, who was well rehearsed for the part because of the protracted cabinet crisis, passed over a note containing the draft terms on 3 August.[23]

Consensus in Japan had been hard to find and was still by no means achieved. But a minimum set of terms had been agreed and would be enough to test the Russian reaction.

REFERENCES AND NOTES

1. *Uchida Yasuya,* p. 90.
2. *Itō-den,* vol. 3, pp. 589–90.
3. Tsunoda Jun, *Manshū mondai to kokubō hōshin,* p. 154f.
4. Ibid., p. 158; Okamoto Shumpei, *The Japanese Oligarchy and the Russo-Japanese War,* pp. 61–2.
5. Okamoto, op. cit., pp. 65–7.
6. Inoki Masamichi, *Hyōden Yoshida Shigeru,* vol. 1, pp. 61–3.
7. Tsunoda, op. cit., p. 158.
8. Bezobrazov's developing interests in the Yalu region are best described in A. Malozemoff, *Russian Far Eastern Policy,* pp. 208–23.
9. E. M. Satow, *Korea and Manchuria between Russia and Japan,* p. 228.
10. Ōyama Azusa, *Nichi-Ro Sensō no gunsei shiroku,* Tokyo, p. 30; Tsunoda, op. cit., pp. 157–8.
11. Segawa to Komura, 15 May 1903, *NGB* 36/1, no. 838.
12. Ōyama, op. cit., p. 31; Tsunoda, op. cit., p. 160.
13. *Meiji Gunjishi.*
14. *Krasnyi Arkhiv,* ('Dnevnik A. N. Kuropatkina'), **2** (1922), p. 43.
15. Tsunoda, op. cit., pp. 160–2.
16. Komura to cabinet, *NGNB,* vol. 1, pp. 210–12.
17. *Kōshaku Katsura Tarō-den,* vol. 2, pp. 119–22.
18. *BD,* vol. 2, nos. 237–8.
19. Kajima Morinosuke, *The Diplomacy of Japan,* vol. 2, p. 101, fn. 7.
20. *BD,* vol. 2, no. 236.
21. MacDonald to Lansdowne, 3 July 1903, FO 46/566.
22. I. H. Nish, *The Anglo-Japanese Alliance,* pp. 265–6.
23. *NGNB,* vol. 1, pp. 212–13.

Chapter 11

RUSSIA'S NEW COURSE AND RENEGOTIATION WITH CHINA (1903)

With the advent of 1903 there was a turning-point in the attitude of Russia towards the far east. Its features included a change of attitude both at home in St Petersburg and at the frontier in China, Korea and Manchuria. It is not easy to define this turning-point. But indisputably it contained the following elements: a change in the balance of forces at the Russian court; the rise and fall of Bezobrazov and his circle; decentralization of power in dealing with east Asian issues and the rise of Admiral Alekseyev. Beyond this, it is hard to go. It is doubtful whether the conventional phraseology of the 'old course' being replaced by the 'new course' is wholly satisfactory. There were too many resemblances between the old and new courses; and there was continuity in some of the key roles, even if Finance Minister Witte was forcibly retired. We shall, therefore, suggest that, while there were continuities, there were also new dimensions and that, even within these 'new dimensions', there were many contradictory elements.

Perhaps ambivalence was of the essence of the tsarist autocracy. If Tsar Nicholas was to maintain his position and prestige, he had to play a balancing game between his various advisers. Hence his dismissal and rejection of the over-weaning, over-bearing and possibly disloyal Witte. But the tsar never sold himself completely to one side. Thus his attraction to Bezobrazov and later to Alekseyev was a partial one. All the while he was balancing the various forces and making compromises very often behind the backs of the participants. Uppermost in his mind were probably the economic crises and the possibility of revolution. The state was too rich, the people too poor; and the autocracy, based on military and police power, was unpopular. Nicholas therefore needed some success to compensate for what he saw as his record of failure. Hence the haphazard decisions: the alternation between reckless courses and more moderate ones, between internationalist courses and ones purely based on Russia's and Romanov interests.[1]

The tsar's search for successes seems to have led him to concentrate in the years after 1900 on Asia to the neglect of Europe. It is not so much

that these were years of startling expansion as that Russia wanted to
hold on to what had fallen into her lap in China so easily in 1900.
Specifically, it was hard for the tsar to order the withdrawal of troops
from Manchuria without risking great loss of face and reputation.
Moreover, to focus attention on Manchuria and Korea cost money
which Russia could ill afford in her uncertain financial position and on
which she would gain no dividend in the short term. Further, by
concentrating on east Asia, Russia was turning her back on the crying
problem of the day, the poverty and hunger of her people. In order to
remedy these, the critics wrote, she ought to have been cultivating the
granary of Europe. *Novoye Vremya,* one of the most penetrating and
thoughtful organs of the press, stated the alternatives for Russia thus:
concentration on Asia *or* concentration at home and in Europe.[2] It
favoured the latter course. In the public debate on the subject it was
being said that the stomach was being sacrificed to the fingertips. In
other words, Russia had a choice between extending her fingertips to
east Asia or attending to pressing problems at home; the eastern
adventures could only be pursued at the expense of the 'stomach'.

To use this vivid imagery, the Russians, by devoting so much
attention to the east, were risking acute stomach ache. There was grave
dissatisfaction with the Russian government over the neglected issues of
poverty and hunger. Hitherto protests had tended to be met by police
repression; but, while this had been effective in the neighbourhood of St
Petersburg and Moscow, it had not been so easy to maintain control in
the countryside and especially in the south by means of police power. It
was widely thought that this could not long continue without some
explosion and that, if this were to be prevented, some of the repressive
powers of the autocracy would have to be removed and a programme of
reforms introduced. This again was a divisive issue among the Russian
leaders. Witte and his group were mildly in favour of reform, while the
emperor and the grand dukes seem rather to have leant towards tougher
repression. This explains why Witte was losing the tsar's favour which
was being shown instead to Plehve, the interior minister and the agent of
repression.

Another symptom of this change appears to have been a rise in the
fortunes of Grand Duke Alexander Mikhailovich, the emperor's
brother-in-law, who began to play a more notable part in court circles
early in 1903. An enthusiastic sailor, he had a reputation for being hard-
working and unusually intelligent. He had connections with Korea
going back to 1898. The emperor allotted him the department of
navigation and ports, a newly-created department of state, which was
transferred from Witte's charge. A bitter opponent of Witte, he sought
to remove all commercial business from the finance ministry and have it
transferred to his own department. But his role, like that of the grand
dukes in general, can only be described in terms of general influence
within the court.

Associated with him was General Alexander Mikhailovich Bezobrazov, an army officer, who had earned a formidable reputation in frontier posts in Iran and west Siberia. Since retirement he had dabbled in various money-making projects on the frontier. He became associated with the grand duke's affairs and was identified as a powerful member of the anti-Witte camp. Bezobrazov had charisma and seems to have enjoyed remarkable access to the tsar's presence, and to have exerted some influence over his thinking. He and his group seem to have been able to manipulate the tsar and his authority. In this Bezobrazov had a valuable ally in St Petersburg in Rear-Admiral Aleksei Mikhailovich Abaza, who was his cousin and was to be appointed in mid 1903 as secretary of the Far Eastern Committee.[3]

Opinions will probably always differ on the 'sinister influence' of Bezobrazov and the conspiracy to which it may have led. I take an intermediate position. Bezobrazov was certainly not all-powerful nor was he, on the other hand, lacking in political clout in the capital. His power was spasmodic, some would say short-lived. Sometimes he convinced the tsar; sometimes he was sent on tour to get him out of the tsar's way. While Bezobrazov's bluff soldierly manner seems to have appealed to the tsar, it excited the opposition of Witte, Lamsdorf and Kuropatkin, who found him to be vain, self-centred and difficult to handle. There had been a running battle between him and the triumvirate since Bezobrazov became involved in the Korean concession project in 1898. His activities received a setback two years later at the hands of Witte who did not favour Korean adventures and managed to prevent independent projects being pursued there outside the control of the ministry of finance. But Bezobrazov was one of the main beneficiaries of Witte's declining fortunes in 1902 as he had been one of his most influential and eloquent opponents.

Yet how meteoric was the 'rise' of Bezobrazov? The evidence is hard to interpret. Typical of this difficulty is the incident in the autumn of 1902 when Bezobrazov was in attendance on the tsar at Livadia in the Crimea and seems to have discussed with him the report presented by Witte on the return from his trip to the far east, and criticized it severely. Thereafter Nicholas decided to send Bezobrazov as special emissary in November with a vague assignment. The tsar ordered Witte to make available large funds through the Russo-Chinese Bank for his stay in Port Arthur. Bezobrazov remained in the east two months. This episode is capable of two interpretations: first that Bezobrazov had the complete backing of the tsar for the enterprises which he was pursuing; or second that this was a good opportunity to get rid of an awkward busybody and give the tsar some breathing-space from his lobbying at a time when important ministerial conferences were being held. Both views can be supported by evidence. Perhaps it will suffice to say that it was another example of the tsar's balancing the influence of factions and lobbies.

Nicholas certainly found some of Bezobrazov's views infectious and exciting. He may have been swayed by his memorandum on far eastern policy:

> Russia should demonstrate her energy and determination. Withdrawal of Russian forces from Manchuria is out of the question. A problem such as this concerns only Russia and China and should not be made a subject for international negotiations. Russia should increase her forces in the Far East with a view to silencing any opposition. She should construct defence works on the Yalu river with the object of forestalling a Japanese attack on Manchuria's flank and making it possible for her to threaten Japan from that region in case Japan attacks. Russia should discard Witte's timid policy which will only lead her into difficulties. Real economic benefit should be obtained from the Far East, and this could be achieved on the Yalu river basin by aiding the East Asian Enterprise Company based on Briner's concession. In Korea, it is possible for Russia to acquire further concessions. With the object of ending American support to Japan and attracting American sympathy for Russia, attempts should be made to become associated with American capital. In Manchuria important industries should be controlled [and arrangements made with the governor-general]. But, in order to soften the dissatisfaction of Americans and others, the Open Door should be observed there for foreigners.[4]

These ideas are quoted at length to indicate how radical was the policy being advocated by the Bezobrazov group and how superficially attractive it could be to the tsar. It was a plausible variant to the 'old course' which was becoming increasingly discredited as its author-in-chief, Witte, fell from grace.

The 'new course' represented innovations not only at the European end but also at the eastern end. One of the features which we shall be noticing is the greater decentralization of power there. That is not to say that it greatly changed the character of the 'Russian team' in the east or enhanced its quality. Nor does it imply that the 'Russian team' had hitherto been weak. On the contrary, we have already quoted Dr George Ernest Morrison, the Peking correspondent of *The Times* of London, who was no mean observer, as saying that the Russian combination was 'one very difficult to compete with'.[5] Who were these talents who drew this praise from Morrison? Pavel Mikhailovich Lessar had gone to Peking in 1901 after winning diplomatic laurels for serving under de Staal at the London embassy and was regarded as a star of the Russian Foreign Ministry though he was suffering from a fatal disease. Basil Kroupensky was also an accomplished diplomat, though a junior one. He had served in China since 1900. Dmitrii Dmitrievich Pokotilov had come to China as a young man in 1888 and become highly proficient in the Chinese language and adept at handling the Chinese. He had been manager of the Russo-Chinese Bank from 1896 to 1903 and director-general of the Chinese Eastern Railway. All commentators speak favourably of his skills. Thus Morrison wrote of him:

The subjection of Li Hung Chang to Russia was largely due to his influence and it would be difficult to over-estimate the services he rendered to his country during the friendly negotiations which have secured the separation of Manchuria, with the fortress of Port Arthur, from Chinese dominion. Probably no abler servant of the Russian Government ever came to the Far East.[6]

His talents were rewarded; and he ended up as his country's minister to China (1905–8). Since Russia's actions were essentially military ones, an important part was played by Colonel Konstantin de Wogack (Vogak), the military attaché for China and Japan, who had taken a large role since the Boxer emergency in northern railway matters. In this he complemented the role of Baron G. G. Ginsberg who was associated with the Peking legation through de Wogack and had enterprises in Manchuria and Korea. He was a director of the Russo-Chinese Bank and chief contractor for the Russian Pacific squadron. From January 1902 he was increasingly involved in Korea, engaged in negotiations for a loan connected with mines, and soon became a vital participant in Bezobrazov's concession on the Yalu. He was described disparagingly by his enemies as a 'Jewish speculator' but he was an active and subtle operator on behalf of Russia.[7]

Slightly outside this group was Admiral Evgenii Ivanovich Alekseyev. He came to prominence first as commander of the Pacific squadron in 1895. Three years later he was appointed as governor of the Kuantung lease territory and commander-in-chief of Russian naval forces in the Pacific. During the Boxer emergency he was appointed by Kuropatkin as an army corps commander. Alekseyev was generally distrusted by the army leaders but enjoyed the favour of the tsar and the grand dukes. Just sixty, he was a bachelor and a hard-working but rather remote official.

This was a remarkable combination of diplomats, bankers, soldiers, sailors and entrepreneurs who were conscious of the new opportunities in the east created by the near-completion of the railways. Whether acting together or separately, they made up a formidable team. Writing of Russian activities, Guber speaks of the 'adventurism' of the time; and certainly there was more than a whiff of frontier adventurism in their actions, beliefs and reports.[8] There had been a Russian tradition of adventure in central and east Asia for several decades and a tendency to act independently of central authority. Dr Morrison, who was no Russophil observer, wrote of the Russian officials in China as not being governed by timidity or fastidiousness and propriety as was the British minister in Peking and his officials. The impression he conveys is that, while the British were tired, the Russians were lively and that, while the Russians were tough-minded, often brutal and insincere, they were more energetic in their actions, more adaptable to their oriental environment and more successful than any other European power.[9] As against that, moves were made to limit individual initiatives. As the rest of this chapter will show, attempts were made because of improved railway communications to bring these disparate elements together at meetings in order to hammer out an acceptable consensus. But even these endeavours did not greatly limit some of the adventurism of the frontier.

There was also an expansion of Russian forces in the east Asian area. Whether this was the result of cries from the periphery or the result of Kuropatkin's initiative from the metropolis cannot be said for sure. At the end of June 1903 the Russians by way of testing the carrying capacity of their new railway sent to Siberia two infantry brigades and two artillery battalions together with appropriate cavalry. Russia thereafter continued to send forces to east Asia. She was also increasing her naval strength in the area. She was improving the fortifications of the naval ports of Port Arthur and Vladivostok and their capacity to accommodate an increased fleet.

But the motive for sending these reinforcements does not seem to have been any expectation of war breaking out with Japan. Russia did not believe that Japan would make war on her; and there is no evidence that she was sending out forces for the purpose of making war on Japan. If anything, the Russians played down the military qualities of the Japanese army and its strike capability. Indeed Colonel Vannovskii, who had occupied the position of military attaché at the Tokyo legation since 1900 and was the man capable of reporting most authoritatively, seems to have taken the view that the Japanese would need about a century to develop a modern army comparable to that of the weakest army in Europe and that their army was one of infants.[10] Whether this was a reference to the Japanese being undersized in comparison to European armies of the time cannot be said. But Vannovskii's views were by no means uncommon in the ranks of military attachés in Tokyo. So persistent were they that one wonders whether the Japanese deliberately tried to plant this idea in the minds of foreign representatives. The gradual expansion of Russian forces can have had little connection with a perceived risk of hostilities with Japan.

KOREAN DEVELOPMENTS

Having tried to show some of the changes in the balance of forces within Russia, we must now turn to Korea. Since 1898 Russia had been keeping a lower profile there; but gradually under the active Pavlov, she was again pressing her case with the Korean court. There was in Korea, as there had been in China, a pro-Russian party, at this time led by Yi Yong-ik. There was still a residual respect for Russia for having given the emperor asylum in her Seoul legation in 1896. In particular the Koreans seem to have found the personality of Weber, the former minister who had returned to Seoul to act at the legation during Pavlov's absence on leave in 1902–3, congenial and sympathetic. On the other side, the Koreans often found the Japanese concession-hunters very trying and difficult to handle and sometimes turned to the Russians to offset their pressure.

As we briefly mentioned in the previous chapter, the focus of Japanese attention turned on Yongampo, a spot on the Korean bank of the Yalu river, where disturbing developments were taking place. The Russians had secured a 'preliminary lease' of the area from a pliant deputy sent up to the place, though its terms were not wholly satisfactory to either the Russians or the Koreans. In June 1903 the headquarters of the timber company was set up there, even though it was recognized that this action would be regarded by the Japanese as provocative. Japan viewed the Yalu enterprise as more strategic than commercial and as a Russian attempt to obtain and consolidate a foothold in northern Korea from which they could contain Japanese activities in the peninsula. This view seemed all the more plausible when the management and work-force seemed to have been drawn from demobilized soldiers. The Japanese, aided by the British, opposed the Yongampo enterprise.[11]

Bezobrazov, with his considerable experience of Korea in the past, had a major hand in this. His enthusiasm for the Yalu concession took shape after his group acquired the interests originally obtained from the Koreans by the entrepreneur, Briner, in 1898. Two timber companies were set up in Vladivostok to exploit the timber rights in valuable forests on both banks of the Yalu river. As soon as Bezobrazov took over the timber companies, he set aside 180,000 roubles for the construction of a sawmill at the mouth of the Yalu and began to build up a labour force. For this purpose he planned to bring large numbers of discharged soldiers to the concession area. Admiral Alekseyev in Port Arthur, however, did not like the shape which this enterprise was taking and only sent 40 out of an expected quota of 300 ex-soldiers. Bezobrazov, who had secured through his relative, Abaza, in the Russian capital permission in principle to proceed on these lines, was furious at this and submitted a critical report.[12]

The Yalu project was running into criticism from all sides. On receipt of the report, the tsar thought it best to recall Bezobrazov from Port Arthur on 2 April. Meanwhile Bezobrazov's enemies in the capital decided to raise the Yalu project for discussion and convened a special conference in St Petersburg on 8 April. They did not wait for Bezobrazov to return but received his views as embodied in a memorandum from Abaza. The Grand Duke Alexander Mikhailovich, who was a sort of protector of Bezobrazov at court and an advocate of the Yalu project and a person whose relations with Witte were far from cordial, was not invited. Witte felt able to resist the more extreme proposals and was supported as usual by Foreign Minister Lamsdorf. On this occasion Kuropatkin, who found Bezobrazov's general ideas on

Korea distasteful, came out in full support of their opposition. It was not only that the three found little to be said for commercial undertakings on the Yalu river and for Bezobrazov's commercial sense but also that they could see little merit in going out of their way to antagonize the Japanese whose hostility to the project was already clear, for such a small commercial return in northern Korea. While agreeing that the company involved in the concession should be purely commercial with only the routine services of government, the conferees wanted to establish themselves on both banks of the Yalu, thereby preventing the opening of the river by others. Against Witte's idea of imposing more control, Kuropatkin proposed that the commander of the Kuantung Leased Territory be given authority over the concessions on both the Korean and Manchurian banks and obtained approval for it. This was an early and surprising anticipation of an increase in powers for Alekseyev.[13]

On 18 April Bezobrazov returned from the east in high style. By this time he may have earned some support for his notions from Alekseyev and may have won the positive support of the tsar because of this. This must be partly explained by the impact of his rumbustious personality on Nicholas. But it was not an overwhelming vote of confidence for there are several witnesses who contend that, when Kuropatkin was sent to the east on a fact-finding mission, he was specifically enjoined by the tsar 'to efface the traces of Bezobrazov's activities'.[14] Kuropatkin's trip removed the member of the triumvirate who carried most weight with the tsar and may therefore have played into Bezobrazov's hands. He benefited from Witte's continuing unpopularity and was supported by Witte's rivals, especially Plehve. In a sense, Bezobrazov seems to have turned the tables on his critics.

The official start of the new course was on 15 May. It was then that Nicholas, without consulting his ministers, appointed Bezobrazov 'state secretary' (in Russian 'stats-sekretar'). From that point on the timber company at Yongampo could not be regarded as a private speculation. It now had official blessing since its president had an official title. Moreover, the manager, Ginsberg, had long-standing connections with the Russian legation in Peking. Even if, as some scholars argue, the appointment of state secretary did not give Bezobrazov a vital role in the state apparatus, it must have had some symbolic significance. It surely implied that the tsar and his advisers were so frustrated by the unwillingness of the existing ministers to seize the opportunity offered by the railway in the east that they had decided to give a token of approval to one who would. On 15 May the tsar, again acting on his own, appointed Admiral Alekseyev as supremo over all departments in the east, thus rationalizing the structure of decision-making there. This too was a mark of favour to one not popular with the St Petersburg triumvirate.[15]

In his instructions to Alekseyev, Nicholas gave some guidelines for the new course (*novyi kurs*). In effect these consisted of two unobjectionable propositions: that the activities of Russian entrepreneurs were to be promoted in Manchuria, especially in areas which were significant politically and militarily, and foreign enterprise was to be excluded; and that, regardless of the expense involved, Russia's defensive capability in the east was to be brought into line with her interests in political and economic fields, thus indicating to the world her resolve to uphold her right to an exclusive sphere of influence in Manchuria.[16] This was the personal policy of the tsar, doubtless nudged by Bezobrazov and Abaza. But it was a positive policy, not dramatic in its novelty, and a gesture of protest against the attitudes hitherto taken by his 'stick-in-the-mud' ministers.

These new instructions reflected a new consciousness of the need for defence expenditure in the east. It was recognized that, despite the vast expenditure in the past, Manchuria, the railway and especially Port Arthur were vulnerable. Whereas Russia had in the past relied on Japan not having the courage to risk confrontation with her unless she occupied fresh territories, this was no longer certain. There was now a determination that there would be land and sea reinforcements and stronger centralized leadership in the east through Alekseyev. The tsar did not carry his ministers with him over the new course and did not try to.

The next landmark was the summit conference held at Port Arthur between 1 and 10 July. It severely taxed the limited hotel resources of the town. From Japan Kuropatkin reached Port Arthur in the cruiser *Askold* and stayed with Alekseyev at his official residence after his exhausting tour of inspection. Bezobrazov arrived by special train from the Russian capital and stayed comfortably in the sidings. The minister in Seoul, Pavlov, arrived with his family by the *Greimyashich* and stayed on board ship, while the minister in Peking, Lessar, sailed in later in the *Zapiak* where he too stayed during the period of the conference. The other delegates included Rosen from Tokyo, Grosse, the head of the Russian civil administration in Niuchuang, Chichagov, the army commander for the Harbin region, D. L. Horvat, director of the Chinese Eastern Railway and commander of the railway police, Vogak, the military attaché at Peking, who had accompanied Kuropatkin to Japan, and Pokotilov. It was a remarkable gathering of experts and showed the systematic way in which the Russians sought to reach some sort of consensus over policy.

During the five sessions of the conference, there was considerable friction, despite the fact that some of the more important participants had met in the capital not long before to work out a national policy. Bezobrazov who had travelled east specially was the outsider, not having been present at the earlier talks. He and those of his persuasion were in a minority. He had received *en route* the tsar's instructions as communicated by his agent Abaza. They stated rather evasively that

Russia would permit Japan to occupy Korea even up to the limits of the Russian timber concessions – a declaration which would be made from strength after Russian forces in the area had been reinforced. Perhaps because he did not like them, Bezobrazov seems not to have transmitted them to the delegates. He was not inclined to pull out of Korea and was in favour of war if Russia was challenged. Kuropatkin and Alekseyev made common cause against this and seem to have obtained majority support. It may be that they discussed the possibility of making Kuropatkin commander-in-chief of the army in the area, while Alekseyev became naval commander-in-chief. For the present that proposal was shelved.[17]

The broad conclusions reached were: (1) not to support with Russian government funds any enterprise either in Manchuria or in Korea (where the Yalu enterprise was to be solely of a commercial character); (2) to carry out the evacuation of Manchuria provided China accepted the new demands which the conference devised. Both points went against the grain of Bezobrazov's thinking, especially the first.

Though Kuropatkin was recalled to Europe without delay, he did manage to fit in inspections at Dalny, Liaoyang, Mukden and Harbin (16–17 July). He returned to Russia with a favourable impression of the capacity and efficiency of Japan's armies. His view of Russia's strength is not so clear. Bezobrazov for his part returned to St Petersburg before Kuropatkin and began to lobby against the findings of the Port Arthur conferences. He submitted a note setting out his dissent with their major conclusions. But by this time his charisma had failed. The tsar was not impressed by his arguments. By 16 August Kuropatkin won acceptance from the triumvirate for his line against Bezobrazov and the latter's influence seems to have faded. Yet he may have had some residual effect on some of the later events. Bezobrazov became ill with his exertions later in the year and retired from the scene. He may have been depressed with the lack of ready success which his enterprises on the Yalu had had. His appearance at the front of the stage was an important and dramatic one but it was shortlived.[18]

The Manchurian and Korean findings of the Port Arthur meeting were subjected to scrutiny by ministers at St Petersburg. Witte, Lamsdorf, and Kuropatkin (by this time returned from the east) met on 14 August and reduced the demands to be made to China from the original ten to five. These revised terms after approval by the emperor were telegraphed to Minister Lessar on 5 September.

In trying to assess the 'new course' as devised in the various conferences up to August, one must conclude that there were vast contradictions within it. There was a gap between the rhetoric of the decisions and the actuality and between the hope and the reality which emerged. The hopes of the majority included: pursuing the Yalu concession but without giving it official support and encouragement; withdrawing from Manchuria gracefully and gradually but only after obtaining guarantees from the Chinese about Russian interests; and pacifying the powers whose opposition to Russian actions had been bitter by contriving some means of giving them assurances and appeasing Japan as far as possible in Korea. By the imperialist standards of the day, these aspirations were reasonable, unexceptionable and moderate. But there was in several respects a gap between these statements and the actual performance. Think for example of the terms which were now to be presented to China and were still very tough. Did this mean that Russia wanted to evacuate or did she merely want to impose terms which China could not accept in order to get a pretext for staying on?

Moreover, there was a gap between the findings of the conferences and the thinking of the executants on the spot, the military groups and the concession hunters. Minister Pavlov in Seoul had no compunction about giving 'official encouragement' to the Yalu concession and clearly did not hold himself bound by the decisions taken at Port Arthur. Thus, he drew up a new agreement for the Yalu concession and used all his powers of persuasion and menace to get the Koreans to sign. He and Baron Ginsberg spent two entire afternoons and evenings trying to persuade the foreign minister and threatening dire consequences if he would not agree. But without success! The Japanese and British ministers in turn threatened consequences still more awful if the Koreans did so agree. But Pavlov's action was not in accordance with the spirit of the Port Arthur decisions.[19]

The proceedings at Port Arthur had been monitored with considerable perseverance by the Japanese, both military and civilian. In the case of civilians it was the consuls at Chefoo and Niuchuang (Yingkow) who bore the main responsibility. In the case of the military, it was left to the naval authorities to make their reports on matters arising in China.[20]

There were many reports of the possible outbreak of war between Russia and Japan (*Nichi-Ro kaisendan*). None seemed to be especially authoritative and some seemed to have been extracted by bribery of Russians in the know. As an example let us cite the report of Consul Segawa at Niuchuang which was telegraphed in English:

> According to private information from Port Arthur, in conference which was held there, Russian Minister of War, and most of military and naval officers insisted upon peace. Imperial messenger [Bezobrazov] and most of civil officers insisted upon war, but the latter was not successful. In Port Arthur, Minister of War intended to leave on Wednesday, but having received telegram from St Petersburg, he has left on Monday in haste.[21]

This was a typical example of much of the intelligence material reported by Japanese agencies in north-east Asia. From what we can understand from the Russian side, it was not a misleading picture of what took place at the five Port Arthur conferences. While to the Japanese Bezobrazov was always a sinister figure who had the ear of the tsar, the fact was that their reports were focused upon Kuropatkin, whom they had observed at close quarters. It would appear that Japan was not seriously misinformed about the outcome of the conferences, despite all the menacing things which were being said and written about it.

DROPPING THE FIREMAN

It will be clear from this chapter that there were in Russia uncertainty as to objectives and confusion as to actions. These were closely related to personal rivalries within the ruling elite. The main influences on the tsar at this time appear to have been the naval grand dukes (Aleksei and Alexander Mikhailovich) who were hostile to Witte and supported Alekseyev and forward policy in the far east, and Plehve, the only member of the council who carried any weight with the tsar and an unapologetic enemy of Witte. These opposed Witte on all fronts, abroad and at home. In the east Witte had been the architect of the railway projects and the genius behind their financing. He was open to criticism for the high costs entailed and the corruption which arose over the contracts. At home, Witte was a man of many political enemies: he was often over-zealous and ruthless, sometimes disloyal and often lacked finesse in his dealings. He lacked social graces at court where his manners were thought to be rough. As had happened between William II and Bismarck a decade earlier, the monarch felt that he was being in some respects outshone by a brilliant and overbearing minister. So Witte was in jeopardy from the jealousy of the tsar. The fireman of the Trans-Siberian railway was in danger.[22]

It was against this background that the emperor staged his *tour de force*. Relying on the cooperation of Plehve and the grand dukes, he issued the ukase on 12 August, establishing the viceroyalty of the far east. Its purpose was to integrate the diplomatic, military and economic administration in Russian territories to the east of Lake Baikal. Admiral Evgenii Ivanovich Alekseyev was appointed to the important office of viceroy with his headquarters at Port Arthur. But his exact functions were ill-defined; and he himself was unclear about the extent of his autonomy.

A watchdog committee, consisting of the tsar, Plehve and the war, foreign and finance ministers and called the Special Committee on Far Eastern Affairs, was to supervise Alekseyev's actions from Europe. Its secretariat was run by Abaza. Thus there would be decentralization in east Asian affairs and experts residing in the area would be able to formulate policy, subject to the ultimate approval, in effect rubber-stamping, of this committee. Because of the tsar's absences from the capital during the autumn, the committee was never to meet even during the critical negotiations with Japan. There was sense and nonsense in this arrangement. It was good sense to make use of the greatly improved telegraphic communication between European Russia and the far east and to have a mechanism for closer consultation and coordination. It was nonsense to link the new arrangement by way of a new committee to the already creaking top-heavy bureaucracy at St Petersburg (or wherever the tsar happened to be). In any event Alekseyev, who already had been given in May very great powers of coordination, did not greatly welcome the new title and almost declined to accept it.

Who were the gainers and who the losers from this change? Lamsdorf, Kuropatkin and Witte were certainly losers because some of their customary functions were absorbed by Alekseyev, who was ill-qualified for diplomatic, army or financial decision-making. (We should in parenthesis state that the existing ministers were not consulted about this change of structure so far as we know.) All three of the old guard lost out in so far as Alekseyev was more expansionist than any of them, even if he was more moderate than the Bezobrazov group.[23] Bezobrazov was in any case forced to retire in September. It is debatable whether he had ever exercised overwhelming influence. He had cashed in on Witte's undoubted unpopularity in ruling circles and had found a ready response among Witte's enemies, notably Plehve. His overall object seems to have been a commercial-political one: to secure Russia's new base in Manchuria by the creation of a buffer territory on both sides of the Yalu which should be financially viable. Bezobrazov was the mouthpiece of this idea. How far he was the leader of the group and how much leverage he had in court circles, it is hard to assess. After he bowed out, he was accorded great stature by Witte in his various writings which sought to lay the blame for the Japanese war and the Manchurian disaster on Bezobrazov's shoulders. He was to be one of many scapegoats for the war; but probably his credentials for this role were not unique.[24]

The question was whether in a country like Russia where control of the periphery from the centre was so lax there would be any check on Alekseyev's activities through the Far East Committee. This body never met and seems in any case to have been packed by Alekseyev's friends and the 'behind-the-scenes' apostles of the 'new course' – the jingoistic Grand Duke Alexander Mikhailovich and Abaza. It was unlikely that such a body could be a major corrective to the policies of the man on the spot, though naturally those in St Petersburg were more aware of financial realities and were not anxious to encourage the great expenditure which a policy of 'adventurism' would entail.

Meanwhile rumours were circulating that Witte had said some uncomplimentary things about the tsar to one of the private secretaries and that these had leaked out.[25] On 28 August Nicholas summoned

Witte into private audience at Tsarskoye Selo and told him that he was being appointed chairman of the council of ministers, which had hitherto been a post of an honorary nature without great responsibility. Behind the immediate issue of the personal insult to a sensitive tsar, there was the more enduring issue that Witte had been growing very powerful and this power had been resented by a jealous tsar. Witte's demotion had been a long time coming. He was astonished and disbelieving when the moment came because he had come to regard himself as indispensable to the administration.

'The triumvirate' which had been the custodian of the 'old course' had collapsed. After Witte, Kuropatkin offered his resignation in protest against the viceregency ukase which reduced the say of the war ministry in dealing with far eastern problems and placed security in the east under a naval officer. The tsar asked him to withdraw it and Kuropatkin agreed to stay on for two months to work the new system. Kuropatkin's diary shows that there was a substantial residuum of goodwill between him and the tsar in their talk of 1 September.[26] The third member of 'the triumvirate', Lamsdorf, had suffered several heart attacks. Although he had been forty years in the ministry's service, he had not the same leadership qualities as Witte and Kuropatkin. With the collapse of 'the triumvirate', a brake had been released.

It was perhaps Lamsdorf and the foreign ministry that were the greatest sufferers. The viceroy was henceforth to have overall charge of diplomatic negotiations with 'neighbouring states', that is, China and Japan. True, this was not as yet clearly defined. But it could only mean that Lamsdorf's wings were being clipped. If the foreign ministry was to retain any great role in eastern policy, this could only result in a 'dual diplomacy'. In months to come Lamsdorf's statements were in some cases found to be contradictory to those of the viceroy for the Far East. Nor did he have to be consulted as a matter of course. Understandably Lamsdorf offered to resign on several occasions but was persuaded to stay on out of a sense of loyalty. It is likely that the grand dukes had contrived this demotion for they had little respect for Lamsdorf; but others have seen the hand of Bezobrazov in it.[27]

Whatever the merits of these changes, it must be said that they were a disaster for the series of important negotiations which was about to open with Japan. Even without a dual diplomacy, Russia often spoke with a divided voice; now that dual diplomacy was more likely to occur, equivocation and buck-passing became the order of the day. Alekseyev, while he was experienced in the east, was inexperienced in conducting international negotiations. Moreover, to leave negotiation to Russia's old China hands meant that the European perspective on the Manchurian-Korean problem was lost. Thus Russian newspapers like *Novoye Vremya* could write that annexation of Manchuria would be fatal because the russification of the territory on the lines of what Russia was doing for her European territories at the time would be a colossal task and an intolerable expense; that it would divert her from her true interests in the 'near east'; and that Russia could develop her interests in the far east without 'possessing territory'.[28] It is doubtful if such views penetrated to the majority of the new negotiating team. To revert to the image at the start of this chapter, the new course pushed decision-making into the hands of those who believed in the fingertips rather than the stomach.

REFERENCES AND NOTES

1. The tsar's policy of 'balance' is well illustrated in A. Malozemoff, *Russian Far Eastern Policy,* pp. 213–18.
2. *Novoye Vremya,* 31 Oct. 1903.
3. R. Quested, *The Russo-Chinese Bank,* p. 11, describes Bezobrazov aptly as a 'court favourite'.
4. B. B. Glinskii, *Prolog Russko-Iaponskoi Voiny,* pp. 589f.
5. Lo Hui-min (ed.), *The Correspondence of G. E. Morrison,* vol. 1, p. 195.
6. *The Times,* 7 June 1903.
7. These men were highly individualistic and it would be wrong to see them as part of a Bezobrazov team or group.
8. A. A. Guber, 'Imperializma', in A. L. Narochnitskii *et al., Mezhdunarodnye otnosheniia na Dalnem Vostoke,* pp. 222–4.
9. Lo Hui-min (ed.) op. cit., vol. 1, pp. 194–6.
10. Kajima Morinosuke, *The Diplomacy of Japan,* vol. 2, p. 93.
11. 'Dubail said that Yongampo was merely a speculation in timber. I said not so, for the President was Bezobrazov [the Russian secretary of state] and the manager Ginsburg, the âme damnée if Wogack'. Satow diary for 24 Dec, 1903, quoted in E. M. Satow, *Korea and Manchuria between Russia and Japan,* p. 245.
12. Malozemoff, op. cit., pp. 211–14.
13. Ibid., pp. 215–17.
14. *Krasnyi Arkhiv* ('Dnevnik A. N. Kuropatkina'), 2 (1922), pp. 41–3.
15. B. A. Romanov, *Russia in Manchuria,* pp. 284–5.
16. Ibid., p. 284.
17. Ibid., pp. 303–5.
18. Ibid., pp. 306–7.
19. Jordan to J. D. Campbell, 29 Aug. 1903, Jordan Papers 3; McLeavy Brown to Morrison, 7 Sept. 1903, in Morrison *Correspondence*, vol. 1, no. 139.
20. *NGB* 36/1, no. 807.
21. *NGB* 36/1, no. 806.
22. Witte is described as 'a very transitory functionary'. Romanov, op. cit., p. 307.
23. Ibid., p. 296: 'Long afterwards they still claimed the right to preen themselves on having up to the last moment fought for the "peaceful" way out and opposed the "adventure" undertaken by new advisers, who had, it seems, "hypnotized the tsar".'

24. Witte to Kuropatkin, 12 Mar. 1904 in 'Perepiska', *Krasnyi Arkhiv,* **19** (1927), pp. 73–4.
25. Hardinge to Lansdowne, 7 Oct. 1905, in Hardinge Papers 6; von Laue, *Witte,* p. 248. It appears to have been the personal action of Nicholas, without consulting his advisers, as was the case with the appointment of Alekseyev as viceroy.
26. *Krasnyi Arkhiv* ('Dnevnik A. N. Kuropatkina'), **2** (1922), pp. 58.
27. Cf. *BD,* vol. 2, no. 250.
28. *Novoye Vremya,* 31 Oct. 1903.

Chapter 12

DIPLOMATIC INACTIVITY (SEPTEMBER–NOVEMBER 1903)

The Korea-Manchuria issue was a complex many-sided one. In the last two chapters we have described the relevant internal developments in Japan and Russia. There was in both countries an expansionist group tussling with a more moderate one which was equally determined to pursue national interests but in ways which would avoid confrontation or offence to other powers. The attainment of rational solutions was often lost because of the factional infighting. By the summer of 1903 the possibility of war emerging between Japan and Russia was being studied on the Japanese side, but probably not on the Russian. In Japan contingency military-naval plans were being pushed forward. But the Russians were also increasing their forces in the area. The Japanese intelligence services were observing this and trying to assess among other things the future potential of the Russian railways' carrying capacity.

In the next few chapters we shall write of the diplomatic negotiations which accompanied the military activities. These too were infinitely complicated. But it is not enough to look at the bilateral negotiations between Russia and Japan. We must also look at the continuing saga of Russia's supplementary demands to China which resulted in the further default of Russia over the third evacuation of her troops from Manchuria. But first we must mention the diplomatic activities of the Open Door powers and in particular the Manchurian aspects of the American and Japanese treaties with China.

OPEN DOOR POWERS BLOCK THE RUSSIAN PATH

From the perspective of the Open Door powers, the situation in Manchuria was gloomy. Dalny, the apple of Witte's eye and his ideal of a commercial port, had failed to develop trade and was, according to Dr Morrison, who spent time there in August, 'being transformed into a garrison city' with 16,000 troops and two war vessels, the *Amur* and *Yenisei*. Since its early promise as a port had not been fulfilled, the Russians were holding on under one pretext and another to Niuchuang. Meanwhile to the west at Port Arthur, Morrison saw ten new barracks of stone and brick under construction and the west harbour being steadily dredged: 'Where two years ago men could wade, battleships now are anchored.'[1] Evidently there was no serious intention to move from the leased territory to north Manchuria.

One way in which Japan and the other powers could deal with the 'monopolization' of power in Manchuria by the Russians was to strengthen the hands of the Chinese. This they could do by insisting on 'Manchurian safeguards' being included in the new commercial treaties which they had been negotiating with the Chinese since the Peking protocol of September 1901 which had brought an end to the Boxer troubles. The way had been led by Britain which had concluded the Mackay treaty with China (September 1902). Japan and the United States were negotiating the revision of their treaties of commerce and navigation with China separately through special commissioners from January 1903 onwards. While the general run of the clauses does not here concern us, it is significant that both countries had included in their demands the opening of further ports in Manchuria. They asked for the opening of Mukden on the Liao river and Tatungkow on the Tatung river, both ports being firmly in the hands of Russia.[2] Initially China was not particularly anxious to open new treaty ports, especially when it would inevitably attract the disapproval of Russia. On the other hand, she was not unaware that, if she accepted such a demand, it would identify outside powers with her cause and possibly improve her prospects of forcing Russia to evacuate Manchuria. But, if China went too far and granted the demand for both ports, it would be interpreted by Russia as an act aimed against her and might lay China open to penalties. This was the main point which held up the conclusion of the two treaties for four months. When, however, the Russians failed to withdraw their troops in the spring, the way was clear for a stronger stance against the Russians.

The Chinese attitude became tougher as it became apparent that the Russians were not going to fulfil their evacuation without additional severe demands. Whereas the Chinese negotiators, Lu Hai-huan, Sheng Hsuan-huai and Wu Ting-fang, together with the elder statesmen, Chang Chih-tung and Yuan Shih-k'ai, who were consulted behind the scenes, had earlier kept their counsel about the Manchurian ports, they gradually became more amenable. In August, they agreed first to the inclusion of secret notes to the effect that Manchurian ports would be opened after the evacuation of Manchuria by Russia. When, however, the Japanese, following the Americans, insisted that a clause should be included in the open treaty to this effect, China conceded even this in September.[3] The American treaty was signed in Shanghai in its Chinese text on 8 October and provided for the opening of Mukden and Antung, while the Japanese treaty signed after an all-night session at 9 a.m. the following morning included the following clause: 'The Chinese Government agree that, upon the exchange of the Ratifications of this Treaty, Mukden and Tatungkow, both in the province of Shengking, will be opened by China itself as places of international residence and trade. (Art. X)' As occurs so often in history, the negotiations over the commercial treaty were an essential part of the background to the main Russo-Japanese negotiations on political and strategic considerations. These reflected the deteriorating relations between Russia and China and the more resolute opposition which China felt strong enough to offer at the behest of the Open Door powers. In reality, the existence of the clause did not alter the situation on the ground in Manchuria; but it gave Japan, as it also gave the United States, some *locus standi*. They might later have to protect the rights that had been conferred on them by the new commercial treaty, even against Russian action.[4]

The Chinese knew that the Russians would not be pleased to see such references to Manchuria in public treaties with the Open Door powers. They had therefore paused and tried to argue that the opening of Mukden and other ports should be included in secret treaties. In this Prince Ching had the support of Yuan Shih-k'sai, the governor of Chihli, who was no coward in the face of Russian menaces but felt that this opening of Russian-held ports would be provocative. Yuan knew that he was in the firing-line and was scared to use his New Model Army so soon after it had been formed in 1902. After the treaties were signed, he recommended the Waiwupu not to ratify the American and Japanese treaties. But his view was not upheld; and the treaties were ratified. The publication of the treaties made the Russians furious. They argued that, since China was not in any position to 'open' Mukden to any foreign country, it was a meaningless and provocative gesture. But the Chinese, having moved cautiously, decided to ride the storm. They now had one argument for use with the Russians in calling for the evacuation of their troops: the three Open Door powers were insisting on China calling for withdrawal of Russian troops.[5]

Uchida Yasuya, the Japanese minister in Peking (1901–6), whose biography is one of the important sources for this period of crisis at the Chinese court, had been encouraging the Chinese in their resistance. Chinese officials had always been varied in their foreign allegiances. Uchida, therefore, played on the feelings of the pro-Japan group. The appointment of Natung as head of the Waiwupu was a sign of increasing Japanese influence. In 1902 and 1903 Uchida had discussed with Japan's friends the possibility of a Sino-Japanese alliance against Europeans. Its appeal was not sufficiently widespread for it to come to anything practical. But it did serve to encourage the Chinese to defy Russia.

Uchida also cooperated with the other diplomats of Open Door powers in Peking in urging the Chinese in their resistance to the Russians. Considering the weakness of their position, the Chinese did respond to this kind of encouragement.[6]

DEVELOPMENTS IN NORTH-EAST ASIA: RUSSO-CHINESE MANOEUVRES

While the slow-moving negotiations were proceeding between China and Russia, little change was taking place on the ground. The Chinese were waiting with eager anticipation for the Russians to fulfil the third stage of their evacuation, knowing that, if they did not pull out, China could not act against them. It had been left that, with the return of Lessar in place of Planson, the Russians would show a more sympathetic face. But on 6 September Prince Ching received new Russian demands. If they were accepted, Russia undertook to put part of the evacuation into immediate effect but to defer evacuation in Kirin and Heilungkiang provinces for from four to twelve months. The conditions imposed on China were that Manchuria should never be ceded to any foreign power, no piece of land should be leased or pledged or disposed of; 'Russia shall construct wharves in different places along the Sungari river and post there necessary troops for the protection of trading vessels'; no special heavy duties would be imposed upon goods conveyed by railway; in order to prevent importation of plague from Niuchuang, necessary measures would be taken in all territories pertaining to the Chinese Eastern Railway, including the employment of a Russian physician.[7]

Prince Ching, aware of China's reputation for feebleness in the face of Russian pressure, had problems to face. Naturally the Russians had given the Chinese an indication that the Japanese were trying to do a deal over Manchuria and Korea by which Russia would have discretion in Manchuria. This implied that China could expect no help from Japan in future over the evacuation. There was also the feeling that, if China responded uncooperatively on this occasion, she would lose the opportunity for an evacuation of the Russian armies. This appears to have been the viewpoint of the empress dowager, who wanted the restoration of Manchuria at almost any price and summoned the prince to the Summer Palace to tell him so. Not unexpectedly the prince preferred to keep his own counsel. He was, however, offered the advice of the Japanese, American and British ministers who all urged him not to act hastily and in any case to oppose the demands.

On 25 September Prince Ching addressed a note to Lessar, refusing the new conditions and insisting that the Russians should first evacuate Chinese territory and then discuss the pledges they sought. The viceroy for the far east, Admiral Alekseyev, as one of his first acts, broke off negotiations; and relations between Russia and China became worse than they had been for a decade. Shortly after the third phase of the evacuation agreement was due to be executed on 8 October, Alekseyev rather provocatively organized a military parade through the streets of Port Arthur. Some Russian ground troops pulled out of Mukden at the time but then reoccupied it about 27 October; and several hundred manned the gates thereafter. No attempt was made to evacuate Heilungkiang as had been laid down in the original treaty.[8]

The world powers who because of their treaty rights considered that they were entitled to some explanation did not receive any. It should be said that Russia gave assurances to the powers through diplomatic channels that she was ready to hand over Niuchuang before long to the Chinese authorities and did not intend to hold on to banking and customs; all she wanted was the formation of an International Sanitary Commission where, in view of her great interests and the proximity of her frontier, she should have a privileged position. But foreigners were interested in Manchurian cities other than Niuchuang. Moreover, the pleading of Russian representatives overseas was often contradicted by events. The Russians seemed to ignore the fact that communications had so much improved in China in recent years and put about statements which were at odds with the facts.[9]

The Chinese for their part kept up their pleas for positive evacuation. They knew of course that they could not use force and had to make the best terms they could. Moreover, they had intelligence that Japan was going to give up her protests over Manchuria in return for receiving a free hand in Korea. This intelligence was inaccurate; but the Chinese deduced that they could not rely on Japanese support. Eventually at the end of the year the Russian minister in Peking told China that Russian evacuation of Manchuria was impossible as in that event Japan would enter Korea which would be a serious menace to Russia's Manchurian railway. Perhaps this was Russia's thinking all along and, despite pious arguments, she never intended to make a full-scale pull-out.

RUSSO-JAPANESE NEGOTIATIONS

The third set of international negotiations was more crucial than the others – those between Japan and Russia. Although Lamsdorf was willing to open negotiations, it was not until 12 August that the Six Articles could be handed by Minister Kurino to Lamsdorf, because the foreign minister was so busy. The articles were in English and the first five read:

1. Mutual engagement to respect the independence and territorial integrity of the Chinese and Corean Empires and to maintain the principle of equal opportunity for the commerce and industry of all nations in those countries;
2. Reciprocal recognition of Japan's preponderating interests in Corea and Russia's special interest in railway enterprises in Manchuria and of the right of Japan to take in Corea, and of Russia to take in Manchuria, such measures as may be necessary for the protection of their respective interests as above defined, subject, however, to the provisions of Article 1 of this agreement;
3. Reciprocal undertaking on the part of Russia and Japan not to impede the development of those industrial and commercial activities respectively of Japan in Corea, and Russia in Manchuria, which are not inconsistent with the stipulations of Article 1 of this agreement.

   Additional engagement on the part of Russia not to impede the eventual extension of the Corean Railway into South Manchuria, so as to connect with the Chinese Eastern Railways and Shanhaikwan-Newchwang lines;
4. Reciprocal engagement that in case it is found necessary to send troops by Japan to Corea or by Russia to Manchuria, for the purpose either of protecting the interests mentioned in Article 2 of this agreement, or of suppressing insurrection or disorder calculated to create international complications, the troops so sent are in no case to exceed the actual number required, and are to be forthwith recalled as soon as their missions are accomplished;
5. Recognition on the part of Russia of the exclusive right of Japan to give advice and assistance in the interest of reform and good government in Corea, including necessary military assistance . . .[10]

By these terms Japan would place Korea entirely under her influence and Russia's forces in Manchuria should not exceed the strength that was necessary and should be withdrawn immediately after the discharge of their duties. These provisions were intended to oppose the Russian policy of exploiting Manchuria and Korea.

Soon after the Japanese terms were passed over came the bombshell of the imperial ukase appointing Alekseyev as viceroy of the far east. In Kurino's view this was issued without the knowledge of Lamsdorf or Witte and was the work of the expansionist party behind the scenes.[11] The British ambassador thought that Lamsdorf was not too unhappy at the development since he no longer wanted to deal with these negotiations with the Japanese. On 23 August Lamsdorf proposed that their negotiations should be transferred to Tokyo. He could not in any case give the tsar's view because he was away for a week at military exercises. Moreover, he now had to consult Alekseyev. When Lamsdorf consulted the tsar on his return, he confirmed that, if Russo-Japanese negotiations were to be dealt with expeditiously, they should be moved to Tokyo on the ground that he would be touring from 31 August onwards and then going abroad direct; and the relevant ministers would not be at St Petersburg. Japan was furious at this, feeling that she was being treated like a colony or a second-rate, subordinate power which was not entitled to normal diplomatic courtesies. At first, the Japanese refused to transfer the negotiations. Under the surface, they thought it was an indignity to receive such a suggestion and probably feared it was some subtle Russian trick. In any case, Rosen, the Russian minister, was not thought to be *persona grata* with officials in St Petersburg or to have their full confidence.[12]

Lamsdorf promised to convey Japan's preference to the emperor at his audience on 31 August. But the Russians asked that Tokyo should be the venue for discussions. Kurino had to admit that there was no other alternative since Lamsdorf himself was due to leave on 10 September to go into attendance on the tsar in Germany. Japan, therefore, accepted Kurino's advice and agreed to the transfer.[13]

Komura was in two minds. On the one hand, Kurino had been two years in Russia and was proving to be popular there. Moreover he had been posted to Paris before that and had plenty of relevant experience for the negotiations which were to take place. On the other hand, Kurino did not have Komura's complete confidence. There had been personal disagreements in the past; and he had once or twice had to reprimand Kurino for exceeding his instructions.[14] Moreover, Kurino, as a protégé of Itō, had the general reputation of being pro-Russian.[15] Despite all this, Komura had hoped that the negotiations would be conducted in the Russian capital in order to keep the Russian court involved in the decisions reached. He failed to understand the Russian court's conception of holiday-making or to sympathize with it and felt that Russia had made a nonsense of the negotiations and decided that too much of a concession should not be made. So, while Komura agreed that the talks would be held in Tokyo and Komura and Rosen were appointed plenipotentiaries on 7 September, the fact was that the Japanese drafts would always be addressed to the Russian foreign ministry in St Petersburg. Japan was thereby insisting that the Russian court should be implicated and should not foist the negotiation on to a junior like Alekseyev.

Rosen himself had his difficulties, being unable to get Alekseyev to commit himself to precise instructions. So he left on board the *Rurik* from Nagasaki in order to have personal consultations with the admiral in Port Arthur on 22 September. They discussed the draft of the Russian counter-proposals exhaustively before Rosen returned on 3 October and handed over the Russian terms which had been approved by his government.[16] The gist was that no part of Korea should be used for military purposes and free passage of the Korean straits should be guaranteed; Russia would recognize Japan's position in south Korea provided that Korea north of the 39th parallel was recognized as a neutral zone; Manchuria and its coastal islands were to be regarded as entirely outside Japan's sphere of interest. No guarantee was given about the evacuation of Russian troops. Komura received the draft with disappointment, seeing it as incompatible with anything Japan had in mind but recognizing that it could be merely an uncompromising statement of Russia's initial position.[17]

Keeping cool and preserving an optimistic exterior in spite of his disappointment, Komura in October held five meetings with Rosen at which amendments were proposed to the Russian terms. But there was little practical outcome. On 30 October such amendments as had emerged from these consultations were officially passed over to Rosen while a copy was sent to St Petersburg for onward transmission to the foreign minister. Japan agreed to set up a 50-kilometre neutral zone on both sides of the Korean frontier with Manchuria where troops should not be sent. In Manchuria, Japan was prepared to recognize Russia's commercial rights but wished to have assurances about her own existing treaty rights there. Admiral Alekseyev, as if to indicate his unconciliatory reaction, reoccupied Mukden with 1000 men late in October and drove out the Chinese troops.

The text was passed over to Prince Obolenskii, the deputy foreign minister, who was acting in Lamsdorf's absence. He first referred them to the tsar at Darmstadt. When Lamsdorf returned, Kurino met him to discuss the terms on 12 November. Ten days later Lamsdorf apologized that he could not refer the matter to the tsar because of the indisposition of the empress. His next audience with the tsar was cancelled because of the tsarina's continued illness. Naturally Kurino asked for urgent attention.[18]

Japan's counter-proposals offered some positive concessions in order to avert the prospect of an immediate war. Following the approach of 12 August, they had called on Russia to recognize Korea as being outside Russia's sphere of interest in return for Japan recognizing that Manchuria was outside her sphere of interest. Japan was ready to accept Russia's political rights there (as distinct from purely railway rights) and her need to take special measures in an emergency. Japan was even willing to consider a neutral zone, provided it operated on both sides of the Yalu. She wanted the concessions made to Russia to be reciprocal, that is, that Japan would be permitted by Russia to enjoy political and strategic rights in Korea, but undertook not to fortify the Korean coastline in a manner which would menace the navigation rights of the Russians. Obviously some relaxation of terms was to be expected in the second stage of negotiations. But, since Komura was a hard-liner, we may speculate whether the more conciliatory approach came from the genro who had held two meetings on 14 and 24 October. Japan's concessions here were greater than anything Russia had offered on 12 October.

When these terms reached Russia, the country was in some disarray over eastern questions. In November a leading Russian diplomat confessed that 'there are two parties in Russia, one for evacuation and the other against, and at the present moment the Russian government does not know its mind'.[19] This assessment by Benckendorff can be further substantiated by some of the memoranda circulating at the time. In a memorandum presented in October to Kuropatkin, a senior general with long experience of Manchuria, General D. I. Subbotich, reached the surprising conclusion that Russia should give up her enterprise in Manchuria; with war now a real possibility, two hundred thousand roubles daily would be required to keep the army in a state of readiness for combat; unfortunately it was already too late to give up her enterprises as fully as was desirable because of the degree to which Russia had become embroiled over the past five years. But the writer thought that it would be quite proper for Russia to give up south for north Manchuria. Naturally a pull-out from an area where substantial investment had been made might stipulate some financial compensation but Subbotich was unspecific on this point. This was an unusual view for a senior Russian officer on the periphery; but he was clearly worried by the consequences of over-extension.[20]

Whether it was under Subbotich's influence or not, Kuropatkin himself addressed a penetrating memorandum to Nicholas II on 23 November. He proposed to return Kuantung to China with Port Arthur and Dalny, to give up the southern section of the Chinese Eastern Railway and to receive in return from China rights in northern Manchuria and 250 million roubles in reparation for the expenses Russia had incurred on the railway and the cities. These views were presented (apart from the tsar) only to Alekseyev, Lamsdorf and Witte, licking his wounds after his enforced retirement in August, but won little approbation. It was unthinkable to Alekseyev that his 'capital' should be sold off to China. Kuropatkin's strange and pessimistic proposal, therefore, lapsed and does not appear to have been raised again.[21]

RUSSIAN EXCURSIONS INTO EUROPE

The movements of the tsar and his entourage in Europe were not without meaning for the far east. Even the meeting of the tsar and the emperor of Austria in the alpine resort of Mürzsteg on 4 October and the signing of the Mürzsteg Punctation can be interpreted as a means of taking tension out of the Balkan situation and allowing Russia to gird her loins for any trouble which was brewing in east Asia. After the tsar's visit to Italy in October, Lamsdorf went to Paris bearing a letter from the tsar to President Loubet This was a letter of reassurance that the Russians were still faithful to the French alliance. The feeling had been growing in Paris that Russia was coming closer to Germany and that the substance of the alliance had been lost, while the sentiment in St Petersburg was that France had been cavorting with Britain too gaily for comfort. Doubtless Lamsdorf was also seeking reassurances from France.

There can be no doubt that the French mood was a complaining one. In Paris Count Lamsdorf was told by Foreign Minister Delcassé that France was kept in the dark over Russia's intentions in east Asia and had not been adequately consulted. Though dislodged from far eastern policy-making, Lamsdorf still tried to impress Delcassé that Russia's demands upon Japan were of a very moderate character but said that he was extremely anxious about how Japan's policy would be affected by her hope of English support. The Frenchman suggested that a little more frankness was desirable and would be calculated to smooth difficulties. Delcassé, who had had the advantage of conversations with British leaders beforehand, said that they were far from desiring to follow a provocative policy; he urged extreme caution on Russia, even suggesting that the Japanese had the better case. Lamsdorf seemed to be in conciliatory mood. In the background there was the suggestion of a new French loan to Russia and, while this gave Delcassé some leverage in his negotiations, he was inevitably having difficulties over the terms with the finance minister, Maurice Rouvier.[22]

Britain, which was already far advanced towards what later became the Anglo-French entente in April 1904, had planted the idea with Lamsdorf through Delcassé that some accommodation could be reached with Russia. This depended on Count Benckendorff who had gone from London to Paris in order to have discussions with his foreign minister. Lamsdorf sent back the message that an endeavour should be made to remove all sources of misunderstanding between Russia and Britain and discuss the various questions outstanding between them – a statement of the utmost cordiality and vagueness.[23] On 17 November Lansdowne saw Benckendorff but concluded that he had not been authorized by Lamsdorf to make any specific proposals and was leaving the initiative with Britain. Speaking more relaxedly to Charles Hardinge at Windsor Castle on 22 November, Benckendorff acknowledged that the moment was ripe for a friendly understanding but insisted that Manchuria should not be discussed since it was an area where Russian interests preponderated and Britain should not press them hard on the subject of evacuation.[24]

Again on the most personal and confidential basis, Lansdowne gave Benckendorff on 25 November an idea of the kind of arrangements which he would be ready to lay before his colleagues and the government of India, covering Afghanistan, Tibet, Manchuria, Persia and Seistan. It is only relevant here to note that Lansdowne was prepared to contemplate some undertakings over Manchuria as part of an overall Anglo-Russian settlement. His line was: we should recognize the predominating interest of Russia as the limitrophe power in Manchuria; we had no desire to interfere with the control of her Manchurian railway system, having agreed in 1899 that railway development in this part of the Chinese empire should fall to Russia; we should not take exception to any reasonable measures of precaution which Russia might adopt for insuring the safety of the line; but we insisted that our treaty rights in all parts of the Chinese empire should be respected and our trade should receive equal treatment in those regions.[25]

After his sojourn in Paris, where he had some uncomfortable moments, Lamsdorf rejoined the tsar who was staying at the tsarina's home. Before her marriage Alexandra had been princess of Hesse-Darmstadt and she liked to return occasionally to her family home on the lower Rhine. Their stay at the palace in Darmstadt was a combination of business and pleasure. On the one hand, the tsar accompanied by Lamsdorf had a meeting with the German emperor at Wiesbaden on 4 November. On the other, they transacted some of the business of state. As an example we may quote one of the incidents which is supposed to have arisen. The tsarina, we are told, received at Darmstadt a telegram from Admiral Alekseyev complaining that Lessar at Peking was not obeying his instructions. The tsar drew up a severe reprimand for Lessar and was only with difficulty persuaded from sending it by Lamsdorf who was in attendance and had a higher opinion of Lessar than he had of Alekseyev.[26]

Towards the end of their stay at Darmstadt, Alexandra, never noted for robust health, fell seriously, even critically, ill. The tsar in remorse refused to attend to state business. Rumour had it that the empress was suffering from acute earache and that the emperor with characteristic concern for her would not meet anyone to discuss the responsibilities of state. Ministers and courtiers were unable to transact their business.

If the Russians found Japanese policy-making quaint, the Japanese certainly found the long absence of the royal family mysterious. They have never fully understood the western attitude towards regular holidays and certainly found the behaviour of the tsarist court and ministers at the peak of negotiations lacking in seriousness. It suggested an attitude of condescension towards an issue to which the Russians evidently accorded a low priority. Dispirited by the lack of progress in the Rosen–Komura dialogue, the Japanese were doubly annoyed at the delays which these forays into Europe entailed. Spring-Rice, left in charge at the British embassy in St Petersburg, made fun of the Russian style of diplomacy: 'Japan asks for an answer. She is told, the emperor is taking a holiday. Then that the Empress is ill; finally that the Viceroy must be consulted. There is no sign that Russia imagines for a moment that Japan would be justified in pressing for an answer, even if the Empress were ill. Everything must wait for that.'[27] We do not know

189

whether Alexandra at the imperial Skernevitsy estates in Poland was indeed sick with earache or with symptoms of pregnancy or with the ailments which came to dominate the last decade of her reign. But there can be no doubt that the Japanese saw them as a mere pretext for delay in vital negotiations.

In a court where ideas of divine right were never absent for long, it was necessary to consult the tsar. Between August and November this was not easy and the exact shape of decision-making was far from clear to participants. Alekseyev and Rosen assumed that they had the prime duty of conducting the negotiations with Japan; and Rosen always insisted that the talks were held 'under the Viceroy's direction'. But in the last resort the tsar had to be consulted at some stage through his ministers and had to give his final approval. The fact that the foreign ministry had a low status under Lamsdorf meant that the issue did not become a major problem. But when late in October Alekseyev seemed to be responding excessively to Japan's and China's 'provocations' by first holding his military parade in Port Arthur and then reoccupying Mukden, the tsar stepped in and cabled him that he did 'not want war between Russia and Japan' and wished all measures to be taken to prevent it occurring. After conferring with Kuropatkin, he clarified the viceroy's powers, reminding him that he could not order mobilization. This curb on Alekseyev's powers did not ease the negotiating process.[28]

REFERENCES AND NOTES

1. *The Times,* 29 Aug. 1903.
2. Sino-Japanese Additional Treaty of Commerce and Navigation, signed Shanghai 9 Oct., ratified 9 Dec, 1903. Ratifications exchanged, 11 Jan. 1904.
3. *NGB* 36/II, no. 975.
4. *NGB* 36/II, no. 947; Bland to V. Chirol, 15 Oct. 1903: 'The *Jiji* [*Shimpō*] reports that the opening of Mukden and Tatungkow is an accomplished fact since the signature of the Treaty but this I cannot believe.... All the imitation of Mackay's lead in these Treaties should be very gratifying to him; the Japanese and US Commissioners have in many instances simply lifted his ideas and the method of their expression bodily from the British Treaty.'
5. *NGB* 36/I, no. 374.
6. Ikei Masaru, *Uchida Yasuya,* pp. 70–1.
7. B. A. Romanov, *Russia in Manchuria,* pp. 462–3, fn. 211.
8. MacDonald to Lansdowne, 29 Oct. 1903, in *BD,* vol. 2, no. 254.
9. *NGB* 36/I, no. 393.
10. *NGNB,* vol. 1, pp. 212–13.
11. *NGB* 36/I, no. 13.
12. *NGB* 36/I, no. 22.

13. Ibid.
14. *NGB* 36/I, no. 398.
15. MacDonald to Hardinge, 18 Jan. 1905, in Hardinge Papers 7.
16. Rosen, *Forty Years,* vol. 1, pp. 222–8.
17. *NGB* 36/I, nos. 27–33; for a comment on the Russian reply, see the remark of King Edward VII: 'Russia wishes to make a good bargain to the detriment of Japan' (FO 46/568, minute by the king, 7 Oct. 1903).
18. *NGB* 36/I, no. 408f.
19. *BD,* vol. 4, no. 181(b).
20. Romanov, op. cit., pp. 28–9.
21. Ibid., p. 27.
22. *DDF,* 2nd series, vol. 3 (1903).
23. *BD,* vol. 2, no. 258.
24. *BD,* vol. 4, nos. 181(a) and (b).
25. *BD,* vol. 4, no. 182.
26. Spring-Rice to Villiers, 26 Dec. 1903, FO 800/23 (Villiers).
27. Spring-Rice to Mrs Roosevelt, 9 Dec, 1903, in S. Gwynn (ed.), *The Letters and Friendships of Sir Cecil Spring-Rice,* vol. 1, p. 373.
28. A. Malozemoff, *Russian Far Eastern Policy,* p. 243.

Chapter 13

FINAL NEGOTIATIONS – CLIMAX AND BEYOND (1903–4)

The situation on the ground in Korea seemed to the Japanese to become daily more serious. The Russian minister was trying to legalize the position of the timber company at Yongampo. The representatives of Britain, the United States and Japan were in varying degrees urging Korea to open the ports on the Yalu river as the best way of dealing with the awkward lumber concession. The Japanese tended to see Yongampo rather as a Russian base of operations against Japanese activities in the peninsula. Thus, there was a message from Minister Hayashi in Seoul on 4 October, reporting intelligence received that the Russians had installed gun emplacements at Yongampo. Colonel C. M. Ducat, military attaché at the British legation in Peking who was visiting Korea and had a high reputation for intelligence work in the area, initially reported that it was merely a semaphore unit. But, after he had discussions with the Japanese, he confirmed that the Russians had been building sites for 5–6 guns.[1]

This information about the gun-sites was valuable propaganda for the group in Japan which favoured an early war. Intelligence from army officers was being allowed to leak out and was inflaming public opinion. Intelligence from diplomats and consuls too was not inconsiderable and may have played down exaggerated reports about the Russian lumber company being merely a military enterprise in disguise. On 11 October another inroad took place. A message from Captain Hino in north Korea alleged that woods which had been brought by the Japanese were being snatched by the Russians. Japanese in the locality wanted Tokyo to send troops and, when this was refused, they did not know what to do. Faced by the prospect of danger, they made preparations to withdraw, sending the women and the sick in advance. In view of the situation on the spot being so uncertain, the Seoul legation sent an agent to carry out an inspection on 22 October on the *Wakaura Maru*. But the company police at Yongampo, using the argument that it was not an open port, did not allow him to land.[2] It was incidents of this kind, trivial in themselves, that brought home the Korean problem to the Japanese people and created bitterness towards Russia.

On 1 October General Tamura Iyozo, the vice-chief of the army general staff, who had been a faithful deputy to General Ōyama, died suddenly and unexpectedly. General Kodama Gentarō was invited by Yamagata to succeed him in strange circumstances. Kodama was home minister and a former governor-general of Taiwan and war minister, and his acceptance would have meant a loss of status for him. But Yamagata argued that the new vice-chief would have to be a man capable of planning and preparing for war. Kodama is said to have accepted the appointment because of the challenge it involved despite the fact that it implied definite demotion in rank and a reduction in salary for him. Sympathetic to the Kogetsukai's anti-Russian views, he took up the post on 13 October with a view to preparing Japan for 'the coming war against Russia' and embarked vigorously on war planning for which he had a natural gift.[3] By 23 October he had drawn up his first strategic plan which would involve Japan in invading Korea in order to confront Russia. He spent the next months pushing his battle plans through the army general staff by his contacts with leaders of the Chōshū clan who dominated the army. He found the army minister, General Terauchi, and the prime minister, General Katsura, to be pliable. He also made headway with politicians through his 'patron', General Yamagata. By the time the Russian counterproposals were delivered in the middle of December, many exchanges of view had taken place within the upper echelons of society and substantial agreement had been reached. But unanimity had not been achieved with the elder statesmen over the critical strategic issue, the need for invading Korea.[4]

Kodama, a man of single-minded dedication and enthusiasm, was frustrated. He found that, as deputy chief of the general staff, he did not take part in critical decisions on national policy nor did he know the details of diplomatic negotiations. He became convinced that the Russo-Japanese negotiations were veering towards peace and devoted some attention to mobilizing opinion by calculated leakages of information damaging to the Russian cause, on the lines of the Yongampo information already mentioned.

Kodama was indefatigable also in business circles. On 17 October he sought an interview with the most powerful businessman, Shibusawa Eiichi, in the hope of winning over the *zaikai,* the commercial and financial world. He tried to demonstrate that Russo-Japanese relations were reaching crisis-point. He recognized Shibusawa as a peace-loving man but the present was not a time when soldiers alone should be worked up. If the *zaikai* was to come round to the advocacy of war, it would show the Russians the determination of a united people.

Shibusawa, we are told, was much impressed by this dynamic soldier although he was well aware of the difficulties which war would inflict on Japan commercially and financially, both short-term and long-term. He promised that he would use his good offices to ensure that the shipping lines would in time of emergency decline to lift private cargo and offer the entire fleet for the objectives of the war. In his own way, Shibusawa gave his whole-hearted support to the army and tried to persuade the NYK and OSK lines to this view.[5]

The army also tried to convert the newspapers. On 10 November a body called the Tōkyoku Mondai Rengō Konshinkai, affiliated to the Union of Contemporary Affairs, held a rally involving prominent newspaper editors. It was attended by Baron Shibusawa, Viscount Miura, Viscount Akimoto and Baron Maejima. The meeting was unanimous that 'Japan has the heaven-sent mission of preserving the peace of the East'; that the government has public opinion on its side; and that it has the sympathy of the world. This supported the views of the seven professors and the Kogetsukai that Japan had made a fatal mistake in not asserting herself in 1895.[6]

Public opinion was indeed rallying behind the government. The estimate of some foreign observers was that opinion in Japan was becoming over-heated and too emotional. Secrecy being impossible to maintain in the Japanese capital, there were wild rumours circulating about the negotiations going badly. The government did not succeed in dispelling them by its over-optimistic press statements. Meanwhile, eye-witnesses were reporting that Japan's situation on the ground, in China as in Korea, was clearly deteriorating. Journalists were criticizing the government's policy of undue caution; and right-wing groups in particular were calling on the government to check Russia's activities.

This all came to a head with the December session of the Diet. The two opposition parties, the Seiyūkai and the Kensei Hontō, had gained ground against the non-party government in the general elections in October 1902 and March 1903. They decided to announce on 3 December that they were forming a party coalition against the Katsura cabinet. The 19th Diet assembled two days later. The emperor presented the customary opening message, exhorting the parliamentarians to support the government in its negotiations with Russia. The Diet members were told nothing specific about the secret talks and felt frustrated at their derisory treatment. In order to register their protest, they decided to exploit the message of thanks which they were due to return to the emperor. They substituted for the usual anodyne reply a more pointed one produced by the president of the House of Representatives, Kōno Hironaka, which included the phrase:

> In this period of unprecedented national uprising, the administration of our cabinet ministers does not accord with the national demands of the time. Internal policies are based simply on temporary, remedial actions,

and opportunities in foreign diplomacy are being missed. We cannot help feeling the utmost anxiety for such misgovernment and therefore appeal to Your Majesty's wise judgement.[7]

The house voted overwhelmingly for Kōnō's draft which, though vaguely worded, was equivalent to a severe vote of censure against the government. Some politicians pulled back from the brink because they did not want to bring the cabinet down. The resolution was taken to the palace but it was not received. On 11 December the house was dissolved and the cabinet lived to fight another day.

The historian has to take note of this demonstration, which criticized the government for not using its opportunities to assert a strong foreign policy. It reminds us that 'popular feeling' was more extreme and more anti-Russian than government feeling. This was an enduring feature of Japanese opinion which has been observed by the historian Kiyozawa Kiyoshi at various points in Japanese history.[8] One cannot say that the Diet was a direct and durable influence on the ultimate decisions of the government. It had been dissolved and was not to reappear before the war was under way. But popular extremism was part of the background which the government could not ignore. Demonstrations of this kind would not disappear, even if the Diet was not available as a forum. The existence of this kind of feeling played into the hands of the tough-liners among Japanese policy-makers and undercut the policy advocated by the genro.

Despite the cautious image which Komura sought to convey, many foreign observers were by the first week of December predicting the likelihood of war. Baroness d'Anethan had described the Japanese as 'most bellicose and equally indignant' on 9 October. Another described the Japanese as 'truculent' later in the year.[9] The Japanese – politicians and newspapers – had set their expectations so high that it was almost impossible to imagine Russia being willing to offer terms commensurate with their demands and expectations were bound to be dashed. On the other hand, Minister Rosen, while admitting that 'the strain of the political situation was beginning to tell on the popular mind', felt that the 'Japanese Press displayed a patriotic and unanimous readiness to take its cue from the Government's lead. It also avoided any abusive and offensive expressions.'[10] The hope of Rosen who certainly did not seek war was that the Katsura cabinet could hold extremist feelings in check.

NEGOTIATIONS REACH CRISIS

This was the background of rising national determination in Japan against which Russia presented her second set of counter-proposals. On

11 December Rosen passed them over to Komura in reply to Japan's set of 30 October. They did not seem to budge much from Russia's earlier position. Alekseyev in Port Arthur had been in almost daily contact by telegram with the others involved in the negotiation – Rosen in Tokyo, Lamsdorf in St Petersburg and the tsar in Poland. It was not just that this caused delay; it failed to give adequate opportunities for consultation on basic policy. In the end, Alekseyev's attitude seems to have been one of no concession but one of hope to prolong the exchanges with Japan. Over Korea, he confirmed Russia's earlier proposal for a neutral zone north of the 39th parallel and thereby rejected the Japanese proposal for a neutral zone on both banks of the Yalu. Russia in her counter-proposals included no mention of Manchuria, which was evidently intended to be outside the bounds of discussion with Japan.[11] This was a reaffirmation of the line which Russia had followed since 1900, namely that it was a bilateral issue between Russia and China only.

The implication was that Man-Kan kōkan had been rejected without putting forward any formula of compromise. This was perhaps the consequence of leaving such a large say in the exchanges to Alekseyev who seemed to be singularly lacking in original ideas and merely dug his heels in deeper and deeper. One British observer, Thomas Hohler, felt that Russia had been unwise to reject Japan's second-round terms.[12] This doubtless reflected the hope of Britain that war would not result from this. But Alekseyev seems to have held the view that Japan would not fight so that little concession need be given during the negotiations.

The British foreign secretary was able to make allowances for the Russian negotiating style. Over Manchuria, Lansdowne thought that Japan had gained – negatively – by the withdrawal of the objectionable Russian counter-proposal VII in the first set, which Japan had sought to suppress in the October talks but without success. On Russia's silence over Manchuria, Lansdowne wrote that

> Russia is now engaged in a protracted negotiation with Chinese as to
> Manchuria and is driving as hard a bargain as she can. It is not
> unnatural that she should be reluctant, while that negotiation is still in
> suspense, to make with Japan a separate bargain as to a part of the
> Chinese Empire on terms advantageous to China.[13]

Lansdowne was therefore able to look dispassionately at the negotiations proceeding in Tokyo. But, apart from this aspect, his sympathies were broadly with the Japanese case.

A genro conference which was convened on 16 December laid down that there were no 'concessions' that Japan could make and that Russia should be asked to 're-examine her position' and reinject Manchuria into the negotiations. That is, Japan was not prepared to climb down and was leaving it to Russia to have second thoughts. There was little hope for a peaceful solution of the Manchurian-Korean problem on a reciprocal basis. With only very slight delay, the Japanese passed over their third counter-proposals which conveyed what were thought to be their final terms on 21 December.[14]

Simultaneously Japan was proceeding with military preparations. On 19 December, General Iguchi of the army general staff expressed the view to the industrious Kodama that Japan would ultimately have to send troops to Korea amounting to one or two divisions and would require special bases; Japan must be determined and must plan for a decisive war (*kessen*). Two days later the government considered and approved a memorandum by Kodama, confirming that there would be no objection at any time to sending an expeditionary force to Korea.[15]

Behind the preparations, a major role was being played by intelligence. The general staff tried to estimate the transport capacity of the Siberian and Chinese Eastern railways for carrying the Russian armies to the east. The calculation was that there could be eight trains to Manchuria in a day. On an estimate of six trains per day, the numbers would roughly match Japan's capacity to send troops by sea to the continent *via* Korea. But, apart from that, there were already six divisions or so in Manchuria; and the Russian forces were thought to be better placed strategically than the Japanese. These points were disadvantageous to the argument for making war so Major Tanaka Giichi of the general staff amended the estimate in the memorandum to six trains in the day, two for arms and four for troops. For his part, the foreign minister was worried that the Japanese army in Korea was limited to four companies, dispersed in all parts, while Russia had vastly superior strength in Manchuria and could use it to attack in Korea at any time.[16]

The risk of making war on a country as vast as Russia could not be taken lightly. Yamagata, who was the genro closest to the army, revealed in letters of 21 December that the elder statesman had been trying to avoid brinkmanship. Katsura clarified the cabinet's position: it would make no war over Manchuria, unless Japan's Korean proposals were turned down. That was several stages in advance of the genro. Yamagata was still not convinced that Japan should go to war over Korea. The prime minister was anxious to proceed with war preparations but could not do so unless he had the support of Itō and Yamagata, now that the genro were fully involved in decision-making. With War Minister General Terauchi, therefore, he visited them at the resort of Ōiso on 24 December and received their blessing to take the next step.[17]

On 26 December the Japanese minister in Seoul, Hayashi Gonsuke, came out in favour of the sending of troops to Korea urgently. It would be best, he argued, for Japan to complete her preparations within the shortest possible time; if they were made little by little, it would inevitably be a warning to Russia and encourage her to take steps of her own, while a faction at the Korean court might seek a treaty of protection from Russia. Hayashi hoped that the method chosen to send the troops would not attract too much Russian or Korean attention.[18]

JAPAN'S NAVY DEMANDS DELAY

The general staff felt that the time was ripe for a joint conference between army and navy leaders to be held. Negotiations with the naval general staff began. When the negotiations with Russia had begun in August, the fleet was called back to Sasebo near Nagasaki for refitting. When the negotiations reached an impasse in December, the first and second fleets were amalgamated to become the combined fleet (*rengō kantai*) and Admiral Tōgō was made its commander. But the naval authorities were still worried about their capacity to carry out the army's expectations, that is, to transport the necessary troops to Korea. The worry was greater because the navy felt that it did not command the Tsushima channel and the Japan sea. To illustrate this, the naval command published at the end of the year a statement of comparative naval strengths in east Asian waters. By a strict interpretation of these figures, Japan was inferior in battleships but superior in cruisers. The Russian strength of nine battleships takes account of the fact that there were Russian reinforcements in the Mediterranean at the end of the year *en route* to the far east. When such reinforcements reached Chinese waters, Russia ought to be able to win a fleet engagement with Japan. But the battleship *Osliaba* was delayed for repair and only the two accompanying cruisers reached the east.[19]

But this was a superiority on paper. Good tactics and good shooting for which Japan was noted might weight the balance in Japan's favour. Then again, many of the Russian ships in Port Arthur were in doubtful shape and had not been rigorously refitted. Being older vessels, they could not compare with the Japanese fleet for speed; and, if they once engaged in battle, they were unlikely to reach Vladivostok, pursued by the Japanese. Japan would also be operating closer to her own shores and bases. All in all, therefore, any Russian superiority on paper which these figures suggest was likely to be less marked in practice. It would appear that Japan was not too inferior, if indeed she was inferior at all, in battleships.

An element of propaganda and illusion entered into these figures. It was part of the debate between the army and the navy over war readiness at the end of the year. The navy, by issuing these figures, was appealing to the public against an immediate war. True, it would suit Japan to fight a winter naval campaign when Vladivostok would be sealed. But the naval anxiety was that Russia had six battleships and six armoured cruisers in Port Arthur, giving her command of the Gulf of Pechihli.[20]

Relative naval strength in the Pacific (Tokyo estimate 30/12/1903)

	Japan	Russia	Britain	US	France	Germany
Battleships	6	9	5	3	0	0
A/cruisers	6	5	2	0	3	1
Cruisers (over 20 kn.)	6	8	2	3	2	1
Cruisers (16 kn.)	12	1	6	2	1	5
Gunboats	2	2	0	0	0	0

The Japanese navy ministry figures do not correspond with those given in the Russian 'Fleet and Maritime Reference Book for 1904' as quoted by I. I. Rostunov (ed.), *Istoriya Russko-Iaponskoi Voiny,* p. 81.

Against the Japanese claim of nine battleships, Rostunov mentions only seven (the older vessels *Petropavlovsk, Poltava, Sevastopol, Peresvet,* and the more modern, *Retvisan, Pobeda* and *Tsezarevich*). This may be partly accounted for by the modern battleship, *Osliaba,* which set off for east Asian waters in December 1903 but was detained in the Red Sea. In the category of armouted cruisers, the Russians acknowledge 6 against the Japanese estimate of 7 (*Rurik, Rossiia, Gromoboi, Variag, Pallada, Diana* and *Askold*).

At the end of the year there was a critical meeting over Japan's strategy in the presence of the genro (Itō, Yamagata, Matsukata and Inoue), the cabinet (Katsura, Komura, Yamamoto and Terauchi), the army general staff (generals Ōyama and Kodama) and the navy general staff (admirals Itō and Ijūin). Yamagata, the most cautious of statesmen, made the crucial speech, speaking both as genrō and as army mouthpiece. In particular, he seemed to be ventilating the ideas of the new vice-chief of the army staff, Kodama, whom he had earlier sponsored: 'What effrontery it is that the Russians are erecting military installations in the neighbourhood of Uiju. As Russia's power increases, she will probably never pull out. I think that we should send troops to Seoul before Russian power in Korea becomes excessive (two divisions) and occupy considerable territory in line with Russian actions.'[21] To this pronouncement by one of the genrō, the navy minister Yamamoto replied. While he understood the reasons for trying to forestall the Russians, he was opposed to the proposed two divisions because Japan was not yet ready for the dispatch of troops and in any case it would be improper to proceed with peaceful international negotiations with Russia while Japan was at the same time sending troops.[22] In the debate that followed, the army agreed that it had come to be accepted in the war of 1894–95 that it could not send troops overseas if the navy did not first say that it was in order. In these strange circumstances the proposal of an elder statesman was overturned by the opposition of a member of the cabinet. Yamagata, of course, did not concede. Eventually he agreed to reduce his proposal to the sending of one mixed brigade; and on this basis the leaders managed to obtain consensus. But this was a much watered-down proposal and less significant as an indication of Japanese motives.

At a cabinet meeting on 28 December the cabinet dealt with a number of problems central to war preparation. They had four days earlier decided to ask Britain for a substantial loan for war purposes, which Britain in due course declined.[23] They arranged for the speedy completion of the Japanese railway from Seoul to Fusan, which required an ordinance of the privy council. They also got the privy council to ratify the emergency regulations for military expenditure. A wider-ranging diplomatic problem was discussed at a further cabinet on 30 December. It was then reinforced for the first time by the chief of the naval general staff, his deputy and Kodama, the deputy chief of army staff. The primary purpose was to debate a critical issue expressed in the draft resolution which was before them thus: 'Although the outcome of the talks with Russia cannot now be foreseen, it is opportune to consider the policies to be adopted towards China and Korea in the event of hostilities and very necessary to make certain that Japan's actions are well thought out.'[24] It was the known wish of some Chinese, and indeed some foreigners, that China should not fail to take part in any battles fought on her territories. What would be Japan's policy towards China in the event of war breaking out? There were broadly two alternatives: to get China to oppose Russia alongside Japan; or to get China to remain neutral and keep out of hostilities. The cabinet adopted the second course and concluded that it was most desirable to confine hostilities to Russia and Japan, otherwise, if China joined in and other powers followed, a world-wide conflagration could not be avoided. Japan's motives regarding China – and indeed her whole philosophy at the end of 1903 – are best seen in the extensive resolution passed at that meeting. A lengthy extract from that document is given here:

[If China starts fighting against Russia], it will tempt the Powers who will try to cash in for themselves by intervening straightaway, while Japan will be so fully involved fighting to the north that she will have no occasion to worry about what is going on elsewhere and will even lose her corner in south China in the end. Needless to say, this is equivalent to our pulling chestnuts out of the fire for someone else ... With Japan about to take up arms against Russia, what she must fear most is an intervention by outside Powers. We must do our utmost to prevent this. From the very start of the negotiations Japan has been moderate and patient and has consequently been able to win the goodwill of Britain, the United States and so on. She must now try not to lose this.

Since Japan has, in spite of her wish for peace at all costs, been forced to go to war, it is best for her as far as possible to limit the fighting to one area and to ensure that the damage and loss that other countries suffer are as small as possible. Although Manchuria will inevitably become the war zone, it is important, in retaining the sympathy of other countries for our cause and giving them no grounds for intervention, to keep China neutral and reduce the impact of war on the China trade of other neutral countries to a minimum.

In this way we should hope to confine the war to Japan and Russia and thus avoid intervention by other countries. Since the war will have its origins in conflict between Japan and Russia only, it is best not to involve other Powers in it. If we were to let China enter the war, the situation would become difficult and we could not be sure that complications might not take place. In view of the Franco-Russian declaration [of March 1902] which was issued as a counterpoise to the Anglo-Japanese alliance, it might be that, if a third country like China were to enter the war against Russia alongside Japan, France would have no alternative but to come to Russia's aid. If France were to help Russia, Britain would also be required to support Japan, thus leading ultimately to the involvement of all world powers. We therefore believe that it would be most opportune if China and all other countries stayed neutral and thus restricted the scope of the war to Russia and Japan. ...

The doctrine of the 'yellow peril' is not too prominent a concern among white people nowadays, but it still persists among some Europeans. There is a risk that it might readily return and induce them to rally together to this far-fetched notion. If, therefore, Japan and China were to join together in any war against Russia, the anxiety over the 'yellow peril' might recur and persuade Germany, France and other countries to intervene.[25]

This memorandum, which is thoughtful and shows how international Meiji Japan was in her thinking, opens a window on Japan's approach at this time. It is primarily concerned, of course, with the possibility that China might want to aid Japan in dislodging Russia from Manchuria. This was to be discouraged in case it brought into play the old Dreibund of 1895 or the Franco-Russian alliance. So any Chinese suggestions for taking part in the war had to be avoided like the plague. It may be added *en passant* that the memorandum contains no mention of the possibility that Korea might offer to assist Japan in resisting and dislodging Russia from her peninsula. Evidently this was thought to be an unrealistic possibility.

On the whole, Japan does not seem to have expected much in the way of foreign intervention. She had probably concluded that France was reluctant to join her ally, though it was hard to guess what France's obligations really were. Germany was unstable in her responses because of the emperor's preoccupation with 'yellow peril' doctrine; but she had made it abundantly clear in the autumn of 1900 that Manchuria was not a major concern of hers. If Japan was to prevent Great Power intervention, it was desirable that mediation and other forms of pre-war interference should be avoided.

On 7 January 1904 the Japanese minister in Peking, Uchida, strongly recommended the Chinese to stay neutral in the event of a Russo-Japanese war.[26]

BOILING-POINT

On 21 December the Japanese had passed over their third set of counter-proposals. These reached Russia by the accustomed routes: Kurino passed them over in the Russian capital, while Komura handed them over to Rosen in Tokyo who then sent them on to Alekseyev in Port Arthur. Japan made it clear that the Russian redraft was unacceptable to Japan and made no compromises. Komura presented a *note verbale* containing four points as Japan's minimum requirements, and insisting on the inclusion of Manchuria among the matters discussed. Alekseyev added his advice on 26 December that 'more concessions to Japan will only lead to a further breach of relations; it would be better in every way that the Tokyo government should gain its objects in Korea without Russia giving her approval'. Lamsdorf, who saw the tsar immediately, was determined to reject Alekseyev's advice which was tantamount to breaking off negotiations, and wanted to continue talking.[27]

As a device to this end, the tsar convened a meeting of interested ministers on 28 December. Under the chairmanship of the tsar, Lamsdorf, Kuropatkin and Grand Duke Aleksei were present. But Pleske, Witte's successor as finance minister, was absent, as was Plehve. There was evidence of the lack of a helmsman who had a clear vision of Russia's objects in Manchuria. The meeting decided against cutting short the negotiations and was forced therefore to include some clause bearing on Manchuria. Kuropatkin, whose voice was probably the strongest, was unrelenting on Korea, wanting neutralization to the north of the 39th parallel, but took his earlier stance on Manchuria: Russia should concentrate on northern Manchuria and not risk a war over the south. In speaking of 'risk', he was hinting that the Chinese Eastern railway in its existing state might not be ideal for military operations, involving large contingents of men. So far Alekseyev's views had won no support. One person who did support him was Admiral Abaza, presumably as secretary of the committee for far eastern affairs. He had been an ally (as well as a relative) of Bezobrazov. He supported Alekseyev's line that Russia should merely allow Japan to take over Korea because this would not injure her true interests in the area; that Japan would merely follow one concession by another demand; and that Russia should not be a party to Japanese encroachment in Korea, which would be internationally unpopular and would not be profitable for the Japanese.[28] St Petersburg gossip suggests that the tsar also supported this view and the recommendations of Alekseyev. But all were agreed on peace. There were thoughts of war and of war preparations. But there was no talk of making war on Japan. According to Kuropatkin's diary, the tsar had led off with the view that war was without doubt to be avoided and time was Russia's friend. There was general agreement for this opinion.[29] Troops had been sent in great numbers to the east and, using the resources of the railways, this process could be continued and expedited. There was therefore a degree of confidence without a spirit of encouraging a resort to war.

It was left to the foreign ministry to prepare the Russian riposte to Japan. Steps were taken to bring home to the tsar the need to appease Japan in some form of words to the effect that Russia had no designs to encroach on the treaty rights in Manchuria of Japan or indeed any other power. The reply was therefore to be above all else conciliatory in tone. It was also to be part of a concerted strategy around the world in so far as Russia assured all the powers with interests in Manchuria that she would not injure their treaty rights. This satisfied no one because most of the powers only enjoyed treaty rights in Niuchuang, a town which was being held under a Russian administration at that time. The two treaties under which additional treaty rights had been negotiated, the Sino-American and Sino-Japanese treaties, were still unratified by China; and ratifications were only exchanged on 11 January 1904.[30]

At the insistence of Komura, Rosen brought over the Russian reply on 6 January 1904. The most important of its six points covered the concession on Manchuria which read: 'Japan recognizes Manchuria and her littoral as being outside her sphere of interest, while Russia, within the limits of that province, will not impede Japan, or any other power, in the enjoyment of rights and privileges acquired by them under existing treaties with China, exclusive of the establishment of settlements.'[31] For reasons already stated, this was unlikely to prove an attractive proposition to the Japanese, who could no longer accept *désintéressement* in Manchuria nor exclusion from settlements.

Even before the Russian reply came through, the Japanese were becoming firmer in their resolve. Many held that there was little point left in conducting further talks. The problems were twofold: the elder statesmen and the navy. Among the elder statesmen, even the Marquis Itō who was the Japanese leader most understanding towards Russia was coming round to despair at the possibility of a settlement with the Russians whom he now distrusted: they had shown little evidence of the desire to compromise which he had expected. So the political opposition to war had almost broken.[32] But the navy's reluctance for an immediate declaration of war was a more serious obstacle. Certain military steps were taken. The *Senji Dai-Honei* (wartime general headquarters) was authorized on 28 December by a number of ordinances. This enabled the army and the navy to sit down together and discuss matters which could not normally be done in peacetime. The *Rengō Kantai* (combined fleet) was authorized at the same time. Initial provision was made for an expeditionary force (*Rinji Hakengun*). Funds were voted for these purposes. Financial provision was made for the completion of the Seoul-Fusan railway, a sizeable expenditure which could not have been passed so easily had it not been regarded as a strategic railway if war came to the Korean peninsula. These developments were not kept secret; and this led to an infinity of speculation about the inevitability and imminence of war.[33]

By the beginning of 1904 the Japanese leaders had lost all confidence in a favourable outcome to the talks with Russia. Nothing short of a miracle could bring about a solution satisfactory to both parties. The Japanese were by no means sure of victory but they were determined not to shrink from their duty as they saw it: for, while their intentions regarding Korea were a matter of Japan's national interest, their intention regarding Manchuria was an aspiration of all the Open Door powers. They were in particular adamant that they would not entertain any proposals for mediation which, they thought, would only cause pointless delay and play into the hands of the Russians.

REFERENCES AND NOTES

1. *NGB* 36/I, no. 178.
2. Ōyama Azusa, *Nichi-Ro sensō no gunsei shiroku*, pp. 37–8.
3. Tsunoda Jun, *Manshū mondai to kokubō hōshin* p. 220.
4. Ibid., pp. 225–7.
5. Okamoto Shumpei, *The Japanese Oligarchy and the Russo-Japanese War*, pp. 91–2.
6. *Taiheiyō ni kakeru hashi,* Yomiuri Shimbunsha, 1970, pp. 135–41.
7. Okamoto, op. cit., p. 90, gives resolution in full.
8. Ibid., pp. 41–2.
9. G. W. Monger, *The End of Isolation,* pp. 134–6.
10. *Forty Years,* vol. 1, 229.
11. *NGB* 36/I, no. 43.
12. Hohler to Spring-Rice, 8 Mar 1904, Spring-Rice papers 1/44.
13. Lansdowne to British cabinet, no date, Cabinet Papers 1.4.
14. *NGB* 36/I, no. 44–5.
15. Note by Kodama, 21 Dec. 1903, in Tsunoda, op. cit., p. 224.
16. *Tanaka Giichi Denki,* vol. 1, pp. 232–3.
17. Tsunoda, op. cit., pp. 226–7.
18. *NGU* 36/I, no. 763.
19. *Japan Times,* 30 Dec. 1903.
20. I. I. Rostunov (ed.) *Istoriya Russko-Iaponskoi Voiny,* p. 81.
21. Japan, Navy Ministry, *Yamamoto Gombei to Kaigun,* p. 145.
22. Ibid., pp. 145–7.
23. I. H. Nish, *The Anglo-Japanese Alliance,* pp. 276–9.

24. Cabinet resolution of 30 Dec. 1903, *NGB* 36/I, no. 50.
25. Ibid.
26. *NGB* 37/38, Nichi-Ro Sensō, vol. 1, nos. 660–1.
27. A. Malozemoff, *Russian Far Eastern Policy,* p. 244.
28. Ibid., pp. 244–5.
29. *Krasnyi Arkhiv* ('Dnevnik A. N. Kuropatkina'), **2** (1925), p. 85.
30. *BD*, vol. 2, no. 270.
31. *NGB* 37/I, no. 20.
32. Itō's memorandum after the genro conference on 30 Jan., Tsunoda, op. cit., pp. 226–7.
33. Furuya Tetsuo, *Nichi-Ro Sensō,* pp. 81–2.

Chapter 14

FINAL NEGOTIATIONS – AN ADVERSARIAL CODA (1904)

A study of the origins of many wars in the past suggests that the final month of negotiations before the outbreak of hostilities is often crucial, dramatic and intense. That was scarcely true in this case. The negotiations from 6 January to 10 February which are the subject of this chapter were in the nature of an adversarial coda. A coda is a musical term describing an independent and often artificial passage introduced after the natural conclusion of a musical work. In our case, the negotiations had come to a natural conclusion without success. They were prolonged not so much with real hope of success as for extraneous and artificial reasons, namely that the sides were not ready for war and wanted to delay matters. Since peace is valuable in itself, the prolongation of peace is also valuable. But this coda, while it is important, introduces little in the way of new material and reiterates old themes.

An imperial conference was held at the palace in Tokyo on 12 January after many private consultations. Its object was to study the latest Russian response which had come in on 6 January. In view of the critical decisions to be made, there were present (for the genro) Itō, Yamagata, Ōyama, Matsukata and Inoue and (for the cabinet) all members except the prime minister who was ill. The heads and deputies of the army and navy general staffs were also in attendance. The emperor was present; and the navy minister, Admiral Yamamoto, was acting prime minister. The conference passed a resolution that 'Russia had made no adequate concession over Korea and had even refused to enter into negotiations over Manchuria, while she was at the same time trying to build up her military strength there'.[1] First there was evidence of some breast-beating. Yamagata is alleged to have told Itō: 'Although we cannot foretell victory or defeat, we must enter the battle confident of victory. If we should by any chance fail, it would be an immeasurable catastrophe for our destiny.'[2] Certainly it was an assembly of anxious but determined men. Second, there was (as Komura reported) 'complete unanimity of opinon'. By this he implied that Itō, who had for three years been the optimist who had held that Russia would be prepared to do a deal, had finally admitted that she had shown no willingness to make any concessions.[3] Itō's sentiments are explained in a memorandum entitled 'Nichi-Ro kōshō ketsuretsu no temmatsu' (An account of the breakdown of Russo-Japanese negotiations) which he wrote in retrospect in February:

> There is no question but that Russia's aim was from the start to increase her military and naval forces and then reject Japan's demands. In this way she could fulfil her ambitions in Manchuria and Korea without interference. This being so, if Japan does not now go to war and defend her threatened interests, she will eventually have to kowtow to the Russian governor of one of her frontier provinces.[4]

Japan decided to send Russia a final ultimatum. The problem was over the expected Russian delay. While there was no deadline set for a reply from St Petersburg, Russia was warned to give an early reply; and Minister Kurino was told to say that the reply should not be unduly or unreasonably delayed. The document was courteously worded but made it clear that modifications to the Russian terms would have to be made 'in order to arrive at a pacific solution of the pending question'. After rejecting the article concerning the neutral zone in Korea, the Japanese agreed that the Russian proposal concerning Manchuria could be accepted but with a number of far-reaching modifications, the main one being the 'recognition by Russia of Korea and its littoral as being outside her sphere of interest'. The grounds for the various amendments had been fully explained on previous occasions and were not repeated. Japan stressed that she was motivated by 'a spirit of perfect conciliation' and invited Russia's reconsideration. These terms were sent to Kurino on 13 January and passed over in St Petersburg three days later.[5] The impression given was one of sweet reasonableness and perhaps it was not clear to contemporaries that it was indeed an ultimatum.

The reason for the delay was a naval one. Here the status of Yamamoto as acting prime minister may have been important. So far as the army spokesmen on 12 January were concerned, they would have been willing to send off the emergency expeditionary force to Korea without delay; but they had to follow the wishes of the navy. The naval view was that it would take longer to assemble the troopships at Sasebo in western Japan. They could not complete preparations before (on one estimate) 20 January or (on another) 26 January. A later estimate postponed the target of readiness into February. This suggests that the delay may have been caused less by the need to gather transports than by the need to form an escort. In particular it was probably connected with the two cruisers just purchased in Genoa. The two cruisers had been built in a Genoese yard for the Argentine in their war with Chile; but the war had been ended by mediation. The ships had been sold to Japan through the British brokers Antony Gibbs on 9 January. Because the

Italian yard was practically a branch establishment of Armstrong Whitworth at Elswick, it was left to the latter to supply the crews for the journey to Japan.[6] This was of course the cause of protests by Russia; but nothing could be done about it in time of peace. Russia was probably unaware of the tie-up between Genoa and Armstrongs. The Japanese navy would only enter upon operations after the ships were well on their way from Europe, placed under Japanese naval officers. Until the ships entered the south China seas, the cautious naval authorities were not agreeable to war being declared. The ships eventually reached Japan on 16 February, were placed under Japanese crews and renamed the *Nisshin* and *Kasuga*. Katsura, restored to health on 24 January, had an audience with the emperor and reported on the options open to Japan:

1. Should Russia accept Japan's proposals, Japan need not start a war;
2. Should Russia reject Japan's proposals, Japan would commence hostilities against Russia immediately;
3. Should Russia accept some of Japan's proposals and make concessions acceptable to Japan, Japan would have to consider its policy further.[7]

RUSSIAN RESPONSE

It was announced on 25 January that the Japanese terms would be referred to a special conference, as had the policy to be adopted for the far east in 1903. This of course involved inevitable delay. But it did imply that the balance of decision-making in Russia had tilted again to St Petersburg and away from Port Arthur. Under the 'new course' of 1903, a greater say had been left to Admiral Alekseyev, though final sanction depended on the tsar and the telegraphic signals passed along the railway systems. At this phase of the crisis blame was coming to be attached to Alekseyev; and influence was being restored to Lamsdorf. Some interpreted this as a defeat for 'the military party'. There was an almost naïve belief in the possibility of a satisfactory settlement through the skills of the foreign ministry. From our knowledge of the determination on the Japanese side, we know that this was misinformation, misjudgement and wishful thinking. In a way the Russians may have been lulled into a sense of false security by hearing Komura say (as we have reported) as late as December that the negotiations were coming along well and that things were under control.

That Alekseyev had forfeited some of the tsar's confidence may be seen in the order of 13 January that no military action should be taken by him without informing the tsar.[8] Evidently it was thought that he was incautious. It is however wrong to imagine that Alekseyev was no longer consulted. The fact was that, until the war started, Port Arthur was the point through which all signals to Tokyo were passed. More than this, he was understood to have the discretion to modify the instructions, though it was understood that this would apply only in the military sphere. While, therefore, Alekseyev continued to have some say and was busily reporting developments, the major decisions were now being left to councils at the European end.[9]

It would appear that Rosen, who had hitherto accepted a role junior to Alekseyev, now became more assertive. On 13 January he passed over to Komura the assurance that Russia had given to all the powers, namely that she would not 'prevent the Powers from enjoying, within the limits of the treaties in force, the rights and advantages which they have acquired under such treaties'.[10] Evidently feeling that this was quite inadequate to satisfy the Japanese, Rosen claims in his autobiography that

the only possible chance of a reversal of [the Japanese decision for war] lay in strengthening the hands of the party which had been standing for a peaceful solution of the crisis . . . . This could only be accomplished by a complete surrender of our position, so obstinately maintained in regard to Korea . . . . I despatched the same evening a telegram to Count Lamsdorf, representing to him the absolute necessity of immediately proposing the return to the original offer of the Japanese Government, made in March 1898, implying the complete surrender of all our pretensions in Korea . . . . No attention was apparently paid to this telegram, as it remained unanswered . . . . [There followed] a couple of weeks more of a fruitless exchange of proposals and counter-proposals.[11]

Obviously Rosen felt that, by offering substantial concessions in Korea, Russia might deflect the Japanese away from overt hostilities. It appears to have struck no responsive chord in St Petersburg.

It is indeed hard to reach a fair assessment of Rosen at this critical time. Reports suggest that for three or four weeks before the outbreak of war he was confined to his room with tympanites (distension of the belly) and never saw any of his diplomatic colleagues. Apart from his own staff, the only person he did see was the legation doctor, Dr Baelz. The British minister reported that he had heard from Rosen's doctor, who was also the consultant to the British legation, that Rosen had told him ten days before the war broke out that 'we had only to mobilize one Division and the Japanese will climb down'. Baelz argued that the Japanese would most assuredly fight; but Rosen would not listen to him or anyone else.[12] In his diary, Erwin Baelz, the German physician, is more discreet, claiming that Rosen had good nerves but was to suffer from intolerable earache the night before his departure from Japan (6 March).[13] It may be therefore that Rosen's advice to his government was not so 'cool' or so liberal as he himself would have us believe.

In St Petersburg they were aware of some of Japan's war preparations. This hardened their hearts against Japan's counter-proposals of 13–14 January. War Minister Kuropatkin, who naturally assumed a special authority in such an emergency, wrote to the tsar on 16 January of the absolute necessity for a neutral zone in Korea north of the 39th parallel. For his part, the tsar thought it monstrous that Japan should be insisting on China's territorial integrity in Manchuria.[14] This was scarcely the language of concession. Yet, when Alekseyev reported further Japanese troop movements and suggested the need for some degree of mobilization, the tsar was quick to respond on 27 January with a statement of Russian policy, namely, if Japan lands in south Korea or on the east coast south of Seoul, Russia will disregard it and will not consider it a *casus belli;* Russia can permit Japan to occupy as far as the mountain range forming the watershed of the Yalu and Tumen rivers.[15] This was to curb the extraordinary powers that Alekseyev had been given as recently as August. It was a sign of a cooling breeze from the west.

On 28 January a sort of strategic conference was held to discuss Japan's terms and formulate a counter-proposal. Urgency was imparted to the meeting by the repeated warnings by the Japanese minister that time was running out. In the presence of Grand Duke Aleksei Alexandrovich, Admiral Avelan, Admiral Abaza, Lamsdorf and Kuropatkin, it was agreed not to mention in Russia's counter-proposals the question of Chinese territorial integrity in Manchuria (to which the emperor had taken such exception); not to insist on the demand for a neutral zone in Korea (this can only be interpreted as a defeat for Kuropatkin); but to insist on retaining the clause about Japan's guarantee not to use Korea for strategic purposes.[16]

On 31 January Lamsdorf told Kurino that it was too early to predict when the reply would be ready. The views of the court and Alekseyev had to be reconciled; and the tsar satisfied. A damaging rumour reached Kurino the following day from a Japanese newspaper correspondent on the spot that Russia had decided not to reply to Japan's ultimatum. While this was denied by Lamsdorf, the report reached Tokyo on the morning of 2 February. The counter-proposals were in fact approved by the tsar that day and sent to Alekseyev for onward transmission to Tokyo.[17]

The last Russian terms are often described as the 'compromise.' We shall not discuss them in detail here because they did not influence the course of negotiations. The text is given in Professor White's book. But Malozemoff writes of them as 'a compromise' indicating Russia's amenable attitude.[18] B. A. Romanov makes one important observation about them which bears examination. He describes how Japan broke off the negotiations 'notwithstanding the fact that Nicholas at the very last moment agreed to the fundamental wording of the Manchurian demand of Japan'.[19] Had this been true, it would have been a great tragedy for the protracted negotiations that they had come so close to fulfilment. But it is not true. It is true that the Russians at the eleventh hour did include two clauses bearing on Manchuria which previously they had solemnly omitted to discuss. But one is merely a statement of Russian demands for an exclusive sphere of interest in Manchuria, which Japan was seeking to challenge. The other was a new addition to the discussion from the Russian side, 'mutual guarantee not to prevent the joining of the Korean and Chinese Eastern railways when these railways reach the Yalu'.[20] Perhaps to some extent this was a desideratum for the Japanese but it was of a low level of priority.

On the whole, the final Russian terms were rather unbending. If, as Romanov and Malozemoff argue, they appeared to be generous in the eyes of the Russians, were they generous for tactical reasons? That is, were they intended to 'put Japan in the wrong, if war breaks out'? One thing is certain, whether they were generous or not, the Russian terms were slow in their formulation. The Russian leaders appear to have been blind to the fact that, the slower the Russian response, the more the Japanese would allege that Russia was merely playing for time, was merely dragging her feet while she increased her war-readiness.

Ironically, Russia's decision, delayed so long in the formulation, was also long delayed in the transmission. The telegram seems to have reached Alekseyev on 3 February. But it is alleged that the Japanese purposely delayed forwarding the coded message to Rosen until 7 February. Whatever the truth of this, it was a fairly purposeless act because Lamsdorf had himself informed Kurino of the instructions that had been sent to Japan on 5 February; and Kurino's account of them reached Tokyo at 5.15 p.m. on that day. Even this channel of communication was pointless because the message seems to have arrived after Japan had sent her telegrams dealing with the breaking of diplomatic relations at 2 p.m. on 5 February.[21] Nor would the contents of the telegrams have altered Japanese thinking. As so many had predicted over the six months of talks, Russia's concessions were too small and came too late.

In fact, the Japanese had brought down the guillotine rather earlier. Having heard that Minister Kurino had been able to obtain no response, a top-level meeting was held on 30 January. It concluded that Russia was merely spinning things out because time was on her side and was working against Japan. A delay of three weeks in replying was regarded as inexcusable; and it was unanimously agreed that a firm response was needed. Even Itō who drafted the resolution held that further negotiations with Russia would merely paper over the cracks and be no long-term solution.[22]

After this, events followed in rapid succession. On 1 February Kodama drew up an appreciation of the Russian army and navy in north-east Asia and circulated it with Chief of Staff Ōyama's comment that Japan must strike first. On 3 February there were meetings of the cabinet and later the cabinet and genro. On the following day an imperial conference in the presence of the emperor was held and took the fateful decision to go to war at once.[23] They may have been influenced in their decision by the intelligence that a large Russian naval squadron had sailed from Port Arthur on the previous day. It was left to the foreign ministry to notify Rosen and Kurino that Japan was breaking off the negotiations and was further breaking off relations.[24]

The most telling point in the Japanese discussions was the intelligence they had received about Russian troop movements in the area. From their comprehensive network in Manchuria, Korea and Siberia, they learnt (for example) that on 21 January about two battalions of infantry and some artillery were sent from Port Arthur and Talien to the northern frontier of Korea; and that on the 28th Alekseyev ordered Russian troops near the Yalu to be placed on a war footing. On 1 February the governor of Vladivostok asked the commercial agent of Japan to prepare to withdraw to Khabarovsk as he was ready to proclaim the coming of war. This sort of information was grist to the mill of those Japanese who wanted to show that Russia was not as peace-loving as she professed.

After the conversion of Itō and Yamagata to the need for war, Komura was in a position to take the next diplomatic steps. Kurino passed over the lengthy telegrams bearing on the breaking off of the talks at 4 p.m. on 6 February. He was required to do this, regardless of whether the long-awaited Russian reply had reached him or not. By this time it had. According to a Russian source, Kurino expressed the hope in a letter to Lamsdorf that the rupture would be short. He was further instructed to leave St Petersburg and move to Berlin, while the Japanese consul at Odessa was to move with his staff to Vienna.[25] The United States was asked to take over responsibility for Japan's affairs. The legation staff eventually left the Russian capital on 10 February. This was equivalent to breaking diplomatic relations rather than a mere rupture of talks. It fell short, however, of being a declaration of war. Indeed Lamsdorf claimed that the talks had been so cordial and their rupture so discreetly carried out that he had no reason to fear that an outbreak of hostilities was about to take place.

The Japanese message on the rupture gave notice of the termination of talks and of Japan's intention to take independent action. Those who understood the coded language of diplomatic communications could see in it a rupture of relations and even a declaration of war. It was stressed that Russia's delay remained 'largely unexplained' and it was difficult to 'reconcile [Russia's naval and military activities] with entirely peaceful aims'. The final document is so important in its implications that it must be quoted at length:

> The successive rejections by the Imperial Russian Government, by means of inadmissible amendments, of Japan's proposals respecting Corea, the

adoption of which the Imperial Government regarded as indispensable to assure the independence and territorial integrity of the Corean Empire and to safeguard Japan's preponderating interests in the Peninsula, coupled with the successive refusals of the Imperial Russian Government to enter into engagements to respect China's territorial integrity in Manchuria which is seriously menaced by their continued occupation of the province, notwithstanding their treaty engagements with China and their repeated assurances to other Powers possessing interests in those regions, have made it necessary for the Imperial Government seriously to consider what measures of self-defence they are called upon to take.

In the presence of delays which remain largely unexplained and naval and military activities which it is difficult to reconcile with entirely pacific aims, the Imperial Government have exercised in the depending negotiations, a degree of forbearance which they believe affords abundant proof of their loyal desire to remove from their relations with the Imperial Russian Government every cause for future misunderstanding. But finding in their efforts no prospect of securing from the Imperial Russian Government an adhesion either to Japan's moderate and unselfish proposals or to any other proposals likely to establish a firm and enduring peace in the Extreme East, the Imperial Government have no other alternative than to terminate the present futile negotiations.

In adopting that course the Imperial Government reserve to themselves the right to take such independent action as they may deem best to consolidate and defend their menaced position, as well as to protect their established rights and legitimate interests.[26]

One has the feeling that this document had been drawn up primarily with the aim of publication after the war ultimately broke out. It was in the nature of a justification and defence of Japan's decision to take the initiative in opening hostilities.

JAPAN, CHINA AND KOREA

Admiral Tōgō received orders to begin operations on 5 February when the squadrons were assembled at Sasebo. The initial operation was to send one squadron to deal with the Russian fleet at Port Arthur and simultaneously to send cruisers to Chemulpo (Inchon), to land troops from transports for the occupation of Seoul and the capture of Korea. The first fleet reached the neighbourhood of Port Arthur on 8 February and squadrons made two surprise attacks on the Russian vessels and put much of the Russian fleet there out of action with their torpedoes. Admiral Tōgō thus acquired command of the seas in the Yellow Sea for Japan. Meanwhile the navy had been engaging Russian ships found in

Japanese waters and on the high seas and had seized them, though the news was deliberately kept from the Japanese people.

The second squadron approached Chemulpo on 8 February. The disembarkation operations were undertaken overnight and completed by the morning of 9 February and the Japanese breathed a sigh of relief. An ultimatum was then presented to the Russian ships in port requiring them to leave or be attacked. The cruiser *Varyag* and the gunboat *Koreetz,* though outnumbered and outclassed, left the harbour. They were attacked and badly crippled. They crept back into Chemulpo; but the commanders decided to sacrifice their ships.

The Japanese operation was of course a violation of Korean neutrality. The Russo-Japanese war was not simply a war between Japan and Russia; it was a war fought over the Russian occupation of Chinese territory, using Korea as one of the zones of operations. Such was Kodama's master plan, as approved by the various decision-making bodies, of 'striking first and striking through Korea'.

The impact of the Japanese strategy on China and Korea had been discussed exhaustively by Japan's leaders on 30 December. The decision taken with regard to China had been to persuade her to remain neutral and dissuade her from taking part in operations. On 7 January Prince Ching agreed that, while China should logically have negotiated on her own behalf with Russia over 'Manchuria', she could in the present circumstances see no other course but to observe neutrality in the event of hostilities between Russia and Japan.[27]

The position with regard to Korea was more difficult. Over the previous years Korea had been calling for world-wide recognition of her neutrality. Fearing that there might be a military flare-up between Russia and Japan over Yongampo in August 1903, the Korean emperor had renewed his appeal to both for a guarantee of neutrality 'so that, if in the future war should break out none of the operations will take place within our borders and we should have no bodies of troops marching through our territory.' Komura evaded discussion of the matter saying on 26 September that it was 'unpropitious and also very untimely to discuss warfare and neutrality now'.[28]

The decision over Korea at the cabinet on 30 December had been that Japan should seek a secret agreement whereby Korea would request Japanese assistance for the security of her imperial family and her independence and, in an emergency, suitable steps on the part of Japan for the security of Korea and especially Seoul. While Minister Hayashi thought that the prospects were good with the emperor and the pro-Japanese members of the court, he feared the Russian troop reinforcements in Seoul might tilt the balance away from Japan. Moreover the Koreans wanted an assurance from Japan that her sole object was the safety of the Korean dynasty and the country's independence, as their experience after the last declaration in 1895 had not been an auspicious one.[29]

The communications of the Russian minister with the outside world were broken by the interruption of Korean telegraphic services largely under Japan's control from mid January onwards. This forced Pavlov to use a mail steamer or a gunboat to neighbouring ports like Chefoo in north Shantung. To the considerable mystification of most governments, a telegram in the French language and originating in Chefoo in the name of the Korean foreign minister was sent round the world. It was a declaration of Korea's intention to observe the strictest neutrality. The eleven Korean diplomats around the world asked the governments to which they were accredited to declare their respect for Korean neutrality. Britain, among others, gave this declaration. This was awkward for Japan. In this gesture of independence the Koreans had been abetted by the Russians and the French; and it was from the office of the French vice-consul at Chefoo (who was also consul-general for Korea) that the telegrams were sent.[30]

Meanwhile as a result of forceful negotiations between Japan and Korea, the secret agreement was signed on 24 January. But almost immediately the Korean emperor insisted that the ratifications should only be exchanged when the Japanese had replied favourably over guaranteeing Korean neutrality. The Japanese minister urged his government to give the necessary assurances even though it seemed superficially to contradict the secret alliance. He felt that the guarantees would be made public while the alliance would be kept secret and so the contradiction and inconsistency would not be openly apparent. Tokyo however did not heed this advice. On 25 January Hayashi was informed that the conclusion of the secret agreement was not considered of such necessity or of such ultimate interest as to require Japan to risk the world's misunderstanding of her position and to prevent her freedom of action in the future. When therefore the Koreans pressed for Japan to acknowledge Korea's neutrality, the Japanese merely stated that they did not propose to reply for the time being.[31]

This was a diplomatic setback for Japan. Her attempt to negotiate a secret alliance was leaked to the Russian minister who opposed it utterly. The rival pro-Russian and pro-Japanese factions at the Seoul court fought the matter out but found that the Russians were the stronger and so the secret agreement had to be dropped. The Koreans very naturally sought to link a Japanese agreement with Japan's acceptance of the inviolability of her territory. From the Japanese point of view, this was a most awkward declaration to be asked to give because the Japanese strategic plan involved the violation of Korean territory in the event of war. The optimum solution for the Japanese would have been for Korea to propose a treaty of alliance which would have invited their armies to come to the aid of Korea against the Russians; but such an invitation was never issued. Hence the Japanese had to face the necessity of invading Korea and violating her territory in fulfilment of their strategic plans.

The worry of the invading Japanese army was firstly with the Koreans and secondly with the Russians. The initial force of 2500 troops which was landed was not likely to be challenged by Korean soldiery. In order to win over the Koreans, the Japanese claimed that the landing 'did not take place before a state of war actually existed between Japan and Russia'. This presumably rests on the doubtful proposition that after the rupture of diplomatic relations a state of war necessarily exists. The Japanese also tried to contend that Korea consented to the landing of Japanese troops at Chemulpo. We can only conjecture that they refer here to the abortive secret treaty. At any rate there was no popular uprising against Japan. For Japan, the danger was rather that the emperor would move to the Russian or French legation for protection. To prevent this, the Japanese minister gave an assurance to the Korean emperor on 8 February that Japanese troops, even if they entered the capital, would neither harm the people nor violate the Imperial Palace.[32]

On the Russian side also there was no likelihood of a military confrontation. There was only a legation guard of less than a hundred troops in Seoul and they were caught unprepared by the Japanese landing. The loss of the two Russian ships at Chemulpo took Minister Pavlov by surprise and, though it seems to be out of character with his outlook in the past, he sought the permission of the Japanese to leave from Chemulpo by a French warship bound for Chefoo. He left Korea, a broken man with his newly-wed young wife, on 12 February, placing Russian property under French protection. Japanese troops supplied the escort to Chemulpo.

On 23 February Japan signed a protocol with the Koreans, pledging to guarantee their independence and territorial integrity and to introduce internal reforms. Japan could take measures if Korea was endangered by the aggression of a third power or by internal disturbances, while Korea promised to give facilities to Japan and put at Japan's disposal such places as were necessary from strategic considerations. Korea was debarred from concluding any arrangement with a third power.[33] The peninsula had therefore come under the military occupation and political protection of Japan.

DECLARATION OF WAR

The imperial rescript on the declaration of war was issued in Tokyo on 10 February. On that day it was circulated to the legations in Tokyo. Baron Rosen, who did not withdraw from Tokyo till 11 February, presumably either received a copy or heard of its contents. There is a slight discrepancy over dates since *The Times* of London reported that it was issued on the 11th, but it did not make any difference to the course of war which had already begun with the Japanese naval actions in Korean and Manchurian waters.[34]

On receipt of the notice breaking off the negotiations, the tsar acted immediately. He ordered the minister at Tokyo and all the legation staff to leave the Japanese capital and thus reciprocated the Japanese action on 7 February. The following day, he held a special conference with Lamsdorf, Kuropatkin, Aleksei Alexandrovich, Avelan and Abaza in attendance. After discussion, they agreed to the Russian declaration issued by Nicholas on 9 February. The important part read:

> We gave our consent to the Japanese proposal to revise the existing Russo-Japanese treaty over Korea. But Japan has informed Russia of her decision to call off the talks and break off diplomatic relations even before the negotiations have ended and the arrival of Russia's final reply. Without giving any warning that the rupture of relations would result in the start of warlike activities, the Japanese government ordered its torpedo boats to conduct attacks on the Russian squadron lying off Port Arthur fort. On receipt of this message from the Viceroy of the Far East, we have issued the order to meet Japan's challenge by force of arms.[35]

Though they are not really itemized in the Russian declaration itself, the events complained of are 'a whole series of revolting attacks on Russian warships and merchantmen'.[36] Russia claimed that the steamer *Rossiya* was seized in the waters of south Korea and the attack on the *Varyag* and *Koreetz* took place before Kurino had presented his note. In addition there was the attack on the fleet at Port Arthur mentioned in the declaration of war. These claims seem to have been spurious; but they became part of the propaganda battle to rally support.

During the discussion of strategic issues on 8 February, Kuropatkin took the view that a landing of Japanese forces at Chemulpo would give the Russians great advantages in initial deployment. The notion presumably was that the Japanese would not make a direct attack on Manchuria and would be bogged down in Korea to some degree and this would give Russia time to pursue her preparations in Manchuria. There was no evidence of a view that Russia could in any way resist Japan in Korea. A carefully-worded telegram was accordingly sent to Admiral Alekseyev:

> It is desirable that the Japanese, and not we, begin military actions. Provided they do not, therefore, direct their operations against us, you should not take any measures against them, whether in landings in southern Korea or on the eastern coast as far north as Gensan. But if the Japanese fleet, with or without landing parties, were to cross the 39th parallel on the western coast of Korea, you may attack without waiting for them to fire the first shot.[37]

These were fairly explicit instructions and took the decision out of the hands of the viceroy. But they were also crafty. Like the Japanese before them, the Russians were preparing their position for the eventuality of war breaking out and were anxious to show themselves as being unprovocative. They were making a bid in advance for the sympathy of world opinion.

Yet there is evidence that the specific nature of these instructions belied the true mood in St Petersburg and the chaos and uncertainty which prevailed. On the evening that the attack on Port Arthur took place, the tsar and tsarina attended the opera. He declined to cancel the arrangements which were under way for a court ball, until the news of the attack and its results were received at midnight on 9 February. When Rosen reported on happenings at Port Arthur, the tsar apparently penned the marginal note: 'This is absolutely absurd'.[38] It would seem therefore that there was wishful thinking in the Russian court up to the last moment that the Japanese would not dare to make war on the mighty imperial forces. Yet preparations were continuing systematically enough. The declaration of war was issued ultimately on 18 February.[39]

Needless to say, Japan's action has come in for many-sided criticism, both contemporary and subsequent. In the white papers issued by both powers after the war began, accusation and counter-accusation were flung at each other on these and other themes. The Japanese case then and now rests with the argument that a declaration of war is not a necessary condition for beginning hostilities and that the breaking of diplomatic relations is enough to enable countries to take independent action, even of a military sort. This was the argument advanced by the Japanese foreign ministry on 3 March: Japan had made it abundantly clear that she would take 'independent action' which implied that she would go as far even as opening hostilities.

Arguments along similar lines were – perhaps not unexpectedly – developed by one of the 'seven professors' who became notorious in the summer of 1903, Takahashi Sakue, Professor of Law at Tokyo University. Writing in the *Kokumin Shimbun,* he cited many cases of modern European wars where the declaration of war did not come before the start of fighting.[40] From later incidents in Japanese history, we know that in a crisis decisions of a military kind were reserved to serving officers by the doctrine of *dokudan senkō* (doctrine of supreme command). Thus military or naval commanders had a large measure of freedom of action over naval encounters or expeditionary forces which would hardly be enjoyed in other countries. One has the feeling that Admiral Tōgō exercised these rights without knowing the finer points about Japan's declaration of war.

The Russian view was that the breaking off of diplomatic relations by no means implied the opening of hostilities. In its note of 20 February in its *Official Messenger* it disputed strongly the view that a state of war existed between Japan and Russia from 6 February onwards.[41]

So divided was opinion in Russia over the war that there were not lacking those who supported the Japanese arguments. While there was plenty of evidence in public demonstrations that a war against Japan was a popular war, there was much evidence of hostility among the intelligentsia. An example which is relevant to the present discussion is a jurist called Pilenko, a lecturer in international law, who worked under Professor Martens at St Petersburg. He argued surprisingly that 'Kurino's note contained not only the rupture of diplomatic relations but also the declaration of war as published in the Japanese White Book .... It is common knowledge that fifty hours elapsed between the rupture and the attack on the Port Arthur squadron.'[42] He goes on to argue that Russia could have used that time by offering Japan certain concessions. It seems to be straining the terms of the Japanese note to call it a declaration of war. But it is none the less interesting that a Russian jurist should interpret it in this way, albeit twelve months later, and say in effect that the Japanese were entitled by the notice given to take the action that they did at Port Arthur.

As defeat followed defeat, Russia became demoralized and a search for scapegoats began. Much controversy surrounded the events of the first ten days of February. In November 1904 Alekseyev, who had been sacked as commander-in-chief, returned to the capital an embittered man and spoke to French newspapermen. He apparently alleged that he had been told that war was not likely to result from the rupture of negotiations.[43] Although we cannot substantiate this point, we have seen that Alekseyev had been warned to abstain from acts which might be interpreted as beginning hostilities. Perhaps he had not been fully alerted to the critical situation that had been reached. In the face of the witchhunt which inevitably overtakes the unsuccessful in war, Alekseyev had to defend his actions in the last week. He did so by trying to incriminate Lamsdorf. Lamsdorf's defence was that by the division of authority introduced in August 1903 the responsibility lay with the viceroy and not with himself. In any case Lamsdorf argued that the Japanese messages were equivocal. The wording of the official notes was vague, deliberately so. Moreover Lamsdorf had received a personal letter in which the Japanese minister, Kurino, had expressed his hope for the speedy resumption of relations. The problem of 'decoding' the communications on both sides was certainly a great one. And Lamsdorf may have been taken in by the courteous tone of the Japanese messages. In turn, Lamsdorf may not have conveyed to Alekseyev the seriousness of Japan's intentions. Having said that, it is also true that Alekseyev must be blamed for not having his own sources of information and intelligence about Japan's actions. There does seem to have been overconfidence in Port Arthur which was singularly blind.

As in many a coda, little new of substance emerged. Old arguments were rehearsed and refuted. But the coda was significant. The two events of January – Japan's final ultimatum and Russia's failure to reply – were critical for the outbreak of the war and for the occurrence of a catastrophe on an immense scale. We have hitherto looked at the coda from the standpoint of the two adversaries. In fact there were many other parties looking on. To them we must turn in the next chapter.

REFERENCES AND NOTES

1. Japan, Navy Ministry, *Yamamoto Gombei to Kaigun,* pp. 189–201.
2. R. Hackett, *Yamagata Amitomo in the Rise of Modern Japan,* p. 226.
3. *NGB* 37/I, no. 45.
4. Tsunoda Jun, *Manshū Mondai to kokubō hōshin,* p. 230, quoting *Zoku Itō Hirobumi Hiroku.*
5. Komura to Kurino, 13 Jan. 1904, *NGB* 37/I, nos. 20–35.
6. Louis of Battenberg to T. H. Sanderson, 3 Feb. 1904, Scott Papers, Add. MSS 52,299, British Library, London; Marquis Ruvigny, *Nobilities of Europe* (Edinburgh 1909).
7. Tokutomi: Iichirō, *Kōshaku Katsura Tarō den,* vol. 2, Tokyo 1917, pp. 197–8.
8. A. Malozemoff, *Russian Far Eastern Policy,* p. 248.
9. Note by Spring-Rice, 25 Jan 1904, Scott Papers, 52,302; 'V Shtabe Adm. E. I. Alekseyeva (Planson diary)', *Krasnyi Arkhiv* **41–2** (1930), pp. 148–56.
10. *NGB* 37/I, no. 34.
11. Rosen, *Forty Years,* vol. 1, pp. 230–2.
12. MacDonald to Hardinge, 30 June 1904, Hardinge Papers 3.
13. Erwin Baelz, *Awakening Japan: Diary of a German Doctor,* entries for 14 Dec. 1903 and 6 Mar. 1904.
14. Malozemoff, op. cit., p. 248.
15. Ibid.
16. Ibid.
17. *Yamamoto Gombei to Kaigun,* pp. 185–7.
18. Malozemoff, op. cit., p. 248; White, pp. 356–8, Fourth Exchange.
19. B. A. Romanov, *Russia in Manchuria,* p. 331.
20. White, op. cit., p. 357.
21. *NGB* 37/I, no. 117; *Japan: Correspondence regarding the Negotiations between Japan and Russia, 1903–4,* pp. 33–6.
22. Itō, 'Nichi-Ro Kōshō Ketsuretsu no Temmatsu': 'From the start the intention of Russia was to build up her land and sea forces, and then to reject the Japanese demands.'
23. Kodama's 'Jōkyō Handan' in Tsunoda, op. cit., pp. 227 ff.
24. Message from Consul Mizuno (Chefoo), 3 Feb. 1904, Tsunoda, op. cit., p. 230; H. G. W. Woodhead diaries (transcribed), 5 Feb. 1904: 'Great excitement today as it is said that the Russian fleet has left Port Arthur. News of war expected all today. I personally think that the fleet left there because the *Kazan,* a transport which left Hong Kong for Port Arthur has not arrived, or else that the Russians want to capture the two new cruisers *Nisshin* and *Kasuga* before they reach Japan.'
25. *NGB* 37/I, no. 121.

26. *NGB* 37/I, no. 122.
27. *NGB,* Nichi-Ro Sensō, vol. 1, no. 661.
28. *NGB* 36/I, no. 700.
29. *NGB* 37/I, no. 368.
30. *NGB* 37/I, no. 333; Fontenay (Chefoo) to Delcassé, 2 Feb. 1904, *DDF,* 2nd series, vol. 4 (1904), no. 235.
31. *NGB* 37/I, nos. 335–42.
32. *NGB* 37/I, nos. 343–7.
33. *NGB* 37/I, no. 376.
34. *The Times,* 22 Feb. 1904.
35. Asakawa Kanichi, *Russo-Japanese Conflict,* pp. 348–51.
36. Ibid.
37. Tsar to Alekseyev, 8 Feb. 1904, in Malozemoff, op. cit., p. 249.
38. Hardinge to Lansdowne, 13 Dec. 1904, Hardinge Papers 46.
39. Official communiqué, 18 Feb. 1904 in Asakawa, op. cit., pp. 348–9.
40. Takahashi rehearsed his exploits in *Manshū mondai no kaiketsu,* published in 1904.
41. *Official Messenger,* 20. Feb. 1904, in Asakawa, op. cit., pp. 349–51.
42. Hardinge to Lansdowne, 13 Dec. 1904, Hardinge Papers 46.
43. Ibid.

Chapter 15

INTERNATIONAL EFFORTS FOR PEACE (1903–4)

A natural question must inevitably be asked: 'Why did the powers not avert this war?' It is a fundamental question in any discussion of the origins of war and is especially relevant in the context of the twentieth century when it is often assumed that the Great Powers have the ability to restrain their political partners in matters like making war. In 1904 there were indeed many and varied efforts at *apaisement* – the maintenance of peace. There was no serious suggestion of convening an international conference or of using some international medium. There were, however, efforts at mediation; the 'good offices' of friendly powers were offered. These were in general favoured by Russia and rejected by Japan. But consultations about a formula which would be acceptable to both sides did take place.

Various alternative formulae were devised by France, Britain and the United States and were put forward by a sort of post-box technique by which they were first put to one side and then to the other. They failed partly because of opposition from Japan but also because they were started too late. They were less than successful also because it proved impossible to arrange for a wide enough coalition of powers to support these international initiatives and exert the necessary influence to prevent war breaking out. The motives of the powers were varied. Certainly the European countries wanted to avoid direct involvement in this war at all costs. So their efforts, though to some extent motivated by a desire for international peace-keeping, were also motivated by self-interest. But in the last resort countries like Germany and Britain found it to be as advantageous to them to stay on the sidelines as it would have been to take serious steps to prevent the war.

Although Japan, as this chapter will show, was opposed to all suggestions of mediation, she was very sensitive about international reactions to her if she ultimately declared war. She wanted to avoid antagonizing powers which favoured the territorial integrity of Korea and China and to confine the war to Russia and Japan. It was necessary for her to find out foreign reactions, both official and unofficial.

Komura, therefore, addressed his ministers in London, Paris, Berlin, Rome, Vienna and Washington early in January:

A clear conception of popular sentiments in Europe and America as well as the disposition of the great Powers are [sic] necessary for the Government to form correct judgement of the situation. You are accordingly desired to exert your best effort in keeping me fully and timely [sic] informed of the general tone of public opinion and any indications of the attitude of the Govt. to which you are accredited. If you think money necessary to accomplish the above end, reasonable sum will be allowed on your application.[1]

The enquiry did not elicit any precise information which greatly influenced Japan's ultimate decision for war. But the replies did suggest that newspapers in London and Washington in general supported Japan's standpoint, while those in Berlin were non-committal. Thus Minister Inoue in Berlin reported that he did not find the leaders in the German press to be of a nature opposed to Japan.[2] But rumours were flying about thick and fast; and the Japanese, who were anxious to get world opinion on their side, were fully stretched in scotching those which reflected badly on them.

Among these were rumours about mediation between Russia and Japan. The Tokyo cabinet had already decided on the line that it would take and informed Britain and the other powers accordingly: 'Russia, if she asks for mediation, does so only to gain time in order to consolidate her position in the east. Consequently mediation, if it were now to be arranged, would result in advantage to Russia.'[3] The Japanese accordingly pleaded that the actions of the Russians indicated their manifest desire to pursue a policy of procrastination so as to give them time to complete their warlike preparations; mediation would serve no purpose other than to gain time for Russia. Britain saw the logic of this argument and did not press for mediation by the outside powers.

THE POWERS AND THE COMING CONFLICT

In the atmosphere of rumour and foreboding, it is necessary to examine how the powers individually regarded the prospect of war between Russia and Japan. Britain did not think that the Manchurian issue was serious enough for her to intervene. That did not mean that there was not a real risk that she would be drawn in, since it was widely expected that Japan would suffer serious losses if war came. Hence Britain had to have a contingency plan, providing for her ultimate involvement in the struggle. This might suggest that Britain would do her damnedest to prevent the war. But the result of such a course might have been to make Britain unpopular with Japan and to divert Russia's energies to the frontiers of India. It was there that Britain had been involved in a seemingly endless series of incidents with Russia over Afghanistan, Tibet and Persia. With the Orenburg–Tashkent railway due to be completed late in 1903, the prospect for future disputes between British India and Russia was very great.

Britain hoped desperately that she would not be involved in the conflict. Her decision in favour of neutrality was not intended to be mere rhetoric to mask her true feelings. The fact was that Britain, having entered into an alliance with Japan and being in the middle of negotiations with France for an *entente,* could still not afford to turn her back on France's ally, Russia. Foreign Secretary Lansdowne had consequently initiated talks in 1903 with the Russian ambassador in London, Count Benckendorff, for a settlement of outstanding questions by patching up traditional areas of disagreement in central and southern Asia. On 1 January 1904 he formulated for the cabinet some heads of agreement which might serve as a basis of discussion with the Russians.[4] This was not seen as being disloyal to the Japanese alliance at a time of crisis for Japan, any more than Japan's approaches to Russia were regarded as inconsistent with it. The crisis that developed in the east had the effect of removing this particular overture to Russia to a back burner. But some sort of *rapprochement* with Russia remained an aspiration in London, even if there was plenty of distrust about Russia's motives and methods. With Britain proceeding with negotiations with France, it was clearly inopportune that relations between her and France's ally, Russia, should deteriorate too much.

The British government considered how to avoid being implicated in the event of war. When Britain heard that Komura had found the Russian redraft of 12 December to be unsatisfactory and presented four amendments and when she learnt that the Japanese cabinet had begun to pass through an emergency military budget, the British cabinet became worried. This led to much activity over Christmas, when the members were widely dispersed and had therefore to communicate with each other in writing. It took in Balfour, Lansdowne, Selborne and Austen Chamberlain and various Committee of Imperial Defence bodies. There had already been detailed discussions of a preparatory nature in the Foreign Office. Significant here is the personal view of Lansdowne and presumably therefore of his Foreign Office subordinates:

> I should like HMG to try its hand as a mediator, or at all events as a friendly counsellor, rather than wait until it can appear on the scene in the role of a 'deliverer'.
>
> I doubt whether her [Japan's] diplomacy is very adroit and I think we ought to help her if we can to get out of the impasse in which she finds herself. The most promising exit would be found in an arrangement under which Russia might enter into an engagement not with Japan alone but with all Powers having Treaty rights.[5]

His colleagues could not be persuaded to adopt this view, which weakened Lansdowne's role in the crisis. Secondly it was proposed by Lansdowne in the knowledge that Japan did not approve of the course he was urging. But this was not the reason for his colleagues' reservations. The First Lord of the Admiralty, Lord Selborne, asked the question: 'Cannot you use France to put pressure on Russia? France must dread war more than we do. I would put forward France or the United States as mediators and not ourselves.'[6] There is, however, no evidence that Britain urged France or the United States to take a special role as mediator. After Britain took a conscious decision not to mediate, she left things to take their own course.

The other Open Door power which might have had a role in mediation was the United States. More than the European powers she had interests in both Korea and Manchuria. Her new minister in Tokyo, Lloyd Griscom, certainly developed a rapport with the Japanese. Washington, while it was developing a concern for things Japanese, took the view that Japan should be left to decide on her own vital interests for herself and to protect them in her own special way. But when there was a proposal on 9 May 1903 for joint action on the part of Open Door powers, the United States asked to be excused.[7]

France was more ready to be of diplomatic service. She was deeply involved in Russian exploits, both as investor in some of them and as political partner. In both respects she was not anxious to see a war in east Asia. Théophile Delcassé, her foreign minister (1899–1906), was a shrewd, calculating and energetic statesman of fifty. He was conscious of a deterioration in the state of the Franco-Russian alliance and wondered whether it was possible to breathe new life into it by direct French mediation with Japan and, more important, to cash in on improving Anglo-French relations by getting Britain to exert some leverage with her ally, Japan. Having an optimistic frame of mind, Delcassé thought it was possible. Encouraged by Russia, he set about soundings with the great enthusiasm of which he was capable. But Delcassé, like Russia herself, seems to have underestimated Japan's determination for war and may have left his intervention too late for any hope of success because he had little sense of urgency.

The odd man out was Germany who had far-eastern interests and was actively promoting world policy. Her problem over acting as honest broker was that her interest was one-sided: she wanted Russia to develop her interests in Manchuria and Korea, even at the risk of a policy of adventure. The kaiser, perhaps because of his obsession with the yellow peril, was inclined to encourage Russia to restrain Japan. Such views were not necessarily shared by the German foreign ministry.[8] But the end result of this split in policy-making was that Germany was likely to sit on the sidelines if war came in east Asia. The Germans were in any case not approached for mediation from either side. Nor did they volunteer any. Germany's isolated position is indicated by this extract from Holstein's letters: 'Nobody approached us with such a proposal [for acting as mediator] for it is known from former official statements that Manchuria could never become a *casus belli* for Germany.... The Russians are in a very embarrassing situation because they see they are isolated.'[9]

The linchpin of mediation efforts was France to whom her ally, Russia, appealed for diplomatic assistance. It must be remembered that these requests emanated from the Russian foreign ministry which (as the French knew) had lost power to deal with east Asian problems because of the decentralization that had taken place in August. Secondly, the French did not wholly approve of Russia's activities in Manchuria. This meant that Delcassé was not wholehearted in his mediation efforts and was anxious not to be trapped into arranging for mediation when only Lamsdorf was anxious for it and those more powerful in Russia dishonoured the attempt. Hence one of the motives behind his mediation effort was concern for France's investment in Russia. The editors of the French documents write that Delcassé exerted himself unceasingly to solve the conflict 'with, at certain moments, the authority, if not the title, of a veritable mediator'.[10]

The starting point was Lamsdorf's visit to Paris at the end of October. According to the French record, Lamsdorf asked Delcassé to speak to Lansdowne in the hope that Britain could calm down her ally. Delcassé said that Britain did not appear to want to stir up her ally but, if she were to calm down, Japan would need some assurances. On this the luckless Lamsdorf hedged, saying that he had spoken to Benckendorff who had come over to Paris for conversations with him. Delcassé, therefore, concluded that 'the powers most interested in the complications which it was possible to foresee hoped that our intervention could usefully be exercised in the interests of peace. I have reasons for thinking that from this point of view also the stay of Count Lamsdorf at Paris will not have been useless.'[11]

On 25 November Delcassé was asked to intervene for Russia in Peking. Some days later the Korean emperor also asked for French intervention. Buoyed up with optimism, Delcassé told the Senate in a speech on 26 December that 'the pacific dispositions of the two sides are not in question. There is no warrant for the alarmist news which has been spreading for some time now.'[12] Despite this, Tokyo sent instructions to its minister to France, Motono Ichirō, who had been in Paris since 1901, that it was not really anxious for outside interference in the negotiations. By this time it was clear that the real hope was not so much for mediation as for 'good offices'; and even this was a dangerous phrase of which the Japanese were very distrustful.

Conscious of the need to win over the goodwill of the powers, Russia on 9 January 1904 tried to assist the progress of good offices by clarifying her position over Manchuria. Lamsdorf distributed a circular letter defining his policy there and guaranteeing the treaty rights of the powers. The underlying purpose of the letter was to make Manchuria an international issue and one that could legitimately be excluded from the purview of the Russo-Japanese talks. Japan turned down this approach, while Britain and the United States raised very serious doubts about it, which suggested that they had reservations about the *bona fides* of the Russian guarantee.[13]

Shortly after, on 12 January, Lamsdorf asked for the good offices of France, if possible with the approval of Britain. This last was a bold move because Russian opinion at the time was becoming very anti-British on account of Britain's assistance to Japan over cruisers. Delcassé was ready to open discussions with Motono in Paris, though Lamsdorf had asked the pregnant question: does Motono speak effectively in the name of his government? On 13 January Delcassé took the initiative tentatively to offer his services and asked Britain to bring pressure to bear on Japan.[14] Interpreting this as a first step towards international mediation, Japan informed Britain that it would serve no purpose but to meet Russia's desire to gain time and by prolongation of the crisis to compel Japan perhaps 'to come to any terms dictated by Russia'.[15] The hope of early Anglo-French cooperation was destroyed when Lansdowne refused to advise the Japanese to abandon their rights in Manchuria and informed Delcassé that several of their demands seemed to be reasonable. The French had held high hopes of joint approaches, perhaps because they were impressed by the speech of King Edward VII in opening parliament on 3 February when he had said: 'My Government will hasten to do all in its power to help towards a pacific solution of the question' of China and Korea.[16] In the event not much materialized.

Lansdowne was under pressure from other quarters apart from France to stop the war. Thus, Sir Claude MacDonald, his minister in Tokyo, suggested on 20 January that the king should bring his private influence to bear on the tsar in the interests of peace, since the tsar appeared to be distancing himself from the war party. The suggestion was put to the king and prime minister. While Lansdowne spoke to King Edward VII about it, he made it clear that 'it would NOT be desirable that he should write'. This was an example of the practice of keeping the monarch out of politics. But the fact that it was discussed suggests that some other route for communicating with the tsar might have been contemplated.[17]

Nor was the general public in Britain inactive. In an initiative on 21 January an influential group of journalists, led by Sir John Gorst and W. T. Stead, who knew the Russian royal family well, called strongly for peace. They prepared petitions addressed to the Russian and Japanese emperors asking them to prevent the war. They too sought to identify Edward VII with the prevention of the war but this proposal was scotched by Lansdowne on the ground that it would not be acceptable to the Japanese who had 'on no less than four occasions expressed their decided objection to mediation'.[18] When the foreign secretary none the less enquired whether Britain could help in finding a solution by ways other than mediation, the Japanese did not take him up.

The question of 'settlements' in Manchuria was the sticking-point in the mediation talks during January. It related primarily to the Sino-American and Sino-Japanese treaties of October 1903 which had given these powers special rights of settlement in Manchuria. Japan complained that she had every right to be consulted over Manchuria and every right to insist on the opening of Mukden and Tatungkow in accordance with her new treaty. Such a claim was incompatible with Russia's conception of her own rights and was not a line likely to be fruitful for the success of mediation efforts. For Russia Manchuria was a matter under negotiation between Russia and China and a subject of bilateral interest exclusive to these two countries. Hence, when Britain tried to include Manchuria in the important round of talks she held with Russia in the autumn of 1903, the Russian ambassador asked Britain not to call for Russian evacuation from that territory: 'there were two parties in Russia, one for evacuation and the other against, and ... the Russian Government did not know its own mind'. Lansdowne went on to stress Niuchuang where Britain had important treaty rights and a considerable trade and asked Russia to fulfil her promises as to the 'opening of other ports in Manchuria and as to the maintenance of the "open door".' Count Benckendorff stated that 'the promise to open other ports would be fulfilled, but he begged us not to press too hard'.[19] It would appear that there would be no change in Russia's stance in the near future.

On 21 January Delcassé put his diplomatic reputation on the line. He informed his minister in Tokyo that various factors had led him to employ himself in assisting an accord which was so desirable and that it was his impression that accord was not 'irréalisable'. The following day he received encouragement in a message from Lamsdorf:

> We are still talking only at Paris, there are no more negotiations except there; in order to avoid any misunderstanding I have stopped corresponding with Port Arthur, as with Tokyo. It is therefore indispensable for me to know if M. Delcassé would not think it fitting to elicit on the part of the Tokyo cabinet instructions putting M. Motono in a position to let him know the intentions of the Japanese government.[20]

These are strange sentiments for Lamsdorf to express. He seems to be saying that there is so little trust between Japan and Russia that talks are not likely to be fruitful between them and that he has little trust also in Russia's own officials in the area. He is hoping that Delcassé's influence may assist in the opening of negotiations in Paris; since Russia's final terms had not yet been passed to Japan, the logic of this is hard to grasp. At all events he was determined to implicate the French and call on their support in the Russian emergency.

If the French mediation were to succeed, a critical factor must be the nature of Russia's last terms and the speed with which her reply was sent to Tokyo. On both these points the Russians let down their ally. They did not consult Delcassé over their last note to the Japanese; nor did they speed up its delivery. Had there been signs of concessions, it might have aided the task of the conciliator. It might also have brought in Britain. Certainly it was one of Delcassé's desiderata that there should be an Anglo-French common front, Britain putting pressure on Japan and France on Russia. But Lamsdorf's approach to Delcassé, though it was humble and desperate enough, did not specify on what points Russia might be willing to make concessions. The French foreign minister, therefore, had no bargaining hand and, when he approached Britain, Lansdowne had to say that the Russian position had not changed in any obvious way; in his view, only substantial Russian concessions could pull Japan back from the brink. This is why Britain gave Delcassé the cold shoulder and why the latter had to let the French initiative lapse.[21]

ELEVENTH-HOUR EFFORTS

While Count Lamsdorf was preparing his final draft, he was launching a diplomatic offensive in Europe by approaching all sources of help and mediation. On 26 January Benckendorff asked Lansdowne directly 'if he could suggest any means by which Russia could satisfy Japan's desire for a pledge that she would respect Chinese sovereignty in Manchuria without the insertion of such a provision in the Treaty which would be a blow to her *amour propre*'. The foreign secretary replied that he feared he had no suggestion to make except an engagement to all the powers which apparently Benckendorff did not like any better.[22] On the following day Paul Cambon, the French ambassador, told Lansdowne that it would be extremely difficult for Russia to negotiate with Japan over recognition of Chinese sovereignty in Manchuria. Russia had always held that this was a subject reserved for herself and China. Could the other powers not bring about some amicable solution? Lansdowne replied that Japan would require a bilateral arrangement of some sort over Manchuria and would not be content with a unilateral declaration. Thus, Britain defended Japan's position and would not resort to putting pressure on her. When Lansdowne saw Minister Hayashi the next day, he told him of the diplomatic activity which had been taking place and mentioned that, if Japan had had second thoughts over the question of mediation, he felt it could be arranged. Though he put this in the most tentative way, Hayashi turned it down most positively, saying that it was just a formula for further delay which Japan could not tolerate.[23]

Early in February Count Lamsdorf himself invited both Britain and France to help in bringing about a peaceful outcome. Lansdowne was willing enough to help but felt that Russia was holding things up with her reply. Delcassé, taking a more optimistic line, was unsuccessful in his overtures with Motono in Paris, London and Tokyo. But he continued to be enthusiastic for peace until the last moment. Through the Russian ambassador, who was well known and well liked in Paris, and Motono who was renowned for his fluency in French, Delcassé kept open communication in some form between two essentially shy negotiators, Russia and Japan,[24]

The Russians took up their cause as actively in London as in Paris. While Anglo-French mediation never took root, there was some hope that Britain individually could, like France, contribute something to a continuation of peace. This was based on the assumption in St Petersburg that Japan looked on Britain as a patron and would accept Britain's advice, if it was offered. The assumption was a complete illusion. But it was in that context that the Russian ambassador, who was popular in British government circles, came to report that Japan had broken off further negotiations and that his country had reciprocated by withdrawing her minister from Tokyo. Despite the rupture of relations, he – and evidently Lamsdorf also – thought that there was still scope for a diplomatic solution. In his view the problem of Korea could be easily settled; but Russia refused to make a treaty with Japan over Manchuria, though she was prepared to make a declaration to all powers, recognizing the integrity of China in Manchuria. Lansdowne's judgement was that this would not be adequate since Japan wanted a treaty commitment. Benckendorff then asked whether he could suggest 'any form in which such an engagement might be embodied other than a treaty between Russia and Japan'. Lansdowne suggested (as he had done previously) a treaty between Russia and China recognizing the sovereignty of China in Manchuria and guaranteed by the powers. Benckendorff's response was to ask whether, if Russia agreed to this, Britain would recommend Japan to accept it. The matter had to be referred to the British cabinet which decided that it was impossible for Britain to intervene. Not to be put off, Benckendorff again asked for endeavours to be made by the powers; but Lansdowne said that events in east Asia had already made intervention by a third power very difficult. In conclusion, Benckendorf claimed to be speaking with some authority from St Petersburg.[25] Although we have no way of checking this, it is possible that Lamsdorf was still hoping for a peaceful way out.

These eleventh-hour efforts find no place in Japanese thinking. The Japanese foreign ministry had already closed its file on Russo-Japanese negotiations some days earlier. It is tragic that the Russians did not know or chose to ignore the determination of the Japanese that war was the only course left open to them. The last-minute talks were in my view genuine but evidence of Russia's blindness and misjudgement.

Could the powers have resorted to tougher measures to prevent the war? Since the diplomatic initiatives of an international kind were too weak and flabby to carry weight, could they have starved the belligerents of funds or weapons or arms in order to make war difficult to fight? In particular, could France have prevented Russia from fighting and Britain prevented Japan from fighting by (say) applying economic or financial sanctions?

These are hypothetical questions to which it is not possible to give a satisfactory answer. But the answer is probably 'No' in each case. France could not have stopped Russia fighting because she was unable to bring much influence to bear on the Russian military party with whom the decision of peace or war really rested. She did not give Russia advance funds which might make the waging of war easy. But she did not, after the war began, observe 'strict neutrality' as rigidly as one might expect. So that she did give the Russian fleet on the way to the far east (for example) the facilities of Djibouti in the Red Sea. She was therefore a neutral benevolent to Russia. But the Russians viewed things differently and felt that France had been an ineffective mediator before war broke out and should have gone beyond 'strict neutrality' when hostilities began.

Similarly Britain could not have stopped Japan because it would have involved too much loss of face after five months' unproductive diplomacy for the Tokyo cabinet not to have gone to war. Prime Minister Balfour would not restrain Japan in case it enabled the Japanese government 'to transfer their welldeserved unpopularity to us'. 'While I would avoid giving any advice to Japan which would enable her to say hereafter that we had got her into war, I would *not* put pressure upon her of any kind to abate her demands.'[26] Britain also would make no commitment over finance on the ground that it was morally an act of war against Russia to do so. As against that, the London cabinet had shown its pro-Japanese stance by the financial aid it had given to purchase the Chilean cruisers. Britain was therefore a neutral benevolent to Japan.[27]

INFLUENCING THE BELLIGERENTS?

In the Russo-Japanese war, as in many other wars before and after, there is frequently heard the glib comment that Russia and Japan were 'egged on' by others to go to war. First, let us consider the evidence for Japan being goaded to action by others. Spring-Rice, reflecting a common view in Russia, Germany and Europe generally, and trying to explain why Japan dared to fight, wrote that 'she was egged on by England and

America'.[28] This was a view to be seen in *Novoye Vremya* and widely held of course in Russian government circles at the time. It has been taken to heart by a generation of historians. Erich Brandenburg wrote in 1923 of the Russo-Japanese war: 'England's vaunted love of peace was not great enough to induce her statesmen to prevent wars in the course of which they might expect considerable advantages for their own country without any risk to themselves'.[29] This view was shared by the Soviet historian, Romanov, who spoke of Japan as being Britain's infantryman. Such a view was also shared by the Soviet expert on this period, A. L. Galperin, and a later generation of historians.[30]

Now there is no doubt that there were advantages to Britain in having Russia tied down in Manchuria – and doubtless in having Japan tied down in Manchuria also. Balfour admitted as much in the note quoted above. But it has to be borne in mind that there was a distinct possibility of Russia moving to Afghanistan and discomfiting Britain in India if Russia were defeated in east Asia. This was not in Britain's best interest because the defence of India was in fact one of the Balfour government's major anxieties – and perhaps even an exaggerated one. It suited Britain better to have Russia anchored in Manchuria where Britain had indeed recognized her standing (so far as railways were concerned) in 1899. If this is accepted, it would have been lunacy to egg on Japan to fight.

Because of Britain's preoccupation with Russia, the degree of commitment towards Japan is less than might be thought. Komura had to ask for an indication of Britain's views on 27 December 'in case we are obliged to take more decisive action',[31] and to request financial assistance or an undertaking thereof. In fact the British cabinet had in the week before Christmas had an exchange of views on these points which are described in my earlier study and are only summarized here. So far as the Russian terms were concerned, the British felt that the Japanese 'must be content with the best they can get as to Korea – the Korean clauses, barring that as to the neutral zone, are upon the whole not unsatisfactory'.[32] Perhaps because of this, the members of the inner cabinet, though they were divided over the issue of mediation, decided to take no initiative to prevent war. So far as involvement in the war was concerned, the cabinet view may be summed up thus:

1. Britain should try to avoid becoming involved over Manchuria and Korea, which were not part of Britain's traditional interests.
2. Since the alliance with Japan required of Britain only neutrality, Britain should follow a policy of strict neutrality;
3. Britain would not make a loan, nor give a guarantee for a loan, nor enter into a private arrangement between the two governments about the nature of future financial assistance.[33]

This may appear to be a tough and calculating attitude towards her Japanese ally. But bear in mind that the British cabinet was under the strong influence of Balfour's pessimism. 'If Japan goes to war', he had written, 'who is going to lay long odds that we are not at loggerheads with Russia within six months?' And again 'if by any unfortunate chance we get dragged in, we shall require every shilling for ourselves'.[34] All in all, Britain neither egged on nor discouraged the Japanese.

There was a pragmatic British attitude towards her obligations under the Japanese alliance. But there was pragmatism also in Japan's response. She quite understood that the war was not likely to come within the purview of the alliance but asked: what kind of assistance could Britain give *outside* the scope of the alliance? Lansdowne was not forthcoming and insisted that he had to consult the prime minister.

Although Britain was tight-fisted and vigilant, the fact was that Russia could not and would not accept Britain's lack of commitment to the cause of Japan. Since this was a period of secret diplomacy, Russia had always presumed that there was more to the Anglo-Japanese alliance than met the eye. It was widely believed that Japan could not fight without explicit offers of British support. Russia's suspicions of the alliance were fed by intelligence received from agents in Japan. They had been told by Alekseyev in May 1903 about 'information that had come to hand from our Japanese secret agents' in code. It was to the effect that Komura's plan for an approach to Russia had been authorized by the highest leaders – as was indeed true – and was about to be put before Britain: Japan must first find out the extent of Britain's willingness to assist Japan in the event of a rupture of her relations with Russia; as soon as the will of the British government was known, Japan could make approaches to the governments of Russia and China.[35] Since the Japanese in due course did approach Russia, it seemed to be the fulfilment of the project and to indicate that they had obtained prior undertakings of support from Britain. As we know, this was not so. Japan went ahead without expressions of support. But Captain Rusin, the naval attaché at the Tokyo legation, was able to substantiate the earlier intelligence. And so by the outbreak of war, Russians were generally convinced that Britain was aiding the Japanese.

Was Japan egged on by the United States? Certainly an important role was being played by Lloyd Griscom, the young American minister in Tokyo, who was trying to justify his rise to top rank in the service by the energies he was showing in the crisis. He seems to have risen to a place of confidence in the minds of Japanese ministers equal perhaps to that of the British minister. Griscom reflected the thinking of his master and knew that his key was to offer the Japanese Washington's support. There is not much evidence from either the Japanese or the American side that he committed great indiscretions which encouraged the Japanese to declare war. But the Japanese were of course cultivating foreign opinion and had financial motives, if no other, for staying close to the United States.[36]

Was Russia egged on by France? There is precious little substance in this. France had two clear objectives: to prevent the war if possible; to keep clear of the war, if not. Her attempt to prevent the war exposed what Frenchmen already knew, that she was not able to control the activities of the autocratic government of St Petersburg, only to exert occasional influence. She was herself anxious to persuade Russia to make concessions for the sake of peace; and Russia was unwilling to consider this to the extent required. Hence, when war came, France entered into the *entente* with Britain, with whose standpoint in the crisis of 1903–4 she had a lot in common. As soon as this came into being, there was talk of some agreement being reached between Britain and Russia. The truth of the matter seems to be that France did not carry enough weight with Russia through her alliance to induce her to start or to stop a war. In the circumstances of the start of a war, a country has to assess its own national interest.

The capacity of one power to influence the course of action of another varies in accordance with the degree of the supplicant's dependence on the first. Russia had traditionally been dependent on French loans for the running of the state. France could have used her financial power if Russia, in anticipation of war breaking out, had applied to France for a war loan. So far as we know, this did not take place. The reasons for this are various. The Russian leaders do not seem to have been expecting an early war. Secondly, Russia was without a finance minister. After Witte's dismissal, Pleske had been appointed but he was no sooner in office than he fell critically ill and gave up in November. Interim arrangements were made; but no new appointment emerged until Kokovtsov was chosen as the new minister in February 1904. It is true that Kokovtsov then called the French bankers to St Petersburg to discuss a war loan. But nothing of a serious kind was done before war broke out.[37] One feels that, if Witte had still been at the helm, more decisive approaches to France would have been made. On the French side also, there were grounds for hastening slowly over any financial approach. French lenders were disillusioned and annoyed at the uses to which previous loans had been put; they wanted railways to be built from the capital to Russia's western frontier, not through Asia to the Pacific coast. So Nelidov, the Russian ambassador in Paris, was not hopeful of securing a loan on the French money market and opposed such initiatives. Behind the bankers the newspapers were deeply hostile to Russia, so much so that, when war started, it was necessary for Russia to spend considerable sums to curry the favour of the French newspaper editors.[38] For these various reasons Russia did not come to the French as a financial supplicant early in 1904. The consequence was that France could not play her financial cards.

France, like Britain, had little enthusiasm for assisting the Russians. If anything, Franco-Russian relations in the months before the war were worse than Anglo-Japanese relations. Delcassé might act as go-between in the Russian interest but there was little popular will to assist the Russians.

None of the powers had much success in restraining the two belligerents. Whether by fraternal advice or by suggestion, the outside powers had little impact on the negotiations. The six months of Russo-Japanese talks were not marked by any great movement in the positions on the two sides. There were really very few negotiating concessions on Russia's part, even in her final terms (which were not delivered to Japan till 7 February). Nor was there any success from any procedures of mediation, largely because of the hostility of Japan. Nor is it clear that the powers could have been more successful in keeping the peace if they had employed stronger tactics like the threat of sanctions or embargoes. The fact was that they did not use them. The internal pressures in Russia and Japan were so great that no major breakthrough seemed to be likely. In these circumstances there was not much scope for outside influences.

Britain and France had to look at the east Asian problem in the context of their global interests. For both of them, the far east was an important, but middle-ranking, zone of concern. Like France, Britain had to maintain a delicate balance between her various interests. Lansdowne is quoted as saying:

> From the very first our political interest had been to prevent the war which would not only expose us to great dangers and loss in Asia itself, but would seriously imperil our good understanding with France which is the most popular event in modern times in England.... As a result [of war breaking out], we all but lost our agreement with France; but it would have been worse if we had broken our word, on which the value of any agreement [like the Japanese alliance] depended.[39]

Delcassé would probably have seen the situation in similar terms. For him as for Lansdowne, Russo-Japanese tension in Manchuria was only part of a multi-dimensional picture. For them it was well-nigh insoluble.

REFERENCES AND NOTES

1. *NGB* 37/I, no. 16.
2. *NGB* 37/I, no. 38.
3. *Katsura-den,* vol. 2, p. 194.
4. Lansdowne, heads of agreement, 1 Jan. 1904, Cabinet papers 1.4.
5. Ibid.
6. Ibid.
7. *NGNB,* vol. 1, pp. 149–50.
8. *Die Grosse Politik der Europäischen Kabinette 1871–1914,* xix(1), Berlin 1922, 5–6; 89.
9. N. Rich and M. H. Fisher (eds), *Holstein Papers,* iv, nos. 818–20.

10. *DDF*, 2nd series, vol. 3, p. vii, editors' preface: 'Would an entente with Britain risk disturbing Russia? The Franco-Russian alliance remains, according to Delcassé's phrase, the cornerstone of France's foreign policy. But the alliance in practice raises delicate problems: Russia's action in Manchuria provokes the protests of Britain, the United States and especially Japan. France is preoccupied with this situation but cannot exercise a moderating influence at Petersburg because Foreign Minister Lamsdorf is eliminated from the direction of far eastern affairs.'

11. Ibid., vol. 4, nos. 45 and 80.

12. Ibid. no. 147.

13. Ibid., no. 163; *BD*, vol. 2, nos. 274–6.

14. Delcassé, asked if he had a New Year resolution, said that he wanted to prevent a war between Russia and Japan. *BD*, vol. 2, nos. 265–8.

15. *NGB* 37/I, no. 59.

16. *NGB* 37/I, no. 112; *BD*, vol. 2, nos. 278–80.

17. MacDonald to Lansdowne, 24 Jan. 1904, FO 800/134.

18. Another apostle of mediation was Ambassador Scott, who wrote 'if we could only muzzle the European press for a short time, and induce the players to show their cards to impartial and friendly bystanders, a way could easily be found to avoid a resort to the arbitrament of war'. (Scott to Sanderson, 6 Jan. 1904, Scott Papers, 52,304.)

19. *BD*, vol. 4, no. 181(b).

20. *DDF*, 2nd series, vol. 4, no. 207. It has to be remembered that Delcassé was only reflecting the optimism that prevailed in St Petersburg about a peaceful outcome. See talks between Boutiron and Spring-Rice, 25 Jan. (Scott Papers 52,302).

21. French opinion was favourable to Russia and distrustful of Japan: there was a great fear that Fukien and Taiwan might become bases for attacks on Indochina. See Suematsu Kenchō, 'Japan and France' in *The Risen Sun* (London, 1905), pp. 298ff.

22. Lansdowne to MacDonald, 29 Jan. 1904, FO 46/576.

23. *Holstein Papers*, iv, no. 820.

24. *BD*, vol. 2, no. 285.

25. Ibid., no. 295.

26. Balfour to Lansdowne, 22 Dec. 1903, Cabinet Papers 1/4/43.

27. I. H. Nish, *The Anglo-Japanese Alliance*, pp. 270–3.

28. Spring-Rice to Satow, 24 Mar. 1904, Satow Papers, 9/15.

29. E. Brandenburg, *From Bismarck to the World War*, London 1926, p. 149.

30. A. L. Galperin, *Anglo-Iaponskii Soiuz*, p. 243.

31. *NGB* 36/I, no. 51; *BD*, vol. 2, no. 265.

32. Lansdowne to Balfour, 22 Dec. 1903, Papers of A. J. Balfour, Add. MSS 49,728, British Library, London.

33. The diplomats were also divided. Ambassador Scott wrote as late as 21 Jan.: 'I really hope that the tide has now turned and that peace is secured for the present . . . . If all turns out as [Plehve] confidently expects, Lamsdorf has at last got the better of the swashbucklers, titled concession-hunters and company promoters who have had a good deal to say to putting the Emperor into the desperate dilemma in which he has got himself.' Scott to T. H. Sanderson, 21 Jan. 1904.

34. Nish, op. cit., p. 276.

35. B. A. Romanov, *Russia in Manchuria,* p. 459, fn. 169, 24 May 1903.
36. L. C. Griscom, *Diplomatically Speaking,* ch. 19.
37. Romanov, op. cit., pp. 324–5.
38. Ibid., p. 340.
39. Spring-Rice to Roosevelt, 1905, in Spring-Rice Papers 9/4.

CONCLUSION

The Russo-Japanese war started in a blaze of controversy with wordy accusations being met by equally wordy counter-accusations. The two governments had been careful about the documents they exchanged because they saw that war, if it came, would have an international dimension and it would be important to win the goodwill of neutral countries. It was the aim of both Russia and Japan to win the battle of words about the causes of the war.

On the Russian side, frequent appeals were made to European press and public opinion in the early months of the war. They were eventually assembled in 1910 into a collection and published in what was known as the Red Book.[1] Information about the inner tensions within Russia came from the report which General Kuropatkin wrote in Manchuria around the end of the war. He was of course a particular expert on the causes and course of the war. Though the report was suppressed when it appeared in Russia, it leaked out to the foreign press in 1906. In defending his own position, Kuropatkin drew attention to the state of Russian military unpreparedness and incriminated Admiral Alekseyev, Finance Minister Witte and the generals who surrounded him at the battle-front. Witte in due course responded in 1911 after a dignified silence by offering his own explanations about General Kuropatkin's version of the Japanese war.[2] While these arguments lifted the veil on the problems of the Russian decision-makers, they did not on the whole add very much to the story of the negotiations.

The Russian cause was not without its advocates in Europe, especially after the early attacks on Port Arthur and Chemulpo. This made it all the more necessary for Japan to publish her White Book entitled *Correspondence regarding the Negotiations between Japan and Russia, 1903-4* which was an English translation of documents presented to the Imperial Diet in March 1904. It was intended to convey the message that the Russians had been most dilatory over the talks and that Japan was justified in taking the course of war that she had followed.[3] This was the main raw material for the truly remarkable *The Russo-Japanese Conflict:*

Its Causes and Issues by Asakawa Kanichi of Dartmouth College which was published in the United States and Britain in November 1904. It had access to very special materials and was literally rushed to the press in order to reach a world audience. Two other presenters of the Japanese case were Baron Suematsu and Baron Kaneko. Suematsu reached London in March and was thereafter engaged in speech-making and article-writing throughout Europe in order to rebut items appearing in Russian-inspired periodicals. His articles found their way into journals like *Nineteenth Century and After* in Britain and corresponding ones on the continent. Eventually the most important of these were assembled in *The Risen Sun,* published in London towards the end of the war. Translations of this work, which was strongly apologetic in tone, were published also in France and Germany. Suematsu's central message was that 'Japan has shown a great moral heroism [in fighting Russia] in the cause of humanity and civilisation.'[4] Suematsu's opposite number in the United States was Kaneko. By contributing articles to the *North American Review,* he was able to combat the arguments of Russian apologists like the ambassador, Count Cassini.[5] Asakawa, Suematsu and Kaneko were able pleaders and enjoyed some success. But they operated in an atmosphere which was remarkably even-handed as between Russia and Japan. Indeed, they may have been sent abroad under the impression that the outbreak of war would generate a fresh growth of the 'yellow peril' doctrine. This did not happen. Although the Russians had loyal supporters throughout the war, the Japanese had from the start grave doubts about the extent of the goodwill towards them from around the world and felt that it had to be fortified by presenting the Japanese case in a favourable light.[6]

Justice cannot be done here to this outpouring of material. Some of the most telling debates relate to matters which cannot be discussed here: for example, whether international law lays down that a formal declaration of war is required before a state of war exists between countries. Since the Pearl Harbour attack this has been a hotly disputed issue over which there is no consensus.

It is necessary to turn to some of the conclusions which suggest themselves as having affected the decision for war and the outbreak of war in both countries. The nature of the Russo-Japanese war was that Japan declared war on Russia on the grounds that Russia had been expansionist in Manchuria and Korea. Russia was expansionist against the weaker states of China and Korea and possibly provocative against Japan. Her expansion was challenged by Japan, first by protest, next by subversion, then by negotiation and finally by war. Russia might possibly have prevented or avoided this war by concessions: she might have honoured her evacuation agreement of April 1902; she might have been more accommodating by improving Japan's position in Korea. In the event she did not honour her evacuation promises and offered only modest concessions too late for any practical outcome.

Russia was at the end of a long road of expansion in north-east Asia. She had passed several milestones: she had acquired the lease for twenty-five years of Port Arthur (Lushun) and its environs in 1898; she had occupied with her troops the critical cities and routes of Manchuria from 1900 to 1904; she had on two occasions failed to withdraw in accordance with her pledges to China in 1902; she had in 1903 taken new initiatives in the north of Korea which were not purely commercial. During the five months of negotiations with Japan in 1903 she showed herself to be unyielding and insensitive.

Yet there are certain points which can be made for the Russian position. Firstly, the Russian expansionist drive, though it may seem to be determined and unidirectional, was in fact diffuse and complicated. It was the result of jostling for power between many parties and individuals who gained and lost the ascendancy from time to time. The basic problem was how to deal with the colossal investment in railways, both the Trans-Siberian and the Chinese Eastern railways, which the Russians had made under the aegis of Sergei Witte. Whatever Witte's propaganda claimed, this was not purely a commercial undertaking because the track had to be guarded by 'police' who were synonymous with 'troops'. These expensive railway projects had failed to yield a profit by 1903; and it was natural that voices should be raised in favour of 'capitalizing' on existing investment by military or other means.

Although Russia had been reinforcing her strength in east Asia by land and sea, she was hardly prepared for war. This was made clear in her official communiqué of 18 February.

> The distance of the territory now attacked and the desire of the Czar to maintain peace were causes of the impossibility of preparations for war being made a long time in advance. Much time is now necessary in order to strike at Japan blows worthy of the dignity and might of Russia.... Russia must await the event in patience, being sure that our army will avenge that provocation a hundredfold. Operations on land must not be expected for some time yet, and we cannot obtain early news from the theatre of war.[7]

The picture here painted was disputed by Japanese intelligence sources which concluded that Russia was already formidable in military and naval terms in east Asia: not less than 30,000 troops had been sent to the Trans-Baikal in the second half of 1903, while two new first-class battleships and two first-class cruisers had been ordered to the far east without any ships there being sent home. The 'official' communiqué, moreover, does not tally with the general confidence expressed by Russian officers themselves. Alekseyev's naval staff could not contemplate the defeat of the Russian far eastern squadron by Japan; and General Kuropatkin, whose frankness we have earlier observed, was more optimistic in 1903 than he had been two years earlier, though strongly impressed with the danger of fighting Japan. Where the Russian army was unprepared in 1904 was in organization and supplies; it was also weak in the fighting spirit of its troops so far from home. It depended very much on the new rail network which proved in February to be seriously deficient in coal. The railways had therefore to suspend ordinary services in order to concentrate on the movement of troops and supplies. They had to do panic buying of coal from Tangshan in north China through Chinwangtao and also from Niuchuang.[8] Thus, by the time the two armies came to confront each other, the unpreparedness had been largely overcome. But there was strong evidence that the reservists in the Russian army did not have a heart for the struggle in Manchuria.

Then there was the unrealistic Russian perception of Japan. Russia's leaders in east Asia seem to have convinced themselves that the Japanese were bluffing and would not ultimately resort to war. Admiral Alekseyev, conscious of a Russian mission in the east, thought it was presumptuous of Japan to challenge this and so made few concessions during the negotiations. A more widespread view in Port Arthur was that the Japanese army would not dare to attack because of its poor calibre.[9] This was of course not a uniquely Russian viewpoint; and, apart from Britain which had a high opinion of Japan's strength by land and sea, it was held by many other foreign observers. But many Russians certainly took a view of Japan which was derisory in comparison with themselves. It may be that this derived from a deliberate policy of secrecy and concealment which the Japanese army applied because of the historic coolness between the two countries.

Our broad view in this study has been that Russia did not want war but by sheer dilatoriness over the negotiations let war occur. She did not want war in the sense that her strategic position was improving day by day with the growth and improvement of her railways and time was on her side. It therefore suited her to stall in negotiations. Because she had little sense of urgency, she did not give positive assurances which the Japanese cabinet might have been happy to latch on to. The Russians were adamant in not negotiating over Manchuria and made only minor gestures over Korea, which failed to acknowledge the importance which Japan attached to that peninsula. Perhaps it was hard for the tsar ever to make concessions. There is much truth in the assessment that 'The Czar wishes peace, but he refused to realise how serious matters were until his constant delay had irritated the Japanese to exasperation.'[10] It was to Russia's advantage to seek peace and employ delaying tactics. It does not seem to have occurred to the cautious and inefficient ministers that their dilatoriness would push even the peace party in Japan to a determination to teach Russia a lesson. Nor were there any pressures from public or newspaper opinion to take the negotiations seriously and avert the war. The people, especially the alienated intelligentsia, were uninformed about the far eastern situation, mentally unprepared for war and indifferent to it when it came. Those like the Poles or the Finns were either disinterested or deeply opposed.[11]

In an attempt to analyse the climate of opinion in European Russia, Cecil Spring-Rice, who spent the early months of the war in Russia, wrote: 'I have seen this Government which had every reason to wish for peace – which was warned by Witte and Plehve and Kuropatkin that war would be useless and dangerous – plunged suddenly into *a wholly preventible war* by the action of a few interested and irresponsible people and the invincible ignorance and conceit of the Directing power' [my italics].[12] There is no evidence as to whom he identified as the 'Directing power'. But Spring-Rice says of the tsar and courtiers that they wanted war to take place in the spring of 1904 when Russia would be so strong that Japan would not be able to fight and would not dare; while 'the outbreak of war [as early as February] found the military party which had brought it on unprepared, and the Emperor almost incredulous'.[13] Possibly Russia was so elated by the eastern railways coming to completion that she did not immediately capitalize on them by building up overwhelming strength in the area. Perhaps there was conceit; certainly there was 'ignorance' despite the visits to the east of Witte and Kuropatkin.

The problem is to pin down the objectives of the 'military party'. General Kuropatkin as war minister had tended since 1900 to favour withdrawal from southern Manchuria, while advocating a much more rigorous occupation of the northern part of the country. But this view was not universally accepted, even in the army. Nor was it acceptable to the navy. Obviously during the period when the tsar fell under the influence of Bezobrazov and his group, the idea of withdrawal lapsed and a policy of greater firmness prevailed both in Manchuria and Korea. But this lasted only a short time; and moderate counsels were in the second half of 1903 able to exert a certain amount of influence. But even they had no clear objectives. Thus, Plehve confessed to Kuropatkin that he did not know where Russia's leaders were heading for.[14] It would appear that civilian ministers were looking for opportunities not to the Balkans but to the east, and were as innately expansionist as the army, even if their conception of expansion was commercial rather than territorial. The truth seems to be that Russia, whether military or civilian, was going through a period of blurred vision.

Japan for her part had also been expansionist though she was not ready to challenge Russia until 1904. She had marked out for herself under the treaty of Shimonoseki a vast area of the south of Manchuria and, while she had been deprived of this by the actions of the three powers, it was presumably still within the 'sights' of some at least of the Japanese leaders. Japan had acted discreetly during the far-eastern crises of 1898 and 1900. She had however been gaining ground on the Russians, both commercially and militarily, in Korea in the years after 1900. She was as much feared by the Chinese and the Koreans as were the Russians. Indeed in Seoul Japan was probably more terrifying. None the less the Japanese entered into negotiations with Russia in 1903 in good faith, hopeful of limiting Russia's encroachments in the area. Although it is unwise of the historian to speculate about hypothetical questions, it is possible that, even if Russia had made concrete concessions over either Manchuria or Korea – which of course she did not – Japan would still have made war in the end though it might not have come as soon as it did. The fact was that Japan herself had ambitions in the area. The older Japanese political leaders like Itō, who still accepted a subordinate role for Japan in world affairs, were not prepared to endorse actions which would lead to the fulfilment of these ambitions at this stage, and were strong enough to control the crisis of 1903–4. But the time would come when they no longer dominated the Japanese stage. Even if the Russo-Japanese negotiations had come to some acceptable formula, it is possible that it might not have lasted very long.

Japan could justly claim in her White Book that she was to some extent operating in February 1904 in the interests of China and Korea. She could also believe that she was acting in accordance with the (unexpressed) wishes of the United States and Britain by taking steps to cut Russia down to size in east Asia.[15] She could argue that, while the three Open Door powers were enthusiastic about giving advice to China, only Japan was sufficiently resolute to confront Russia herself in the interest of all three. Japan could further claim that she had been willing to resolve the issue in an amicable spirit but that the Russians had proved to be impossible to negotiate with.

Japan has to bear an awesome responsibility in two respects. Firstly she was the first to declare war. This she did as a conscious act. To be sure, the tsar had given instructions that Russia was to be careful not to do anything that might be interpreted as a declaration of war or as an excuse for the other side to declare war. But the fact was that Japan was ready and willing – and first. She felt that her friends would be understanding about the declaration if they heard the full story of the many months of frustrating negotiation which had produced no tangible result from the Russian negotiators. Secondly, she executed an act of war before the actual declaration of war had been made. This point has already been argued. While the Japanese were convinced of the necessity of this act, most of the powers – even the sympathetic ones – looked askance at it.

In the Japanese view of things, the main justification of the war was Russian expansionism and intransigence during negotiations. But there can be little doubt that Japan was not simply defensively intentioned and that she wanted a stake in Korea for herself and, from her Korean foothold, wanted a share in the Chinese cake as it crumbled. In the hypothetical eventuality that Russia had offered concessions, it is doubtful how readily they would have been accepted unless they had been of overwhelming proportions. Both belligerents had designs on territorial expansion in Manchuria. Japan fought both to curtail Russia's retention of the south of Manchuria and to protect her own interests in Korea and China with a view to replacing Russia in Manchuria in the long term. Considering the sense of threat that she felt from the eastward penetration of the Russian railway system, she was remarkably patient in negotiation. Perhaps it was this patience which led the Russians to conclude that the Japanese were not serious about making war, not determined enough. Misconceptions exist in all countries before wars break out. Japan did not err by deliberately creating a false impression. It was Russian blindness which failed to detect Japan's war-mindedness which other countries saw quite clearly.

Compared to the Russians, the Japanese services were ready for hostilities. They chose the time for opening hostilities in the light of their military and naval position. The initiative was theirs; they chose the ground and the pace of the war. Surprise was an important weapon in their armoury. There were of course faint hearts. Among the top leadership the navy was not prepared to be pushed into a precipitate war, nor was Marshal Yamagata fully confident of victory. But massive strategic preparations had been made since the summer of 1903 and at lower levels there was confidence. At the same time the Japanese were not looking far ahead so that they did not consider the problem which became paramount in 1905: what would happen if Japan was so successful that she defeated the Russians decisively and could not pursue them because of shortage of manpower and armaments? A foreign observer writing in 1904 foresaw this dilemma:

> One cannot seriously believe that Japan would ever invade Manchuria, unless, indeed, she be caught by the madness with which the gods first visit those whom they wish to destroy; but if ever her army did occupy Moukden she would only find another Moscow in the ancient capital of the Manchus, and when all is said and done what would be the use? She could never hope to hold the Liao valley for ever against Russia . . . . The conclusion is that as far as Manchuria is concerned, Russia is even now more or less invulnerable.[16]

In the planning that took place, these remote possibilities were not explored. Japan's military planners were preoccupied with finding beachheads in Korea and Manchuria.

Japan's population of 45 million was mentally prepared for war against Russia. The press and through it the public had a fair idea of the negotiations which had been proceeding and were much more bellicose than the government. Indeed the ministry had to restrain the people from its enthusiasm for war by painting a deceptively favourable impression of the progress which negotiations were making. It had to preserve this front because the elder statesmen were not persuaded of the need for war until the end of 1903. Undue enthusiasm for war was held in check among the military and the people because of these elder statesmen who tried not unsuccessfully to keep the situation under their control.

PERSONAL FACTORS

War is not made by abstract, impersonal forces. It is necessary, therefore, to look at the men behind the Russo-Japanese war on both sides. Fortunately we can deal briefly with the Japanese personalities involved since an excellent study by Professor Okamoto has already appeared in English on this subject.[17] It is desirable to mention those who were behind an early war and those who exercised a restraining influence.

Those who were prepared to accept the necessity and the risk of war were the army, the cabinet and some sections of public opinion. Within the army there had been long-term hostility to Russia; but the actual planning of a war did not take shape before 1903 and is associated with the figure of General Kodama. There were, however, tensions within the army between the cautious General Ōyama, who as a genro came under the influence of Itō's persuasive arguments, and those who wanted to take up arms before the rail network gave Russia too great an advantage. But even Ōyama as chief of the general staff had come round to accepting as a long-term strategic objective Japan's absorption of Korea within her empire.

Through the figure of General Katsura himself, the army had some leverage within the Katsura cabinet. But Katsura was a cautious military bureaucrat. The pace towards war would probably have been slower if it had not been that the strongest and most competent member of his cabinet was Foreign Minister Komura. Before entering the cabinet he had been a diplomat, specializing in China and Russia. As a minister he resisted the influence of the inner clans, Satsuma and Chōshū, and contested the interference in government of the elder statesmen, especially Itō and Inoue. Opposed to political parties, he tended to find his friends among members of the Kokumin Dōmeikai and even made contact with the right-wing Kogetsukai through his underlings, Yamaza Enjirō and Honda Kumatarō.[18] It would appear that, unlike most Japanese diplomats, he had a conception of war as an instrument of his political strategy. While he behaved quite properly in the conduct of his negotiations with Russia in 1903, it is unlikely that he thought that there would be a peaceful outcome.[19]

Those who discouraged the idea of war with Russia – or at least of an early war – were Itō Hirobumi and Inoue Kaoru, who affected decision-making through the body of elder statesmen. As we have seen, they had advocated the need for an *entente* with Russia in order to settle the problem of Manchuria from 1901 onwards. While they were as determined to take Korea for Japan, they were prepared to make a trade-off with Russia over Manchuria, which was in their eyes less vital for Japan and not worth fighting for. Komura and others with like views did not feel that Japan's national interest could contemplate a separation of Manchuria from Korea. Outpointed by the genro in political gatherings, Komura spent the second half of 1903 in negotiations with Russia in order to please the elder statesmen but was probably sceptical that his talks could succeed. Hence the atmosphere of Japan in the year before war broke out was one of division and discord. These served as a brake on the aspirations of the early war party.

The issue was resolved early in the New Year when Itō, the leader of the peace party, lost confidence in the good faith of the Russian negotiators. He came round to the view that war was inevitable. In an account of the failure of the negotiations between Russia and Japan, he explained his position thus:

> Undoubtedly Russia's aim had from the start been to increase her naval and military forces and to ignore Japan's demands, thus securing her ambitions in Manchuria and Korea without opposition. This being the case, if Japan had not stood up for her threatened interests by force, she would ultimately have had to take orders from a Russian frontier potentate. This would have meant that we were fiddling while Rome was burning.[20]

He expressed it later in a letter to the British foreign secretary: 'The high-handed policy of the Russian Government of late has obliged us to begin to think seriously of our future safety . . . . I need only assure you that we have tried our best for the maintenance of peace and that we had [sic] failed.'[21] As a result of this conversion, the anti-war group dispersed. While there were differences of emphasis thereafter, they were of a less fundamental nature.

As Itō's opposition melted, restraint was advocated from another quarter, the navy. It was not that the navy was opposed to the taking of Korea in general or the army's plan for a continental expedition to Korea in particular. It did however insist that Japan should try to ensure command of the seas beforehand. The navy was determined not to be taken for granted. There was a long history of army–navy tension of which this was only the latest example. The army, because of its dependence on the navy for transports to convey troops to Korea and Manchuria and for naval vessels to escort them there had to wait until the navy declared the moment right for starting the operation. Meanwhile the foreign ministry had to spin out the negotiations. Because of the strong personality of the navy minister, Admiral Yamamoto, the army had no alternative but to accept him as the pace-setter.[22]

Although it had no effect on the actual outbreak of hostilities, we should record among the forces for restraint the activities of the pacifist groups in Japan. In general popular opinion was strongly anti-Russian and favourable to war. There were hardly any supporters for chambers of commerce or merchant houses who pointed out the disadvantages and risks of war for Japan. The pacifist wing was a still small voice. The newspaper *Yorozu Chōhō* contained from the time of the Boxer uprising onwards a number of articles which justified pacifism and criticized the warrior tradition. The editor, Kuroiwa Ruikō, accepted articles of a controversial kind from Christians like Uchimura Kanzō and socialists like Kōtoku Shūsui, who came out in opposition to war. In October 1903 when sales began to suffer because of the unpopularity of the anti-war articles, Kuroiwa altered the paper's policy in favour of the war effort. The anti-war writers resigned from the company and set up immediately a new paper, *Heimin Shimbun* (Commoners' News) which tried to reverse the tide of war fever which was engulfing the Japanese islands. When it continued its attacks on the war policy of the government after fighting began, the government tried to close the paper but it obtained a reprieve in the courts from the press law. It was not until January 1905 that *Heimin Shimbun,* the mouthpiece of the socialist anti-war message for just over one year, discontinued publication.[23]

THE RUSSIAN DIMENSION

It is hard to make an assessment of the role of the tsar and to disentangle his views from those of his servants. The impression that comes through from foreign correspondents who entered into his family circle is of a warm and sympathetic man. Wide in his international interests for family reasons, he was diligent over diplomatic reports and kept a close check on the conduct of foreign affairs. He was so sensitive and religious that he detested the idea of war and violence. The tone of the minutes of council meetings over which he presided is peaceful. Yet, while he was not warlike, he was in general inclined towards expansionism in Asia. It is hard to reach any conclusion other than that it was he who opposed concessions or reconciliation on the part of Russia which would have prevented the outbreak of war with Japan. Valentine Chirol of the London *Times* who was privy to much of the information circulating in the British Foreign Office, was probably expressing a well-informed opinion when he wrote: 'That the Tsar himself – still entirely dominated by Alexeieff – had been throughout and is today the head and front of the war party is to me beyond doubt.... Like many very weak men,

Nicholas II is sometimes mulishly obstinate, and he sees visions! a very dangerous foible in an autocrat.'[24] How the war party or the military party operated – if indeed they existed – is not something that is easy to analyse, any more than it is easy to estimate the influence that the grand dukes exerted over the tsar. Living at Tsarskoye Selo outside St Petersburg, he was more vulnerable than most to the narrow circle of associates which surrounded him. Nicholas was proud of his position at the head of the armed forces and could on occasion be disdainful of civilian opinions when they contradicted military ones. He was conscious of being the autocrat of the Russias; and there are grounds for believing that he could be unyielding and uncompromising when it came to discussing Russia's interests and dignity as he conceived them to be. Thus, he probably favoured holding the line in both Korea and Manchuria in the fateful summer of 1903.

Naturally, whenever a country is involved in a war which is unsuccessful and full of humiliating defeats, there is great back-biting and mutual criticism. Certainly Russian officials made errors of omission and commission. Let us look first at those most implicated in the far-eastern establishment, whether at St Petersburg or at the periphery at Port Arthur or at the legations in the far east.

First place must go to Alekseyev, the laird of Port Arthur, of whose personality there is remarkably little in foreign memoirs. Spring-Rice refers to him in the words of Satow as the 'bluff and hearty Admiral Alexeiff' to gratify whose ambition ('and that of a few more') they had been spending a huge amount of money.[25] A protégé of the grand dukes, Alekseyev had been appointed commander of the Pacific squadron in 1895 and was given the extra assignment of the governorship of the Kwantung leased territory three years later. During the Boxer emergency he was made an army corps commander, thus combining military, naval and civilian ranks. Ambition he may have had but there seems to be evidence that he did not want the greater powers which were conferred on him in August 1903, when the tsar appointed him viceroy of the Far Eastern Provinces. Nor is there evidence that he was adventurous. He appears to have been highly suspicious of Bezobrazov and his group and of Minister Pavlov and his set of entrepreneurs and to have restrained their actions. He was, however, a believer in holding Port Arthur so that he was several degrees more expansionist than Kuropatkin who wanted to pull out of the south of Manchuria which he regarded as indefensible. From the standpoint of the Russian drift towards war, the main criticism of Alekseyev is that he bungled the negotiations with Japan by guiding the Russian side of the negotiations in a direction that the Japanese could not remotely accept. When negotiation failed and war approached, he may have contrived to hold up reports from Lessar and Rosen which drew attention to the dangers which Russia was running by risking hostilities with Japan.[26]

In this Alekseyev must be partnered with Rosen who must be judged an enigmatic character. We know from Griscom's memoirs and from MacDonald that Rosen was a pleasant person and well liked by the Japanese. We know from his autobiography that he was not liked by Lamsdorf and probably Witte with whom he had disagreements on policy.[27] He was a party to all the important committee decisions on far-eastern policy in 1903 both in St Petersburg and at Port Arthur. He was called for consultation with Alekseyev in September and himself conducted the intricate discussions with Komura in October and November. He tells us that Komura only lost his cool once. This may have misled him about the temper of Japanese opinion. Certainly he cannot escape blame for failing to alert either Alekseyev or St Petersburg to the seriousness of developments at the end of the year. MacDonald in another letter wrote that he had been interested to read that Rosen had

> said the Japanese had gone quite mad with war fever and would listen to
> nothing. This is quite untrue; Rosen was convinced that the Japanese
> were bluffing and would not fight. He said to his great friend in Tokio –
> the Doctor of this Legation – 10 days before the war broke out – 'we
> had only to mobilize one Division and the Japanese will climb down'.
> This friend who is a German and who has lived 30 years in Japan said to
> him the Japanese would most assuredly fight. But [Rosen] would listen
> to nobody.[28]

This evidence, though admittedly hearsay evidence, seems to confirm what seems plausible from other evidence, namely that Rosen had a complacent view about Japan's capacity and Japan's intentions.

It was with some astonishment to Rosen that he was received on his return home with hostility at the foreign ministry but with signal evidence of favour from the tsar himself. While this may have been due to Rosen's services in staving off the crisis with Japan, it was more probably due to the fact that the emperor was going through a phase of coolness towards Lamsdorf at the time. It was with even greater astonishment that Japan learnt that Rosen had been appointed as ambassador to Washington in 1905 in advance of what was to be the important peace conference at Portsmouth. He was relatively successful in this post and stayed on at the embassy until 1911. Rosen saw that Russia's destiny lay in the development of Siberia and in her relations with Asia. This perception arose from his special experience in these areas and his corresponding lack of experience in Europe.[29] But he did not press this world view aggressively on his government for he was timid in advice. He was shrewd in judgement and remained popular with his diplomatic colleagues in Tokyo.

When we pass to Korea, the key figure was supposed to be that of Minister Pavlov. While Russia's star was supposed to be receding in Korea, Pavlov seems to have considered it to be his role to keep it shining brightly and to achieve this by any means. The Japanese considered his methods to be objectionable. There was firstly the tension over Masampo; then Russia's scheme for Korea's neutralization – a concept which was intolerable to Japan; and finally the single-minded pursuit of the Yalu concessions. He was certainly a thorn in the flesh of the Japanese. He was not prepared to accept a secondary role for Russia – in this he was supported by many Russians – and was a difficult person to deal with.[30] British observers seem to have shared Japan's views of Pavlov; and it may be instructive to quote the assessment by John Jordan, the minister, of his responsibility for the Japanese invasion of the peninsula:

> Pavlov is in my opinion largely responsible for what has taken place. He had trod very heavily upon Japan's tender corn – Corea – and treated very cavalierly all the courteous overtures that were made to him to smooth matters by letting Corea open the Yalu. My firm conviction is that had Russia kept in Seoul a man of Waeber's temperament, her position here would not have suffered and things would never have come to the present pass. She has courted the arbitrament of war where time and quiet methods were all in her favour.[31]

This seems to be a fair indictment, though it is tinged with some anti-Russian bias.

Over Manchuria and China we need mention only Lessar, Planson and Bezobrazov. Over Manchuria they did not count for the decisions were taken from Port Arthur by Alekseyev and his circle. This at least was the judgement of British Minister Satow, who argued that the Russians had blundered badly in taking things out of Lessar's hands to put them in the less experienced hands of Alekseyev. But Lessar, though brilliant, was a dying man and was not able to find a solution to the Manchurian problem.[32]

Many would give Bezobrazov pride of place in this roll-call. From Kuropatkin in his *Zapiski* through Glinskii, the biographer of Witte, to Romanov and later Soviet historians, the authors have blamed him for sinister activities in the east and malign 'influence' with the tsar at home. In particular, he worked with the tsar's blessing for the extension of Russia's influence on the Yalu and in Korea and for a firm rejection of Japanese opposition. By his own boundless energy, he was able to promote his schemes both in the capital and in the east. With some adroitness he managed to insinuate his cousin, Admiral Abaza, into court circles and into the office of secretary of the so-called far-eastern committee. While the committee was a non-starter, Abaza was able to establish a role for himself as its senior official. In many studies General Bezobrazov is the main scapegoat for Russia's expansion. In the period of his maximum influence from November 1902 to August 1903 there is no doubt that he planted the idea of expansionism in Korea and Manchuria, which was continued by other hands after his retirement. But the fact is that he was out of power at the time of negotiation and did not influence its course. On 14 January 1904 he left St Petersburg to join his family in Geneva, scarcely the action of an ambitious man, greedy for power in an approaching war. On the critical issue which led to war – Japan's insistence on assurances over Manchuria – Bezobrazov had no voice (though he doubtless had views). To say that Bezobrazov caused the war would surely be a misjudgement; to say that he contributed to the failure of the Russo-Japanese negotiations in their early stages would not be an exaggeration.

Of the St Petersburg advisers of Nicholas II, we must observe the triumvirate Lamsdorf, the diplomat, Kuropatkin, the general, and Witte, the Finance minister forced into retirement. Though there was internal bickering between them, they had some mutual respect and tried to reach a consensus, for example against Bezobrazov, the outsider. But it was still possible for the tsar to 'divide and rule' and get his own way with them. Against Count Lamsdorf the greatest accusations have been made by Rosen: 'It has been the cruel fate of our unfortunate country that the headship of our foreign department should have been left to purblind incompetence and pompous self-sufficiency.'[33] This was a general complaint from someone who was not a well-wisher. Rosen also added a specific complaint, namely that Lamsdorf withheld from Alekseyev the news of the rupture of relations between Tokyo and St Petersburg and thus contributed to the losses of the Russian fleet outside Chemulpo and Port Arthur and to Japan's gaining command of the seas. Though this accusation was common knowledge in the Russian capital, Lamsdorf survived. Yet there is evidence that the tsar cooled greatly towards him during the war period. It would appear that this may have been due to these criticisms.

Foreign diplomats had mixed feelings about Lamsdorf. In his favour, it was agreed that he was hard-working, knew his job, had accumulated an abundance of experience over forty years and was affable and conciliatory. Against him, it was alleged that he was devious, lying, evasive, mystical. All these qualities have been illustrated in this study when on countless occasions he denied the existence of a Russo-Chinese treaty over Manchuria. Perhaps a more serious underlying complaint was that he did not defend his corner: he allowed the emperor to alienate the foreign ministry's power to Alekseyev in August 1903 with disastrous effect.[34] Thus the Russian institution most sensitive to peace had no strong voice during the critical months.

Where Lamsdorf was reticent, Kuropatkin was vocal, a great writer of reports, letters and diaries. Written privately, they have been published and are an essential source for this whole period.[35] Kuropatkin's remarkable career owed much to his popularity which carried him through as Lamsdorf was carried through by his timidity. Kuropatkin was expansionist and a believer in armies and railways. But he was a cautious professional who was no believer in war for the sake of glory. As war minister, he was a party to Russia's decision to occupy Manchuria in 1900. Indeed, he thought it a divine opportunity. But when it ran into resistance he had second thoughts. Alone among the top Russian leaders (apart from the tsar himself), he had visited Japan and formed a high opinion of the army he had seen there and of the navy at Nagasaki. He was therefore a cautious voice in the councils at Port Arthur (July) and St Petersburg. Soon after his return he reaffirmed the opinion that Russia should develop in northern Manchuria and should therefore withdraw from the south; but this never became orthodoxy; and the negotiations with Japan were conducted on a different basis. Kuropatkin always claimed along with Lamsdorf that he had argued against war. Whereas Lamsdorf was low in the ladder of influence with the tsar, Kuropatkin was at times relatively high. Yet he did not succeed in impressing the emperor with a sense of urgency. Almost incredibly he became army commander early in the war (March), determined that he would retreat to the north until reinforcements came. But this course of action led him to one of his disagreements with Alekseyev until the latter was forced to resign in favour of Kuropatkin as commander-in-chief. Kuropatkin himself lost the battle of Mukden in March 1905 but asked to become a corps commander under the new commander-in-chief, Linievich. After the war he was to become administrator of central Asia. So he too, like Rosen and (for a short term) Lamsdorf, continued in the service of the tsar. They survived the ignominy associated with taking Russia into an unsuccessful war, as could only happen in an autocracy.

What was Witte's relationship with the outbreak of war? In a technical sense there was none. He was out of power, fulminating in retirement with a sinecure that gave him honour without influence. Yet, as chairman of the council of ministers, he was still a formidable political figure; when he spoke, it was with authority. On the other hand, he was no longer the indispensable force in Russian decision-making. But the roots of the war went deep into the soil of the 1890s when Witte was the most prominent national leader: 'a man who has for over ten years faithfully and truly served the autocracy with the full force of his natural abilities and all the experience he had brought over from the private-capitalist "camp" ... the actual guiding spirit of Russian diplomacy in the far east'.[36] His policy of peaceful expansion into Manchuria was only marginally different from that of the 'military party': they were prepared to use force and to pursue expansion into Korea. Witte had created the railway as a commercial outlet; others were carrying it forward for objectives unintended by him. The other accusation was that made by the disillusioned Kuropatkin writing his campaign report in 1905 on the lost war. In considering various causes of unpreparedness for war against Japan, he made a bitter attack on Witte for his parsimonious financing. In due course after it had been published, Witte prepared a stinging defence of himself.

A tell-tale factor about the energetic Witte in his unwelcome retirement was his desire for self-justification. Brooding, intriguing and scheming, he developed an obsessive desire to vindicate himself. Charles

Hardinge of the British embassy described how 'he fishes for his own advantage in troubled waters and he is likely to stir up the mud until his position is assured'. And again:

> Witte himself is very anxious to convince foreign public opinion that he is in no way responsible for the Manchurian adventure. He asked me the other day if I would give a copy of a telegram which O'Conor (a former ambassador) sent reporting an interview with him in which he described the Manchurian adventure as a *bêtise*. There is no doubt that, whatever may have been Witte's original views, he was responsible for the sinking of vast sums of money in Kharbin, Dalny and elsewhere and did his utmost to make the Manchurian *bêtise* a success.[37]

There is much justice in Hardinge's assessment: Witte could not disclaim having some responsibility.

The men of Japan made war, not confidently but deliberately. They were cool and calculating, not bloodthirsty or emotional. The men of Russia – the tsar and his ministers – were not at all lovers of war. They hoped that they could secure their objectives by peace and certainly did not think that there was a high risk of war started by Japan. Untested in recent wars, they had no reason to doubt their capacity, even in a colonial environment. The person who held the unenviable office of tsar had the supreme power and had to make the decisions. There was a signal lack of coordination in the advice he received from the military and civilians on key issues; and he became the victim of cliques. Although shrewd and conscientious, Nicholas II was unsure of himself and, faced with the terms presented by the Japanese, he sanctioned an unconciliatory line of approach which doubtless gave him a false feeling of strength. He maintained an unyielding posture throughout the months of negotiations and did not show any awareness of the dire consequences to which this policy would lead. Nicholas was not alone in his blindness. The machinery of state was quite inadequate to deal with the affairs of empire in Europe and the vast empire in Asia at the same time. The experiment of decentralization by leaving critical decisions to Admiral Alekseyev was disastrous and had to be reversed in January 1904. But even the shortcomings of the imperial system in coping with the events of 1903–4 were not remedied after defeat in 1905.

THE ISSUES

Cecil Spring-Rice described the Russo-Japanese war as 'a preventible war'[38] into which the Russians slid unconsciously. This is easy to write; but it is difficult to imagine an acceptable solution to the problems at issue short of near capitulation by Russia. Yet it is something to which the historian must address himself seriously. Let us take a final overview of the issues on which common ground could not be found.

Over the basic problem of Korea, the Japanese defined their position very clearly. In the cabinet resolution of 30 December 1903, it was agreed:

> It is inevitable that we should keep Korea under our thumb by force whatever happens but, as it is desirable for us, if possible, to justify our actions, we should try to conclude an offensive-defensive alliance with the Koreans or a treaty for their protection as was done during our war with China (1894–5). We have been taking steps to prepare the ground for such treaties and will continue to do so in future. We cannot, however, be sure that we will manage this; and, even if we do succeed, success will ultimately rest on military force, since the Korean emperor cannot be relied on to comply with such treaties. Our Korean policy, in short, depends either directly or indirectly, on conducting military operations and must be determined in accordance with military criteria.[39]

While no mention of Russian activities is made in this resolution, it is clear that Japan wanted supremacy in the peninsula and would only achieve it by removing Russian influence from the court and the territory as a whole.

Korea had been a Russian appendage for almost a decade. The Russian position on Korea is very hard to define because it was a subject of divided opinions. In St Petersburg there was the division between the expansionists and the others (including expansionists who had no interest in Korea). There was also the division between European Russia and the frontiersmen, including entrepreneurs like Ginzburg and diplomats like Pavlov. Whereas Russia had entered into several treaties with Japan giving the Japanese more and more say in the peninsula, there was no diminution of activity on the part of Russian functionaries in Seoul. Her agents, taking advantage of the anti-Japanese feelings in Korea, were always exerting pressure in Seoul to obtain fresh concessions in the north or the south of the country. The scholar, Romanov, considers Korea not to have been regarded as one of Russia's significant national interests and implies that it could have been dispensed with. But the archives in European Russia may be misleading on that point; the situation on the ground suggests that it was a vital national objective. It is hard to imagine Admiral Alekseyev giving in over Russia's right to the passage of the seas around the south of Korea or the tsar over-ruling him about this. Basically it suited Russia to keep the peninsula divided.

Over Manchuria, there was a divided house in both countries. In Russia there was the 'Kuropatkin school' which wanted Russia to hold on to the defensible north and the 'Alekseyev school' which wanted to maintain Russia's existing position in both north and south. In any event these disagreements need not concern us further since both groups in Russia considered Manchuria to be a matter for discussion with

China but not with Japan. This excluded the possibility of compromise over the Three Eastern provinces.

Over China, Japan proclaimed that her prime object was to bring within her sphere of influence the southern region adjacent to Fukien province. But this was a low priority compared to improving her position in Korea. She was not talking about seeking a sphere of influence in Manchuria at this stage. As early as 30 December, the cabinet recorded that 'it is advantageous to confine the area of fighting to one region . . . . Manchuria will have to be the frontline'. But it was equally of interest to China to get the Russians out of Manchuria. The cabinet concluded that 'the present leaders of China are divided between those who favour coalition with Japan and those who wish to maintain neutrality and will thus be unable to make up their minds if the Russo-Japanese negotiations break down'.[40] On balance, it was better for Japan that China should remain neutral.

The Japanese military leaders were ready to invade Manchuria and had no thought of confining their operations to Korean territory south of the Yalu. This suggests that Manchuria was a prime object of Japan in going to war. For some Japanese, a major concern was revenge against Russia for the Three-power Intervention of 1895 and the object was the recovery of the Liaotung peninsula and the expansion of markets there. Certainly Japan was closely preoccupied with the schedule of Russian troop withdrawals from the Three Eastern provinces. As against that, the more influential statesmen, and especially the elder statesmen, were reluctant to take the risks involved in going to war with Russia and wanted to use Manchuria as a trade-off for improving Japan's hold over Korea. But Itō mentioned only Korea at the time of his abortive visit to St Petersburg in 1901 and Izvolskii at the Tokyo legation was preoccupied with schemes for Korean neutralization. Hence the possibility of trading off Russia's dominance in Manchuria for Japan's dominance in Korea really never became a talking-point.

If the two sides could not find an agreeable basis for compromise, it is hard to see how the war can be described as 'preventible'.

In its origins, the Russo-Japanese war stands in interesting contrast to other wars. It was not the result of economic pressures, for example the scarcity of resources for the number of people. Certainly Japan was the initiator: she also suffered from a shortage of raw materials and a rapidly growing population. But Korea was not sought for her raw materials or as a place to locate surplus population. Nor was Manchuria at this stage a place for great overseas settlement by Japanese or indeed of great commercial activity (if one excludes Niuchuang). Nor can one say that Japan was in a state of social distintegration and was seeking war as a way of diverting attention from domestic problems. There was not in 1904 an appeal to xenophobia or nationalism or war-lust on the part of the Japanese people in order to deflect them from thoughts of poverty, revolution or political discontent. Certainly Japan was suffering from teething troubles over the activities of political parties; but it would be a distortion of the facts to suggest that resort to war was intended to divert the people from insuperable political difficulties. By a paradox, Russia, it could be argued, was in a state of social disintegration. But there is no evidence that this prompted the tsar to look to war as a way of uniting the nation. A war in far-off Manchuria did not initially have much impact on European Russia. While the war became popular in Japan, there is little evidence that it ever was in Russia.

The decision for war in both countries was taken on a narrow basis and probably owed most to strategic considerations. It was not taken as the result of nationwide emotion for war. The factors which seem to have weighed most were security and fear of armament policies on the part of the other party. These weighed most because in both countries the military-naval authorities had a considerable say in the decision for war, the Kodama group in Japan and Admiral Alekseyev in Russia. These fears were in some respects justified. Both countries had increased their military and naval strength over a decade. The Japanese feared the increase in Russian power in east Asia since 1900, especially after the railways came into operation. Some Russians did record Japan's military growth but the general reaction of the Russian military seems to have been to discount her army and navy. In retrospect it would appear that Japan exaggerated the potential menace of Russia's military and naval power in 1903 or it may be that she merely professed to do so for propaganda purposes. Her sources of intelligence information were very comprehensive and accurate. But elements of distortion crept in since it was necessary to sell the idea of war to some of the top leadership. Russia of course had sources of information; but for some reason which is not clear she was not so skilful in evaluating Japan's strengths and weaknesses. It is doubtful whether Russia could have learnt more since the Japanese military were intent on keeping their preparations secret.

Inextricably linked with strategic considerations was the question of alliances. The Russo-Japanese war took place at the height of the secret alliances in world history. But it would be wrong to imagine that the Franco-Russian alliance or the Anglo-Japanese alliance caused the war. The European allies of the Russo-Japanese belligerents were the main external supporters of their allies but did not wield control over them in either case. Indeed it can be argued that the Anglo-Japanese alliance narrowed the scope of any war. Lord Lansdowne argued that 'although not intended to encourage the Japanese Government to resort to extremities, [it] had, and was sure to have, the effect of making Japan feel that she might try conclusions with her great rival in the Far East, *free from all risk of a European coalition* such as that which had on a previous occasion deprived her of the fruits of victory.' [my italics][41] Japan feared above all the reappearance of the Russo-German-French coalition of 1895 which was prevented by the British alliance and the Anglo-French *ententes*. She could take her decision for war with a fair prospect of a straightforward two-party conflict. The events of 1895 with which this study began hung like a cloud over the events of 1904.

REFERENCES AND NOTES

1. By 'Red Book', I refer to 'Malinovaia Kniga' (literally, Crimson Book).
2. A. N. Kuropatkin, *Zapiski* (1909), translated as *The Russian Army and the Japanese War*; S. Yu. Witte, 'Explanations about Kuropatkin's version of the Japanese War' (1911).
3. The English language version of the Japanese White Book was widely distributed throughout the world.
4. Suematsu Kenchō, *The Risen Sun* (London 1905), p. x.
5. The standard work is Matsumura Masayoshi, *Nichi-Ro Sensō to Kaneko Kentarō*.
6. *NGB*, Nichi-Ro Senso, vol. 1, no. 529, Motono to Komura, 7 Feb. 1904: 'Tendency of public opinion in France is generally against us. Although I am doing my best to attract French public opinion to our side, it seems to me of urgent necessity to defend ourselves in a manner suitable to our position before the world.'
7. Asakawa Kanichi, *The Russo-Japanese Conflict*, p. 349.
8. Two obvious weaknesses of the Russian position were the poor communication between the two groups of troops in Primorsk and Liaotung; and the icing of Vladivostok, the far eastern headquarters, despite the use of powerful icebreakers.
9. *d'Anethan Dispatches*, p. 158.
10. Spring-Rice to Roosevelt, 4 Feb. 1904, Spring-Rice Papers.
11. Witte's analysis was 'at the start of the war there was a flash of patriotism (in many cases artificial). If the war had ended in a few months, it would even have strengthened the Russian spirit.... But the war has gone sour ... and now all the leading intellectuals and many others have gone against it'. 'Perepiska S. Iu. Witte i Kuropatkina', in *Krasnyi Arkhiv*, **19** (1927), p. 74. Certainly revolutionaries rejoiced in the war, hoping that they could make capital out of it.
12. S. Gwynn (ed.) *The Letters and Friendships of Sir Cecil Spring-Rice*, vol. 1, p. 405.
13. Ibid., p. 402; I. I. Rostunov (ed.), *Istoriya Russko-Iaponslcoi Voiny*, p. 34.
14. Kuropatkin, 'Dnevnik' in 3 parts, in *Krasnyi Arkhiv* (1922–25).
15. 'The war in the Far East was not in reality a conflict which had arisen merely out of a dispute between the two combatants. It was rather to be ascribed to the general revolt of all the civilized peoples of the earth against the perfidy and insincerity of Russia, who for many years past has sought to outwit and overreach the other Powers. It was because Japan felt all along that her interests, more than those of any other country, were involved ... [that she] resolved that she would take up the cudgels, and

was content to do battle with Russia single-handed, in advance of the other nations whose prospects were similarly jeopardized.' Suematsu Kenchō, *The Risen Sun* (London, 1905), pp. 90–1.

16. H. J. Whigham, *Manchuria and Korea.*

17. Okamoto Shumpei, *The Japanese Oligarchy and the Russo-Japanese War.*

18. Okamoto, 'A phase of Meiji Japan's attitude toward China: The case of Komura Jūtarō'.

19. In answer to Galperin's claim that Komura was not negotiating seriously, it seems that he did try to make a success of the negotiations (even if he was despondent) and to keep down the temperature of public opinion while talks were proceeding.

20. Itō, 'Nichi-Ro Kōshō Ketsuretsu no Temmatsu' in *Zoku Itō Hirobumi Hiroku,* p. 166.

21. Itō to Lansdowne, 9 Feb. 1904, FO 800/134.

22. From Dec. 1903 to Feb. 1904 Yamamoto was the critical decision-maker. Japan, Navy Ministry, *Yamamoto Gombei to Kaigun,* pp. 155–211.

23. Nobuya Bamba and J. F. Howes, *Pacifism in Japan;* Okamoto, *Oligarchy,* pp. 93–4.

24. Chirol to Morrison, 24 June 1904 in Lo Hui-min (ed.), *The Correspondence of G. E. Morrison,* vol. 1, 265–6.

25. Satow to Spring-Rice, 11 Jan. 1904, in Gwynn, op. cit., p. 392.

26. Sanderson to Scott, 24 Feb. 1904, Scott Papers 52,299.

27. L. Griscom, *Diplomatically Speaking,* p. 204.

28. MacDonald to Hardinge, 18 Jan. 1905, Hardinge Papers 7. 'Rosen was an enigma to me for why he did not warn his people to be prepared for serious trouble I cannot make out. Personally I liked him very much but the lady was a holy terror.' MacDonald to Hardinge, 30 June 1904, Hardinge Papers 3.

29. Rosen, *Forty Years,* vol. 1, pp. 205–6.

30. *d'Anethan Dispatches,* pp. 158, 173.

31. Jordan to J. D. Campbell, 15 Feb. 1904, Jordan Papers 3.

32. Gwynn, op. cit., p. 392.

33. Rosen, *Forty Years,* vol. 1, pp. 241–2.

34. A damaging criticism of Lamsdorf was that he allowed policies to be pursued behind his back with which he disagreed.

35. Kuropatkin, 'Dnevnik,' appeared in three large slabs in *Krasnyi Arkhiv* (1922–5).

36. B. A. Romanov, *Russia in Manchuria,* pp. 256–7.

37. Hardinge to Lansdowne, 4 Jan. 1905, and to T. H. Sanderson, 12 April 1905, Hardinge Papers 6.

38. Gwynn, op. cit., p. 405.

39. *NGNB,* vol. 1, cabinet resolution, 30 Dec. 1903.

40. Ibid.

41. Lansdowne to the king, 18 April 1904, FO 800/134.

SELECT BIBLIOGRAPHY

This is not primarily an archival study. I have, however, consulted a number of British manuscript collections of which the private papers are set out briefly below.

THE BRITISH LIBRARY, LONDON
Sir Charles Stewart Scott, ambassador to Russia, 1898–1904 (Ass. MSS 52,294–52,310).
PUBLIC RECORD OFFICE, LONDON
Sir Ernest Mason Satow, minister to Japan, 1895–1900, and to China, 1900–6 (Gifts and Deposits 30/33).
Sir John Newell Jordon, consul-general, 1896–1901, and minister to Korea, 1901–6 (FO 350).
Sir E. Grey, Lord Lansdowne, F. H. Villiers, C. Hardinge, C. Spring-Rice (FO 800).
LIBRARY OF THE SCHOOL OF ORIENTAL AND AFRICAN STUDIES, LONDON
Chinese Maritime Customs, especially papers of Cecil Arthur Verner Bowra.
Sir Mortimer Durand, ambassador to the United States, 1903–7 (MS 257,247).
CHURCHILL COLLEGE, CAMBRIDGE
(Sir) Cecil Spring-Rice, chargé d'affaires at embassy to Russia, various times, 1900–5.
UNIVERSITY LIBRARY, CAMBRIDGE
(Sir) Charles Hardinge, secretary to embassy, 1898–1903, and ambassador to Russia, 1904–6 (HP 3–8).
UNIVERSITY OF TORONTO LIBRARY, TORONTO, CANADA
(Thomas Fisher Rare Book Library)
John Otway Percy Bland, secretary of Municipal Council, International Settlement, Shanghai, correspondent of *The Times* in China.
MITCHELL LIBRARY, SYDNEY, NEW SOUTH WALES
Dr George Ernest Morrison, correspondent of *The Times* in Peking, 1897–1912.
HOUGHTON LIBRARY, HARVARD UNIVERSITY
William Woodville Rockhill, delegate to Peking Conference, 1900–1, and minister to China, 1905–9.

STERLING LIBRARY, YALE UNIVERSITY
Anson Phelps Stokes, of the Committee on Japanese Peace Plans, 1904–5, and correspondent of Asakawa Kanichi. Yale University archives, on doctorate for Itō Hirobumi, 1901.
BRITISH LIBRARY OF ECONOMICS AND POLITICAL SCIENCE
Alfred Edward Hippisley, Chinese Maritime Customs, collection of books.

MONOGRAPHS

Dmitrii I. Abrikosov, *Revelations of a Russian Diplomat,* Seattle 1964.
Alexander (Grand Duke), *Once a Grand Duke.* New York 1932.
Christopher Andrew, *Theophile Delcassé and the Entente Cordiale.* London 1966.
Albert d'Anethan, *The d'Anethan Dispatches from Japan, 1894–1910* (G. A. Lensen, ed.). Tokyo 1967.
d'Anethan (Baroness), *Fourteen Years of Diplomatic Life in Japan: Leaves from the Diary of Baroness Albert D'Anethan.* London 1912.
Asakawa Kanichi, *The Russo-Japanese Conflict: Its Causes and Issues.* Boston 1904.

Erwin Baelz, *Awakening Japan: Diary of a German Doctor.* New York 1932.
Nobuya Bamba and John F. Howes, *Pacifism in Japan.* Kyoto 1978.
John Barber, *Soviet Historians in Crisis, 1928–32.* London 1981.
Constantine A. Benckendorff, *Half a Life: Reminiscences of a Russian Gentleman.* London 1955
Torsten Burgman, *Svensk Opinion och Diplomatii under Rysk-Japanska Kriget, 1904–5.* Uppsala 1966.

Cambridge History of China, vol. 10, 1800–1911, parts 1 and 2 (J. K. Fairbank and D. Twitchett, eds).
Paul H. Clyde, *International Rivalries in Manchuria, 1689–1922.* Columbus 1928.
D. N. Collins, 'Franco-Russian alliance and Russian railways, 1891–1914' in *Historical Journal,* 16 (1973), 777–88.
Hilary Conroy, *The Japanese Seizure of Korea, 1868–1910.* Philadelphia 1960.
Olga Crisp, 'The Russo-Chinese Bank: an episode in Franco-Russian relations' in *Slavonic and East European Review,* 52 (1974), 197–212.
Olga Crisp, *Studies in the Russian Economy before 1914.* London 1976.
John D. Crump, *The Origins of Socialist Thought in Japan,* London 1983.

David Dallin, *Rise of Russia in Asia.* New York 1950.
A. I. Dmitriev-Mamonov and A. F. Zdziarskii (eds), *Guide to the Great Siberian Railway.* St Petersburg 1900.
J. M. Dorwart. *The Pigtail War: American Involvement in the Sino-Japanese War, 1894–5.* Amherst 1975.
Charles Drage, *Servants of the Dragon Throne.* London 1966.

Mark Elvin, 'Mandarins and Millenarians: reflections on the Boxer Uprising of 1899–1900' in *Journal of the Anthropological Society of Oxford,* **10** (1979), 115–38.

J. K. Fairbank, K. F. Bruner and E. M. Matheson (eds), *The I. G. in Peking: Letters of Robert Hart, Chinese Maritime Customs, 1868–1907* (2 vols). Cambridge, Mass. 1975.

Olavi K. Fält, 'The picture of Japan in Finnish underground newspapers during the Russo-Japanese War' in I. H. Nish and C. Dunn (eds), *European Studies on Japan.* Tenterden, Kent 1979, 130–4.

Olavi K. Fält, 'Collaboration between Japanese intelligence and the Finnish underground during the Russo-Japanese War' in *Asian Profile,* **4** (1976).

M. H. Fisher and N. Rich (eds), *Holstein Papers.* 4 vols, London 1955–63.

France: *Documents Diplomatiques Français, 1870–1914,* 1st and 2nd series.

Edmund S. K. Fung, *The Military Dimension of the Chinese Revolution.* Canberra 1980.

Michael Futrell, 'Colonel Akashi and Japanese contacts with Russian revolutionaries in 1904–5' in G. F. Hudson (ed.), *St Antony's Papers, no. 2, Far Eastern Affairs* (1967).

S. Galai, 'The impact of the Russo-Japanese War on the Russian Liberals in 1904–5' in *Government and Opposition,* **1** (1965), 85–110.

Dietrich Geyer, *Der russische Imperialismus, 1860–1914.* Göttingen 1977.

David Gillard, *The Struggle for Asia, 1828–1914: A Study in British and Russian Imperialism.* London 1975.

Great Britain, *British Documents on the Origins of the War, 1898–1914* (G. P. Gooch and H. W. V. Temperley, eds), vols 1, 2 and 4.

Lloyd Griscom, *Diplomatically Speaking.* London 1941.

Stephen Gwynn (ed.), *The Letters and Friendships of Sir Cecil Spring-Rice,* 2 vols. Boston 1929.

Roger Hackett, *Yamagata Aritomo in the Rise of Modern Japan, 1838–1922.* Cambridge, Mass. 1970.

Reginald Hargreaves, *Red Sun Rising: the Siege of Port Arthur.* London 1962.

Fred Harrington, *God, Mammon and the Japanese: Dr Allen and Korean-American Relations, 1884–1905.* Madison, 1944.

Seiji Hishida, *The International Position of Japan as a Great Power.* New York 1905.

Alexander Hosie, *Manchuria: Its People, Resources and Recent History.* London 1904.

Michael H. Hunt, *Frontier Defence and the Open Door: Manchuria in Chinese-American Relations, 1895–1911.* New Haven 1973.

Michael H. Hunt, 'The forgotten occupation: Peking, 1900–1' in *Pacific Historical Review,* **48** (1979), 501–29.

Michael H. Hunt, *The Making of a Special Relationship: The United States and China to 1914.* New York 1983.

Inouye Yūichi, 'Russo-Japanese relations and railway construction in Korea, 1894–1904' in G. Daniels (ed.), *Proceedings of the British Association for Japanese Studies,* 1979, 87–97.

Akira Iriye, *Pacific Estrangement: Japanese and American Expansion, 1897–1911.* Cambridge, Mass. 1972.

Italy, Defence Ministry, *Documenti Italiani Sulla Guerra Russo-Giapponese (1904–5)* (Antonello F. M. Biagini). Roma 1977.

Marius Jansen, 'Konoe Atsumaro' in A. Iriye (ed.), *The Chinese and the Japanese.* Princeton 1980.

Japan, *Correspondence Regarding the Negotiations between Japan and Russia (1903–4),* presented to the Imperial Diet, March 1904.

Geoffrey Jones and G. Gerenstain (eds), *Foreign Capital in Russia* by P. V. Ol'. New York 1983.

Kajima Morinosuke, *The Diplomacy of Japan, 1894–1922,* 3 vols. Tokyo 1976–8.

Kambe Masao, *Der russisch-japanische Krieg und die japanische Volkswirtschaft.* Lipzig 1906.

George Katkov *et al.* (eds), *Russia Enters the Twentieth Century 1894–1917.* London 1971.

E. G. Kemp, *The Face of Manchuria, Korea and Russian Turkestan.* London 1910.

E. S. Kirby, *Russian Studies on Japan.* London 1980.

Lionel Kochan, *Russia in Revolution, 1890–1918.* London 1966.

A. N. Kuropatkin, *The Russian Army and the Japanese War,* 2 vols. London 1909.

William L. Langer, 'The origins of the Russo-Japanese War' in C. E. and E. Schorske (eds), *Explorations in Crisis: Papers on International History,* Cambridge, Mass., 1969, 3–45.

Theodore H. von Laue, *Sergei Witte and the Industrialization of Russia.* New York 1963.

George A. Lensen, *The Russo-Chinese War.* Tallahassee, 1967.

George A. Lensen, *Balance of Intrigue: International Rivalry in Korea and Manchuria, 1884–99,* 2 vols. Tallahassee, 1982.

Dominic C. B. Lieven, *Russia and the Origins of the First World War.* London 1983.

Lo Hui-min (ed.), *The Correspondence of G. E. Morrison,* 2 vols. Cambridge 1976.

Andrew Malozemoff, *Russian Far Eastern Policy, 1881–1904.* Berkeley 1958.

Miyazaki Tōten, *My 33 Years' Dream* (Etō Shinkichi and Marius Jansen, eds). Princeton 1982.

Mutsu Munemitsu, *Kenkenroku: A Diplomatic Record of the Sino-Japanese War, 1894–5* (G. M. Berger, ed.). Tokyo 1982.

Ian Nish, 'Japan and China: the case of Weihaiwei, 1894–1906' in *Bulletin of Fukuoka UNESCO Association* (1973), 29–35.

Ian Nish, 'The three-power intervention of 1895' in A. R. Davis and A. D. Stefanowska (eds), *Austrina,* Sydney, 1982, 204–25.

Ian Nish, 'Naval aspects of the Anglo-Japanese Alliance' in (Keio) *Hōgaku Kenkyū* (1983).

Ian Nish, 'Britain and the three-power intervention, 1895' in John Chapman (ed.), *Proceedings of the British Association for Japanese Studies,* 1980, 12–26.

Ian Nish, 'Itō in St Petersburg, 1901' in G. Daniels (ed.), *Europe Interprets Japan*, Tenterden, Kent 1984, pp. 90–5.

Ian Nish, 'Japanese intelligence at the time of the Russo-Japanese War' in C. Andrew and D. N. Dilks (eds), *The Missing Dimension*. London 1984.

Ian Nish, *The Anglo-Japanese Alliance: A Study of Two Island Empires*. London 1966.

Nobori Shomu and Akamatsu Katsumaro, *The Russian Impact on Japan: Literature and Social Thought*. Los Angeles 1981.

F. G. Notehelfer, *Kōtoku Shūsui: Portrait of a Radical*. Cambridge 1971.

Okamoto Shumpei, 'A phase of Meiji Japan's attitude toward China: the case of Komura Jūtarō' in *Modern Asian Studies,* 13 (1979), 431–59.

Okamoto Shumpei, *The Japanese Oligarchy and the Russo-Japanese War*. New York 1970.

W. J. Oudendyk, *Ways and By-ways in Diplomacy*. London 1939.

Paul Pelliot, *Carnets de Pékin, 1899–1901*. Paris 1977.

R. Pipes, *Russia under the Old Regime*. London 1974.

Don C. Price, *Russia and the Roots of the Chinese Revolution, 1896–1911*. Cambridge, Mass. 1974.

Rosemary K. I. Quested, *The Russo-Chinese Bank: a Multi-national Financial Base of Tsarism in China*. Birmingham 1977.

Rosemary K. I. Quested, 'An introduction to the enigmatic career of Chou Mien' in *Journal of Oriental Studies,* Hong Kong, 16 (1978), 39–48.

Rosemary, K. I. Quested, 'A fresh look at the Sino-Russian conflict of 1900 in Manchuria' in *Journal of the Institute of Chinese Studies,* Chinese University, Hong Kong, 8 (1978), 159–91.

Rosemary, K. I. Quested, *Matey Imperialists?: The Tsarist Russians in Manchuria 1895–1917*. Hong Kong 1982.

Hans Rogger, *Russia in the Age of Modernization and Revolution, 1881–1917*. London 1983.

Boris A. Romanov, *Russia in Manchuria, 1892–1906* (trans. Susan Jones). Ann Arbor 1952.

Roman R. Rosen, *Forty Years of Diplomacy,* 2 vols. London 1922.

Ryū Shintarō, 'Ikebe Sanzan' in *Japan Quarterly,* 12 (1965), 379–87.

Ernest M. Satow, *Korea and Manchuria between Russia and Japan* (G. A. Lensen, ed.), Tallahassee 1966.

Hans Schwabe and Heinrich Seemann, *Deutsche Botschafter in Japan, 1860–1973*. Tokyo 1974.

Hugh Seton-Watson, *The Russian Empire, 1801–1917*. Oxford 1967.

T. G. Stavrou (ed.), *Russia under the Last Tsar*. Minneapolis 1969.

John J. Stephan, *Sakhalin: a History*. Oxford 1971.

Benedict H. Sumner, *Tsardom and Imperialism in the Far East and Middle East, 1880–1914*. London 1942.

Chester C. Tan, *The Boxer Catastrophe*. New York 1967.

Harmon Tupper, *To the Great Ocean: Siberia and the Trans-Siberian Railway*. London 1965.

Teddy J. Uldricks, 'Tsarist and Soviet Ministry of Foreign Affairs' in Zara Steiner (ed.), *The Times Survey of Foreign Ministries of the World.* London 1982, 511–22.

D. Mackenzie Wallace, *Russia,* 2 vols. London 1912.
Denis and Peggy Warner, *The Tide at Sunrise: a History of the Russo-Japanese War, 1904–5.* London 1974.
Ken-shen Weigh, *Russo-Chinese Diplomacy, 1689–1924.* Shanghai 1928.
J. N. Westwood, *A History of Russian Railways.* London 1964.
Henry J. Whigham, *Manchuria and Korea.* London 1904.
John A. White, *The Diplomacy of the Russo-Japanese War.* Princeton 1964.
Sergei Yu. Witte, *The Memoirs of Count Witte* (A. Yarmolinsky, ed.). London 1921.
H. G. W. Woodhead, *Adventures in Far Eastern Journalism.* Tokyo 1935.
Aitchen K. Wu, *China and the Soviet Union: a Study of Sino-Soviet Relations, 1618–1950.* London 1950.

L. K. Young, *British Policy in China, 1895–1902.* Oxford 1970.

Edward H. Zabriskie, *American-Russian Rivalry in the Far East, 1895–1914,* Philadelphia 1946.

For a more exhaustive bibliography, readers should consult Lensen, *Balance of Intrigue,* pp. 941–84.

MONOGRAPHS IN JAPANESE

Abe Kōzō, 'Manshū mondai wo meguru Nichi-Ro kōshō' in *Kokusai Seiji,* 1965, 30–51.
Fujimura Michio, *Nisshin Sensō.* Tokyo: Iwanami 1973.
Furuya Tetsuo, *Nichi-Ro Sensō.* Tokyo: Chūō Kōron 1966.
Harada Katsumasa, *Mantetsu.* Tokyo: Iwanami 1981.
Hiratsuka Atsushi (ed.), *Itō Hirobumi Hiroku.* 2 vols, Tokyo 1928–30.
Hiratsuka Atsushi, *Shishaku Kurino Shinichirō den.* Tokyo 1942.
Ikeda Kiyoshi, *Nihon no Kaigun,* 2 vols. Tokyo 1966.
Ikeda Kiyoshi, *Kaigun to Nihon.* Tokyo: Chūō Kōron 1981.
Inouye Yūichi, 'Nichi-Ro sensōji ni okeru Nihon no gunyō tetsudō kensetsu mondai' in *Gunji Shigaku,* **16** (1980), 9–20.
Itō Hirobumi, *Kimitsu Nisshin Sensō* (from Hisho Ruisan), Tokyo: Hara Shobō 1967.
Itō Masanori, *Kokubōshi.* Tokyo 1941.
Japan, Foreign Ministry, *Gaimushō no 100-nen,* 2 vols. Tokyo 1969.
Japan, Foreign Ministry, *Nichi-Ro Kōshōshi.* Tokyo 1944.
Japan, Foreign Ministry, *Nihon Gaikō Bunsho,* especially volumes 24 to 38, including the sub-series on the Boxer Disturbances and the Russo-Japanese war.

Japan, Foreign Ministry, *Nihon Gaikō Nempyō narabi ni Shūyō Bunsho.* 2 vols, Tokyo 1955.

Japan, Foreign Ministry, *Komura Gaikō*shi, 2 vols. Tokyo 1953.

Japan, Navy Ministry, *Yamamoto Gombei to Kaigun.* Tokyo; Hara Shobō 1966.

Kajima Morinosuke, *Nihon Gaikōshi,* especially vols 1–9.

Kimitsu Nichi-Ro senshi. Tokyo: Hara Shobō 1974.

Kurobane Shigeru, *Sekaishijō yori mitaru Nichi-Ro Sensō.* Tokyo: Shibundō 1972.

Kurobane Shigeru, *Nichi-Ro Sensō to Akashi Kōsaku.* Tokyo 1976.

Kurobane Shigeru, *Nichi-Ro Sensō Shiron.* Tokyo 1982.

Matsumura Masayoshi, *Nichi-Ro Sensō to Kaneko Kentarō: Kōhō gaikō no Kenkyū.* Tokyo: Shinyūdo 1980.

Matsumura Masayoshi, 'Portsmouth Kōwa Kaigi to Nihonjin tokuhain' in *Hōgaku Kenkyū* 1983.

Matsumura Masayoshi, 'Nichi-Ro sensō to Nihon no kōhō gaikō' in *Gunji Shigaku,* **16** (1980), 2–8.

Meiji Gunjishi, from Meiji Tenno Go-denki Shiryō

Muneta Hiroshi, *Heitai Nihonshi: Nisshin Nichi-Ro Sensō-hen.* Tokyo: Shin Jimbutsu Ōraisha 1974.

Ōe Shinobu, *Nichi-Ro Sensō no Gunji Shiteki Kenkyū.* Tokyo 1976.

Nakayama Jiichi and Shinobu Seisaburō, *Nichi-Ro Sensō no Kenkyū,* Tokyo 1959.

Ōyama Azusa (ed.), *Yamagata Aritomo ikensho.* Tokyo: Hara Shobō 1966.

Ōyama Azusa (ed.), *Nichi-Ro Sensō no Gunsei Shiroku.* Tokyo 1973.

Ōyama Azusa (ed.), 'Nichi-Ro Sensō to Eikō (Yingkow) Senryō' in *Kokusai Seiji,* 1965, 52–66.

Sakane Yoshihisa, *Aoki Shūzō Jiden.* Tokyo 1966.

Shiba Gōrō, *Hokkyo (Peking) rōjō* (Ōyama Azusa, ed.). Tokyo, Heibonsha 1965.

Shidehara Kijūrō. Tokyo: Shidehara Heiwa Zaidan 1955.

Shimomura Fujio, *Nichi-Ro Sensō.* Tokyo: Jimbutsu Ōraisha 1966.

Tani Kanjō, *Kimitsu Nichi-Ro Senshi.* Tokyo: Hara Shobō 1974.

Tanaka Giichi Denki, 3 vols. Tokyo 1958.

Toyama Saburō, *Nisshin-Nichi-Ro-Daitōa Kaisenshi.* Tokyo 1979.

Tsunoda Jun, *Manshū Mondai to Kokubō Hōshin.* Tokyo: Hara Shobō 1967.

Tabohashi Kiyoshi, *Nisshin Seneki Gaikōshi no Kenkyū, 1894–5.* Tokyo: Tōkō Shoin 1951.

Uchida Yasuya. Tokyo: Kajima Heiwa Zaidan 1969.

Uchiyama Masakuma, *Gendai Nihon Gaikoshi ron.* Tokyo: Keio 1971.

MONOGRAPHS IN RUSSIAN

A. I. Alekseyev, *Osvoenie russkimi lyudmi Dalnego Vostoka i Russkoi Ameriki, do kontsa XIX veka.* Moscow 1982.

B. Ia, Avarin, *Borba za Tikhii Okean.* Moscow, 1952.

A. I. Dmitriev-Mamonov, *Putevoditel po Velikii Sibirskoi Zheleznoi Doroge.* St Petersburg 1902.

G. V. Efimov, *Velikii kitaiskii revolyutsioner-demokrat Sun Yat-sen*. Leningrad 1961.

A. L. Galperin, *Anglo-Iaponskii Soiuz, 1902–21 gg*. Moscow 1947.

K. A. Gamazkov and T. M. Angora (eds), *Iaponiya: voprosy istorii*. Moscow 1959.

B. B. Glinskii, *Prolog Russko-Iaponskoi Voiny*. Petrograd 1916.

I. Ia. Korostovets, *Rossiia na Dalnem Vostoke*. Peking 1922.

Krasnyi Arkhiv. Moscow, 1922–39:

'Dnevnik A. N. Kuropatkina', **2** (1922), 5–117.

'Tsarskaya diplomatiya o zadachakh Rossii na Vostoke v 1900g', **18** (1926), no. 5, 3–29.

'Perepiska S. Iu. Vitte i A. N. Kuropatkina v 1904–5 gg', **19** (1927), no. 6, 64–82.

'V Shtabe Adm. E. I. Alekseyeva (Planson diary)', **41–2** (1930), 148–208.

'Pervye shagi russkogo imperializma na Dalnem Vostoke, 1888–1903', **52** (1932), no. 3, 34–124.

'Nakanune Russko-Iaponskoi Voiny, 1900–2', **63** (1934), no. 2, 3–54.

I. A. Mikhailov (*et al.*), *Kitaiskaia Vostochnaia Zheleznaia Doroga*. St Petersburg 1913.

A. L. Narochnitskii (*et al.*), *Mezhdunarodnye otnosheniia na Dalnem Vostoke* (2 vols), vol. 1, 16th century to 1917. Moscow 1973.

P. I. Ostrikov, *Imperialisticheskaia politika Anglii v Kitae v 1900–4 gg*. Moscow 1978.

S. A. Rashevskii (Colonel), 'Dnevnik: Port Artur, 1904' in *Istoricheskii Arkhiv*, Moscow, vol. x, 1954.

B. A. Romanov, *Rossiya v Manchzhurii, 1892–1906*. Leningrad 1928.

B. A. Romanov, *Ocherki Diplomaticheskoi Istorii Russko-Iaponskoi Voiny, 1895–1907*. Moscow 1947.

I. I. Rostunov (ed.), *Istoriya Russko-Iaponskoi Voiny, 1904–5 gg*. Moscow 1977.

Russko-Kitaiskie otnosheniya (1689–1916). Moscow 1958.

Sbornik diplomaticheskikh dokumentov mezhdu Rossiei i Iaponiei, St Petersburg 1907.

O. K. Smirnova (ed.), *Sbornik dokumentov po istorii SSSR: Period imperializma*. Moscow 1977.

S. L. Tikhvinskii, 'Manchzhurskoe Vladychestvo v Kitae' in *Manchzhurskoe Vladychestvo v Kitae*. Moscow 1966.

S. N. Valk, 'Boris Aleksandrovich Romanov' in *Istoricheski Zapiski*, **62** (1958), 269–82.

D. C. Vishnevskii (*et al.*), *Khabarovskii Krai*. Khabarovsk 1965.

S. Iu. Witte, *Vospominaniya tsarstvovaniye Nikolaia II*, vol. 1, Berlin: Slovo-verlag 1922.

Vladivostoka, 1860–1960. Vladivostok 1960.

P. A. Zaionchkovskii, *Samoderzhavie i russkaya armiya na rubezhe XIX–XX stoletti, 1881–1903*. Moscow 1973.

S. E. Zakharov, *Tikho-okeanskii Flot*. Moscow 1966.

E. M. Zhukov, *Mezhdunarodnye Otnosheniia na Dalnem Vostoke, 1870–1945 gg*. Moscow 1951.

MAPS

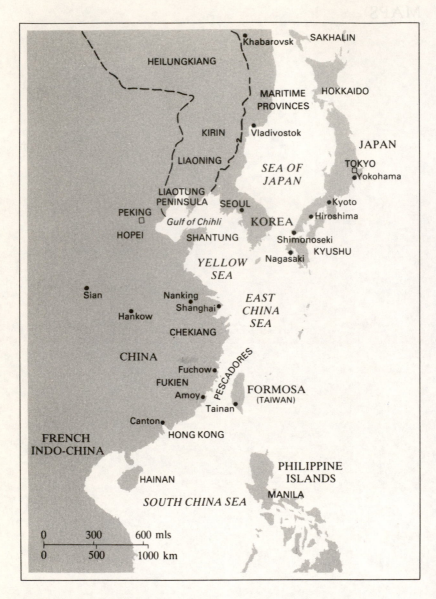

MAP 1.   Japan and the China Sea

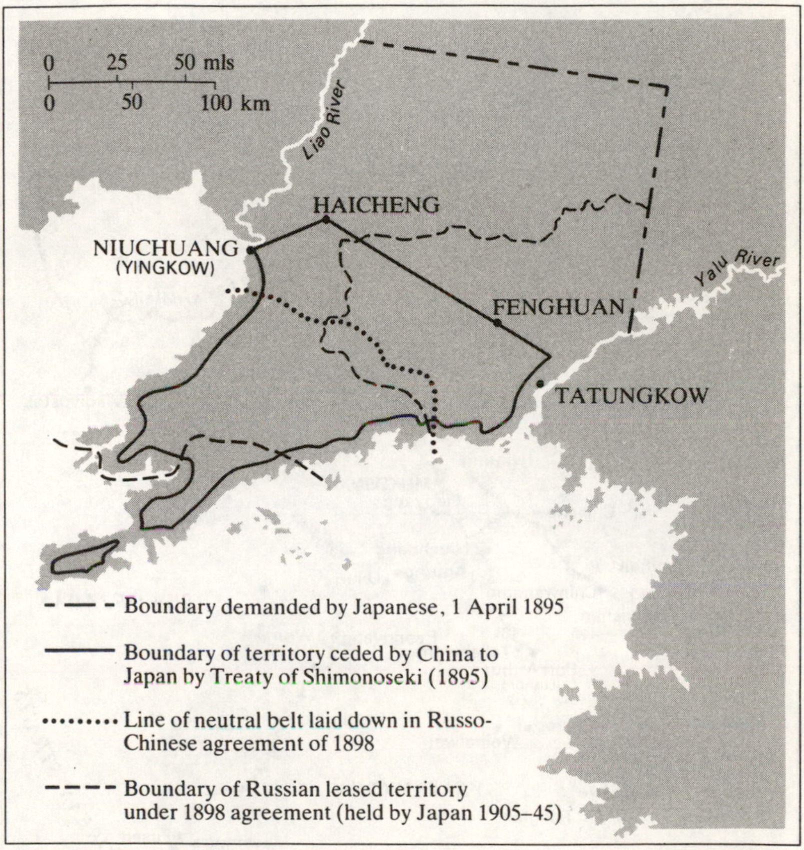
0 25 50 mls
0 50 100 km
Liao River
HAICHENG
NIUCHUANG
(YINGKOW)
Yalu River
FENGHUAN
TATUNGKOW
Boundary demanded by Japanese, 1 April 1895
Boundary of territory ceded by China to Japan by Treaty of Shimonoseki (1895)
Line of neutral belt laid down in Russo-Chinese agreement of 1898
Boundary of Russian leased territory under 1898 agreement (held by Japan 1905–45)

MAP 2. Fengtien Province of China

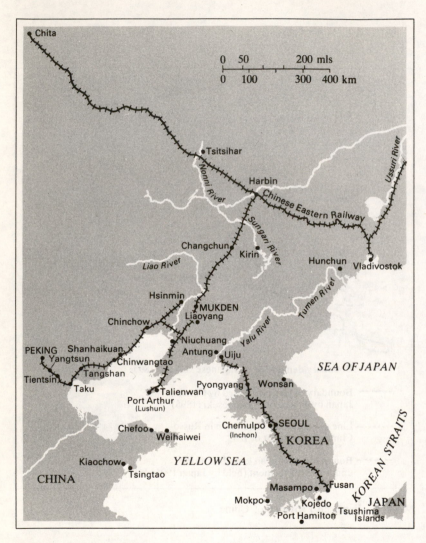

MAP 3.   North-east Asia

INDEX